Critical Terrorism Studies

In response to the growth of a critical perspective on contemporary issues of terrorism, this edited volume brings together a number of leading scholars to debate the new subfield of 'critical terrorism studies'.

In the years since the 9/11 attacks, the study of terrorism has undergone a major transformation from a minor subfield of security studies into a large standalone field, and is probably one of the fastest expanding areas of research in the Western academic world. However, much of the literature is beset by a number of problems, limiting its potential for producing rigorous empirical findings and genuine theoretical advancement. In response to these weaknesses in the broader field, a small but increasing number of scholars have begun to articulate a critical perspective on contemporary issues of terrorism. This volume brings together a number of leading scholars to debate the need for, and the shape of, this exciting new subfield. The first part of the volume examines some of the main shortcomings and limitations of orthodox terrorism studies, while the second examines exactly what 'critical' terrorism studies would look like. Contributors from a variety of methodological and disciplinary perspectives give this volume diversity, and it will lay the foundations for, and provoke debate about, the future research agenda of this new field.

This book will be of much interest to students of critical security studies, terrorism studies and international relations.

Richard Jackson is Reader in the Department of International Politics, Aberystwyth University, where he is also Senior Researcher at the Centre for the Study of Radicalisation and Contemporary Political Violence (CSRV). He is the founding editor of the journal, *Critical Studies on Terrorism*. **Marie Breen Smyth** is Director of the Centre for the Study of Radicalisation and Contemporary Political Violence at Aberystwyth University. She is a Reader in International Politics and co-editor of the journal, *Critical Studies on Terrorism*. **Jeroen Gunning** is Lecturer in International Politics at Aberystwyth University, Deputy Director of the Centre for the Study of Radicalisation and Contemporary Political Violence and co-editor of the journal, *Critical Studies on Terrorism*.

Critical terrorism studies
Series Editors: Richard Jackson, Marie Breen Smyth and Jeroen Gunning
Aberystwyth University, UK

This book series will publish rigorous and innovative studies on all aspects of terrorism, counterterrorism and state terror. It seeks to advance a new generation of thinking on traditional subjects, and investigate topics frequently overlooked in orthodox accounts of terrorism. Books in this series will typically adopt approaches informed by critical-normative theory, post-positivist methodologies and non-Western perspectives, as well as rigorous and reflective orthodox terrorism studies.

Terrorism and the Politics of Response
London in a time of terror
Edited by Angharad Closs Stephens and Nick Vaughan-Williams

Critical Terrorism Studies
A new research agenda
Edited by Richard Jackson, Marie Breen Smyth and Jeroen Gunning

Critical Terrorism Studies
A new research agenda

**Edited by Richard Jackson,
Marie Breen Smyth and Jeroen Gunning**

LONDON AND NEW YORK

First published 2009
by Routledge
2 Park Square, Milton Park, Abingdon, Oxon OX14 4RN

Simultaneously published in the USA and Canada
by Routledge
270 Madison Ave, New York, NY 10016

Routledge is an imprint of the Taylor & Francis Group, an informa business

Transferred to Digital Printing 2009

© 2009 Selection and editorial matter, Richard Jackson, Marie Breen Smyth and Jeroen Gunning; individual chapters, the contributors

Typeset in Times by Wearset Ltd, Boldon, Tyne and Wear

All rights reserved. No part of this book may be reprinted or reproduced or utilised in any form or by any electronic, mechanical, or other means, now known or hereafter invented, including photocopying and recording, or in any information storage or retrieval system, without permission in writing from the publishers.

British Library Cataloguing in Publication Data
A catalogue record for this book is available from the British Library

Library of Congress Cataloging in Publication Data
A catalog record for this book has been requested

ISBN10: 0-415-45507-3 (hbk)
ISBN10: 0-415-57415-3 (pbk)
ISBN10: 0-203-88022-6 (ebk)

ISBN13: 978-0-415-45507-7 (hbk)
ISBN13: 978-0-415-57415-0 (pbk)
ISBN13: 978-0-203-88022-7 (ebk)

This book is dedicated to Fiona Leggat
Conflict resolution facilitator
7 November 1975–14 June 2008

Contents

List of illustrations ix
Notes on contributors x
Acknowledgements xii

Introduction: the case for critical terrorism studies 1
RICHARD JACKSON, MARIE BREEN SMYTH AND
JEROEN GUNNING

PART I
The contemporary study of political terrorism 11

1 **Mapping terrorism studies after 9/11: an academic field of old problems and new prospects** 13
  MAGNUS RANSTORP

2 **Contemporary terrorism studies: issues in research** 34
  ANDREW SILKE

3 **In the service of power: terrorism studies and US intervention in the global South** 49
  SAM RAPHAEL

4 **Knowledge, power and politics in the study of political terrorism** 66
  RICHARD JACKSON

PART II
Critical approaches to the study of political terrorism — 85

5 Exploring a critical theory approach to terrorism studies — 87
HARMONIE TOROS AND JEROEN GUNNING

6 Emancipation and critical terrorism studies — 109
MATT McDONALD

7 Middle East area studies and terrorism studies: establishing links via a critical approach — 124
KATERINA DALACOURA

8 The contribution of anthropology to critical terrorism studies — 138
JEFFREY A. SLUKA

9 Social movement theory and the study of terrorism — 156
JEROEN GUNNING

10 The contemporary 'Mahabharata' and the many 'Draupadis': bringing gender to critical terrorism studies — 178
CHRISTINE SYLVESTER AND SWATI PARASHAR

11 Subjectivities, 'suspect communities', governments, and the ethics of research on 'terrorism' — 194
MARIE BREEN SMYTH

12 Critical terrorism studies: framing a new research agenda — 216
RICHARD JACKSON, MARIE BREEN SMYTH AND JEROEN GUNNING

Bibliography — 237
Index — 270

Illustrations

Figures

2.1	Books published with 'terrorism' in the title, 1995–2007	35
2.2	Collaborative research: percentage of articles with two or more authors	39
2.3	Percentage of terrorism research articles applying statistical analysis	41
2.4	Percentage of research articles focusing on al-Qaeda	42
2.5	Percentage of research articles focusing on militant Islamist terrorist groups	42
2.6	Percentage of research articles focusing on suicide terrorism	43
2.7	Percentage of research articles focusing on CBRN terrorism	44
2.8	Percentage of research articles with a historical focus	46

Table

8.1	Percentage of deaths of civilians in Northern Ireland, 1969–88	143

Contributors

Marie Breen Smyth is Director of the Centre for the Study of Radicalisation and Contemporary Political Violence (CSRV) at Aberystwyth University, and a Reader in International Politics and co-editor of the journal, *Critical Studies on Terrorism*. She is author of *Truth and Justice After Violent Conflict: Managing Violent Pasts* (2007).

Katerina Dalacoura is Lecturer in International Relations at the London School of Economics and Political Science. She is author of *Islam, Liberalism and Human Rights: Implications for International Relations* (2003) and *Engagement or Coercion: Weighing Western Human Rights Policies towards Turkey, Iran and Egypt* (2003).

Jeroen Gunning is Lecturer in International Politics at Aberystwyth University, Deputy Director of the Centre for the Study of Radicalisation and Contemporary Political Violence and co-editor of the journal, *Critical Studies on Terrorism*. He is author of *Hamas in Politics: Democracy, Religion, Violence* (2007).

Richard Jackson is Reader in the Department of International Politics, Aberystwyth University, and a Senior Researcher at the Centre for the Study of Radicalisation and Contemporary Political Violence (CSRV). He is the founding editor of the journal, *Critical Studies on Terrorism*, and the author of *Writing the War on Terrorism: Language, Politics and Counterterrorism* (2005).

Matt McDonald is Assistant Professor of International Security in the Department of Politics and International Studies at the University of Warwick. He is editor (with Anthony Burke) of *Critical Security in the Asia-Pacific* (2007).

Swati Parashar is completing her doctoral research at the Department of Politics and International Relations, Lancaster University, UK, on gendered constructions of women militants in South Asia. She is editor of *Maritime Counter Terrorism: A Pan Asian Perspective* (2007) and co-editor, with Wilson John, of *Terrorism in South East Asia – Implications for South Asia* (2005).

Magnus Ranstorp is the Research Director of the Centre for Asymmetric Threat Studies at the Swedish National Defence College. He is the author of *Hizb'allah in Lebanon* (1996) and other numerous articles and monographs on terrorism. His most recent edited book is *Mapping Terrorism Research: State of the Art, Gaps and Future Direction* (2006).

Sam Raphael is Lecturer in International Relations at Kingston University London.

Andrew Silke is Professor of Criminology and the Director of Terrorism Studies at the University of East London. He has published extensively on terrorism, crime and policing, and is author of *Terrorists, Victims & Society: Psychological Perspectives on Terrorism and Its Consequences* (2003) and *Research on Terrorism: Trends, Achievements and Failures* (2004).

Jeffrey A. Sluka earned his PhD from the University of California at Berkeley, and is an Associate Professor in the Social Anthropology Programme at Massey University, New Zealand. He is author of *Hearts and Minds, Water and Fish: Popular Support for the IRA and INLA in a Northern Irish Ghetto* (1989), and editor of *Death Squad: The Anthropology of State Terror* (2000).

Christine Sylvester is Professor of Women's Studies and Professorial Affiliate of Politics and International Relations at the Lancaster University, UK. She is author of four books, including *Feminist International Relations: An Unfinished Journey* (2002) and *Feminist Theory and International Relations in a Postmodern Era* (1994), and co-edited (with Dennis Pirages), *Transformations in the Global Political Economy* (1990).

Harmonie Toros is completing her doctoral research at the Department of International Politics of Aberystwyth University, researching the role of negotiations and dialogue in the transformation of conflicts involving terrorist violence.

Acknowledgements

In the present political and cultural context, the pursuit of a 'critical' approach to the study of terrorism can be a lonely and at times, precarious undertaking. Consequently, we are deeply grateful to the many institutions, organisations, colleagues, and friends who have supported our endeavours. We have greatly appreciated the sense of solidarity and intellectual excitement that is developing among the world-wide community of 'critical' scholars of 'terrorism'. We are also very thankful to those who have engaged with our ideas, challenged them and questioned our arguments; this has been enormously helpful in developing our broader approach.

In addition to our highly capable fellow contributors to this volume, and among many others, we would especially like to thank the following people for their support, encouragement, and engagement with this project: Jim Auld, Maggie Beirne, Ruth Blakeley, Ken Booth, Michael Boyle, Robert Brecher, Anthony Burke, Stuart Croft, Steve Crosby, Donatella della Porta, Helen Dexter, Sue Eckert, William Eubank, Frazer Egerton, Mike Foley, Janine Fullerton, Ayla Gol, Adrian Guelke, Jamal Harwood, Eric Herring, Paddy Hillyard, John Horgan, George Kassimeris, Bob Lambert, Andrew Linklater, Daniel McCarthy, Hazel McCready, Michael McPhee, Monica McWilliams, Arzu Merali, John Mueller, Brendan O'Duffy, Padraig O'Malley, Inderjeet Parmar, Zahid Parvez, Jennifer Pederson, Nick Rengger, John E. Richardson, Mike Ritchie, Piers Robinson, Paul Rogers, Jago Russell, Jamil Sherif, Michael Stohl, Doug Stokes, James Vaughan, Stellan Vinthagen, Nicholas Wheeler, Leonard Weinberg, Carrie Rosefsky Wickham, Rorden Wilkinson, Michael Williams, Richard Wyn Jones, and Joseba Zulaika. We are also grateful to many colleagues and friends in the British International Studies Association (BISA) Critical Studies on Terrorism Working Group, and to our enthusiastic students and post-graduate teaching assistants. We are also thankful for the supportive and professional staff at Routledge, especially Andrew Humphrys for his unwavering support of our project.

Finally, we want to say a special thanks to our families, partners, and close friends for supporting and encouraging our work, and for accepting our absences while we toiled on this project. All of our endeavours, including this book, would mean very little without the love and support of our extended communities of affection. In particular, we would like to acknowledge Michelle Jackson, who also ably assisted us with editing the manuscript, David and Kathryn Wells, Margaret and Murray Borthwick, Peter and Kathryn Bremner, Janet Gunning, Margaret Ames, and Ken Sparks.

Richard Jackson, Marie Breen Smyth and Jeroen Gunning

Introduction
The case for critical terrorism studies

Richard Jackson, Marie Breen Smyth and Jeroen Gunning

Critical approaches to the study of terrorism are not new. As Jeffrey A. Sluka notes in this volume, anthropologists have for decades adopted a sceptical view of the dominant discourse and modes of study of those deemed 'terrorists', and as a consequence, much of the anthropological literature challenges commonly held assertions about the nature and causes of terrorism (see also Zulaika and Douglass, 1996). Similarly, during the cold war a number of mainly left-wing scholars explored how the emerging field of terrorism studies was both politically biased towards the West and appeared to function ideologically to legitimise the involvement of Western governments in the suppression of left-wing movements in parts of the developing world (Chomsky and Herman, 1979; Herman, 1982; Herman and O'Sullivan, 1989; George, 1991a). However, critical approaches such as these have taken place largely outside of the main scholarly activities of what we would identify as the traditional terrorism studies field. Certainly, such critical research has rarely been published in the main terrorism studies journals or included in its conferences, and to date, it has arguably failed to influence the general focus and approach of mainstream, international relations-based terrorism research.

More recently, it has been possible to detect a growing sense of unease from many different quarters with both the state of much current terrorism studies research output, and the practical outworking of Western counterterrorism policies – which are often rooted in, or at least legitimised with reference to, the orthodox terrorism studies literature. Within the mainstream field, for example, a number of recent reviews by established and respected scholars of the truly voluminous output following the 11 September 2001 terrorist attacks bemoan the generally poor quality of much terrorism research (see Silke, 2004a; Ranstorp, 2006a; and both in this volume). Similarly, the mixed achievements of the global war on terror, together with its morally disturbing and counter-productive aspects such as foreign invasion, the Guantanamo Bay internment camp, extraordinary rendition, the use of torture, and the erosion of civil liberties, has engendered a growing sense of political disquiet and dismay. Scholars, security practitioners, media pundits, and politicians are now openly questioning widely accepted 'wisdom' about terrorism in ways that were quite unthinkable in the early years following the 2001 attacks (see, for example, Black, 2008).

It was against this backdrop, and inspired by the experience of Critical Security Studies (see Williams and Krause, 1997; Booth, 2004), that a small group of scholars, including the editors of this volume, deliberately set out to stimulate, encourage, and more clearly articulate the nascent but observable 'critical turn' that was starting to become more visible within the broader terrorism studies field. Apart from the strong intellectual case laid out here and elsewhere, we believe that the present historical juncture presents an extraordinary opportunity to develop a critically-oriented approach to the study of political terrorism, in large part because disillusionment with the existing field of knowledge and practice has opened up the intellectual, political, and discursive space that is necessary for the articulation of new ideas, questions, approaches, and paradigms.

Our ambitious project to encourage the widespread adoption of an openly and self-consciously 'critical' approach to the study of terrorism has thus far involved several distinct strands of activity. First, in relation to teaching activities, we have developed a number of critically-oriented modules and courses at undergraduate and graduate levels (including the first Masters in terrorism studies in the world), supervised critically-oriented doctoral research, and encouraged colleagues in other institutions to develop critically-oriented terrorism-related teaching programmes. In addition, we are in the process of preparing an introductory textbook for teaching a critical approach to understanding terrorism. Partly in response to our efforts, but also related to some of the broader developments we have mentioned above, critical approaches to terrorism are now being taught at an increasing number of universities.

A second strand of our activities has involved convening a number of conferences, seminars, and panels at international conferences on the subject. For example, in October 2006, a conference entitled 'Is it Time for a Critical Terrorism Studies?' was held at the University of Manchester, United Kingdom. Bringing together around fifty scholars from the UK, Europe, and North America, the purpose of the meeting was to discuss the development and potentialities of a self-consciously 'critical' approach to the study of terrorism. Since then, panels on critical terrorism studies or critically-oriented panels organised by critical terrorism studies (CTS) scholars have been convened every year at the annual British International Studies Association (BISA) conference and the International Studies Association (ISA) annual convention. In 2008, CTS scholars at Aberystwyth University organised three Economic and Social Research Council (ESRC)-sponsored seminars on aspects of the phenomenon of 'terrorism' that have remained understudied in traditional terrorism research.[1] In addition, key CTS scholars have presented papers at numerous other public seminars, talks, and conferences on aspects of critical approaches to the study of terrorism.

A third strand of activity has involved the establishment of networks of critically-oriented scholars. In addition to several informal networks maintained by individual CTS scholars, in 2006 we formally established the Critical Studies on Terrorism Working Group (CSTWG) within BISA as a way of linking critically-oriented scholars in a global network, organising events, providing solidarity and mutual support, encouraging collaborations, and providing a focus for research activities.[2] The network has expanded to around 100 scholars from the UK, Europe, North America, and Australasia, and now has links with other networks such as the Network of Activist Scholars of Politics and International Relations (NASPIR),[3] the University of Goteborg Resistance Studies Network,[4] and the Terrorism Research Initiative (TRI).[5]

A fourth important dimension of our broader project has been the establishment in 2005 of the Centre for the Study of Radicalisation and Contemporary Political Violence (CSRV) in the Department of International Politics, Aberystwyth University.[6] An openly 'critical' research centre supported by a distinguished international advisory board, CSRV houses several active CTS scholars, as well as the journal, *Critical Studies on Terrorism* (see below). The Centre aims to advance the scholarly study of the use of political terror through a variety of educational and research-based activities, and to support local and international networks and collaborative relationships with academia, government, policy makers, 'suspect communities', donors, politicians, human rights advocates, and other stakeholders in terrorism research.

One of the most significant initiatives we have undertaken so far is the establishment of a new, international, peer-reviewed academic journal called *Critical Studies on Terrorism*, published by Routledge.[7] Since its first issue in 2008, the journal has generated debate and a high level of interest in the wider International Relations field and is increasingly cited by terrorism researchers. The central aim of the journal is to create space and a focus for the publication of robust, innovative research on terrorism, and to encourage fruitful intellectual engagement between critical and orthodox accounts of terrorism. Importantly, another new journal, *Dynamics of Asymmetric Conflict*, is starting to have a similar positive impact.

Finally, we have attempted to publish a range of articles and papers in different formats and locations, including conference papers, journal articles, and online material, which explore a critical approach to the study of political terrorism (see Breen Smyth, 2007; Gunning, 2007a, 2007b; Jackson, forthcoming, 2008a, 2008c, 2007e, 2007f; Jackson *et al.*, forthcoming). We also convened and subsequently published two major symposiums on critical terrorism studies in *European Political Science* (2007) and *Critical Studies on Terrorism* (2008). These symposia brought together a diverse and distinguished group of scholars to explore some of the main issues and challenges raised by our critical project. The present volume is part of this broader attempt to develop a core academic literature on CTS.

Aims of the book

In this broader context, the specific aim of this volume is to bring together an eminent group of scholars to explore, first, why a new 'critical' approach to the study of political terrorism is needed and, second, what such an approach might entail in terms of its ontology, epistemology, methodology, normative standpoint, ethics, contribution to policy, its relation to other disciplines, and most importantly, its future research agenda. We accept that articulating a clear, achievable, and relevant research agenda is the litmus test of any new approach.

It is not enough to simply point out what is lacking in current research; a clear and realistic alternative must also be provided. In essence, our primary purpose was to make the case for critical terrorism studies in a much clearer and more developed form than we have up to this point. We hope that the following chapters will go some way towards this goal, while at the same time opening up and stimulating new questions, issues, debates, relationships, and collaborations.

At the same time, and as the line-up of contributing scholars clearly demonstrates, a central aim of this project was to put into practice our own call for widening the disciplinary basis of terrorism research and including voices and perspectives that are frequently missing in the orthodox literature. To this end, we asked scholars from a range of disciplinary and methodological approaches to contribute, including political science, anthropology, psychology, international relations, area studies, conflict resolution, and feminist studies, as well as both established and younger researchers, and critical and orthodox scholars. The intention was to enrich and enliven the analyses with multiple and diverse perspectives. We believe that such a multi-disciplinary and methodological interface is essential for generating new ideas and insights.

In tandem with these broader aims, we also recognised a pressing need to engage with the existing terrorism studies field in a new, more dialogic manner than some of our critically-oriented predecessors. We are fully cognisant that previous efforts to influence the field have been largely unsuccessful; many of the criticisms made in the 1980s and 1990s, particularly by left-wing scholars and anthropologists, are still, unfortunately, valid today. In part, this previous failure was the result of a tendency by some critically-oriented scholars to couch their critique in polemical and therefore alienating terms, and the fact that many of them originated outside of the field they were criticising. There was also a certain unwillingness to engage in respectful dialogue with orthodox scholars of terrorism; it often appeared to be a case of throwing rocks from the sidelines. Acutely aware of the potential for a similarly unhelpful outcome in this case, we view the call for a critical approach to the study of terrorism as an opportunity for dialogue and debate, conducted in a respectful manner, and occurring primarily within the central concerns, issues, approaches, and scholarly activities of the broader field. We believe that our efforts to date, including this volume, reflect and express this spirit of inclusive, respectful dialogue.

Finally, we should make it clear that our intentions in this project are not to bifurcate or splinter the field, establish political or ideological dividing lines, or create a set of competing intellectual factions. Nor is it our intention to simply replace an established orthodoxy with a new orthodoxy. Rather, our hope is to generate real dialogue and debate, open up new questions and areas of research, and re-energise, revitalise and improve the contemporary study of political terrorism.

Overview of the book

We suggest that making the case for CTS entails two simultaneous steps. In the first place, it requires demonstrating that there are sufficient weaknesses and problems in current research modes to justify a new approach. Second, and more importantly, it necessitates the articulation of a new set of ontological, epistemological, methodological, and research commitments that in combination constitute a new analytical approach to the study of political terrorism.

To this end, we have organised the volume in two parts. The first, 'The contemporary study of political terrorism', examines the broader field of terrorism studies in terms of its main research practices, its primary output and 'knowledge', recent developments, and some of its key problems and challenges. The four chapters in this section clearly demonstrate that there are genuine reasons to be dissatisfied with the present state of terrorism studies, and that a new approach is indeed necessary. The second part of the book, 'Critical approaches to the study of political terrorism', focuses on elaborating an alternative critical approach. Collectively, the eight chapters in this section outline the central elements, key features, foundations, priorities, challenges, and future research agenda of the CTS approach.

Specifically, in Chapter 1, 'Mapping terrorism studies after 9/11: an academic field of old problems and new prospects', Magnus Ranstorp provides an overview of the current state of terrorism research seven years after the terrorist attacks on the United States. He suggests that, although there are some positive signs of lessons being learned, the field continues to suffer from a number of perennial problems, including: the lack of genuine debate over substantive issues and accepted knowledge; over-reliance on secondary material and the failure to generate new data; the dominance of an 'invisible college of scholars' – an epistemic community – and the frequency of one-time research visitors to the field; a disproportionate focus on al-Qaeda-related terrorism and a lack of research on historical and conceptual dimensions of terrorism; the lack of multi-disciplinarity in terrorism research; and the corrosive effects of 'embedded expertise', including the failure to rigorously question the knowledge and credentials of so-called terrorism 'experts'.

In Chapter 2, 'Contemporary terrorism studies: issues in research', Andrew Silke presents a systematic analysis of research published in the two core terrorism studies journals, *Terrorism and Political Violence* and *Studies in Conflict and Terrorism*, since 2001, as a way of assessing the current state of the field. The data analysis is a follow-up to similar research on the state of the field during the 1990s (see Silke, 2004d); the results reveal a very mixed picture. Although there are some positive improvements in the quantity of collaborative research and the use of statistical analysis, for example, there are continuing problems in the wider literature with an over-emphasis on topics related to al-Qaeda, suicide terrorism, and WMD terrorism, a lack of historically-based research, and a continuing heavy reliance on literature review-based research.

In Chapter 3, 'In the service of power: terrorism studies and US intervention in the global South', Sam Raphael presents some of the results of an in-depth analysis of the output of thirty-one leading terrorism studies scholars. His results demonstrate that a great deal of the primary output of the field is politically biased and distorted by the silences on, and failure to study systematically, cases of terrorism by both states and non-state groups allied to Western powers. He suggests that these problems are primarily the result of an uncritical reliance on official sources of information. More worryingly, Raphael's analysis demonstrates that orthodox terrorism studies scholars and their academic research has frequently been used to legitimise coercive intervention in the global South against movements and groups perceived to be opposed to Western interests. In this way, the orthodox field functions ideologically in the service of existing power structures.

Chapter 4, 'Knowledge, power and politics in the study of political terrorism', by Richard Jackson, involves a discourse analysis of some of the main assumptions, narratives, accepted knowledge, and knowledge-generating practices of the orthodox field. Jackson's findings suggest that much of the most widely accepted knowledge about terrorism in the field is open to challenge and provides a poor foundation for further research, public debate, or policy-making. He also finds a number of problematic research practices and state-scholar relationships which undermine the independence and credibility of the field. Some of these practices and relationships are rooted in the field's origins in counter-insurgency studies. More importantly, like Raphael, he also finds that the 'knowledge' generated in the field functions ideologically to reify existing hierarchies of power and promote particular hegemonic projects.

Chapter 5, 'Exploring a critical theory approach to terrorism studies', opens the second part of the book. In this chapter, Harmonie Toros and Jeroen Gunning turn to Frankfurt School Critical Theory, as seen through the lens of Welsh School Critical Security Studies, to delineate the contours of a comprehensive, theoretically-grounded framework for conceptualising and studying 'terrorism'. Such an approach, Toros and Gunning argue, provides a way of thinking about terrorism which both recognises the term's ideological function and acknowledges that there is a form of behaviour that can, within specific discursive and structural contexts, be understood as 'terrorist', thus creating a bridge between critical and orthodox approaches. Employing a Frankfurt-via-Welsh School Critical Theory perspective, they suggest, serves to address many of the shortcomings identified in the first section of this volume (lack of self-reflexivity, de-contextualisation, statism, dearth of fieldwork, and the like) by providing a (deepening) ontology, a (broadening) epistemology, and a methodology based on emancipatory praxis which makes (contextualised) human beings, rather than the state, the primary referents, while rejecting the notion of an objective, context-independent social science.

In Chapter 6, 'Emancipation and critical terrorism studies', Matt McDonald explores the possibility of developing an emancipatory approach to the study of political terrorism, in part through an analysis of the development of Welsh School Critical Security Studies. He argues that emancipation can most usefully be understood as a process (rather than an endpoint) of freeing people from unnecessary structural constraints and the democratisation of the public sphere. He goes on to examine what an emancipatory approach to the study of terrorism might look like through the prism of four key related questions which are central to any 'critical' approach: whose voices are marginalised and empowered by the process of defining and responding to terrorism? What are the immanent possibilities for emancipatory change in contemporary practices of terrorism and counterterrorism? Who are the most vulnerable in relation to terrorism and counterterrorism? And what would emancipation look like in the context of contemporary practices of terrorism and counterterrorism?

In Chapter 7, 'Middle East area studies and terrorism studies: establishing links via a critical approach', Katerina Dalacoura explores some of the ways in which area studies, and Middle East studies in particular, can contribute to the critical terrorism studies project. She argues that a greater focus on history, context, and local knowledge can help to overcome mono-causal explanations of terrorism, such as the 'religious terrorism' thesis, and can provide necessary nuance to the understanding of social movements like Hamas and Hezbollah. Dalacoura then goes on to explore how CTS can contribute to Middle East studies, primarily by providing a framework through which to examine politically and normatively sensitive subjects related to politics and society in the region.

In Chapter 8, 'The contribution of anthropology to critical terrorism studies', Jeffrey A. Sluka outlines some of the main ways in which the anthropological study of terrorism can contribute to the development of the critical terrorism studies approach. He suggests that anthropology's ethnographic methods, its commitment to direct participant-observation in the communities studied, its humanist concern for ethics and, most importantly, its cultural critique, means it has much to offer CTS. Sluka then explores some of the main contributions that anthropological studies on terrorism have already made to the critical approach, before sketching out a future research agenda guided by the concerns that an anthropological approach brings to the study of terrorism.

In Chapter 9, 'Social movement theory and the study of terrorism', Jeroen Gunning puts forward the argument that social movement theory (SMT) is both an appropriate tool to study (oppositional) organisations engaged in terrorist tactics and can make a significant contribution to overcoming some of the weaknesses of terrorism research. He shows how adopting an SMT framework can serve to broaden the focus of terrorism research by: placing violence in its social and temporal context of social movement and state dynamics; offering a multi-level analytical framework which combines macro-structural with meso-organisational and micro-motivational explanations; and bringing under-studied areas such as the relationship between identity and interests, and the impact of state violence and internal group dynamics on militancy, into sharper focus. Gunning then demonstrates how employing an SMT framework can help to deepen terrorism research by helping to address the 'Orientalist' bias that haunts some aspects of terrorism research, particularly on militant Islamist organisations and, more fundamentally, by increasing terrorism research's self-reflexivity and theoretical rigour.

In Chapter 10, 'The contemporary "Mahabharata" and the many "Draupadis": bringing gender to critical terrorism studies', Christine Sylvester and Swati Parashar explore the different ways in which feminist research and perspectives can contribute to the critical terrorism studies research agenda. They argue that women have too often been painted out of the dominant pictures of terrorism or reduced to stereotypical roles (such as victims in need of counterterrorist protection), and that avoiding gender frameworks in examining questions of security and violence is a sure way to prevent critical thinking. They employ the Indian Sanskrit epic, Mahabharata, as a metaphor through which to foreground crucial issues, such as: the place of women in international relations and security studies; women's roles in terrorist and counterterrorist violence; and women's political agency in making, joining, avoiding, and resisting terrorism/counterterrorism. They conclude that CTS needs to broaden its focus and remit, and democratise the kinds of voices who can contribute to its knowledge and understanding.

In Chapter 11, 'Subjectivities, "suspect communities", governments, and the ethics of research on "terrorism"', Marie Breen Smyth examines some of the main ethical and methodological challenges facing critical scholars in collecting primary data on political violence and terror. The experience of 'suspect communities' and the need for researchers to consider the vulnerability of research participants is highlighted. The chapter addresses issues of access, safety, protection of sources and data, risks of seizure or misuse of data collected, and the subjectivity of the researcher, the myth of objectivity, including the perception of 'contamination' of researchers by association with armed (non-state) actors, and the converse problems of association with or accepting funding from governments. The chapter uses the example of the Economic and Social Research Council's (ESRC) New Security Challenges research funding programme to uncover key differences between various disciplines and sectors within the field. Specific challenges faced by scholars seeking to establish a critical approach are discussed, including political attack and intimidation, facing allegations of support for terrorism and the potentially resultant marginalisation, exclusion, and loss of place in scholarly and policy circles. However, the chapter also points to the more positive experiences of critical scholars. The chapter concludes by exploring some of the implications for the practice of research and the shape of a research agenda for critical scholars of terrorism.

The volume culminates in Chapter 12, 'Critical terrorism studies: framing a new research agenda', where the editors bring the preceding analyses together and elucidate the main features and elements of the CTS project. They summarise its core commitments and assumptions, reflect on the main obstacles and challenges for its wider adoption by scholars in the field and, most importantly, sketch out a future research agenda. One of the central arguments of this final chapter is that CTS is not simply a call for better research or the adoption of a particular set of political values. Rather, CTS provides a distinct approach and orientation that marks it out from most of the orthodox terrorism studies literature by virtue of its ontological orientation, its ethical-normative commitments, particularly in terms of emancipation, its reflexivity, and its core research focus and priorities.

Notes

1 Details of these conferences can be found on the Centre for the Study of Radicalisation and Contemporary Political Violence (CSRV) website, available at: http://users.aber.ac.uk/mys/csrv/index.htm.
2 The CSTWG Home Page can be accessed at: www.bisa.ac.uk/groups/7/index.asp.
3 The NASPIR Home Page can be accessed at: http://naspir.net/.
4 The University of Goteborg Resistance Studies Network Home Page can be accessed at: http://resistancestudies.org/.
5 The TRI Home Page can be accessed at: www.terrorismanalysts.com/pt/.
6 The CSRV Home Page can be accessed at: http://users.aber.ac.uk/mys/csrv/index.htm.
7 The *Critical Studies on Terrorism* journal Home Page can be accessed at: www.tandf.co.uk/journals/titles/17539153.asp.

Part I
The contemporary study of political terrorism

1 Mapping terrorism studies after 9/11

An academic field of old problems and new prospects

Magnus Ranstorp

Introduction

For almost thirty years the terrorism studies field occupied a marginal position within mainstream academic circles. Only a handful of academics toiled away individually to provide some social scientific meaning and order out of a catalogue of acute terrorism crisis events as they unfolded across time and contexts. This intellectual effort was largely preoccupied with immediate events, academics being engulfed in making sense of evolving trends and in trying to predict what new waves of terrorism would appear on the horizon. Towards these ends, researchers developed various theories of terrorism. They focused principally on the causes of the phenomenon, the evolution and dynamics of terrorist groups, and how to deal with it from a state perspective (Maskaliunaite, 2004). Some argued that 'the very fact that the subject of terrorism is studied from so many different angles may well be an advantage and not a shortcoming of the field' (ibid.). It requires increasingly interdisciplinary collaboration, as terrorism in the age of globalization and increased complexity can be characterized, in the words of Nancy Hayden, as a 'wicked problem' (Hayden, 2006). As such, it requires knitting together a range of disciplinary approaches outside of international relations and security studies. This social and behavioral research is inherently difficult to conduct as it is 'socially constructed, culturally specific and changing' (Stohl, 2005: 28). Others scathingly 'characterized the field of terrorism studies as stagnant, poorly conceptualized, lacking in rigor, and devoid of adequate theory, data, and methods' (Stampnitzky, 2007a). As Alex Schmid and Berto Jongman lamented back in 1988: 'there are probably few areas in the social science literature in which so much is written on the basis of so little research' (Schmid and Jongman, 1988).

A principal cause for this critique is the surprisingly few research inventories conducted over the years designed to fundamentally question theories, assumptions, and knowledge production. This type of state-of-the-art research inventory is necessary for preparing the next wave of research. My own anthology, *Mapping Terrorism Research* (2006a), convinced me that every new researcher entering the field of terrorism studies ought to produce their own critique and research inventory as a precursor for any further research – to fundamentally question established epistemological and methodological approaches. Far too few self-reflexive books, chapters, or journal articles actually exist taking stock in a unifying sense of the terrorism studies field to account for what we know; how we know what we know; and what research questions we ought to focus on in terms of individual and collective research efforts. Even fewer exist which address the theory and methods of studying terrorism. One explanation for this absence pertains to the relative absence of debate among the orthodox terrorism scholars. This 'invisible college' of terrorism researchers often recycled empirical information, some with questionable credibility and precision, and interchanged contexts, frequently without sufficient regard for situational, political, social or security specificity. As argued by Martha Crenshaw, researchers should try to avoid 'constructing general categories of terrorist actors that lump together dissimilar motivations, organizations, resources and contexts' (Crenshaw, 2000: 405). Often disparate evidence is woven together selectively to suit the case without regard for specific context. Relying on each others' work alongside government and media reports produced an ever-expanding intellectual quilt that had a tendency to grow in size, but less in layered intellectual depth. The same mantras or analogies – as exemplified by Brian Jenkins' 'terrorism likes a lot of people watching not a lot of people dead' (see Jenkins, 1998) – appeared across the terrorism studies literature without anyone ever critically questioning what it really meant and the social scientific basis or qualitative/quantitative method for getting to this conclusion. This problem has been underscored by Michael Stohl who accurately pointed towards what:

> Popper (1934) might caustically designate as 'wisdom' rather than 'science'. Thus, the assembled wisdom might be correct but the demarcation between wisdom and science that would allow proposing the necessary conjectures, collecting the appropriate data and subjecting these conjectures and data to tests which might arguably demonstrate their falsifiability has not yet met the standards of social science epistemology.
>
> (Stohl, 2005)

As complained by Schmid and Jongman, much of the writing in terrorism studies is 'impressionistic, superficial, and at the same time often also pretentious, venturing far-reaching generalizations on the basis of episodal evidence' (Schmid and Jongman, 1988).

Another exceptionally perceptive explanation offered to account for the absence of introspective critiques within the terrorism studies field is made by Lisa Stampnitzky. Convincingly, she argues that this absence is due to the fact there are no barriers of entry to the terrorism studies field and 'that a high proportion of those writing on the topic have no significant background in the topic' (Stampnitzky, 2007a). Unlike area studies or more professionally specialized social scientific disciplines where there is greater rigor in peer-review practices and professionalized barriers of entry, any retrained Soviet specialist or international relations generalist can in theory and practice become a specialized terrorism 'expert' overnight. As outlined by Andrew Silke, there were 490 articles in the two core terrorism studies journals in the period 1990–9 with 83 percent written by one-time authors (Silke, 2003).

The transitory nature of the field of terrorism studies can provide the seeds of intellectual vitality. However, it can also be a major drawback as very few one-time contributors are ambitious enough to critique the field of study or command enough knowledge to do so. The case made by Stampnitzky about no or low barriers of entry into terrorism studies is supported by Avishai Gordon's study that suggests that 'core journals in terrorism studies had significantly higher rates of contributions from non-academic authors than journals in political science or communication studies' (Gordon, 2001). Hence, even journalists, like Peter Bergen, without PhD or social scientific training in methodology or theory but with privileged access from the terror frontlines, have become the new form of 'pseudo-academic' terrorism expert. As noted by Stampnitzky,

> terrorism expertise is constructed and negotiated in an interstitial space between academia, the state, and the media. The boundaries of legitimate knowledge and expertise are particularly open to challenges from self-proclaimed experts from the media and political fields, and this has had significant consequences for the sort of expert discourses that tend to be produced and disseminated.
>
> (Stampnitzky, 2007b)

The terrorism studies field relies on peer-review as a means of quality control, but suffers from the very absence that drives academic knowledge forward – against-the-grain theories and rigorous intellectual debates and critiques among scholars. Much of the literature does not engage with alternative schools of thought or theory-building. The majority of debate is currently occurring in book review sections and rarely encompasses rigorous critique of the validity of theories or methodology. However, even where articles are peer-reviewed, the peers reviewing may lack the expertise, as so much 'terrorism knowledge' is fragmented. Few terrorism experts are really qualified to authoritatively comment on the internal structures of different terrorist groups across different contexts. However, as pointed out by Ken Booth: 'diversity and debate is not therefore a problem for Terrorism Studies, but a sign of life' (Booth, 2008: 67). It is essentially in the post-9/11 era that these types of essential and major academic debates have been surfacing with widely different schools of thought. Many of these debates have been sparked as a response to the construction of databases and from these have emerged analyses that go against the grain of widely-held assumptions and challenge the main orthodoxy.

Debates and databases: challenging the orthodoxy of terrorism theories

Among the first *major* debates in the post-9/11 period was that sparked by Robert Pape's *Dying to Win: The Strategic Logic of Suicide Terrorism* (2005). Originally an expert on airpower (again reinforcing Stampnitzky's point about no barriers to entry of the field), Pape argues in his book that rather than religious motivation, 'what nearly all suicide attacks have in common is a specific secular and strategic goal: to compel modern democracies to withdraw military forces from territory that the terrorist consider to be their homeland' (Pape, 2005: 4). Pape based this analysis from examining every known case of suicide terrorism from 1980 to 2005, which encompassed 315 attacks from eighteen different campaigns. Modestly referring to his database as 'the first complete universe of suicide attacks worldwide, one that includes every attack in which at least one terrorist killed himself or herself while attempting to kill others' (ibid.), Pape's theory on suicide terrorism was critiqued in some quarters on methodological grounds in terms of 'artificially setting suicide terrorism apart from other forms of political violence' (Kiras, 2007: 227); data collection and codification procedures; and for not distinguishing between 'traditional (localized) and contemporary (globalized) patterns of suicide attacks' – the causes of the globalization of martyrdom (Moghadam, 2006: 707–729; Atran, 2006: 127–147; Crenshaw, 2007: 133–162). Nevertheless, Pape's contribution was important evidence-based research amassed in his own database, though there was wide disagreement about what conclusions could be drawn from the data. As Pape underscored, 'knowledge alone will not win the war on terrorism but solid, reliable knowledge is indispensable' (Murphy, 2005).

Interestingly, the second *major* debate erupting among terrorism scholars came in the aftermath of the publication of Marc Sageman's second book, *Leaderless Jihad: Terror Networks in the Twenty-First Century* (2008). A follow-up to his groundbreaking book, *Understanding Terror Networks* (2004), in which he constructed a detailed biographical database of 172 terrorists and advanced the 'bunch of guys' theory where people became terrorists by joining groups and influencing each other to commit terrorism, *Leaderless Jihad* was scathingly attacked by Bruce Hoffman who suggested that it could be 'more scientifically rigorous had he employed essential and basic tools of social science research and built on the core theories of social and terrorist networks' (B. Hoffman, 2008: 133–138). Although Hoffman's critique centered on the fallacy of grassroots terrorism (as al-Qaeda was 'on the march'), the debate was primarily motivated by Sageman's chapter on methodology in which he dismissed much of the existing literature as unscientific because it 'relies too much on narrowly explanatory case studies and profiles of leading terrorist figures, is too heavily dependent on information gleaned from government sources', and amounts to 'nothing more than arguments made for the sake of scoring political points' (ibid.).

Furthermore, Hoffman criticized Sageman for not explaining 'how his collection of data conforms to the scientific standards of academic inquiry that he finds so lacking in the work of most terrorism scholars' (ibid.). Responding to Hoffman's charge that he 'has a surprisingly curt discussion on methodology', Sageman shot back that he could not find any methodology at all in Hoffman's own book, *Inside Terrorism* (B. Hoffman, 1998). Notwithstanding what the *New York Times* described as 'a bitter personal struggle between two powerful figures in the world of terrorism, forcing their followers to choose sides' (Sciolino and Schmitt, 2008),

Sageman makes a salient point, in that 'disagreements among experts are the driving force of the scientific enterprise' (Sageman and Hoffman, 2008).

Evidence-based research should be at the core of terrorism research. As argued by Sageman: 'there is no substitute for careful scrutiny of primary sources, field research, and analysis of court documents (in which suspected terrorists challenge government claims)' (ibid.). The pre-9/11 literature on terrorism has been criticized for its over-reliance on recycled secondary sources and for academics being ensconced in ivory towers, instead of field research and talking to actual terrorists. As Andrew Silke showed, only roughly eleven percent of articles published in the period 1990–9 contained significant amounts of primary source interviews; the majority of articles relied exclusively on secondary sources (Silke, 2003). A principal problem with relying only on secondary material is naturally that no new information is generated, thereby complementing existing knowledge rather than pushing the research envelope in new directions. At the same time, terrorism researchers ought to be cautious about the scientific limits of relying on, and drawing over-generalised conclusions from, interviews with terrorists or former terrorists, especially when matched from different contexts, different degrees of involvement, and under different interview conditions. Some useful and limited insights can be made as long as the methodology is sound, as illustrated by John Horgan's interviews (since 2006) with twenty-eight former terrorists spanning thirteen organizations (including five extremist Islamist groups) about why they left the groups (Ripley, 2008). Similarly, Jeroen Gunning's use of interviews in shedding further light on Hamas's inner workings and the ideological framework of its members is another useful illustration of where primary research can unearth new and significant knowledge (Gunning, 2007c).

Since 9/11, the terrorism studies field has entered into what some observers have called a golden age (Shepherd, 2007). An explosion of academic and other literature addressing terrorism has appeared worldwide. In 2001, according to the social science index, little more than 100 articles were published in the main journals and 'that figure had almost trebled by the following year and has carried on rising ever since, with more than 2,300 citations recorded last year (2007)' (Crace, 2008). Andrew Silke has 'indicated that a new book appears nearly every six hours, and Richard Jackson notes that, during this period, peer-reviewed papers have increased by approximately 300%' (Lentini, 2008: 133). New, innovative and interdisciplinary journals dealing with terrorism-related issues and research have appeared that promise to provide new theoretical and interdisciplinary insights and perspectives on the phenomenon, from *Critical Studies on Terrorism* to *Dynamics of Asymmetric Conflict*. An array of new, exciting research centers, focusing on terrorism and political violence, have eclipsed older and more established university centers whose programs are seen to be stagnant and even decaying. For example, West Point's Combating Terrorism Center and the Norwegian Defence Research Establishment (FFI) are staffed with regional area specialists and Arabic-speakers, and regularly provide the latest cutting-edge in-depth analysis and highly granulated documents on various dimensions of extremist Islamist groups.

Equally, the Centre for the study of Radicalisation and Contemporary Political Violence (CSRV) at Aberystwyth University constitutes an important intellectual platform creating space for critical research on terrorism, while the National Consortium for the Study of Terrorism and Responses to Terror (START) collaboration spearheaded by the University of Maryland is ploughing new ground in quantitative analysis, as well as contributing to new pathways in understanding the ways in which radicalization can lead to terrorism. Web-based portals knitting together expertise are also usefully contributing to on-line journals on the subject of terrorism, and expanding the universe for old and new students of terrorism studies to exchange analysis and perspectives more quickly and with greater frequency.

After 9/11, the shift of terrorism studies to center stage is visible in many ways. Scattered disciplinary expertise across departments in universities is often knitted together to create new centers of terrorism expertise, degree programs, or on-line degrees (Attwood, 2007). This trend, however, is problematic since there are few evaluation mechanisms or comparative reviews about the quality and methods of teaching terrorism studies within the field itself. As such, the orthodoxy of terrorism studies often prevails, as students are consuming a digest of the same standard introductory texts that rarely challenge conventional wisdom or provide new analytical angles or challenging perspectives. In the long-term, this paucity will stymie the intellectual vibrancy of the terrorism studies field. In short, there is no 'gold standard' of what constitutes the appropriate pathway to terrorism studies.

The steady proliferation of terrorism publications after 9/11 has not necessarily increased a balanced analytical focus. According to Andrew Silke, excessive focus on suicide terrorism has contributed to skewing the research focus on certain issues at the peril of ignoring other forms of terrorism and in different historical, political, and social contexts other than the contemporary Arab world or south Asia (Silke, 2004c). Conceptual issues such as the definitional debate and the history of terrorism continue to be largely ignored. A key problem is that current terrorism research efforts can be compared to a game of children's football where all the players are rushing after the ball (the latest terrorism trends) without a strategy, rather than marking different players or utilizing different areas of the pitch.

Although recent years have seen some major leaps in the quantity, and to some extent, quality of research output, terrorism studies research suffers from serious shortcomings as it needs to further develop theoretically and methodologically. As authoritatively argued by terrorism studies doyenne Martha Crenshaw, the problem is that the field

> is probably still plagued by the enduring challenges posed by a lack of definition (what terrorism constitutes); the inability to build a cohesive integrated and cumulative theory (built around larger data-sets and over longer time periods) and the event-driven character of much research.
> (Crenshaw, 2000: 405)

There are some signs that terrorism studies has attracted scholars intellectually capable of bridging adjacent social science disciplines and breaking new ground in terrorism research. Technological developments also offer some considerable promise in providing new avenues to break down disciplinary boundaries. However, much of the criticism levied at the terrorism studies area prior to 9/11 remains relevant today, principally a symptom of the legacy of how the terrorism studies field was created thirty years ago and how it has developed over time.

The emergence and legacy of the field of terrorism studies

The field of terrorism studies has been largely the confines of a rather varied collegiate of scholars hailing from diverse disciplinary backgrounds since its emergence as a specialization in the mid-to-late 1970s. Largely atomized and peripheral to the major disciplinary debates within the social and behavioral sciences, and confined to a few dozen core scholars worldwide, it is not surprising that there has been a relative absence of core debates and critical challenges of assumptions necessary to intellectually push the field forward with new waves of innovative research. This is not to belittle the Herculean efforts made by a few core academic specialists who steadily ploughed forward along the academic 'road less traveled'. They did succeed in establishing the boundaries of the field and working towards some core assumptions and concepts, theories, and methods. As recently identified by Alex Schmid, only a handful of scholars took terrorism seriously in the early 1970s, but 'each of these scholars brought something new to the study of terrorism' (Schmid, 2007). From Ted Gurr's *Why Men Rebel* in 1970 and David Rapoport's book in 1971 linking religion and terrorism, to Martha Crenshaw's seminal article on 'the concept of revolutionary terrorism' in 1972 and the establishment of the RAND terrorism research program by Brian Jenkins that same year, among the most influential academics were Paul Wilkinson and his book *Political Terrorism* published in 1974 that brought 'much needed conceptual clarity and historical depth which had largely been missing until then' (ibid.).

In this book and the subsequent seminal work, *Terrorism and the Liberal State* in 1977, Paul Wilkinson underscored the necessity of balancing civil liberties with security concerns when liberal democracies were under assault from terrorism – a continuous preoccupation throughout his sixteen monographs and of even greater relevance in the post-9/11 period. Together with Walter Laqueur's books and anthologies on the history of terrorism and guerrilla warfare (see for example, Laqueur, 1977), a small core group of scholars provided the necessary historical context and conceptual clarity of this emerging subfield within Security Studies. Some would argue that this historical focus was limited to discussing historical examples of terrorism, as opposed to providing in-depth historical contexualisation of each terrorist episode. In 1977, a new journal, *Terrorism: An International Journal*, edited by Yonah Alexander, signaled the arrival of a specialized area of inquiry.

It had been the concept of the 'urban guerrilla' appearing within liberal democracies in the 1970s that had generated the necessary academic interest in understanding its nature, causes, and effects. Stefan Aust's seminal contribution, *Der Baader Meinhof Complex* in 1985, provided an impressively detailed insight into the German terrorist zeitgeist of 1970–7, while less rigorously researched and conspiratorially motivated books, such as Claire Sterling's 1981 book, *The Terror Network: the Secret War of International Terrorism*, became popular in American quarters as it claimed that the Soviet Union was a major source of backing behind terrorist groupings worldwide. A handful of academics and journalists shed light on various aspects of the emerging phenomena of terrorism, but often without rigorous social science methods or ironclad scientific quality. As lamented by Ted Gurr in 1988: 'most of the (terrorism) literature consists of naïve description, speculative commentary, and prescriptions for "dealing with terrorism" which could not meet minimum research standards in the more established branches of conflict and policy analysis' (Gurr, 1988: 115–154). This stemmed partially from the fact that the terrorism research community was very small in size and, as such, rarely provided avenues for intellectual collisions either due to self-preservation or the vast interdisciplinary landscape of complex social behavior exhibited by different forms and types of terrorism. It was also due to the fact that terrorism and terrorism scholars generally were not being taken seriously by the mainstream academic disciplines of the time and this had, in turn, an adverse effect on debate and the quality of scientific rigor.

As outlined by Edna Reid and Hsinchun Chen in their extensive mapping exercise of the terrorism research domain, there were forty-two core researchers in all between 1965 and 2003 using the Institute for Scientific Information (ISI) citation database (Reid and Chen, 2007: 42–56). This 'invisible college' of terrorism researchers revolved around eight American and two British academics, who constituted the top ten core terrorism researchers, and who influenced the evolution of the field and its orthodoxy. Many of the same core terrorism researchers continually met and presented their findings at the same conferences for over two decades. Their analysis and thinking about the evolution of terrorism largely evolved into veritable 'group think' that moved with the changing contours of the threat of terrorism as it shifted and changed focus per decade. As observed by Leonard Weinberg, 'terrorism research has tended to focus on the here and now' (Weinberg, 2008). In many ways the field of terrorism research has evolved in an event-driven fashion. As rigorously documented and analyzed by Lisa Stampnitzky, the rise and production of terrorism and the way this new field of knowledge was shaped became largely influenced by the creation of terrorism chronologies and databases, as well as terrorism conferences where networks of experts from different disciplines and backgrounds came together from 1972 onwards.

The establishment of the Cabinet Committee to Combat Terrorism by President Nixon in late 1972 provided a contract to RAND to 'provide a broad understanding of the origins, theory, strategy, and tactics of modern terrorism' (Stampnitzky, 2007b). Among the principal projects in RAND was the creation of a chronology of 'international terrorism events' (Jenkins, 2002). Other chronologies and databases followed, with the creation of the University of Michigan ITERATE project, as well as by the CIA and Hero (Historical Evaluation and Research Organization). Yet, as pointed out by Stampnitzky, 'techniques of quantification served both to communicate the magnitude of the problem and also to establish the scientific legitimacy and necessity of its analysis, and thus, also, the need for "terrorism experts"' (Stampnitzky, 2007b). This origin provided the grounds for opening up a number of issues about the political agenda of those setting up these committees and funds, the effect of this on the agendas of this research community, and the role of this research community in framing (and to an extent perpetuating the high visibility of) the threat. In other words, there was an in-built political dimension to knowledge production, which in turn had an effect on the emerging theories and methodologies developed and used.

Similarly, terrorism conferences served to create new networks and constitute a community of interest among nascent individual terrorism scholars from different social science backgrounds. As Stampnitzky observed, those invited to a State Department conference on terrorism in 1976 had done some limited research specifically on terrorism and 'many of the most prominent experts were located in relatively peripheral institutional locations – none were in tenured or tenure-track positions at major research universities, and even at think tanks such as RAND, terrorism research was a relatively peripheral endeavor' (ibid.: 20–21).

Many of those present at the 1976 conference on terrorism would become pivotal scholars, establishing the field as they wrote books and articles about the terrorist phenomenon, sought research funding, and supervised a growing cadre of doctoral students specializing in terrorism-related topics. In many ways, this evolution became the seed for the creation of 'an influential and exclusive "epistemic community"', a network of specialists with a common world view about the cause and effect relationships which relate to their domain of expertise...' (Stone, 1996: 86).

As Edna Reid has shown, different phases have occurred in the evolution of terrorism studies since the real 'take-off' stage between 1972 and 1978 (Reid, 1997: 91–106). The period 1986–90 was marked by a decline in the number of publications, the level of collaboration, and the extent of research funding. During this period, Reid showed that a small and close-knit group of twenty-four scholars produced the majority of publications (from ten to thirty-four books and articles each). This influential 'club' of terrorism researchers was responsible for establishing the principal conceptual and methodological boundaries of successive waves of research. A major problem of research in the pre-9/11 period was methodological, as researchers tended to create closed and circular research systems where they relied on each others' work which was synthesized and functioned in a constantly reinforcing feedback loop (ibid.). As argued by Reid, terrorism studies 'indicates a static environment, the same hypothesis, definitions and theories continue to be analyzed, assimilated, published, cited, and eventually retrieved' (ibid.).

Another major problem for the terrorism studies field was that a majority of articles were authored by one-time research visitors to the field, thereby preventing cumulative theory-driven contributions or debate within the terrorism studies community. Although Hoffman is correct in recognizing that 'science is cumulative' (Sageman and Hoffman, 2008) within terrorism studies, only a handful of academic scholars have spasmodically bothered to take stock as to what the cumulative amounts to in terms of challenging assumptions and in measuring how much new knowledge has been actually generated over the last thirty years. As observed by Vallis *et al.*, 'there is no unified, systematic, and comprehensive framework within which to combine these studies in a way that can integrate the individual, the group, and the society together in a research context' (Vallis *et al.*, 2007).

Terrorism studies in the post-9/11 period

Since 9/11, terrorism research has flourished tremendously, drawing in diverse scholars from different social and behavioral disciplines. The amount of terrorism-related literature is staggering and hard to keep up with, as new books, journal articles, and anthologies are published every day. As systematically collated by Lum, Kennedy and Sherley, 14,006 articles were published between 1971 and 2002 of which 6,041 were peer-reviewed (Stohl, 2005). Of these articles, 'approximately 54% were published in 2001 and 2002' (Lum *et al.*, 2006). This veritable avalanche of studies has usefully energized the terrorism studies field with new intellectual talents offering fresh analytical angles and contextual and cultural depth. Some areas studies experts and newcomers to terrorism studies are making innovative contributions, like Quintan Wiktorowicz, Muhammed Hafez, Glenn Robinson, and Jeroen Gunning, mainly (but not always) Arabists and marrying Middle Eastern studies with social movement theory to offer new insights into processes leading to violent radicalization (Wiktorowicz, 2004a, 2005; Hafez, 2003; Robinson, 1997, 2004; Gunning, this volume). Similarly, Brynjar Lia has made an extraordinary contribution to understanding Abu Musab al-Suri and other revolutionary theoreticians within the context of al-Qaeda's strategy and tactical thinking (Lia, 2007) and Montasser al-Zayyat, the famous Muslim Brotherhood lawyer, has written on the biography and thinking of Ayman al-Zawahiri (Zayyat, 2005). All newcomers to the terrorism studies field, Marc Sageman, Robert Pape, James A. Piazza (Piazza, 2008: 28–39), and Edwin Baaker (Baaker, 2006) to name a few significant contributors, have constructed their own detailed databases of the life histories of terrorists and/or incidents from which they have drawn analysis and trends. At the same time, it is hardly surprising that the 9/11 attacks led to an almost impenetrable mountain of contributions that could be generously characterized as highly speculative in nature and without a high degree of rigorous scientific standard.

In comparison to Andrew Silke's review in 2004 which evaluated the terrorism studies literature between 1990 and 1999, it is clear that 9/11 had a predictably profound effect on the research agenda. Only seven out of 102 articles that were collectively published between the period 2000 and 2001 in both *Terrorism and Political Violence (TPV)* and *Studies in Conflict and Terrorism (SCT)* related to Muslim extremism or an associated Middle East terrorism topic. In other words, there was extraordinarily limited research on al-Qaeda-related topics before 11 September 2001. My own analysis of Bin Laden's Declaration of War published in 1998, which was the first peer-review article to appear on the subject, ominously warned that this phenomenon was part and parcel of unfolding forces across the Middle East and that the West was ill-equipped to deal with the issue (Ranstorp, 1998: 321–330). However, much literature on militant Islamist extremism was fragmentary and lacked analytical breadth or depth. After the 9/11 incident, it took the terrorism research community until 2003-4 to begin publishing significant numbers of analytical articles on al-Qaeda in the two core terrorism studies journals, illustrating the struggle for most non-Middle Eastern Studies specialists to appropriately bound the research problem and to find adequate and original data to support their approaches. However, the terrorism studies field does not lack appropriate empirical information on terrorism, as there is, in the words of the former head of the UK Joint Terrorism Analysis Centre (JTAC), 'an ocean of signals and open-source information' (JTAC, 2006).

By contrast, in 2007 alone, almost half of all articles (thirty-nine of eighty) were devoted to al-Qaeda or a 9/11-related topic such as martyrdom, suicide-bombings, or Muslim extremism. In fact, some have argued that the research agenda has disproportionately inflated the focus on certain topics such as al-Qaeda, suicide-bombing, and the threat of WMD (chemical, biological, radiological, nuclear, and explosive weapons (CBRNE)) terrorism. And yet, few studies exist on the polymorphous nature of al-Qaeda that capture the way different layers are structured and connected to each other and the way the regional and local affiliations interact with core al-Qaeda elements and to different conflict zones (see Byman, 2007; Baaker and Boer, 2007). While it is true that 'terrorism exists as a rhizome, it is inherently nomadic' (Anselmi *et al.*, 2004), this has meant that al-Qaeda means simultaneously everything and nothing – a catch-all phrase for trying to describe complexity and anything unknown. Similarly, as argued by Gary Ackerman, the WMD studies literature has reached something of an 'interpretative impasse', in which terrorism researchers reiterate the same stale assumptions and mix different CBRN agents indiscriminately with each other and without regard for the specificity of context (Ackerman, 2005).

The analytical overexposure on al-Qaeda-related topics is matched by a paucity of work on the history of terrorism and theoretical/conceptual aspects. Only six articles were published on aspects relating to terrorism prior to the 1960s in the period 2000–7, which illustrates the tendency of terrorism studies 'towards a-historicity, presuming that "terrorism" began on 11 September 2001 and ignoring the historical experiences of numerous countries and the already burgeoning literature on "terrorism" published prior to 2001' (Breen Smyth, 2007: 260). Similarly, there were only seven articles on definitional aspects in this same time period, whereas there were only one or two articles addressing major theoretical dimensions in understanding terrorism. David Leheny is one of the few academics who have argued that Constructivism, through the role of symbolism, strategic signaling, and social movement theory, could be a useful vehicle to more closely connect the sphere of international relations theory with terrorism studies (Leheny, 2002: 57–70). Alexander Spencer argues that the two core journals in terrorism studies do not 'contain articles that are directly concerned about applying international relations (IR) theory to terrorism and a brief look at six leading IR theory journals seems to confirm this trend' (Spencer, 2006: 181). At the same time, he points out that international terrorism is part of the discipline of international relations (ibid.). This theoretical lacuna has meant that few terrorism researchers have applied any theoretical approach explicitly or robustly and, similarly, methods are sparingly discussed or applied rigorously in most studies on terrorism. In other words, there is little self-conscious, sophisticated engagement with theoretical developments elsewhere and even less rigorous application of explicitly visible methodologies by the terrorism research community as a whole.

As perceptively pointed out by Jeroen Gunning, this theoretical paucity can be explained by the fact that many 'who publish elsewhere do not wish to be identified with "terrorism studies"' (Gunning, 2007a: 380). Very few heavyweight IR scholars or Middle East studies specialists elect to publish in any of the two core terrorism studies journals. As argued by Gunning, the reasons *may* be the contested nature of the concept itself and the belief – widespread outside 'terrorism studies' – that 'terrorism studies' is a 'theoretically barren' and ideologically compromised field (ibid.: 381). In other words, it can probably be attributed to the fact that many non-specialists are turned off by the political bias and analytical shallowness on offer (see also Raphael, this volume), as they often complain that similar empirical tapestries are woven together *without* much reference to other literature, critical debates, or interviews in the field with actual terrorists.

A principal reason for the absence of overarching theories and methods is that terrorism is characterized by contradictory assumptions underpinning different levels of units of analysis and across different disciplines within social sciences. It is situated awkwardly between the often clashing ontologies and epistemologies that are used by different subjects and disciplines. As underscored by Vallis, Yang and Abbass's extensive review of the social science literature on terrorism,

> some of the findings of research into the political, social and cultural bases of terrorism is contradictory. That is to say, political science views of terrorism as a form of instrumental rational choice contradict psychological and social explanations of terrorism that view terrorism as a 'product' rather than choice.
> (Vallis *et al.*, 2007)

An important conclusion derived from this research review is that a multidisciplinary analysis is critically needed and that integration of 'the group, individual and societal levels' offers a robust approach, while focus on terrorism decision-making 'processes' and rational choice theories 'offered the highest level of prediction and causal explanation' (ibid.; see also Gunning in this volume).

A principal outcome of the non-terrorism specialist interest in terrorism in the post-9/11 period has been a dramatic expansion of different perspectives from cognate disciplines within the social sciences. This has produced positive effects, as it has drawn in new analytical approaches from cultural anthropology, modeling, and complex adaptive systems to name a few. There is also much more focus on evidence-based research as a vehicle for more rigorous quantitative as well as qualitative research results (J. Ross, 2004).

Over the last three decades, terrorism studies have been criticized for the event-driven nature of research efforts and its policy-driven character. The problem of perceived 'embedded' terrorism expertise existed well before 9/11, but the subsequent dramatic policy focus on terrorism has contributed to even more attention being paid to the nexus between policymakers in the corridors of power and terrorism expertise. As correctly argued by those advocating a critical terrorism studies approach, there is a danger that terrorism studies 'is a largely co-opted field of research that is deeply enmeshed with the actual practices of counterterrorism and the exercise of state power' (Jackson, 2007e: 245). There is a critical issue to bear in mind, namely, that terrorism research may be perceived to be co-opted by government interests and the associated risks of becoming an uncritical mouthpiece of state interests, rather than speaking truth to power (Gunning, 2007b: 240). It is critical to maintain an independent and non-operational role as a researcher in relation to the highly contentious term 'terrorism' and its essence as a subject matter.

The various sensational revelations of terrorist plots, many of which are still unverifiable through documentation, are illustrative of the problematic relationship between terrorism research and policymakers. The claims by Rohan Gunaratna that the 11 September 2001 hijackers planned to hijack a plane and crash it into Big Ben and the House of Commons is illustrative of many unsubstantiated claims by terrorism experts allegedly based on privileged government access that go unchallenged (CNN, 2002). This and other unverifiable claims, often highly publicized at the time of revelation, can often be confused with scientific fact and migrate into so-called 'knowledge'. It is starkly illustrative of the corrosive problem of 'embedded expertise' that provides those critical of the field with ample ammunition to conduct assaults on the science. As poignantly argued by A. Jones, the problem with this is that 'researcher-policy maker relations often devolve into "slightly incestuous echo-talk"' (Jones, 2007), where policymakers and researchers are mutually reinforcing each others' claims as authoritative. Identification of boundaries is in the interest of both the terrorism researcher and policymakers. However, the post-9/11 milieu has produced even greater dangers of a new breed of 'embedded expertise' that exploits crevices in the undergrowth of terrorism studies field that provide them with enough grip to push forward effectively various duplicitous agendas under the guise of 'honest' social scientific projects. As acknowledged by John Horgan, 'the unfortunate popularity of the study of terrorism has drawn a lot of opportunists who do not do serious work' (Horgan, 2008: 58).

The art of masquerading evidence in terrorism research

As Bruce Hoffman poignantly pointed out in a *Foreign Affairs* article, criticism about the field of terrorism studies is 'neither new nor unjustified' (B. Hoffman,

2008). In particular, Hoffman invoked the damning critique made thirty years ago by Professor Michael Howard, who charged that terrorism studies had 'been responsible for more incompetent and unnecessary books than any other outside ... of sociology. It attracts phoneys and amateurs as a candle attracts moths' (ibid.).

Howard's assessment can be considered as true today as it was thirty years ago. A major global strategic surprise event like 9/11 is bound to attract unscrupulous characters, pseudo-academics alongside outright fraudsters, often masquerading behind a thin facade of privileged access to secret sources, often unverifiable in contravention to standard academic praxis. In most cases, this type of rumor intelligence (RUMINT) masquerading as scientific evidence lacks any acceptable academic rigor. Additionally, journalistic speculation or even inaccuracies in reporting events as they unfold, move effortlessly from fiction to becoming established facts. Rarely are these empirical facts investigated or challenged with enough effort. Even rarer are those instances when these well-established facts are investigated to further develop a greater degree of granularity in both detail and context. This becomes especially troublesome as these established 'empirical' facts become continuously reused in other academic contexts to fit ready-made assumptions and arguments. Blurring boundaries between journalism and academic expertise, facts or fiction obfuscate the reliability of data and erode serious terrorism research based on rigorous theory-building and the use of sound methodologies. Good journalism and interesting reporting should not be *confused* with academic rigor or scientific standards.

Within terrorism studies, there are sometimes no bounds to the ingenuity of experts, and at times, outright deception and fraud. Perhaps the most celebrated and outrageous case is that of the Frenchman, Alexis Debat, who managed to rise from being a journalist reporter to the position of Director of the Terrorism and National Security Program at the Nixon Center in Washington DC, as well as contributing editor to *The National Interest*. In an extensive exposé by the French news media *Rue 89* in June 2007, it was revealed that Debat had made up several bogus interviews with former US President Bill Clinton, former US Secretary of State Colin Powell, New York Mayor Michael Bloomberg, Microsoft founder Bill Gates, former Federal Reserve Chairman Alan Greenspan, and former UN Secretary-General Kofi Annan, for the French magazine, *Politique internationale* (B. Ross, 2007).

After resigning from *ABC News* as a terrorism consultant, after it was discovered he did not hold a PhD from Sorbonne University as he had claimed on his résumé, a series of other claims also proved fraudulent, such as: being a former advisor to the French Ministry of Defence on Transatlantic Affairs; having been Director of the Scientific Committee for the Institut Montaigne (Paris); 'working on the largest manuscript ever written on the history of the Central Intelligence Agency'; and working with RAND, among many other cases (Bourcier and Lesnes, 2007).

This 'mythomaniac analyst' case, as dubbed by *Rue 89*, casts a dark shadow over the terrorism studies field. The fact that Alexis Debat went unchallenged for over five years in terms of faking interviews and rising to prestigious academic positions without postgraduate research qualifications illustrates the case that there is a real absence of critical rigor in questioning expertise and the way in which work is conducted and verified in a scientifically acceptable fashion. It would be easy to disregard the Debat case as the exception rather than a trend that negatively exposes terrorism studies to criticism. Unfortunately, he is far from alone.

Another illuminating case is that of Evan Kohlmann, who authored *Al-Qaida's Jihad in Europe: The Afghan–Bosnian Network* (2004). Considering himself an academic and a 'micro-historian' (Mills, 2008), Kohlmann skillfully mastered the 'art of court diving', volunteering to become an expert witness for the prosecution where he gains access to all discovery material, which in turn, through snowballing is reused in his analysis elsewhere. There is, of course, nothing innately wrong with this practice. However, as underscored by David Miller, Kohlmann

> has risen almost without a trace. With no expertise beyond an undergraduate law degree and an internship at a dubious think-tank, he has become a consultant to the US department of defence, the department of justice, the FBI, the Crown Prosecution Service, and Scotland Yard's SO-15 Counter Terrorism Command.
>
> (Crace, 2008)

Subsequently, without any PhD degree in a cognate social science subject or few publications in any peer-reviewed scholarly journals, Kohlmann managed to testify as an expert witness in at least ten federal terrorism trials in the US and in six criminal (terrorism) cases in Europe. In one terrorist trial, Kohlmann was put forward as an expert witness on the Bangladeshi Islamist party *Jamaat-e-Islami* in *USA* v. *Aref and Hossain* (Northern District of New York, 2006). However

> under cross examination it transpired that he had never written any papers on the party, nor been interviewed about the group. He had never been to Bangladesh, could not name the country's Prime Minister nor the name of the leader of *Jamaat-e-Islami*.
>
> (Mills, 2008)

Similarly, Kohlmann, who speaks some basic Arabic but has never been to Afghanistan or Pakistan, appeared before the first Guantanamo military commission in the case of Salim Hamdan (Bin Laden's chauffeur) in 2008. In this case, Kohlmann testified that the Office of Military Commission (OMC) had commissioned him to produce a seven-part, ninety-minute video about the evolution of al-Qaeda containing a select collage of violent images which he edited, produced, and narrated himself and which was shown at the trial and is planned to be shown in subsequent Guantanamo military commissions. Handsomely paid $45,000 for the film and his testimony, Kohlmann admitted that the OMC had

> changed his proposed name of the film from the "Rise of al-Qaeda" to "The al-Qaeda Plan" in order to draw closer comparison to "The Nazi Plan'', a

famous documentary movie produced during the Nuremburg trials by the US-led prosecution team.

(Muhammad Ally, 2008)

The fact that the prosecution needs to rely on what they themselves describe as a 'self-made al-Qaeda expert' as one of their principal witnesses, undermines severely the credibility of the proceedings and makes mockery of the principle of scientific expertise. Furthermore, it should bewilder most observers that a 'self-made al-Qaeda expert' becomes the custodian in the portrayal of the evolution of al-Qaeda, rather than seasoned scholars with superior knowledge and decades of experience in the region. Probably the answer is simply a financially-driven pliability to stay on message for the prosecution that would not easily exist with a reputable academic with his or her hard-earned reputation at stake.

A principal problem with charlatans and self-proclaimed terrorism expertise in a court of law setting is that 'calling expert witnesses in legal cases is predicated on the assumption that the evidence given will be objective and factually correct – governed by the principle of professional, scientific neutrality' (Crace, 2008). The court records show contradictory evidence, as only a handful of self-proclaimed experts become 'hired guns' for the prosecution without regard for any scientific rigor or principles of impartiality.

One of the most celebrated self-proclaimed al-Qaeda terrorism experts in the post 9/11-period is Sri Lankan-born Rohan Gunaratna, author of *Inside al Qaeda*, who was paid $53,700 as the principal prosecution witness in *USA v. Hassoun, Jayyousi and Padilla* at the United District Court in Florida June/July 2007. Dubbed by the British *Observer* as 'probably the least reliable expert on al-Qaeda' (Bright, 2003), Gunaratna was thoroughly exposed by the Australian newspaper, *The Age*, as making dubious and incorrect claims about his numerous affiliations (Hughes, 2003). Additionally, questions have been raised as to the reasons why Gunaratna continues to downplay his role as a former researcher at St Andrews University when he otherwise engages in self-promotion about his affiliations.

Gunaratna's cavalier attitude and mockery of rigor in academic research and scholarship was evidently displayed during his testimony at the trial in 2007. His testimony under oath claimed that it was academically acceptable to use classified sources that could not be identified or substantiated, because 'if you name that source, the next week that source will be killed. So sometimes you cannot identify a source ... sometimes there is no opportunity for citations' (*USA v. Adham Amin Hassoun, Kifah Wael Jayyousi, Jose Padilla*, 2007a: 82–83). At the same time, Gunaratna acknowledged under cross-examination by the defence lawyers that sound research and scholarship relied on three characteristics: 'accuracy, impartiality, honesty' (ibid.: 99–100). The problem with Gunaratna's approach to evidence through interviews is threefold, as explicitly documented by the 2007 court testimony: (1) it leaves scope to believe some interviews were fabricated; (2) that he cannot locate them in time nor (broadly without compromising security) place; and (3) that the circumstances of his interviews were dubious at times, as they involved tortured and imprisoned terrorist suspects before their cases had gone through any court of law.

Contrary to the claim on the jacket of *Inside al Qaeda* (a title 'borrowed' from Bruce Hoffman's 1998 book, *Inside Terrorism*) where Gunaratna claims he worked on al-Qaeda for over five years prior to 9/11, it is clear that he began working on the issue of Bin Laden and al-Qaeda in earnest only a few months prior to August 2001, when he published an article in *Jane's Intelligence Review* (Gunaratna, 2001). For four years prior to 9/11, he was a postgraduate research student at St Andrews University working on a thesis about Diaspora groups which did not include any analysis of militant Islamist movements; nor did he during this time period claim any specialized expertise on Islam, the Middle East, or Bin Laden. As pointed out by Peter Cronau

> a Sri Lankan, Gunaratna cut his teeth working for the Sri Lankan government from 1984 to 1994 researching and writing about the bloody Tamil separatist conflict. Much of what he now writes he sees through the prism of that conflict.
>
> (Cronau, 2003: 202)

Without Arabic or Urdu language skills, Gunaratna claims to have visited the Middle East region extensively in the past and to have interviewed terrorists. However, as admitted during the Padilla trial, he first visited Israel in 1999 or 2000 and had never been to Lebanon, Egypt, Saudi Arabia, or Yemen, despite the fact that he claims to have interviewed 200 terrorists for the book. When pressed about this in the 2007 Padilla trial, he admitted they were actually not hardcore terrorists but rather 'sympathizers.'

Another major revealing discrepancy relates to Gunaratna's belief that a majority of interviews with these terrorists cited as anonymous sources in undisclosed locations could be judged acceptable within sound and rigorous scholarly standards. When pressed by the defense lawyers on the witness stand, 'a huge number of sources in your book cannot be checked by other authorities unless they have inside information from you?' – Gunaratna simply replied: 'I agree' (*USA* v. *Adham Amin Hassoun, Kifah Wael Jayyousi, Jose Padilla*, 2007a: 158–159). The fact is that there is no information at all about these sources which would allow for some form of corroboration.

Under oath in testimony riddled with contradictions and exaggerations, Gunaratna revealed that he did not follow robust ethical codes of conduct or concern for protecting human subjects when interviewing terrorists. Specifically, Gunaratna claims to have 'debriefed' terrorists in detention facilities without them having court proceedings and to have interviewed detainees who had been *tortured* while in detention (ibid.: 178–179), sometimes for research purposes and at other times being 'engaged in some projects for various governments' (*USA* v. *Adham Amin Hassoun, Kifah Wael Jayyousi, Jose Padilla*, 2007b: 110–111). In particular, Gunaratna has repeatedly used alleged CIA interrogation reports of captured senior al-Qaeda operatives held in secret detention facilities, such as

Khalid Sheikh Mohammed, as a source for scholarly articles, even though the detainee was subjected to 'hundreds of different (interrogation) techniques in just a two-week period soon after his capture' (Mayer, 2008) in 2003. It is doubtful that Gunaratna can produce these documents – if they exist at all. Moreover, this kind of unethical behavior and murky water seriously undermines not only the credibility of Gunaratna, but also casts a dark cloud over the entire terrorism studies community as to the general perception of their ethical codes of conduct during interviews. Critically, the terrorism research community ought to ponder why it is comfortable in using information gathered under torture.

Gunaratna also admitted that he worked very closely with a number of intelligence services. As underscored by him in court testimony, 'you cannot become a terrorism specialist unless you have access to government collectors' (*USA* v. *Adham Amin Hassoun, Kifah Wael Jayyousi, Jose Padilla*, 2007a: 181–182). It is very clear that Gunaratna has never heeded or heard of the famous advice by Schmid and Jongman that researchers should not confuse their roles: 'his role is not to "fight" the terrorist fire; rather than a "firefighter"', he should be a student of combustion' (Schmid and Jongman, 1988: 179). As an 'embedded academic', Gunaratna admitted that there was no way of verifying intelligence information compared to information that had gone through a court of law (*USA* v. *Adham Amin Hassoun, Kifah Wael Jayyousi, Jose Padilla*, 2007a: 182–183). Yet Gunaratna has repeatedly shown poor academic judgment, publishing an article in *Playboy* magazine, as well as in the number of many poorly substantiated claims best exemplified by his contested testimony during the 9/11 Commission Hearing when a senior CIA official came out contradicting his claims (Carr, 2003). This is not to acknowledge that Gunaratna does offer some useful analysis; however, the principal problem remains that it is virtually impossible to decipher what is fact or fiction from his research claims or to triangulate his sources. Less than scientific conduct has sullied and overshadowed more substantive and scientifically more rigorous research efforts. In fact, the absence of scientific criticism of Gunaratna within the terrorism studies community is not only ethically and scientifically indefensible, but also illustrative of the fact that the orthodox terrorism studies community is still relatively embryonic and underdeveloped. It also vividly shows that a world of mutually reinforced camaraderie is often valued over scientific scrutiny of methods, theory, and data. It is also indicative that the terrorism research community frequently adopts a common worldview, as it does not readily critique those who produce arguments that support accepted knowledge. In essence, this invisible college has lost track of the fact that 'strong research deals with events critically, evaluates all potential alternatives and arrives at a conclusion that is methodologically and empirically sound' (D. Jones, 2006).

Some of the aforementioned 'self-anointed' terrorist experts are part of a growing phalanx of what some have called 'terrorologists' (see George, 1991a; Herman and O'Sullivan, 1989) 'who sell a toxic brew of cultural stereotypes and pop psychology packaged in pseudo-academic jargon' (Ahmad, 2008). They represent a minority within the terrorism studies field, but have had major visibility from media appearances and for their flagrant disregard for standard scholarly and ethical codes of conduct. In some way, they have had an inverse positive effect in highlighting the crucial importance of ethical codes of conduct when dealing with a complex social and behavioral science such as terrorism research. They also underscore that the terrorism studies field has low or no barriers of entry, unlike other social science areas where there is a high degree of professionalisation and clearly regulated barriers of entry. As such, it is critical that more established and more credible terrorism scholars assume a greater responsibility for the integrity of research findings; they need to engage more critically with colleagues who violate research standards, as they would never let their undergraduate students get away with this type of masquerading of evidence. It is incumbent upon them that they challenge and expose dubious research agendas and findings rather than, as now, silently sweeping it under the carpet in a bandwagon fashion.

Conclusion: future directions?

As Marie Breen Smyth has highlighted, there are some troublesome features with terrorism research, such as the tendency of 'a-historicity, presuming that "terrorism" began on 11 September 2001 and ignoring the historical experiences of numerous countries and the already burgeoning literature on "terrorism" published prior to 2001' (Breen Smyth, 2007: 260). This division is underscored by Bruce Hoffman's observation that 'on 9/11, of course, Bin Laden wiped the slate clean of the conventional wisdom on terrorists and terrorism, and, by doing so, ushered in a new era of conflict – as well as a new discourse about it' (quoted in ibid.). Only a few of us have had the benefit and hindsight of having been involved in terrorism studies research before and after 9/11. It is very clear that terrorism studies research is beginning to mature, and to produce sufficient self-reflexivity and debate among scholars from different disciplinary backgrounds. New interdisciplinary journals such as *Dynamics of Asymmetric Conflict*, as well as *Critical Studies on Terrorism*, are just an illustration that a critical mass of perspectives is beginning to emerge that challenges analytical approaches, but which will only serve to benefit and enrich the field. This willingness to intellectually engage with opposing views and perspectives between those advocating a 'traditional' approach to terrorism studies and those arguing that a juncture exists necessitating a 'critical turn' is only beginning to emerge. In part, this is due to the fact that the 'critical terrorism studies case' has only recently gotten off the ground. It is also dependent on the willingness of 'traditional' terrorism researchers to examine the merits of, and to engage in a vigorous debate about, the core issues surrounding 'critical terrorism studies'. Although a pathway has been ploughed by John Horgan and a few others into this debate (Horgan and Boyle, 2008), it is less certain whether other more orthodox-minded terrorism researchers will be willing or intellectually ready to follow or whether they will simply continue the same epistemic pathway as always trodden. This would be a great pity, as orthodox terrorism experts continuously need to question their own assumptions and approaches in order to move the field forward. In this sense critical terrorism studies offer a valuable pathway in a Coxian sense, 'calling into question prevailing social relationships and institutions' (Booth, 2008: 71).

Terrorism is an immensely contested concept and a complex social and behavioral phenomenon. Much research needs to be done in a multidisciplinary fashion to deepen existing knowledge and to push the envelope in new directions. More research needs to be collated about the multivariate causes of terrorism more broadly which builds on the few but excellent studies that are available (Bjørgo, 2005; Lia, 2005; Lia and Skjølberg, 2000, 2004; Newman, 2006.). Similarly more research needs to explore the issue of radicalization leading to terrorism and the connection to the preventative strands of countering radicalization itself and the hard effects of counterterrorism efforts. As I have argued elsewhere, it is important to capture the 'causative dynamic interaction which in turn changes the terrorists' behavior and choice of tactics' (Ranstorp, 2006a). As such, more research effort is needed to explore the role of innovation; group dynamics; how and why terrorism ends; decision making within terrorist groups and in counterterrorism; effective crisis management procedures; and public reactions to terrorism. Additionally, understanding the role of ideology, the constituent parts of al-Qaeda's narrative, and efforts to counter these ideological dimensions on the global and local levels in an age of globalization could provide fruitful research avenues that bridge interdisciplinary research into cultural anthropology, information operations, communication studies, and other cognate areas. Similarly, as argued by Vallis *et al.*, 'the "framing" and definition issue in terrorism needs further work, especially with regards to the social constitution of terrorism as a phenomenon' (Vallis *et al.*, 2007). Often the most exciting terrorism research findings are located on the periphery between related cognate social sciences.

Intelligence studies, for example, offers a real prospect for further cross-fertilization with terrorism studies, as both fields struggle with locating methodologies to better handle analytical complexity in the face of growing global uncertainty. Similarly, recognition that cultural anthropology can provide a deeper granulated perspective into communicative aspects and symbolism would significantly enrich terrorism studies. To date, few studies exist that capture this culturally vital dimension, offering a richer and more nuanced insight into al-Qaeda's signaling behavior in a fragmented globalization media environment.

Boundless research horizons have opened up as a result of 9/11, which has moved terrorism studies from the periphery to center stage. Much rich knowledge exists on various dimensions of terrorism that needs to be explored in greater analytical depth and through interdisciplinary breadth. Taking intellectual stock as to the state of the art of terrorism research and where there are problems and prospects is essential in order to reflect on past achievements and where research needs to head. Terrorism research has come a long way, but has even further to journey in different directions. The time has come for more rigorous research inventories and exploration of multidisciplinary approaches into terrorism as a complex social and behavioral phenomenon. In turn, this multi-disciplinarity requires self-reflexivity about methodology, ontology, and epistemology to work. Otherwise, you end up with mutually contradictory findings with no way of adjudicating between them or resolving them. More orthodox terrorism studies ought to recognize that vigorous debates, critical self-reflexivity, and alternative analytical assumptions and approaches do not constitute a threat to knowledge production, but instead, are essential ingredients for moving the next wave of pioneering research forward. After all, this is the very essence of the academic enterprise.

2 Contemporary terrorism studies
Issues in research

Andrew Silke

Introduction

The aim of this chapter is to provide a general review of research published in the core terrorism studies journals between 1990 and 2007. As such, this chapter seeks to build on a long history of past reviews and assessments of the literature (Reid, 1983; Schmid and Jongman, 1988; Merari, 1991; Silke, 2004c) which have attempted at various points to assess the state of the art on this subject. Terrorism has never been an easy subject to study or research. In particular, relentless (and ongoing) conceptual and definitional disagreements, a shortage of experienced researchers, and a general lack of funding for studies have all presented formidable obstacles. Indeed, in the 1990s, there were probably only about 100 researchers across the world researching and writing on terrorism on a regular basis (Silke, 2004c). One consequence of such an environment is that studies which are expensive in terms of funds or time have been scarce as the resources have not been present to carry them out. This has hindered the progression of the field and much work is simply rehashing old data or providing primarily descriptive or exploratory analysis.

Since the terrorist attacks of 9/11, interest in – and funding for – terrorism-related research has increased enormously. The number of researchers both in terms of postgraduate students and more established professionals has increased enormously.

Thus, this review hopes to shed light on what are the key issues in the core journals in a post-9/11 world and whether there are any indications that old problems and limitations are as prevalent as in the past.

The massive rise in funding and manpower has, not surprisingly, led to a similarly enormous rise in publications on the subject. Figure 2.1, for example, shows the huge increase in books on terrorism. The figure illustrates the number of non-fiction books with the word 'terrorism' in the title which have been published since 1995. By June 2008, 2,281 non-fiction books with 'terrorism' in the title had been published since September 2001.[1] In comparison, prior to September 2001 only 1,310 such books had been published in entirety. In short, most of the published work on terrorism has been created in the past seven years.

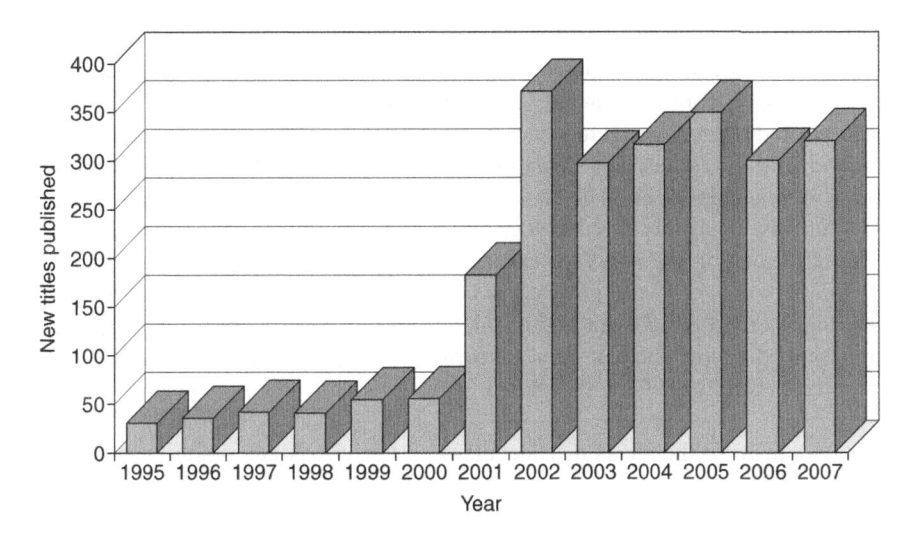

Figure 2.1 Books published with 'terrorism' in the title, 1995–2007.

The huge rise in books has been accompanied by a similarly impressive increase in journal articles. For 2000, the International Bibliography of the Social Sciences recorded 133 articles on 'terrorism'. For 2007, this had risen to 502 articles. Even bigger increases occurred elsewhere. PsycINFO – which includes information from nearly 2,000 journals in the social sciences – recorded just twenty-five articles on 'terrorism' in 2000. In 2007, 556 articles on the subject were recorded. The older journals have also increased their output: the journal *Studies in Conflict and Terrorism* brought out four issues per year prior to 9/11; it now publishes on a monthly basis. There has also been growth in new specialist journals joining the field, with titles such as *Critical Studies on Terrorism* and *Dynamics of Asymmetric Conflict* launched in recent years. Beyond the core terrorism studies journals, articles on the subject in other journals have also increased hugely across the board (Czwarno, 2006).

Naturally, this survey of the increased literature should not be seen as exhaustive. There are many books and journal articles which are related to terrorism which do not have 'terrorism' in the title. For example, many books have been written about the Irish Republican Army (IRA) in the past thirty years. For many observers, the IRA is a terrorist organization (and was certainly proscribed as such in many jurisdictions). Indeed, the group was the most heavily researched and discussed organization in the core terrorism journals prior to 9/11 (and remains the second most discussed group today) (Silke, 2006). Nevertheless, extremely few of the many books on the group had 'terrorism', 'terrorist', or even 'terror' in the title. Almost all of the books which are standard reading for anyone who has a serious interest in understanding the IRA would be missed if those words were relied upon to identify them (see Coogan, 1987; Bishop and

Mallie, 1987; Sluka, 1989; B. O'Brien, 1993; Toolis, 1995; Collins, 1997; O'Doherty, 1998; Harnden, 1999; Bowyer Bell, 2000; English, 2003; etc.).

This state of affairs is partly a consequence of the serious – and arguably irresolvable – problems which remain with the term 'terrorism' itself. There is still no wide agreement within academic circles on what exactly is meant by 'terrorism', and indeed the recent emergence of 'Critical Terrorism Studies' is partly a reflection of this. The question as to what constitutes terrorism, and who is a terrorist, is deeply problematic. There is still no precise and agreed definition of terrorism, and some writers have concluded that 'it is unlikely that any definition will ever be generally agreed upon' (Shafritz *et al.*, 1991). It is not my intention here to get side-tracked in a definitional debate, but rather to stress that the use of the term fluctuates and 'terrorism' means different things to different people. As Gearty (1991: 6) has noted:

> The major difficulty is that identifying a terrorist is not simply a matter of ticking off items on a checklist of violent attributes. The label itself is inevitably value-laden. Its meaning is moulded by government, the media and in popular usage, not by academic departments. The word resonates with moral opprobrium and as such is, as far as the authorities and others are concerned, far too useful an insult to be pinned down and controlled. The manipulators of language are no respecters of academic integrity, and, simply to keep up, political scientists who believe a definition is possible have had to broaden their attempts so extensively that the exercise becomes rather pointless.

Combining a massively growing wider literature to serious problems and debates over what 'terrorism' actually is, is a recipe for confusion and acrimony. Nevertheless, in an effort to help provide a framework for understanding the literature, this chapter represents the latest in a series of articles by the author which have reviewed some aspects of research on terrorism (Silke, 2001, 2004c, 2006).

The first set of these papers focused on research carried out in the 1990s (Silke, 2001). That initial review found that many of the traditional problems associated with research on terrorism continued to eat away at the field's foundations during the 1990s. These problems centered on a shortage of experienced researchers, a large proportion of transient researchers who were often very poorly aware of previous research in the area, a lack of more rigorous data-gathering methods and data analysis. Early reviews, such as Schmid and Jongman's famous work in 1988, had long appreciated that despite the fact that a very sizable body of literature had accumulated on terrorism, the substance of this writing was often very poor indeed. As Schmid and Jongman (1988: 177) noted: 'Much of the writing in the crucial areas of terrorism research ... is impressionistic, superficial, and at the same time often also pretentious, venturing far-reaching generalizations on the basis of episodal evidence.' In examining the quality of research on terrorism, Schmid and Jongman noted that 'there are probably few areas in the social science literature on which so much is written on the basis of so little research'. They estimated that 'as much as 80 percent of the literature is not research-based in any rigorous sense; instead, it is too often narrative, condemnatory, and prescriptive' (Schmid and Jongman, 1988: 179).

My first review showed that this pessimistic state of affairs was largely unchanged (Silke, 2001, 2004c). During the 1990s, 68 percent of the research was found to be based on the literature-type reviews criticised by Schmid and Jongman. Further, the related long-running shortage of terrorism researchers also continued to weaken the area. While the backgrounds of researchers may be relatively diverse, there has in general been a consistent lack of researchers to carry out investigative work in the area. Since it emerged as a clear and substantial topic of study, terrorism has suffered from a near-chronic lack of active researchers. The 1990s review found that terrorism studies had 40 percent fewer authors contributing to articles compared to fields such as criminology (where many of the same research issues and limitations also apply). The lack of researchers meant that less expensive (in terms of time and effort) data gathering and data analysis methods were being used with consequent concerns over the quality and reliability of the findings.

The next review added analysis of research in the first three years following 9/11 (Silke, 2007). While this showed that some distinct changes had taken place in the field, the old problems were still very much present. That said, three years is a very short space of time in research terms. A survey by Garvey, Lin and Tomita (1979), for example, found that on average it took researchers thirteen months to complete a study and write up the results for submission to a journal. Once submitted, it took on average another fifteen months before the article actually appeared in print. The result is that it can often take nearly two and half years between research starting and the findings actually making it into print in a journal. Thus, the previous review arguably really only assessed the initial wave of research started in the direct aftermath of 9/11, and it is perhaps not terribly surprising that the old, long-running problems were still very much in evidence. This review follows on directly from the one ending in 2004, and now considers the research published in the core journals between 2005 and 2007.

Arguably the best way to identify trends and patterns in research efforts is to examine the published literature produced by active researchers. While the literature on terrorism is relatively young in academic terms – existing in a meaningful sense only since the late 1960s – Schmid and Jongman (1988: xiv) noted that by the time of their review it had nonetheless grown far beyond the scope 'of one single researcher [to] survey the field alone'. Indeed, the two Netherlands-based writers pulled in the assistance of over fifty other researchers in order to complete their review.

As already indicated, the situation today is considerably more intimidating. Hundreds (if not thousands) of academic journals have published at least one article relating to some aspect of terrorism in the past ten years. A review which incorporated every such journal would be a formidable undertaking. Fortunately, the presence of two long-established journals which have an explicit and primary focus on terrorism research provides an accessible medium to gauge the state of research. These journals are *Terrorism and Political Violence* (TPV) and *Studies in Conflict and Terrorism* (SICAT). Taken together, and bearing in mind their separate editorial teams and largely separate editorial boards (though there is some overlap in this respect) the two journals can be regarded as providing a reasonably balanced impression of the research activity and interests in the field.

However, it is important to note that many active researchers have not published in these two journals and have instead preferred to publish elsewhere. It would be a mistake to assume that all of the key researchers publish in these journals or that the journals reliably represent the nature of most research on the subject. Some other reviews of the field have tried to address this issue by incorporating a wider range of journals. Increasing the quantity of journals however is not necessarily a guarantee of increasing the reliability of a review. Czwarno (2006) for example, reviewed twelve journals in her survey. These included both SICAT and TPV but also included other journals which only rarely published terrorism related pieces. Czwarno reported that from 1993 to 2001, only 1–3 percent of the articles published in most of the journals she reviewed were on terrorism. The approach adopted here is to take a tighter focus and review only those journals which publish primarily and consistently on terrorism (and for both TPV and SICAT the clear majority of their articles are routinely focused on terrorism-related subjects).

Consequently, this paper presents the results of a review of the published output of the primary journals in the area from 1990 to 2007. Academic journals have a surprisingly diverse range of content. For the two journals under consideration here, this includes articles, research notes, editorials, book reviews, conference reports, review essays, database reports, and official documents and reports. The most immediate question facing a surveyor is how much of this material should be considered? In deciding this, the main criterion has to be which items are consistently the best indicators of significant research activity and effort? This review follows the lead of the UK's Research Assessment Exercise (RAE), which has judged that peer-reviewed journal articles provide a good measure of the broad quality of research work. As with the previous reviews, it is hoped that a review of this nature can be both of interest and of practical value to other writers and researchers on the topic, and that it may also help to establish the broader context in which individual research efforts occur and help illustrate how the field is evolving in the aftermath of 9/11 and the so-called 'global war on terror'.

Trends in data-gathering and analysis

One of the most serious problems facing research on terrorism has been the long-running shortage of experienced researchers. As a field, terrorism studies has struggled to attract new researchers and then hold onto them. The review of research in the 1990s clearly showed that compared to other academic areas such as criminology (which faces many similar challenges to the study of terrorism), research on terrorism was dependent upon the work of far fewer researchers. In a review of leading criminology journals, it was found that 497 articles had been written by a total of 665 authors (Cohn and Farrington, 1998). For the terrorism journals in the 1990s, 490 articles were written, but this was the output of just 403 authors. This was a far lower level compared to the criminology journals and indicated a smaller

Issues in research 39

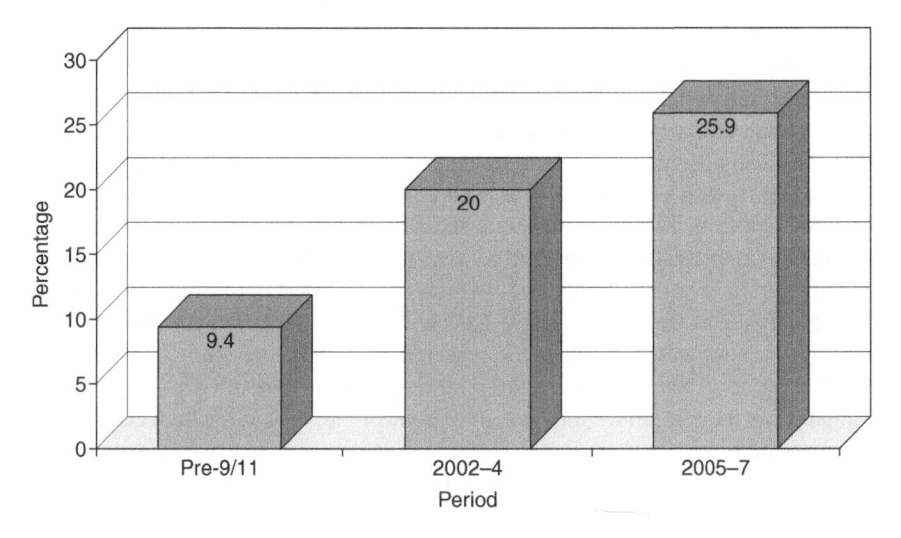

Figure 2.2 Collaborative research: percentage of articles with two or more authors.

pool of active researchers. The figure also highlighted the lack of collaborative research. As Figure 2.2 shows below, less than 10 percent of articles published before 9/11 were the work of two or more researchers. The vast majority of studies were being carried out by individual researchers working alone. This is a far lower level of collaborative research compared with leading journals in fields such as psychology and criminology. It is worth noting however – as one of the editors to this volume pointed out – that levels of collaborative research vary across disciplines and that political science journals, for example, traditionally have lower levels.

Nevertheless, it is important to remember the interdisciplinary nature of terrorism studies, and the historic lack of collaborative work can at least partly be attributed to the long-running shortage of funding available in this area. Collaborative research is more dependent on research grants. Without funding, researchers are much more restricted in what they can aspire to and are much more likely to have to squeeze the research effort in-between other activities. There are knock-on consequences of such a situation: limited resources mean that research which involves more time and effort will be avoided. Instead, researchers will focus on quicker and cheaper approaches. Quick and cheap is fine to a certain extent, but inevitably if a field is heavily dependent on such work, serious questions about the reliability and validity of any findings must emerge.

Following 9/11, however, there has been a major increase in collaborative work. This reflects both the increased interest among researchers (new and old) for the area, and the increased availability of funding for research on the subject. As Figure 2.2 shows, collaborative work in the first three years after 9/11 more than doubled. Encouragingly, this level rose higher again between 2005 and 2007, so that now nearly 26 percent of the research is collaborative study. This is a level almost three times higher than the pre-9/11 average.

The natural following issue is whether the increasing number of researchers and increased funding has led to any improvements in data gathering and analysis. Since the 1950s, all of the social science disciplines have experienced a rapid increase in the use of statistics. People are extremely complex, and their behavior and thoughts are the result of a confusing interaction of emotions, motivations, learned behaviors, and genetically determined traits. Consequently, social science researchers typically have to work with very 'noisy' data where there are potentially a vast number of factors exerting an influence on any one behavior, event, or trend.

Statistical analysis has emerged as a way for researchers to determine which factors genuinely are important and which are not. Descriptive statistics enable the researcher to summarize and organize data in an effective and meaningful way. Inferential statistics allow the researcher to make decisions or inferences by interpreting data patterns. Inferential statistics are regarded as particularly valuable, as they introduce an element of control into research which can help to compensate if relatively weak data collection methods were used. In experimental designs control is normally achieved by randomly assigning research subjects to experimental and control groups. However, this can often be very difficult to achieve in real world research and, consequently, the lack of control throws doubt on any association between variables which the research claims to find. Inferential statistics though can help to introduce a recognized element of control, so that there is less doubt and more confidence over the veracity of any findings (Frankfort-Nachmias and Nachmias, 1996).

It is no coincidence that some of the most significant and influential books published on terrorism since 9/11 have been ones which have made extensive use of statistics to support the authors' arguments. Such key works include Marc Sageman's (2004) *Understanding Terror Networks*, Robert Pape's (2005) *Dying to Win*, and Ronald Clarke and Graeme Newman's (2006) *Outsmarting the Terrorists*. While many might disagree with some elements of these books, there can be no denying that each has had a considerable impact both in the research communities, and (even more importantly) among policy-makers and other practitioners. It is highly unlikely that these texts could have been as influential if they had not provided and relied heavily on statistical evidence to support the arguments being made.

Figure 2.3 though shows that these books are still relatively unusual within terrorism research (and perhaps this partly helps to explain their unusual impact). Only a small minority of studies included either descriptive or inferential statistics prior to 9/11. Just 19 percent of articles had such analysis to support any arguments. This is not surprising given the heavy reliance on literature review methods in the field. Such methods limit the opportunity to use statistics and, to a degree, using statistics is dependent on the nature of the data gathered. Strong statistical analysis will only do so much when the data collection methods are flawed and limited. In the immediate three years after 9/11, there was a definite improvement in the situation with almost 26 percent of articles using statistics. This level, however, has declined slightly and in the most recent period had dropped to 25 percent. Perhaps more encouraging is

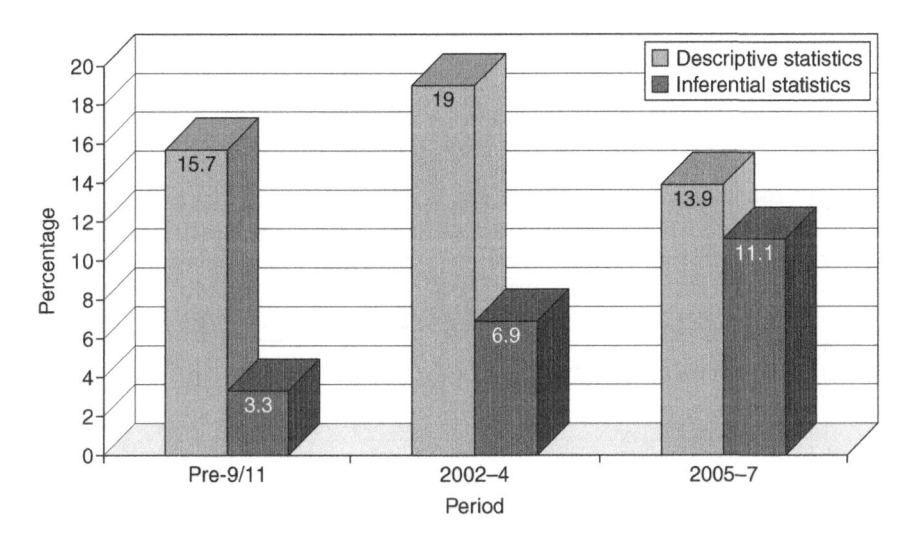

Figure 2.3 Percentage of terrorism research articles applying statistical analysis.

the very substantial growth in inferential statistics in research (going from 3.3 percent to 6.9 percent and now to over 11 percent of articles in just seven years). Inferential statistics are now being used almost four times more often today to help analyse data which is an important and positive shift.

One of the most notable findings in the previous reviews of the research literature was just how little research was focused on al-Qaeda in the ten years prior to 9/11. Al-Qaeda was an active and growing organisation in this period and was responsible for several high profile terrorist attacks, including the highly destructive bombings of US embassies in Africa in 1998 and the well-publicised attack against the USS *Cole* in 2000. Yet, despite what in hindsight seems quite a significant trajectory, the group attracted almost no research attention. As Figure 2.4 shows, in the years prior to 9/11, al-Qaeda was the subject of only 0.5 percent of research articles. In the core journals this represented only two articles (al-Qaeda was mentioned briefly in other articles but in only two was the organization a major focus for the research). The criteria used when judging the focus of an article was that the paper had to be primarily about one or at most two groups. It was not sufficient that a group was briefly mentioned or received discussion of a page or two. There had to be substantial evidence that the group was a major focus of the article.

This failure to notice the growing significance of al-Qaeda has been noticed by other reviewers, most especially Czwarno (2006), who found that the lack of attention paid to the organization was mirrored across a wide range of journals and was not simply a failing of the two core specialist journals.

As Figure 2.4 emphasizes, the neglect preceding 9/11 has been replaced by a surfeit of interest in the years after that date. In the first three years in particular, there was a very heavy focus on al-Qaeda, with roughly one in every seven

42 A. Silke

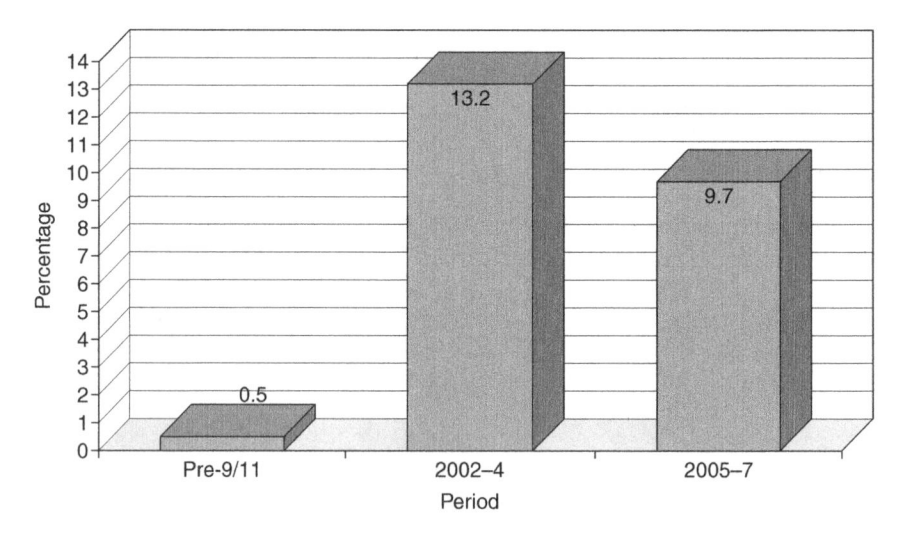

Figure 2.4 Percentage of research articles focusing on al-Qaeda.

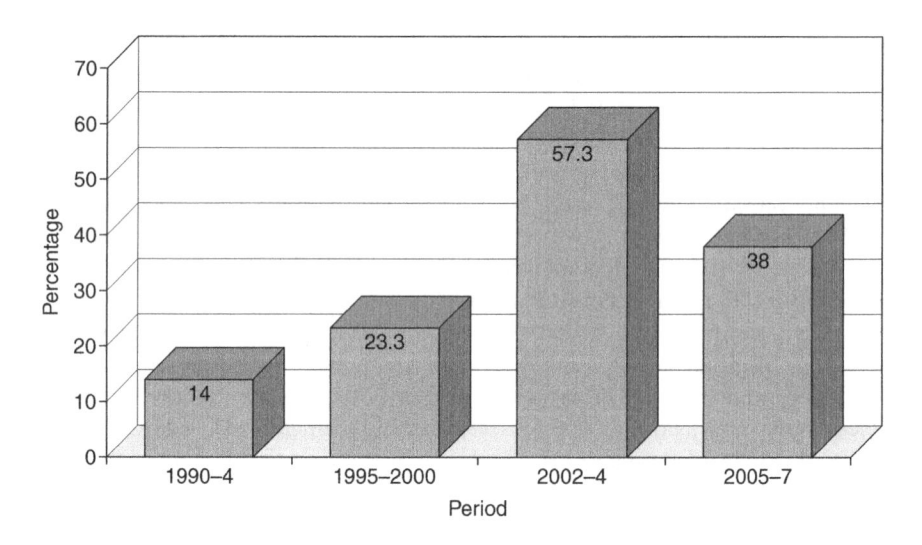

Figure 2.5 Percentage of research articles focusing on militant Islamist terrorist groups.

articles published in the core journals focused on the organisation. It is interesting to note that this very high level of interest declined somewhat in the next three years. Al-Qaeda is still unquestionably the most heavily researched group, but the focus is not as intense as before.

A somewhat similar trend is seen in Figure 2.5. Some articles considered several different groups which shared similar ideologies, backgrounds, activities, and the

Issues in research 43

like. However, if the article examined more than two groups, it was not considered for Figure 2.4. In order to take account of these articles, Figure 2.5 describes all of the articles which were focused on discussing particular Islamist terrorist groups (either individually or as a group). Thus, Figure 2.5 incorporates articles also seen in Figure 2.4. The figure clearly shows that the terrorist groups attracting the most research attention have been extremist Islamic groups such as al-Qaeda, Hamas, Islamic Jihad, and Hezbollah. While the research literature clearly missed the growing significance of al-Qaeda, it would be unfair to say that the research community was entirely unaware of the growing importance of Islamist terrorism. Figure 2.5 shows very clearly that research on Islamist terrorist groups has been steadily increasing over the past two decades. In the first half of the 1990s, 14 percent of articles were focused on some aspect of Islamist terrorism. This rose to over 23 percent in the latter half of the 1990s, representing a significant increase in research attention on this area. Since 9/11, however, Islamist terrorism has completely dominated the field. Nearly 58 percent of the entire literature was on this subject (almost two out of every three articles) in the first three years after 9/11. This very heavy focus on Islamist-related terrorism has slackened somewhat in the most recent period. At 38 percent, these groups still by far attract the most attention, but it has fallen from the overwhelming attention after 9/11.

Research on terrorist tactics

Suicide terrorism is not a new phenomenon, but prior to 9/11 it was certainly relatively ignored by terrorism researchers, considered more of a curiosity than a major subject for analysis. Figure 2.6 shows that only a tiny proportion of articles looked at this issue – only 0.5 percent of articles – a bare handful. That

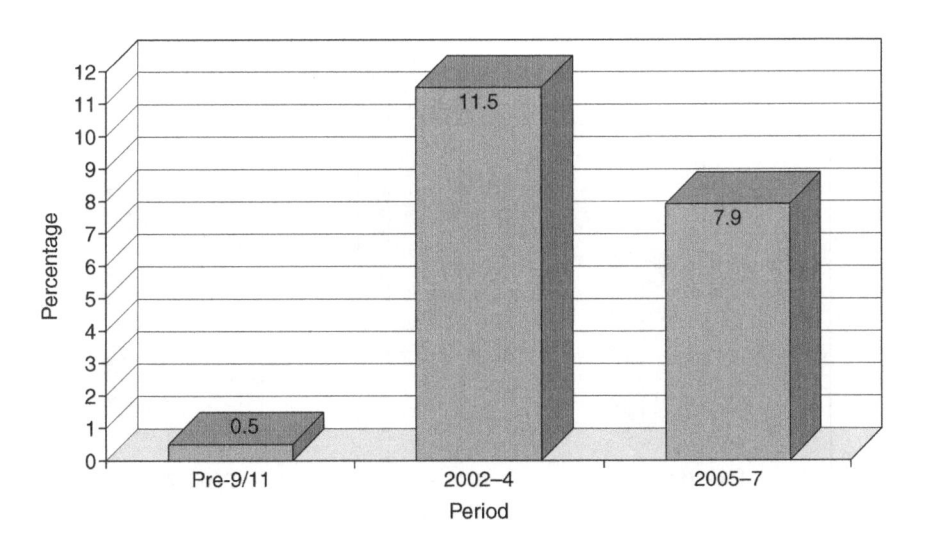

Figure 2.6 Percentage of research articles focusing on suicide terrorism.

44 A. Silke

however changed in the aftermath of 9/11, the most directly devastating terrorist attacks of all time (at least by non-state actors), and accomplished through the use of suicide tactics. Not surprisingly, in the first three years after 9/11, nearly 12 percent of all articles looked at suicide terrorism. For every one study carried out prior to 9/11, twenty-three were published in the three years afterwards.

As with the heavy focus on al-Qaeda and Islamist terrorism, interest in suicide terrorism has slackened somewhat in recent years. Currently, just under 8 percent of all articles are looking at this tactic. This is still vastly higher than the level of interest shown in the 1990s; arguably it is justified given that the number of suicide attacks in the 2000s has been vastly higher than during the 1990s or 1980s (Pape, 2005; Hafez, 2007; Silke, forthcoming).

The increased work being focused on suicide terrorism is arguably both overdue and useful. However, increased research is also being focused on other aspects of terrorism which are less obviously of growing importance. Of particular concern was the rapid growth in research investigating the (potential) use of Chemical, Biological, Radiological, and Nuclear weapons (CBRN) – also often referred to as weapons of mass destruction (WMD) – by terrorists. Figure 2.7 shows that the amount of research focused on CBRN terrorism more than doubled in the first three years after 9/11.

Yet why did this happen? After all, 9/11 was not a CBRN attack. Nearly 3,000 people may have been killed, but the hijackers did not use a nuclear bomb to cause the carnage, they did not spray poisonous chemicals into the atmosphere or release deadly viruses. They used box-cutters. Nevertheless, CBRN research experienced major growth in the aftermath.

Arguably, CBRN research has always been over-subscribed. Prior to 9/11, nearly six times more research was being conducted on CBRN terrorist tactics

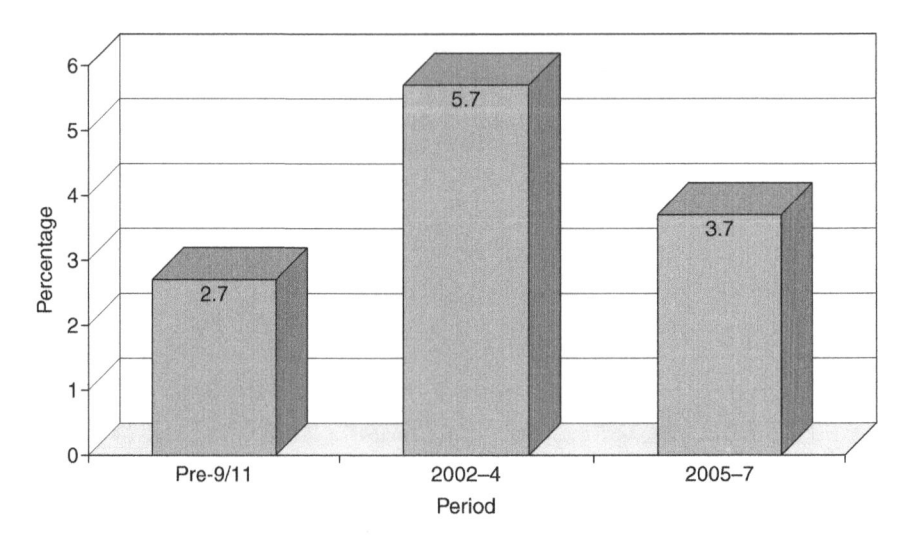

Figure 2.7 Percentage of research articles focusing on CBRN terrorism.

than on suicide tactics. Indeed, no other terrorist tactic (car-bombings, hijackings, assassinations, and the like) received anywhere near as much research attention in the run-up to 9/11 as CBRN. If the relatively low amount of research attention which was given to al-Qaeda is judged to be the most serious failing of terrorism research in the years prior to 9/11, the relatively high amount of research focused on the terrorist use of CBRN must inevitably be seen as the next biggest blunder.

To date, in the few cases where terrorists have attempted to develop CBRN weapons, they have almost always failed. In the handful of instances where they have actually managed to develop and use such weapons, the highest number of individuals they have ever been able to kill is twelve people. In the list of the 300 most destructive terrorist attacks of the past twenty years, not a single one involved the use of CBRN weapons. Yet somehow, one impact of the 9/11 attacks was that CBRN research – already the most studied terrorist tactic during the 1990s – actually managed to attract even more research attention and funding, doubling the proportion of articles focused on CBRN in the journals.

A degree of research looking at CBRN terrorism is justified. Instances such as the 1995 Tokyo subway attack and the post-9/11 anthrax letters show that CBRN attacks *can* happen (albeit only rarely). Such attacks have never caused mass fatalities however, and the popular acronym of Weapons of Mass Destruction (WMD) in describing CBRN weapons is desperately misleading. Despite the rarity – and the extreme unlikelihood of terrorists being able to accomplish a truly devastating attack using these weapons – CBRN remains a popular topic for government and funding bodies. They will award research grants for work on this topic when other far more common and consistently far more deadly terrorist tactics are ignored. This popularity with funding sources partly helps to explain the continuing high profile of CBRN in the literature. It has to be acknowledged, however, that some articles on the subject in the core journals are actually arguing that the issue *is* blown out of proportion and does not warrant the research funding it has and continues to receive (see Claridge, 1999; Leitenberg, 1999).

Those who had hoped that 9/11 – a stunning example of how non-CBRN weapons can be used to kill thousands of people – might then have heralded at least a modest shift away from CBRN research, would have been disappointed by the initial reaction. Thankfully, the 2005–7 period shows an improvement and the level of research on CBRN dropped notably, though it is still receiving more attention than prior to 9/11 (and still remains the most heavily researched terrorist tactic after suicide attacks).

Some conceptual issues

Terrorism research has never been especially good at exploring the past. Prior to 9/11, only 3.9 percent of articles examined non-contemporary terrorism and less than half of these looked at terrorism prior to 1960. We know that terrorism is not a recent phenomenon and that it has been occurring in some form or another

46 *A. Silke*

for over 2,000 years (Asprey, 1994). Yet this wider context is almost entirely ignored, as terrorism research is increasingly driven by a need to provide a short-term, immediate assessment of current groups and threats. Efforts to establish more contextualised and stable guiding principles have been almost entirely side-lined. As Figure 2.8 shows, very little research explores past terrorist conflicts. Before 9/11, only one article in twenty-six looked at historical conflicts. In the immediate aftermath of 9/11, interest in historical cases effectively collapsed and not even one article in fifty was focused away from current events.

It is natural and reasonable that, in the years immediately after the most destructive terrorist attacks in recorded history, the research field should focus heavily on the now, on current issues, actors, and events. Such a strong focus on contemporary issues, however, runs the real risk of losing an understanding of the broader context of terrorist conflicts, patterns, and trends and without such awareness important lessons can be missed.

Thankfully, Figure 2.8 suggests that research is beginning to show increased interest in historical cases again. These still account for a very small proportion of the research – and are still considerably below pre-9/11 levels – but at least indicate a change in the right direction.

Conclusion

What then are the overall conclusions to take away from this review? As we approach the end of the first decade of the twenty-first century, has terrorism studies improved in any way with regard to the problems which blighted so much past effort? The short answer – based on this review of the core journals – must

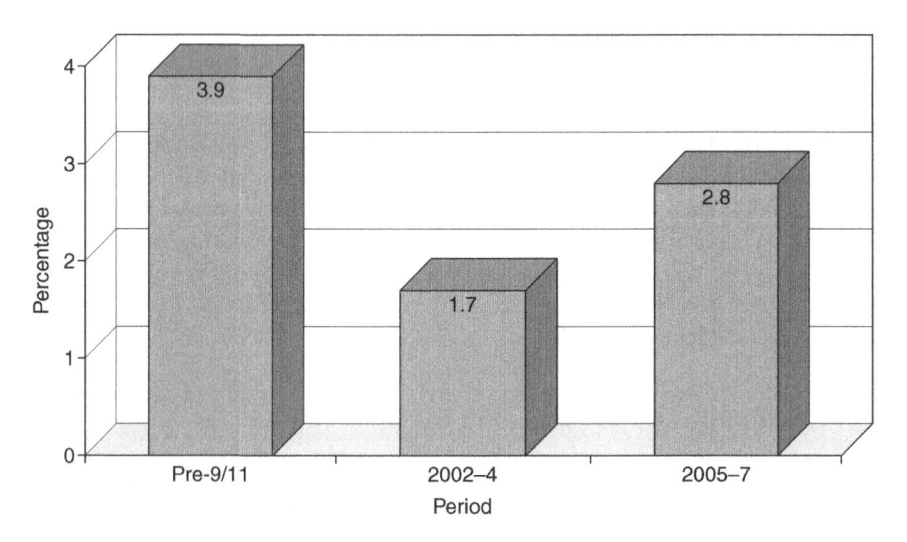

Figure 2.8 Percentage of research articles with a historical focus.

Issues in research 47

be a qualified yes. There are signs that research published in recent years is less opinion-based and more rigorous in methodology and analysis. The range of data-gathering methods is arguably still quite limited, but perhaps slightly less limited than in the past. There is certainly more evidence of researchers attempting to improve the reliability of findings and conclusions through the inclusion of statistics and inferential analysis.

The core journals, then, show evidence of steps in the right direction. The journals, of course, are entirely dependent on what is submitted to them. I remember speaking to one editor in the 1990s who confessed that his heart always sank slightly when yet another article on the IRA landed on his desk. He would have loved more variety in the journal, but all he was sent – he lamented – were pieces on the IRA. When the journal was then criticised for focusing too much on the IRA, some people interpreted this as possibly political bias on the part of the editors. At another time, similar points were made with regard to the limited range of methodologies being published. 'We do want more variety', he commented. 'We simply don't get it.'

There are signs now that the core journals are getting more variety than before. The articles on the IRA still continue to flow in, but perhaps not in quite the numbers of old. Given that the journals do not commission articles and do not pay authors for their contributions, their selection choices will always be limited to what the wider academic community feels interested in researching, writing, and submitting.

Prior to 9/11, the study of terrorism was carried out on the periphery of academia. The funding available for researchers was extremely limited and the number of researchers prepared to focus a substantial element of their careers on the subject was paltry. In most cases, it was harmful to an academic or research career to follow such interests and most of those who were genuinely interested in the subject found that they had to incorporate other issues into their work in order to remain professionally viable. September 11 has brought much greater interest in the subject of terrorism and for the first time the possibility of an expanded core of dedicated researchers exists. It is likely that the field and the amount of research being conducted will continue to grow over the coming years. It is not certain however, whether this growth will be sustained or even if the gains made in the first years since the New York and Washington attacks will not be eroded over the coming decade.

This survey has found that 9/11 had a very clear impact on research on terrorism, both in terms of how research was carried out and in terms of what it was focused on. The field displayed a very heavy shift in research looking at al-Qaeda, Islamist terrorism, suicide tactics, and CBRN terrorism, to the extent that other subjects were effectively drowned out or sidelined. Had terrorism studies persisted with such a lop-sided focus, real issues over its credibility and reliability would have emerged.

Fortunately, the very heavy attention seen in these areas in the first three years after 2001 has slackened considerably in the following three years. All of these subjects are still receiving more attention than they did prior to 9/11, but not to the crushing extent seen in the 2002–4 period. In previous reviews, I was concerned that these heavy biases would remain and that ultimately they would prove damaging for the field. This latest review suggests that is not happening, and the field overall appears to be showing signs of beginning to stabilise from the profound impact of 9/11 and its aftermath.

On a more clearly positive note, this review has also found that some of the positive trends seen immediately after 9/11 – more researchers and more detailed data analysis – have been maintained. It is clear that more researchers are working on the subject than before and there has been a real and continuing increase in collaborative studies. This allows studies to be more ambitious in both data collection and data analysis. At the moment, although there is no real evidence that the field is significantly shifting away from its heavy reliance on literature review-based research, there has been a much more promising increase in the use of descriptive and inferential statistical analysis. The use of inferential statistics on terrorism data in particular has nearly quadrupled since 9/11, a trend which can only help improve the reliability and validity of the conclusions being reached by researchers. Admittedly, this is an increase starting from an extremely low level indeed, but it is unquestionably a major step in the right direction.

While it is understandable that the field would show heavy biases in focus in the immediate aftermath of 9/11 and the war on terror, any objective analysis must still regard the current state of the literature as still quite skewed in that direction. It is worth recognising as well, though, that the field is showing signs of generally moving in the right direction when comparisons are made with the results of the first review carried out three years after 9/11 (Silke, 2007). Compared with this chapter, that earlier review found a higher level of CBRN research, less historical research, less collaborative work, less variety in research methods, and less use of inferential statistical analysis. In short, on almost all of the key issues considered here, the first three years were less satisfactory than a review which includes the full five years after 9/11. The differences between these two reviews in most cases are small, but they exist nonetheless. The hope is that they represent a swing in positive directions, a change of direction which can be maintained and built upon.

Note

1 The data was derived from a search of the www.amazon.com database of non-fiction books carried out on June 10, 2008.

3 In the service of power
Terrorism studies and US intervention in the global South

Sam Raphael

Introduction[1]

Over the past thirty years, a small but politically-significant academic field of 'terrorism studies' has emerged from the relatively disparate research efforts of the 1960s and 1970s, and consolidated its position as a viable subset of 'security studies' (Reid, 1993: 22; Laqueur, 2003: 141). Despite continuing concerns that the concept of 'terrorism', as nothing more than a specific socio-political phenomenon, is not substantial enough to warrant an entire field of study (see Horgan and Boyle, 2008), it is nevertheless possible to identify a core set of scholars writing on the subject who together constitute an 'epistemic community' (Haas, 1992: 2–3). That is, there exists a 'network of knowledge-based experts' who have 'recognised expertise and competence in a particular domain and an authoritative claim to policy-relevant knowledge within that domain'. This community, or 'network of productive authors', has operated by establishing research agendas, recruiting new members, securing funding opportunities, sponsoring conferences, maintaining informal contacts, and linking separate research groups (Reid, 1993, 1997). Regardless of the largely academic debate over whether the study of terrorism *should* constitute an independent field, the existence of a clearly-identifiable research community (with particular individuals at its core) is a social fact.[2]

Further, this community has traditionally had significant influence when it comes to the formulation of government policy, particularly in the United States. It is not the case that the academic field of terrorism studies operates solely in the ivory towers of higher education; as noted in previous studies (Schmid and Jongman, 1988: 180; Burnett and Whyte, 2005), it is a community which has intricate and multifaceted links with the structures and agents of state power, most obviously in Washington. Thus, many recognised terrorism experts have either had prior employment with, or major research contracts from, the Pentagon, the Central Intelligence Agency, the State Department, and other key US Government agencies (Herman and O'Sullivan, 1989: 142–190; RAND, 2004). Likewise, a high proportion of 'core experts' in the field (see below) have been called over the past thirty years to testify in front of Congress on the subject of terrorism (Raphael, forthcoming). Either way, these scholars have fed their 'knowledge' straight into the policymaking process in the US.[3]

The close relationship between the academic field of terrorism studies and the US state means that it is critically important to analyse the research output from key experts within the community. This is particularly the case because of the aura of objectivity surrounding the terrorism 'knowledge' generated by academic experts. Running throughout the core literature is a positivist assumption, explicitly stated or otherwise, that the research conducted is apolitical and objective (see for example, Hoffman, 1992: 27; Wilkinson, 2003). There is little to no reflexivity on behalf of the scholars, who see themselves as wholly dissociated from the politics surrounding the subject of terrorism. This reification of academic knowledge about terrorism is reinforced by those in positions of power in the US who tend to distinguish the experts from other kinds of overtly political actors. For example, academics are introduced to Congressional hearings in a manner which privileges their nonpartisan input:

> Good morning. The Special Oversight Panel on Terrorism meets in open session to receive testimony and discuss the present and future course of terrorism in the Middle East.... It has been the Terrorism Panel's practice, *in the interests of objectivity and gathering all the facts*, to pair classified briefings and open briefings.... This way we garner the best that the classified world of intelligence has to offer and the best from *independent scholars* working in universities, think tanks, and other institutions...
>
> (Saxton, 2000, emphasis added)

The representation of terrorism expertise as 'independent' and as providing 'objectivity' and 'facts' has significance for its contribution to the policymaking process in the US. This is particularly the case given that, as we will see, core experts tend to insulate the broad direction of US policy from critique. Indeed, as Alexander George noted, it is *precisely because* 'they are trained to clothe their work in the trappings of objectivity, independence and scholarship' that expert research is 'particularly effective in securing influence and respect for' the claims made by US policymakers (George, 1991b: 77).

Given this, it becomes vital to subject the content of terrorism studies to close scrutiny. Based upon a wider, systematic study of the research output of key figures within the field (Raphael, forthcoming), and building upon previous critiques of terrorism expertise (see Chomsky and Herman, 1979; Herman, 1982; Herman and O'Sullivan, 1989; Chomsky, 1991; George, 1991b; Jackson, 2007g), this chapter aims to provide a critical analysis of some of the major claims made by these experts and to reveal the ideological functions served by much of the research. Rather than doing so across the board, this chapter focuses on research on the subject of terrorism from the global South which is seen to challenge US interests. Examining this aspect of research is important, given that the 'threat' from this form of terrorism has led the US and its allies to intervene throughout the South on behalf of their national security, with profound consequences for the human security of people in the region.

Specifically, this chapter examines two major problematic features which characterise much of the field's research. First, in the context of anti-US terrorism in the South, many important claims made by key terrorism experts simply replicate official US government analyses. This replication is facilitated primarily through a sustained and uncritical reliance on *selective* US government sources, combined with the frequent use of *unsubstantiated assertion*. This is significant, not least because official analyses have often been revealed as presenting a politically-motivated account of the subject. Second, and partially as a result of this mirroring of government claims, the field tends to insulate from critique those 'counterterrorism' policies justified as a response to the terrorist threat. In particular, the experts overwhelmingly 'silence' the way terrorism is itself often used as a central strategy within US-led counterterrorist interventions in the South. That is, 'counterterrorism' campaigns executed or supported by Washington often deploy terrorism as a mode of controlling violence (Crelinsten, 2002: 83; Stohl, 2006: 18–19).

These two features of the literature are hugely significant. Overall, the core figures in terrorism studies have, wittingly or otherwise, produced a body of work plagued by substantive problems which together shatter the illusion of 'objectivity'. Moreover, the research output can be seen to serve a very particular *ideological function* for US foreign policy. Across the past thirty years, it has largely served the interests of US state power, primarily through legitimising an extensive set of coercive interventions in the global South undertaken under the rubric of various 'war(s) on terror'. After setting out the method by which key experts within the field have been identified, this chapter will outline the two main problematic features which characterise much of the research output by these scholars. It will then discuss the function that this research serves for the US state.

Methodology

Literally thousands of academics have published on the subject of terrorism over the past thirty years, with scholarly activity mushrooming since 9/11. In order to explore the research output from 'terrorism studies', it is important to identify the core figures within the field according to a clear methodology. In doing this, I have used various measures of peer assessment as a basis for establishing those experts who are considered key *from within the field*. This is based upon an acceptance of peer review as the central mechanism for generating accepted knowledge within the social sciences, as well as the *intra-network* process by which peers are initially selected for this gate-keeping role (Kochen *et al.*, 1982). Key within this was a desire to identify those experts who have occupied a central role in the field for a substantial part of the thirty years during which the research community has existed. By undertaking an in-depth survey of the two 'core journals' of the field (*Terrorism and Political Violence* and *Studies in Conflict and Terrorism*) between 1979 and 2004, I have identified those who have held editorial positions for extended periods of time, as well as those who have published prolifically in these vehicles.[4] These results have been triangulated with each other, and with the results of a seminal questionnaire sent to approximately 200 terrorism scholars in the mid-1980s which asked the recipients (amongst other questions) who they considered to be the 'leading figures in the field' (Schmid and Jongman, 1988).

As a result, I have identified a group of thirty-one individuals who have played a central role in this research community for a significant portion of its existence. Each of these 'experts' fulfils at least two of the following three conditions: authoring at least three articles in the core journals between 1979 and 2004; participating on the editorial board of a key journal for at least five years during this period; or receiving three or more citations from Schmid and Jongman's questionnaire. Triangulation of these metrics serves to remove particular anomalies from the sample, such as those asked to join the editorial board of a core journal not because of their perceived centrality to the field, but because of their wider reputation in international affairs.[5] The thirty-one experts identified via this method include, in alphabetical order: Yonah Alexander, Michael Barkun, J. Bowyer Bell, Peter Chalk, Ray Cline, Richard Clutterbuck, Ronald Crelinsten, Martha Crenshaw, Franco Ferracuti, Ted Gurr, Bruce Hoffman, Alison Jamieson, Brian Jenkins, Robert Kupperman, Walter Laqueur, Neil Livingstone, Ariel Merari, Abraham Miller, John Murphy, Dennis Pluchinsky, Jerrold Post, Magnus Ranstorp, David Rapoport, Xavier Raufer, Alex Schmid, Richard Schultz, Michael Smith, Ehud Sprinzak, Grant Wardlaw, Leonard Weinberg, and Paul Wilkinson. Those familiar with the field would no doubt acknowledge that these experts have, together, proved crucial in shaping the study of terrorism for the past thirty years.

The problems associated with the research output of terrorism studies do not characterise the entire work of all thirty-one core experts. Some, such as Crenshaw and Crelinsten, and to a lesser extent Schmid and Sprinzak, have at times adopted an agenda which critiques the general reliance on US government sources and which addresses some of the silences laid out in the present chapter. Indeed, it is possible to find examples of all of the key figures producing research which does not directly serve the ideological function identified here (see Horgan and Boyle, 2008: 56). Notwithstanding this fact, however, a comprehensive survey of the output from these key scholars leads to the unavoidable conclusion that they *overwhelmingly* work to legitimise US 'counterterrorism' policy. One may be able to identify specific passages which buck the trend in this regard. However, such instances are rare in the context of the millions of words and thousands of publications cumulatively produced by these experts.

Overall, following the methodology set out by Haas (1992: 35), the ideological function described here is identified by this study as a result of the detailed examination of a wide range of publications authored by the key figures in the field. I surveyed literally hundreds of publications, ensuring a balanced inclusion of the scholars' major monographs, refereed-journal articles, and other publications (including Congressional testimonies and newspaper interviews), released across the thirty years during which the field has existed. When examining these sources, attention was paid to discussions regarding the nature of terrorism from the South which supposedly presented a threat to the interests of the US and its allies, as well as to the policies which were recommended in response. Where claims were made, the presence and content of any citations were analysed to reveal the empirical basis of the research. They were also overlaid with US government analysis of the same subject, in order to identify the degree to which the expert research confirmed or challenged this. By a wider reading of relevant literature, the study also revealed the silences which run through the research output.

Given present space constraints, analysis will be focused on ten of the key experts who have testified to Congress at some point in the past thirty years, thus feeding their 'independent' knowledge directly into a central policymaking forum. These individuals are, in alphabetical order: Yonah Alexander, Peter Chalk, Ray Cline, Bruce Hoffman, Brian Jenkins, Robert Kupperman, Walter Laqueur, Neil Livingstone, Ariel Merari, and Paul Wilkinson. References to particular publications by these experts, cited here to support the argument, are necessarily illustrative rather than all-encompassing. Likewise, there is room here merely to outline the broad characteristics of the literature, and the mechanisms by which academic 'knowledge' on terrorism works to legitimate US 'counterterror' interventions in the global South. A more comprehensive account of the extent of the bias, and its often-complex position within the field, can be found in a forthcoming major study (Raphael, forthcoming).

The problem of sourcing

The first significant characteristic of the core literature which ensures a legitimisation of policy is its often uncritical use of certain key US government sources, alongside the extensive (re)production of 'facts' with little or no empirical basis. Many of the official documents and speeches used are highly political, with US administrations frequently presenting a particular understanding of the reality of terrorism in order to gain support for a specific set of interventions. Likewise, the continuous repetition of mere assertions, which take on appearance of 'facts', works to further distort the academic value of the research, and when these are aligned with official assertions, contribute to the overall legitimisation of policy. This characteristic is evident at many points throughout the literature; several examples of it in operation are highlighted here to provide an indication of its pervasiveness and significance.

Terrorism studies literature published during the cold war overwhelmingly replicated the claims made by the Reagan administration that there existed a network of radical states throughout the South, ultimately supported by Moscow. This network was supposedly united in opposition to Washington and worked together to sponsor subversion and terrorism in order to undermine US interests (see Haig, 1981; Shultz, cited in Omang, 1984; Reagan, 1985). Such claims formed a central plank of US foreign policy analysis within Washington during the 1980s and provided the intellectual backdrop to an extensive set of 'counterterror' interventions throughout the South. Echoing official analysis, the core figures overwhelmingly signed up to some version of the 'Soviet network theory' (amongst many, see Livingstone, 1980; Alexander, 1980; Elad and Merari, 1984; Kupperman and Taylor, 1985; Wilkinson, 1985: 74). Almost all experts reached a broad consensus regarding the Soviet use of 'surrogate or "proxy" forces to test the resolve of the West and to put pressure on the noncommunist world without running the risk of all-out war' (Livingstone, 1980: 16). The Kremlin was claimed to support 'terrorist operations that attempt to tear down the fabric of Western society and weaken other nonsocialist governments' (Alexander, 1985: 106). Moreover, this support was not undertaken on an ad hoc basis: 'there exists a *carefully developed international terrorist infrastructure* that serves Moscow's foreign policy objectives of destabilising non-Communist governments' (Cline and Alexander, 1984: 55, emphasis added).

However, when this consensus analysis is examined in detail, with attention paid to the specific claims that facilitated such wide-ranging conclusions regarding Soviet sponsorship, it becomes clear that little evidence was presented that stood independent from key US government officials. As just one example, Cline and Alexander (1984: 29–30) base their analysis overwhelmingly upon 'congressional reports and other files of evidence' presented by the Reagan administration. The entire foundation of their 'Soviet network' theory is therefore reliant on highly political sources of information. For instance, that the Kremlin was behind the purported Cuban sponsorship of terrorism was a claim made repeatedly by the authors, despite the fact that it relied solely on the remarks of extreme anti-Communist Senator Jeremiah Denton that the Soviets 'seem to direct certain Cuban activities' (Cline and Alexander, 1984: 72–73). Likewise, their claim that Libyan support for terrorism – such that it exists – forms part of an identifiable Soviet-centred network is based upon the remarks of the State Department's spokesman who spoke of the 'surrogate use of Cubans and Libyans to assist terrorist organisations' (1984: 21), as well as a newspaper article which, when examined, refers to 'intelligence experts' who 'suspect Libya of ... laundering Soviet money and disbursing it to terrorist groups' (Chaze, 1981, cited in Cline and Alexander, 1984: 21).

To more fully examine the reliance on problematic government sources in the context of the 'Soviet network theory' subscribed to by the experts, their analysis of 'communist-inspired' terrorism in Central America will now be explored. This is not the only example of relevance, but it provides a good insight into the pervasiveness of the problem. The cold war terrorism literature examined the terrorist threat in Central America in some depth, and echoing the claims made by the Reagan administration (see for example, Haig, cited in Pearce, 1982: 184), it overwhelmingly argued that such terrorism stemmed from the revolutionary objectives of the Sandinista regime in Nicaragua, backed up with ideological and material support from Cuba, Libya, and the Soviet Union. For example, Kupperman and Taylor (1985: 210) claimed that '[v]iolence and counterviolence have increased rapidly throughout the region as the Sandinistas and their supporters execute a long-term design to export totalitarian revolution'.

Indeed, the Sandinistas have 'engaged in subversive activities against neighbouring countries' (Elad and Merari, 1984: 55).

However, as elsewhere, such claims are either entirely unsupported or rely solely on publications or speeches originating from a high-level within the US government. These include President Reagan himself, the US State Department, the Pentagon, and the Kissinger Commission (see for example, Boyd, 1985; Enders, 1982; State Department, 1983; Pentagon and State Department, 1983; National Bipartisan Commission on Central America, 1984).[6] In particular, key documents released by the State Department, which purported to demonstrate external influences in El Salvador are used entirely uncritically by the literature. Thus:

> In February 1981 the US Department of State issued a White Paper citing *definitive evidence* of support given to Salvadoran rebels in late 1979 and early 1980, immediately after the Communist takeover in Nicaragua, by the Soviet Union, Cuba, East Germany, and their allies.... The evidence, drawn from captured guerrilla documents and war matériel and corroborated with intelligence reports, *leaves no doubt* that the Communist role was to provide direct and decisive support to Marxist factions in their effort to install a Communist regime against the will of the Salvadoran people.
> (Cline and Alexander, 1984: 22, emphasis added)

Indeed, several experts claimed explicitly that the Sandinistas were pursuing a 'revolution without borders' (see for example, Gonzalez *et al.*, 1984: 12–13; Cline and Alexander, 1986: 68). This phrasing was lifted from the title of a State Department (1985) White Paper, where it was provided as an alleged excerpt from a speech by the Sandinista, Tomas Borge, and used repeatedly by US officials to prove the expansionist and subversive nature of Nicaraguan foreign policy (Stokes, 2003: 89).

Key claims made by the literature in relation to terrorism in Central America were supported by *no independent evidence whatsoever*; they were either unsupported assertions or referenced back solely to US government sources. Such claims included the following: the logistical support provided to terrorists via the Cuban, Nicaraguan, and Libyan embassies in Panama (Alexander, 1989: 40); the presence of Nicaraguan and Cuban officials at the unification negotiations of the Guatemalan guerrilla groups (Elad and Merari, 1984: 28); Cuban support for Honduran terrorists (Livingstone, 1983a: 97); the provision of Cuban and Nicaraguan weapons and training to the FMLN in El Salvador, and the further transfer of these weapons from the FMLN to terrorist groups throughout the region (Cline and Alexander, 1986: 51); the arms deliveries from Libya to the Salvadoran guerrillas (as opposed to the sovereign state of Nicaragua) (Alexander, 1986: 11–12); the military training provided by Libya to the group (Cline and Alexander, 1984: 70); the operation of three training camps by the Palestine Liberation Organisation (PLO) in Nicaragua for teaching terrorist tactics to revolutionaries from El Salvador and other Latin American countries

(Livingstone, 1983b: 8); and the Spanish group ETA's staging of terrorist operations in the region on behalf of the Salvadoran guerrillas (Livingstone and Arnold, 1986: 20). In addition, ostensibly independent secondary sources cited by the terrorism experts are often themselves based upon uncritical readings of US government documentation (for example, Leiken, 1982, cited by Kupperman and Taylor, 1985: 210, is based largely upon State Department, 1981).

This reliance by key experts on US government sources (if any) when discussing communist-supported terrorism in Central America is not prima facie problematic. In actuality however, the body of research is built upon an uncritical acceptance of the Reagan administration's propaganda efforts to justify its military intervention in the region. Indeed, key evidence, such as that compiled by the administration regarding the shipment of arms to Salvadoran rebels by Cuba and the USSR through Nicaragua (State Department, 1981), was quickly revealed to form part of a 'public relations war'. These documents were 'quintessentially political', in that they were 'designed not so much to clarify the international dimensions of the Salvadoran civil war as to provide a justification for the Reagan administration's determination to cast the issue of El Salvador in East–West terms' (LeoGrande, 1981: 43–47). Not only were these claims designed to persuade public and elite opinion in the United States of the necessity of military aid to the Salvadoran and Honduran governments and to the Contras fighting in Nicaragua, but careful scholarship has also demonstrated many of them to be exaggerated, mis-contextualised, inconsistent, or even wholly inaccurate (see for example, Petras, 1981; LeoGrande, 1984: 252–254). Indeed, Human Rights Watch (1990) was clear that 'US pronouncements on human rights exaggerated and distorted the real human rights violations of the Sandinista regime', whilst the International Court of Justice (1986) found that although the US government 'contended that Nicaragua was actively supporting armed groups in El Salvador', it could only 'infer the provision of aid from Nicaraguan territory, especially up to early 1981, [and] it remained to be proved, given the circumstances characterising that part of Central America, that the Nicaraguan government was at any time responsible'. Of particular note, given its repetition by several terrorism experts, the use by administration officials of the Borge's phrase 'a revolution without borders' as proof of the Sandinistas' expansionist plans was revealed to be a misrepresentation of what Borge said. The actual words uttered by Borge reveal an entirely different meaning: 'This revolution transcends national boundaries. Our revolution has always been internationalist … *this does not mean that we export revolution*' (Marcus, 1982: 132, cited in Stokes, 2003: 90, emphasis added).

A similarly heavy reliance on official sources and unsubstantiated assertion characterises core terrorism research in the post-cold war era. Again, there is space only for a few illustrative examples. Indicative of scholarship in the 1990s dealing with state-sponsorship of terrorism is Hoffman's monograph (B. Hoffman, 1998: 191–196), which provides analysis of a very narrow set of states (those designated as sponsors by the US State Department). Moreover, this analysis is remarkably similar to that produced by government officials, a fact which is unsurprising, given the extent to which he draws upon the key government annual report on terrorism

The US in the global South 57

to demonstrate Iranian, Libyan, and Syrian sponsorship (State Department, 1997). Furthermore, this was complemented by the use for support of a 'recent high-level discussion paper circulated within the American intelligence community' when discussing ongoing Libyan sponsorship (Hoffman, 1998: 191); an assessment of 'Israeli and American intelligence sources' when considering the scale of Iranian arms shipments to Hezbollah; allegations by Secretary of State Warren Christopher regarding Iranian funding to Islamist groups (Jehl, 1996, cited in B. Hoffman, 1998: 194); and a presentation by, and personal discussions with, State Department officials regarding the groups training in the Bekaa Valley (Hoffman, 1998: 195). There is limited independent sourcing to back up the claims made, with many solely reliant on official sources. A similar picture can be found in many other core publications dealing with the subject of post-cold war state-sponsored terrorism, almost all of which focus exclusively on the sponsors outlined by the State Department, with official sources or simple assertions forming the majority of the support (see for example, Laqueur, 1999: 156–183; Wilkinson, 2002: 21, 63–65).

US government employees and documents are not the only official sources relied upon by the literature: over the past thirty years many of the claims made by the core experts find support from government agencies in pro-US states which are directly fighting the 'terrorist' threat and which are supported to do so by Washington. This can be seen throughout cold war scholarship where, for instance, Elad and Merari rely upon nothing other than a South African 'security force spokesman' as evidence that members of a national liberation movement (the South West African People's Organisation, SWAPO) had admitted to undertaking training in the Soviet Bloc (BBC, 1982, cited in Elad and Merari, 1984: 18). The release of such information came as high-level South African officials declared that the country was 'not going to sit back until it is too late to secure our survival' against the threat of a communist takeover in neighbouring South-West Africa (now Namibia) (Associated Press, 1982); a pretext for an acceleration of the national security state against a supposed 'total onslaught' (Minter, 1994: 37). Again, the clearly political nature of such sources is left unacknowledged and unchallenged in the core literature.

Likewise, Chalk's understanding of the nature of terrorism in Colombia and his consequent mirroring of US government analysis which consistently and overwhelmingly focuses on the activities of the FARC and ELN guerrilla groups (Stokes, 2005; State Department, 1997), is heavily influenced by Colombian military briefings and interviews with Colombian defence officials (Rabasa and Chalk, 2001). This is regardless of the fact that the Colombian Defence Ministry was at the time engaged in a sustained campaign to persuade the US to remove official distinctions between 'insurgents' and 'drug traffickers' and allow funding to flow to campaigns against both. That this interest may lead Colombian officials to overplay the nature of the threat posed by leftist insurgents is a possibility not considered by Chalk, who deploys their claims uncritically in order to build an analysis closely mirroring that of the US government.

58 S. Raphael

The above examples are merely indicative of a wider manifestation of this reliance on official sources and on unsubstantiated assertion, in order to produce an analysis which mirrors directly that emerging from high-level officials in the US government.

The problem of silencing

Alongside the problem of sourcing lies the problem of silencing. Key actors and campaigns of terrorism are systematically ignored by the core experts, particularly, in the context of this chapter, those which have received ideological or material support from Washington. And this is true despite the fact that such examples clearly fit the consensus definition employed by the majority of experts whereby terrorism is:

1   violence (or the threat thereof); which is
2   instrumental, as opposed to aimless; and conducted for
3   political (i.e. non-personal) ends; in order to
4   influence an audience wider than the immediate target(s), generally through the creation of fear; achieved through
5   the deliberate and systematic violation of the established norms surrounding the use of force.[7]

This definition clearly encompasses state as well as non-state acts of terror and could easily be applied to many aspects of US-led 'counterterrorism'. The use of violence targeted against noncombatants in order to influence a wider audience has long been a hallmark of 'counterterrorism' supported by the US. For example, the use of terrorism by pro-US security forces in Central America was systematic and was documented as such at the time. Amnesty International (1984: 155–156), for example, received 'regular, often daily reports identifying El Salvador's regular security and military units as responsible for the torture, "disappearance" and killing of non-combatant civilians from all sectors of Salvadoran society'. The use of disappearance and torture was widespread throughout pro-US states in the region during the 1980s, often carried out by security forces trained and armed by US forces (see Blum, 1995). Such tactics are clearly terrorist in nature, given the fact that 'it is a strategy designed primarily to induce extreme fear in a target population. It is a strategy of terrorism and is understood as such by the populations of targeted societies' (Stohl, 2006: 10). None of this was discussed at the time by the core experts and there has only been the odd, brief acknowledgement of this record since (see for example, Wilkinson, 2002: 68).

Likewise, expert discussion of state assassinations of foreign dissidents – a tactic clearly considered terroristic – has been restricted solely to those governments identified as terrorist-sponsoring by the US government. Thus, the Soviet Union and other Communist countries have 'used the weapon of international terrorism as a means of silencing and intimidating exiled dissidents and hunting down those alleged to have betrayed the Party' (Wilkinson, 1984: 293). Syria has arranged for the assassination of enemies and 'allies' alike (Alexander, 1986: 6), whilst Iraq, Iran, and Libya have also engaged in such activities (B. Jenkins, 1985: 11; Laqueur, 1999: 178–179). However, there is little or no discussion of, for instance, apartheid South Africa's extensive assassination campaign which was 'exercised quite openly by the apartheid government, especially against leaders of the liberation movements who were not based in South Africa but abroad' (K. O'Brien, 2001: 108). Neither was there any analysis of the multinational Operation Condor which

> became the most sinister state-sponsored terrorist network in the Western Hemisphere, if not the world. Those targeted went far beyond members of the militant Southern Cone guerrilla movements ... they included civilian political figures from the region, and Latin American exile leaders living in Europe and the United States.
>
> (Kornbluh, 2003: 324)

A similar silence has greeted the clear use of terrorism by US-supported 'counterterrorist' forces operating in the post-cold war era, notably in Colombia, Turkey, and Israel. Thus, the use of terrorism by Colombian paramilitary groups receives little attention when compared to analyses of the left wing guerrilla movements, despite the fact that they have consistently been responsible for over 70 per cent of all terrorist attacks in the country (State Department, 2000). In contrast, the RAND database, maintained in part by Hoffman and Jenkins, attributes to the guerrillas more than twice the number of fatalities than it does to the paramilitaries, which were apparently responsible for only 12 per cent of incidents between 1998 and 2004.[8] Where such violence is acknowledged, any discussion is exceedingly brief (see for example, Laqueur's (1999: 189) passing reference to the 'activities of counterinsurgency gangs'), and crucially, collaboration between these groups and Colombian security forces is rarely mentioned at all. This collusion has been extensively documented, with Human Rights Watch, for instance, clear that there exists 'abundant, detailed and compelling evidence that certain Colombian army brigades and police detachments continue to promote, work with, support, profit from, and tolerate paramilitary groups, treating them as a force allied to and compatible with their own' (Human Rights Watch, 2001: 1).

Likewise, the systematic use of terrorism by Turkish 'counterterrorist' forces throughout the 1990s, and US complicity in this has been extensively documented (see van Bruinessen, 1996; Gabelnick et al., 1999), but receives little to no treatment by the core literature. In a similar vein, Israel's extensive use of targeted killings, often directed against noncombatants and clearly employed as a strategy for installing fear in a wider target population, is largely ignored by the experts. Evidence regarding the use of this strategy is widespread and exists in relation to Israeli actions during its occupation of Lebanon, during the first and second intifadas, and during the Oslo Peace Process (see Fisk, 1992: 559–578; Human Rights Watch, 1993; B. Morris, 1999: 591–592; Byman, 2006).

Overall, and in parallel with the silences regarding these forms of terrorism, the literature fails to acknowledge and analyse the role that the US has played in supporting these 'counterterror' campaigns. US support for aggressive 'counterterror' campaigns throughout the South and its complicity in many instances of state terrorism which result, either through the training of host security forces in assassination and torture techniques or through the waiver of human rights conditionalities in order to continue the funding of abusive militaries, has been well-documented elsewhere (see Klare and Kornbluh, 1989; Human Rights Watch, 2002; Stokes and Raphael, forthcoming).

Likewise, the less-frequent but still significant use by Washington of insurgent forces to destabilise unfriendly regimes is almost totally ignored by the core experts. During the cold war, substantial support was provided to anti-government forces operating in Nicaragua, Angola, Afghanistan, and elsewhere (Copson and Cronin, 1987; Klare, 1989; Hiro, 2002: 179–264). This has been mirrored by the overt support provided to the Northern Alliance in the winter of 2001–2 against the Taliban regime in Afghanistan (Rose *et al.*, 2001), whilst recent rumours of aid to anti-Tehran groups operating out of post-2003 Iraq potentially represents a continuation of this strategy (Hersh, 2006). Such forces have often employed terrorism as a central strategy, making the silence in the literature significant. For example, very little attention was paid to the use of terrorism by the Contras who received extensive US support in their campaign against the Sandinista regime – and this is the case even though the group shifted the focus of their campaign from early attempts to engage Sandinista military forces to widespread covert sabotage of key economic installations in Nicaragua, as well as systematic attacks on non-combatants (Taubman, 1983). Americas Watch concluded in 1985 that 'there can be no doubt, on the basis of what we heard and saw, that a planned strategy of terrorism is being carried out by the contras along the Honduras border' (quoted in Chomsky, 1985: 12–13). Indeed, by the end of the 1980s, Human Rights Watch (1990) confirmed that 'the *Contras* were major and systematic violators of the most basic standards of the laws of armed conflict, including by launching indiscriminate attacks on civilians, selectively murdering non-combatants, and mistreating prisoners'. Evidence regarding this, as well as similar uses of terrorism by other US-backed forces, is largely written out of the core literature.

Alongside this silencing of US-backed terrorism throughout the South, the core literature also consistently fails to provide an adequate understanding of the armed movements which it does focus on, through silencing the local social and political contexts within which they operate. 'Leftist' movements throughout Latin America during the 1980s, the continuing resistance in Colombia, the history of Turkish separatism, even the 'global jihadi movement' – all are discussed in terms of their internal dynamics, motivating ideology, targets, tactics, and strategies, with very little said about the social and political conditions from which they arise and are often sustained. Indeed, core experts are often sceptical about the desirability of discussing such conditions at all. Jenkins (B. Jenkins, 2003: 5), for instance, is clear that whilst the US should 'help resolve conflicts that give rise to terrorism such as that in Northern Ireland and the Middle East', there is 'little convincing evidence to demonstrate that addressing the so-called root causes of terrorism – oppression, poverty, lack of education – has a causal impact on reducing terrorism'.

This 'decontextualisation' can be seen clearly in relation to research on the various groups employing armed resistance against Israel. Palestinian movements (both secular and 'Islamist'), as well as the Shiite Hezbollah, are overwhelmingly represented by the experts as the aggressors, driven almost entirely by the dictates of an unwavering and fundamentalist ideology. Thus, such groups are responsible for a 'dramatic rise in fundamentalist Islamic-inspired terrorism', the influence of which has been 'the primary driving factor behind savage civil conflicts and violence' in the Occupied Territories and Lebanon (Chalk, 1999: 155, 2000: 20–21).

These groups have been increasingly understood through the lens of the 'new terrorism' thesis which emerged throughout the 1990s and has been outlined in greatest depth by Hoffman (B. Hoffman, 1989a, 1998: 87–129 and 197–205, 1999). Within this overall framework, Hoffman views Islamic groups as the clear aggressors in the Middle East: although Hezbollah and Hamas perceive themselves as fighting 'an entirely self-defensive struggle', the experts cast their struggle 'in terms of an all-out war from which there can be no respite until the enemy is totally and utterly vanquished' (B. Hoffman, 1998: 95–98). Activists are 'engaged in what they regard as a "total war"', which sanctions wide-scale terrorism (B. Hoffman, 1989a: 369–370). This fundamentalist Islamist ideology and the armed struggle which emerges from it, it is suggested, has its roots firmly in Tehran's aim of 'extending the fundamentalist interpretation of Islamic law espoused in Iran to other Muslim countries' (B. Hoffman, 1998: 95–98). Indeed, for Laqueur (1999: 134), the emergence of both Hamas and Hezbollah 'was, of course, not accidental; it was another part of the fundamentalist wave occurring in the Muslim world', with the rise of Hezbollah 'directly connected with the victory of Ayatollah Khomeini and his followers in Iran'. And as a result, these groups work uncompromisingly towards the 'complete destruction of the Israeli state', and thus view the 'present peace process' as tantamount to 'a wholesale betrayal of Islamic interests' (Chalk, 1999: 156–157). This can be seen not least in the suicide campaign waged by Hamas and the Palestinian Islamic Jihad (PIJ) in the mid-1990s, which, it is claimed by the experts, was designed to destroy the chances of peace through undermining the Oslo process (see for example, Merari, 2000).

Absent from all analysis produced by the core experts on these issues is any real consideration of the history or conditions of occupation within southern Lebanon, the West Bank, and the Gaza Strip. This massively skews and distorts the picture painted of the motivations for armed resistance. Thus, the 'rejectionist' groups are seen to be opposed to the Oslo process due to a simple, unrestrained hatred of Israel. There is no acknowledgement of how the process itself has been inherently destructive, by for example, facilitating a year-on-year increase in settlement populations in the West Bank (B'Tselem, undated; Said, 2000). Terrorism experts also spend a great deal of time charting Israeli casualties at the hands of these armed groups. Chalk (2000: 23) found that 460 acts of terrorism were carried out in Israel and the Occupied Territories in the years following Oslo, claiming more than 265 Israeli lives – which 'represents the largest number of Israeli dead from terrorism in any comparable period since the birth of the State in 1948'. Likewise, Laqueur (2003: 102) found that over a period of fifteen years Hezbollah had taken the lives of around 800 Israeli soldiers and their allies in the South Lebanon Army (SLA). In neither case does the author acknowledge the extensive destruction wrought by the Israeli military and their paramilitary allies on the occupied populations, nor the fact that this occupation has directly resulted in substantially more Palestinian and Lebanese deaths than the Israeli casualties cited.

Together, these silences pervading the literature ensure that official understandings of the threat from terrorism have been largely unchallenged by the field. This characteristic of the research output is significant and works to legitimise US policies undertaken in 'response'. How this is so in practice will be explored in the final section.

The ideological functions of the field: legitimising US 'counterterror' interventions

Through replicating official analyses of the terrorist threat facing the US and its allies, and through failing to acknowledge the role that US-led 'counterterrorism' policies have played in sustaining and promoting terrorism in the South, the literature has long worked to legitimise these policies. This has been so as a result of omission – of the silencing of a great deal of facts and perspectives relevant to the study of terrorism – as well as more overt policy prescriptions laid out by the experts. This was evident during the cold war when the experts tended to recommend a wide set of coercive interventions in the region, broadly aligned to those undertaken by the US government. For instance, Kupperman was clear that:

> If [arresting suspects and diplomatic sanctions on sponsors] were to fail, which is quite likely, the administration must then confront the problems of using covert force, including eliminating the bombers and their leaders. If such operations were to be undertaken, Congress must share responsibility. Otherwise, another 'Iran-Contra' debacle would assuredly arise. If covert operations, in particular assassination by executive order, remain proscribed, certain allied secret services would be less squeamish. In any case, the terrorists must be sent a clear message.
>
> (Kupperman and Kamen, 1989)

In particular, the US needed to continue 'to provide security assistance and military training' to the government in El Salvador and elsewhere, through 'expanded military training programs in the United States, the School of Americas, and individual central American countries', in order to 'improve the capabilities of local military organisations to engage in counterinsurgency, the defence of economic targets, and nation-building' (Gonzalez et al., 1984: 31–33). According to Livingstone (1984), US policy should also be directed to providing aid to 'governments resisting

Soviet- or proxy-backed insurgents or terrorists. This support should take the form of economic, police, and military aid, including supplying training to counterinsurgency and counterterrorist forces, [and] the introduction of US military advisors'. Likewise, several core experts advocated continued assistance to the Contras. According to Cline and Alexander (1986: 67–68), the 'US policy for countering terrorism by aid to anti-Sandinista insurgents' is motivated by 'collective defence of people fighting for their freedom [and] is impeccable and fully justified in international law', as 'enshrined in Article 51 of the UN Charter'. The US should 'provide training, arms, and materiel to resistance forces in ... Nicaragua; and we should design psychological operations to buttress that resistance' (Livingstone, 1984). Indeed, 'Somoza was a bad guy, but these guys are worse. The right thing in my judgement is to overthrow that government. Whether the contras or the United States should go in and throw them out, I'm not prepared to say' (Livingstone, cited in MacPherson, 1986).

A similar overt legitimisation of US coercive intervention characterises post-cold war terrorism studies. This can be seen not least in relation to research on terrorism in Colombia, where for example, experts recommend the (cautious) application of a '[t]raditional counterinsurgency strategy [which] would support improved tactical intelligence, the creation of crack fighting units, and increased air mobility' (B. Jenkins 2000/1: 53–55). Indeed: 'Without external assistance, Colombia cannot defeat the guerrilla-gangster Minotaur that consumes it. It is in our national interest to help' (B. Jenkins, 2001). Chalk sees the 'US program of military assistance to El Salvador during the Reagan administration' as a relevant model for the necessary aid to Colombia, given that it 'succeeded in transforming the unprepossessing Salvadoran military into a force capable of turning back a formidable guerrilla threat'. Assistance required includes measures 'to move forces out of static defence, to the extent possible, and remake them into mobile units to retake the initiative from the guerrillas', which in turn will require 'the development of rapid reaction capabilities, including transport and attack helicopters ... and intelligence collection' (Rabasa and Chalk, 2001: 95–96).

Likewise, Israeli counterterrorist policy and US support for it has long been overtly legitimised by the core experts, with, for instance, Hoffman (B. Hoffman, 1989b) asserting that 'Israel should not be condemned, but be praised for its bold' policies against Hezbollah, given that 'we should accept that no progress will be made in the struggle against terrorism until the terrorists' state sponsors are held accountable for their aid and encouragement'. More recently, Jenkins has been clear that whilst it is 'easy to deplore Israeli tactics in the West Bank (such as the razing of buildings and neighbourhoods or the deporting of terrorists' family members)', given the problem of suicide bombings 'precisely what alternatives suggest themselves in the current environment?' (P. Davis and Jenkins, 2002: 29).

In sum, core terrorism experts tend to legitimate US-led and US-supported counterterrorism policies through insulating them from critique and openly supporting them. This function does not apply in all cases, but there is no doubt that it is served in a systematic fashion throughout the literature. And given the close relationship between these experts and state power in the US already discussed, it is a function of huge significance for the formulation of counterterrorism policy in Washington.

Conclusion

As mentioned, the analysis presented in this chapter forms part of a wider project examining the research output from the core figures within terrorism studies (Raphael, forthcoming), and in a paper of this length the examples provided are necessarily illustrative. However, suffice it to say that the problematic features of the literature described here are at play throughout the field, in a variety of specific contexts. If nothing else, this fact points to the need for a 'critical turn' in terrorism studies. As the US continues to lead a worldwide 'war on terror' throughout the global South with profound consequences for the human security of populations in this region, it is vital to continue to investigate the role of 'independent, objective' academic experts in the policymaking process. Furthermore, and crucially, it is necessary to continue to subject their output to critical analysis in order to reveal the ways in which expert 'knowledge' on terrorism, considered to originate outside of politics, in fact relies upon the claims and analyses of deeply political actors and institutions.

A 'critical' study of terrorism should also work to expose the silences present in current mainstream research, particularly regarding the terroristic nature of many aspects of US-led and US-supported 'counterterrorist' policy. Once exposed, there is an urgent need to engage in substantial, rigorous research on the subjects silenced thus far. It is vitally important to understand how practices and policies in past and current 'wars on terror' utilise terrorism as a strategy of political violence, whether directly by the US itself (for example, in Iraq) or more often by its state allies (in Colombia, Turkey, the Occupied Territories, and elsewhere). In sum, there exists a clear research agenda for 'critical terrorism studies' which will be of great importance in coming years: to reveal the ideological function served by much core terrorism research and to challenge this through undertaking rigorous research into major instances of terrorism in the modern world; instances which have thus far been almost wholly ignored.

Notes

1 Thanks are due to the editors of this volume, along with Ruth Blakeley, Doug Stokes, and Vanessa Cooke, all of whom provided invaluable suggestions for strengthening this chapter.
2 For the purposes of this chapter, the terms 'field' and 'research community' will be used interchangeably.
3 The same is true, albeit to a lesser extent, with respect to other governments in the West (in particular, the UK and Israel). However, this chapter will focus solely on the relationship between experts and US state power.
4 For these two publications as the 'core journals' of the field, see Gordon (1998) and Silke (2004c). *Studies in Conflict and Terrorism* arose from the merger of the two

initial core journals in the field: *Terrorism* (established 1977) and *Conflict* (established 1978).
5 A full discussion of the selection methodology can be found elsewhere (Raphael, 2008).
6 The Kissinger Commission was, according to Hufford (1985), the 'single best reference for understanding the Reagan Administration view on Central America'.
7 See Raphael (2007) for a detailed discussion of how the core experts uniformly arrive at this 'consensus definition' and the various strategies they subsequently employ to exclude state terrorism from the analysis.
8 RAND Database, accessed 24 July 2007.

4 Knowledge, power and politics in the study of political terrorism

Richard Jackson[1]

Introduction

Terrorism studies was once a relatively minor specialist subfield of security studies and international relations. Today, it exhibits all the characteristics of a major stand-alone academic field, having its own: dedicated scholarly journals (*Terrorism and Political Violence, Studies in Conflict and Terrorism* and more recently, *Critical Studies on Terrorism*); graduate and post-graduate teaching and research programmes at most major universities in America, Europe, and the Asia-Pacific; a growing number of dedicated research centres and think tanks; a coterie of widely recognised scholars and experts; regular academic conferences; and an accepted body of literature, including a number of widely cited core texts.[2] It is, in many ways, comparable to fields like criminology, Middle East studies, and intelligence studies, particularly in that it comprises research and scholars from a variety of different disciplines and approaches coming together to examine a common subject. Moreover, in the past ten years or so, terrorism studies has evolved into one of the fastest expanding areas of research in the Western academic world, with literally thousands of new books, articles, reports and dissertations published every year (see Gordon, 2004: 109, 1999; Silke, this volume). Perhaps more importantly, it has consolidated itself as a field of genuine political and cultural influence. Its leading scholars and think tanks regularly provide expert advice to officials at the highest levels of Western states and appear regularly as commentators in the news media.

As with any academic field, terrorism studies is in large part constituted by an identifiable and fairly consistent set of shared assumptions, narratives, and labels about its primary subject – a widely and broadly accepted body of 'knowledge' concerning the definition, nature, effects, threat, causes, and responses to the phenomenon called 'terrorism' – as well as an accepted array of knowledge-generating practices. These narratives, assumptions, and knowledge-generating practices function to define the field's ontological, epistemological, methodological, and ethical-normative approaches and can be found in much of the field's primary output, particularly by its leading scholars (see Raphael, this volume). In addition, they are reproduced continuously in conferences, seminars, media commentary, public reports, databases, and expert testimony to official bodies.

Knowledge, power and politics 67

The aim of this chapter is to provide a general critical analysis of the broader semantic field or discourse of terrorism studies, particularly in terms of its core labels, narratives, and assumptions, or, its widely accepted 'knowledge'. As such, it seeks to build upon and corroborate a number of previous studies on the primary knowledge claims and research practices of the field (see Stohl, 1979; Herman, 1982; Schmid and Jongman, 1988; Herman and O'Sullivan, 1989; George, 1991a; Reid, 1993; Zulaika and Douglass, 1996; Silke, 2004a, this volume; Burnett and Whyte, 2005; Ranstorp, 2006a, this volume; Raphael, this volume). The main conclusions to be drawn from the analysis presented here, and the main arguments I wish to advance in this chapter, are that, in the first place, much of the accepted knowledge about terrorism in the field is highly contestable and open to debate. It therefore provides a weak basis for further scholarly research, public policy-making, and public debate. Second, the accepted knowledge of the field is in many instances politically biased, but more importantly, it functions ideologically to reinforce and reify existing structures of power in society, particularly that of the state, and to promote particular elite political projects. As a consequence of these weaknesses, there is an urgent need for a revitalising 'critical turn' within the broader terrorism studies field.

The chapter is organised into three parts. In the following section, I provide a brief overview of the methodological approach I have employed in my research. In part two, I summarise some of the main assumptions, narratives, labels, and knowledge practices of the field. The third part of the paper critically analyses the terrorism studies discourse, employing both a first order critique which examines its central assumptions and narratives on its own social scientific terms, and a second order critique which explores the wider ideological effects of the discourse. In the conclusion, I reflect on the main implications of the study's findings for the field, particularly in light of the call for a more reflective and normatively-oriented 'Critical Terrorism Studies'.

The analysis of discourse[3]

The approach I have utilised to examine the discourse of terrorism studies falls broadly under the mantle of discourse analysis (see Milliken, 1999; Laffey and Weldes, 1997; Purvis and Hunt, 1993; Yee, 1996). Discourse analysis is a form of critical theorising which aims primarily to illustrate and describe the relationship between textual and social and political processes. It is particularly concerned with the politics of representation – the manifest political or ideological consequences of adopting one mode of representation over another. In this case, I am concerned with the ways in which the subject of terrorism and counterterrorism is represented, narrated, and studied within the terrorism studies field.

Although discourse theorising is employed within a range of different epistemological paradigms, including post-structuralist, postmodernist, feminist, and social constructivist approaches, it is predicated on a shared set of theoretical commitments (Milliken, 1999). Broadly speaking, these include: an understanding of language as constitutive or productive of meaning; an understanding of discourse as structures of signification which construct social and political realities, particularly in terms of defining subjects and establishing their relational positions within a system of signification; an understanding of discourse as being productive of subjects authorised to speak and act, legitimate forms of knowledge and political practices and, importantly, common sense within particular social groups and historical settings; an understanding of discourse as necessarily exclusionary and silencing of other modes of representation; and an understanding of discourse as historically and culturally contingent, intertextual, open-ended, requiring continuous articulation and re-articulation and, therefore, open to destabilisation and counter-hegemonic struggle.

The specific research presented in this chapter summarises and extends an ongoing research programme on the academic, political, and cultural discourses of terrorism (see Jackson, forthcoming, 2007a, 2007b, 2007c, 2007d, 2006, 2005). The discourse analytic technique employed in all these studies, including the present one, proceeded in two main stages. The first stage entailed an examination of texts identified as relevant to the study. In this case, the primary units of analysis or 'data' were more than 100 academic monographs, articles in core terrorism studies and international relations journals, papers presented at major international conferences, and reports and websites from terrorism studies think tanks and research institutions.[4] Employing a simple 'grounded theory' approach, the analysis began by selecting a sample of widely-cited terrorism books and articles from recognised leading scholars (see Raphael, this volume), followed by samples of articles from the core terrorism studies journals, international relations journals, widely-cited think tank publications, and conference papers. Each text was then examined for its core labels, assumptions, narratives, and discursive formations, particularly as they related to the nature, causes, and responses to terrorism. The analysis was considered complete when the addition of new texts did not yield any significant new insights or categories.

The second stage of the research involved subjecting the findings of the textual analysis to both a first and second order critique. A first order or immanent critique uses a discourse's internal contradictions, mistakes, misconceptions, and omissions to criticise it on its own terms and expose the events and perspectives that the discourse fails to acknowledge or address (see Milliken, 1999). In such critique, it is not uncommon to use the evidence or arguments of one text to critique another, or even to use different parts of the same text or author to highlight contradictions or alternative explanations. The point of this form of internal critique is not to establish the 'correct' or 'real truth' of the subject, but rather to destabilise dominant interpretations and demonstrate the inherently contested and hence political nature of the discourse.

A second order critique on the other hand, entails reflecting on the broader political and ethical consequences – the wider ideological and historical-material effects – of the representations in the texts. In part, it involves an exploration of the ways in which the discourse can function as a 'symbolic technology' (Laffey and Weldes, 1997) that can be wielded by particular elites and institutions to:

Knowledge, power and politics 69

structure the primary subject positions, accepted knowledge, common sense, and legitimate policy responses to the actors and events being described; exclude and de-legitimise alternative forms of knowledge and practice; naturalise a particular political and social order; and construct and sustain a hegemonic 'regime of truth'. A range of specific discourse analytic techniques can be employed in second order critique: genealogical analysis, predicate analysis, narrative analysis and deconstructive analysis (Milliken, 1999).

It is important to note that when we examine a discourse as a broad form of knowledge and practice, it is never completely uniform, nor is it necessarily entirely coherent or consistent. Rather, it always has porous borders and often contains numerous exceptions, inconsistencies, and contradictions by different speakers and texts. Many terrorism studies scholars for example, upon a close reading of their individual texts, express more nuanced arguments and viewpoints than are necessarily presented here. In addition, orthodox terrorism scholars sometimes engage in fairly vigorous debates and disagreements (see Ranstorp, this volume), although these rarely involve questioning fundamental underlying ontological, epistemological, or methodological assumptions about the primary subject.

The important point is not that each text or scholar can be characterised in the same uniform way or even that these scholars agree on a broad set of knowledge claims; as suggested, there are ongoing debates within the field about a great many key issues. Nor is there any suggestion that individual terrorism studies scholars are engaged in some kind of 'bad faith' conspiracy to promote a particular political agenda or ideological viewpoint (Horgan and Boyle, 2008). It is, rather, that taken together as a broader discourse and a body of work that presently has political and, importantly, cultural, currency, the narratives and forms of the discourse function to construct and maintain a specific understanding of, and approach to, terrorism and counterterrorism and the 'knowledge' generated in the field has certain academic, political, and social effects.

Narrative and 'knowledge' in terrorism studies

In a field as quantitatively large and fast-growing as terrorism studies, there is a potentially vast array of different labels, narratives, and assumptions about the broader subject. However, perhaps due to its very recent origins or its roots in security studies, the particular terrorism studies texts examined in this research displayed a surprisingly restricted and fairly consistent set of characteristics; and there were few major deviations from the dominant narratives, assumptions, and methodological approaches I and others have identified. In this section, I summarise some of the main characteristics of the discourse within a number of distinct clusters related to the conceptualisation and study of terrorism, its perceived threat, its roots and causes, and the core responses to terrorism. Obviously, there are a large number of elements of the discourse not discussed below, or only in passing, due to limitations of space.

The nature and study of terrorism

In the vast majority of texts I examined, the central concept of the field – terrorism – is conceptualised and understood solely or primarily as a form of illegitimate non-state political violence. The construction of terrorism as a form of non-state violence is sustained by two common conceptual practices. First, a surprising number of scholars, including some leading scholars, adopt an actor-based definition of terrorism in which the nature of the actor determines the character of the violence. For example, Bruce Hoffman, a leading figure in the field, argues that terrorism involves violence 'perpetrated by a subnational group or non-state entity' (B. Hoffman, 1998: 43). This is in keeping with the US State Department's highly influential definition of terrorism as 'premeditated, politically motivated violence perpetuated against noncombatant targets by subnational groups or clandestine agents, usually intended to influence an audience' (quoted in Martin, 2003: 33).

A second and more common practice among scholars involves defining terrorism as a strategy of political violence which any actor can employ, including states, but then failing to examine the vast amount of terrorism perpetrated by states in any systematic manner. Walter Laqueur, arguably one of the founders of terrorism studies, is emblematic of this practice: he openly accepts that states practice 'terrorism from above' and have killed many more people and caused far more material and social destruction than 'terrorism from below', but then argues that this is simply not the terrorism he wishes to examine (Laqueur, 1977: 6). Most texts in the field however, do not contain any such acknowledgement; they simply proceed to examine only the terrorism perpetrated by non-state actors (see also, Raphael, this volume; Silke, 2004d). A recent introductory text for example, typical of the burgeoning terrorism literature published today, does not contain a single mention of state terrorism (Sloan, 2006).

An important consequence of these conceptual practices is that terrorism comes to be understood and studied solely as a form of violence carried out by non-state groups, and terrorism by states remains unstudied and mostly invisible (see Jackson, 2008a). When state terrorism is discussed, it is usually limited to descriptions of 'state-sponsored terrorism' by so-called 'rogue states' (Jackson, 2007b). Further, the subsequent silence on the direct use of terrorism by state actors within the terrorism studies literature underpins a mostly unspoken belief that Western liberal democratic states in particular never engage in terrorism as a matter of policy, but only occasionally in error or misjudgement (see Blakeley, 2008). It is also frequently argued that violence by states is de facto legitimate, and therefore cannot be terrorism.

Lastly, the majority of terrorism studies texts take as their starting point the assumption that terrorism is a phenomenon that can be understood and studied fairly objectively and can be explained using traditional social scientific methodologies. Consequently, the majority of terrorism studies research tends to adopt a positivist ontology and employ empirical methodologies involving the collection of observable quantitative, case study, and historical data. Related to this, in the vast majority of studies, scholars rely on secondary information gathered from news media, government sources, or intelligence agencies (Silke, 2004d; Silke, Ranstorp, Raphael, Breen Smyth, this volume). Great store is put in large 'objective' databases on terrorism for example, such as the RAND-MIPT (Memorial Institute for the Prevention of Terrorism) Terrorism Incident Database (RAND, 2006), which are then widely used to develop statistical models and investigate correlations. In combination, these underlying assumptions and conceptual practices construct a widely accepted 'knowledge' that terrorism is a relatively unproblematic form of non-state violence that can be objectively identified, measured and systematically studied.

The terrorist threat narrative

Perhaps the core sustaining narrative of the field is that non-state terrorism poses a significant and existential threat to modern societies and without significant investment in counterterrorism it could have catastrophic consequences for Western states and wider international stability. In most texts, it is viewed as self-evident that terrorism remains 'one of the most significant threats to the Western world in general and US national security in particular' (Mishal and Rosenthal, 2005: 276). Marc Sageman, a leading terrorism scholar, similarly argues: 'A new type of terrorism threatens the world, driven by networks of fanatics determined to inflict maximum civilian and economic damages on distant targets in pursuit of their extremist goals' (Sageman, 2004: vii). Government officials and state-linked scholars, in particular, are apt to suggest that terrorism is such a potent force that it threatens to destroy Western democracy, social stability, the entire Western way of life, and the international system itself (see Jackson, 2007c).

Other related narratives and assumptions which are virtually ubiquitous across the literature include the argument that al-Qaeda, purportedly the primary non-state terrorist group operating in the world today, is a formidable, globally networked foe with tens of thousands of trained 'jihadists' and millions of supporters, and that there are sleeper cells of jihadists and fifth columnists within Western societies ready and waiting to attack. For example, Jessica Stern, a recognised terrorism 'expert', asserted that 'by September 11, 2001, between 70,000 and 110,000 radical Muslims had graduated from Al Qaeda training camps' (Stern, 2003: 260), while a popular textbook suggested that there may be between 35,000 and 50,000 'Al Qaeda operatives' in the world today, many of them in 'independent "sleeper" cells committed to waging holy war against the West' (Martin, 2003: 194, 198). Similarly, it is frequently asserted as common sense that non-state terrorists are eager and willing to use weapons of mass destruction, and that there are 'rogue states', such as Iran, Syria, North Korea, and, until recently, Iraq, who would be willing to provide WMD to terrorists as means of waging proxy warfare against the West.

Tied in with the broader threat narrative is a growing literature on what has been called a 'new terrorism' (see B. Hoffman, 1998; Laqueur, 1999; Kegley, 2003). The 'new terrorism' thesis[5] suggests that driven by hatred, fanaticism, and extremism rather than by political ideology or rational calculation, today's 'new' religiously-inspired terrorists are determined to cause mass casualties among civilians, are driven to sacrifice themselves in murderous suicide attacks, would be willing to employ weapons of mass destruction, and are not amenable to traditional forms of negotiation and dialogue. It is therefore a more murderous and dangerous form of terrorism than the world has ever seen before. Jessica Stern has argued that 'religious terrorist groups are more violent than their secular counterparts and are probably more likely to use weapons of mass destruction' (Stern, 2003: xxii). Similarly, Daniel Byman, another leading terrorism scholar argues that due to its religious worldview, 'appeasing al-Qaeda is difficult in theory and impossible in practice' (Byman, 2003: 147).

In sum, these frequent narratives within the literature construct the widely accepted 'knowledge' that non-state terrorism represents a major security threat to the international community and to democratic societies in particular, in part because their inherent freedoms make them more vulnerable to terrorist infiltration and attack. Moreover, these narratives construct a common sense and widely, though not totally, accepted 'knowledge' that contemporary terrorism is a new and deadlier form of terrorism than any encountered previously, one which creates an exceptional state of emergency requiring 'new' counterterrorism measures to defeat and which cannot be dealt with using negotiation and dialogue, methods which have been previously successful in dealing with the 'old' ideological and nationalist terrorism.

The origins and causes of terrorism[6]

A surprising number of terrorism studies texts promote the view that the roots and causes of terrorism lie in individual psychological abnormality, and religious or ideological extremism engendered through processes of 'radicalisation'. Although theories of individual psychopathology among terrorists have fallen out of favour among most leading scholars in recent years, the notion that terrorist behaviour is rooted in the personality defects of individuals remains close to the surface of most texts, not least in the notion that weak-minded, uneducated, or emotionally vulnerable young Muslims fall prey to indoctrination and brainwashing – so-called 'radicalisation' – by terrorist recruiters operating through *madrasahs*, radical mosques, or extremist internet sites (see Haqqani, 2002). Related to this, it is not uncommon to find texts which argue that 'Islamic' suicide bombers are primarily young men driven by sexual frustration and impotence. In a much-cited text on contemporary 'religious terrorism' for example, Mark Juergensmeyer states that 'the young bachelor self-martyrs in the Hamas movement ... expect that the blasts that kill them will propel them to a bed in heaven where the most delicious acts of sexual consummation will be theirs for the taking' (Juergensmeyer, 2000: 201). In any case, such narratives construct the accepted knowledge that terrorists are different and abnormal and, more importantly, that their actions are rooted in their personalities rather than other factors related to their political situation, strategic calculation or experiences of oppression and humiliation.

Knowledge, power and politics 73

During the cold war, many terrorism studies texts suggested that the roots and causes of terrorism lay within communist ideology and the direct involvement of the Soviet Union (see Raphael, this volume). Claire Sterling's (1981) popular book, *The Terror Network*, for example, posited the existence of a global terrorist network sponsored by the Soviets that was behind many of the revolutionary and anti-colonial movements. As Sam Raphael illustrates in this volume, a great many of the leading terrorism studies scholars at the time subscribed to the 'Soviet network theory' of terrorism.

In many ways, the cold war focus on left-wing ideology was replaced by what is now a vast and growing literature on the religious origins of terrorism, particularly as it relates to Islam (see Jackson, 2007a). Based on David Rapoport's (1984) initial formulation of 'religious terrorism', the discourse of 'Islamic terrorism' argues that the roots and causes of much of the al-Qaeda-related terrorism today can be found in '*Islamic* extremism'. Walter Laqueur for example, suggests that while there is 'no Muslim or Arab monopoly in the field of religious fanaticism … the frequency of Muslim- and Arab-inspired terrorism is still striking' (Laqueur, 1999: 129). Similarly, a prominent counterterrorism think tank publication argues that 'in the Islamic world one cannot differentiate between the political violence of Islamic groups and their popular support derived from religion … the present terrorism on the part of the Arab and Muslim world is *Islamic in nature*' (Paz, 1998, emphasis added). Marc Sageman argues in relation to al-Qaeda: 'Salafi ideology determines its mission, sets its goals, and guides its tactics' (Sageman, 2004: 1). In sum, and similar to narratives of individual deviance, these narratives construct the widely accepted 'knowledge' that contemporary terrorism is primarily rooted in and caused by religious extremism and fanaticism, and not in rational calculation or other political, cultural, and sociological factors.

Responding to terrorism

A final set of assumptions and narratives within the broader literature relates to questions about how to respond to terrorism. Following the logic of the preceding notions of the existential threat posed by the 'new terrorism', as well as the fanatical nature and origins of religiously-inspired terrorism, it is frequently argued in the literature that 'new' methods of counterterrorism are required for its control, and that there are justifiable reasons to employ any means necessary, including torture, targeted killings, and restrictions on human rights, to deal with the threat (see Jackson, 2007d). Rohan Gunaratna, Paul Wilkinson, and Daniel Byman, all major figures in the field, for example, have openly condoned the extra-judicial assassination of terrorist leaders as a potentially effective method of counterterrorism (see Gunaratna, 2003: 233–235; Wilkinson, 2002: 68; Byman, 2006, 2007). At the very least, it is commonly accepted that coercive instruments, including sanctions, pre-emption and military force, are both legal and effective forms of counterterrorism (see for example, Shultz and Vogt, 2003; Byman, 2003). Often unstated, but appearing as a subtext, it is implicitly assumed that non-violent responses to terrorism such as dialogue and

74   R. Jackson

political reform are simply bound to fail in the current context (see Toros, forthcoming).

More specifically, as I have shown elsewhere (Jackson, 2005), the global counterterrorism campaign known as the 'war on terror' is based on a particular series of defining narratives. The most important narrative at the heart of the war on terror is the notion that the attacks of 11 September 2001 amounted to an 'act of war'. This narrative in turn, logically implies that a war-based counterterrorism strategy is both necessary to counter the threat and legal under international law. Consequently, a great many terrorism studies texts take it as axiomatic or common sense that the war on terror, and force-based counterterrorism in general, is both legitimate and efficacious. In this way, the notion that responding to terrorism requires force and counter-violence, and sometimes even war and torture, has come to assume a form of widely accepted 'knowledge'.

In short, the assumptions, narratives and knowledge-practices I have described above, and quite a few more besides, collectively make up much of the widely accepted body of terrorism 'knowledge', or, the discourse of terrorism studies. This 'knowledge' is reproduced, often with little deviation from the central assumptions and narratives, continuously in the field's journals, conferences, and in literally thousands of publications every year by academics and think tanks. Furthermore, as Michael Stohl has recently illustrated, many of these core narratives or 'myths', as he terms them, have proved to be extremely durable over several decades (see Stohl, 1979, 2008).

A critical analysis of the terrorism studies discourse

Having briefly outlined some of its main characteristics, the purpose of this section is to provide a critical analysis of the broader terrorism studies discourse employing a first and second order critique. The main argument I wish to advance here is that most of what is accepted as well-founded 'knowledge' in terrorism studies is, in fact, highly debatable and unstable. More importantly, this 'knowledge' functions ideologically in society to reify existing power structures and advance particular political projects.

First order critique

As explained earlier, a first order or immanent critique employs the same modes of analysis and categories to criticise the discourse on its own terms and expose the events and perspectives that the discourse fails to acknowledge or address. From this perspective, and employing the same social scientific modes of analysis, terminology, and empirical and analytical categories employed within terrorism studies, as well as many of its own texts and authors, it can be argued that virtually all the narratives and assumptions described in the previous section are contestable and subject to doubt. There is not the space here to provide counter-evidence or arguments to all the assumptions and narratives of the wider discourse; I have provided more detailed counter-evidence to many of them

Knowledge, power and politics 75

elsewhere (see Jackson, 2008a, 2008b, 2007a, 2007b, 2007c). It must instead suffice to discuss a few points which illustrate how unstable and contested this widely accepted 'knowledge' is. The following discussion therefore focuses on a limited number of core narratives, such as the terrorism threat, 'new terrorism', and counterterrorism narratives.

In the first instance, the conceptual practices which construct terrorism exclusively as a form of non-state violence are highly contestable. Given that terrorism is a violent tactic in the same way that ambushes are a tactic, it makes little sense to argue that some actors (such as states) are precluded from employing the tactic of terrorism (or ambushes). A bomb planted in a public place where civilians are likely to be randomly killed and that is aimed at causing widespread terror in an audience is an act of terrorism regardless of whether it is enacted by non-state actors or by agents acting on behalf of the state (see Jackson, 2008a). It can therefore be argued that if terrorism refers to violence directed towards or threatened against civilians which is designed to instil terror or intimidate a population for political reasons – a relatively uncontroversial definition within the field and wider society – then states can also commit acts of terrorism. Furthermore, as I and many others have documented elsewhere (for a summary, see Jackson, 2008b), states have killed, tortured, and terrorised on a truly vast scale over the past few decades, and a great many continue to do so today in places like Colombia, Zimbabwe, Darfur, Myanmar, Palestine, Chechnya, Iraq and elsewhere. Moreover, the deliberate and systematic use of political terror by Western democratic states during the colonial period, in the 'terror bombing' of World War II and other air campaigns, during cold war counter-insurgency and pro-insurgency campaigns, through the sponsorship of right-wing terrorist groups and during certain counterterrorism campaigns, among others, is extremely well documented (see, among many others, Gareau, 2004; Grey, 2006; Grosscup, 2006; Sluka, 2000a; Blakeley, 2006, forthcoming; Blum, 1995; Chomsky, 1985; Gabelnick *et al.*, 1999; Herman, 1982; Human Rights Watch, 2001, 2002; Klare, 1989; Minter, 1994; Stokes, 2005, 2006; McSherry, 2002).

The assumption that terrorism can be objectively defined and studied is also highly questionable and far more complex than this. It can be argued that terrorism is not a causally coherent, free-standing phenomenon which can be identified in terms of characteristics inherent to the violence itself (see Jackson, 2008a). In the first instance, 'the nature of terrorism is not inherent in the violent act itself. One and the same act ... can be terrorist or not, depending on intention and circumstance' (Schmid and Jongman, 1988: 101) – and depending on who is describing the act. The killing of civilians, for example, is not always or inherently a terrorist act; it could perhaps be the unintentional consequence of a military operation during war. Terrorism is therefore a social fact rather than a brute fact, and like 'security', it is constructed through speech-acts by socially authorised speakers. That is, 'terrorism' is constituted by and through an identifiable set of discursive practices – such as the categorisation and collection of data by academics and security officials, and the codification of certain actions in law – which thus make it a contingent 'reality' for politicians, law enforcement officials, the media, the public, academics, and so on. In fact, the current discourse of terrorism used by scholars, politicians and the media is a very recent invention. Before the late 1960s, there was virtually no 'terrorism' spoken of by politicians, the media, or academics; instead, acts of political violence were described simply as 'bombings', 'kidnappings', 'assassinations', 'hijackings', and the like (see Zulaika and Douglass, 1996). In an important sense then, terrorism does not exist outside of the definitions and practices which seek to enclose it, including those of the terrorism studies field.

Second, an increasing number of studies suggest that the threat of terrorism to Western or international security is vastly over-exaggerated (see Jackson, 2007c; Mueller, 2006). Related to this, a number of scholars have convincingly argued that the likelihood of terrorists deploying weapons of mass destruction is in fact, miniscule (B. Jenkins, 1998), as is the likelihood that so-called rogue states would provide WMD to terrorists. A number of recent studies have also seriously questioned the notion of 'new terrorism', demonstrating empirically and through reasoned argument that the continuities between 'new' and 'old' terrorism are much greater than any differences. In particular, they show how the assertion that the 'new terrorism' is primarily motivated by religious concerns is largely unsupported by the evidence (Copeland, 2001; Duyvesteyn, 2004), as is the assertion that 'new terrorists' are less constrained in their targeting of civilians.

Third, considering the key narratives about the origins and causes of terrorism, studies by psychologists reveal that there is little if any evidence of a 'terrorist personality' or any discernable psychopathology among individuals involved in terrorism (Horgan, 2005; Silke, 1998). Nor is there any real evidence that suicide bombers are primarily driven by sexual frustration or that they are 'brainwashed' or 'radicalised' in mosques or on the internet (see Sageman, 2004).

More importantly, a number of major empirical studies have thrown doubt on the broader assertion of a direct causal link between religion and terrorism and, specifically, the link between Islam and terrorism. The Chicago Project on Suicide Terrorism for example, which compiled a database on every case of suicide terrorism from 1980 to 2003, some 315 attacks in all, concluded that 'there is little connection between suicide terrorism and Islamic fundamentalism, or any one of the world's religions' (Pape, 2005: 4). Some of the key findings of the study include: only about half of the suicide attacks from this period can be associated by group or individual characteristics with Islamic fundamentalism; the leading practitioners of suicide terrorism are the secular, Marxist-Leninist Tamil Tigers, who committed seventy-six attacks; of the 384 individual attackers on which data could be found, only 166, or 43 per cent, were religious; and 95 per cent of suicide attacks can be shown to be part of a broader political and military campaign which has a secular and strategic goal, namely, to end what is perceived as foreign occupation (Pape, 2005: 4, 17, 139, 210). Robert Pape's findings are supported by other studies which throw doubt on the purported religion-terrorism link (see Bloom, 2005; Sageman, 2004; Holmes, 2005).

Lastly, there are a number of important studies which suggest that force-based approaches to counterterrorism are not only ineffective and counterproductive, but can also be damaging to individuals, communities, and human rights (see Hillyard, 1993; Cole, 2003). Certainly, there are powerful arguments to be made against the use of torture in counterterrorism (Brecher, 2007; Scarry, 2004; Jackson, 2007d), and a growing number of studies which are highly critical of the efficacy and wider consequences of the war on terrorism (see, among many others, Rogers, 2007; Cole, 2007; Lustick, 2006).

In sum, much of what is accepted as unproblematic 'knowledge' in terrorism studies is actually of dubious provenance. In a major review of the field, Andrew Silke has described it as 'a cabal of virulent myths and half-truths whose reach extends even to the most learned and experienced' (Silke, 2004b: 20). However, the purpose of the first order critique I have undertaken here is not necessarily to establish the real and final 'truth' about terrorism. Rather, first order critique aims simply to destabilise dominant understandings and accepted knowledge, expose the biases and imbalances in the field, and suggest that other ways of understanding, conceptualising, and studying the subject – other ways of 'knowing' – are possible. This kind of critical destabilisation is useful for opening up the space needed to ask new kinds of analytical and normative questions and to pursue alternative intellectual and political projects.

Second order critique

In contrast to first order critique, second order critique involves the adoption of a critical standpoint outside of the discourse. That is, based on an understanding of discourse as socially productive or constitutive and fully cognisant of the knowledge-power nexus, a second order critique attempts to expose the political functions and ideological consequences of the particular narratives, practices, and forms of representation enunciated within the dominant terrorism studies discourse.

In the first place, it can be argued that terrorism studies fulfils an obvious ideological function because, as Jeroen Gunning (2007a) has convincingly shown, the dominant 'knowledge' of the field is an ideal type of 'problem-solving theory'. According to Robert Cox, problem-solving theory 'takes the world as it finds it, with the prevailing social and power relationships and the institutions into which they are organised, as the given framework for action', and then works to 'make these relationships and institutions work smoothly by dealing effectively with particular sources of trouble' (Cox, 1981: 128–129). In this instance, problem-solving theories of terrorism do not question the extent to which the status quo and the dominant actors within it – the hierarchies and operation of power and the inequalities and injustices thus generated – could be implicated in the very 'problem' of terrorism itself or the many other forms of violence which it is inextricably bound up with.

The problem-solving character of the field is illustrated most prosaically by the ubiquitous efforts of virtually every terrorism studies scholar to provide research that is 'policy relevant' and which will assist the state in its efforts to defeat terrorism, and by the widespread tendency to uncritically accept the state's categorisations, definitions, dichotomies, and demonisations (see Toros and Gunning, this volume). Andrew Silke's study concluded that a great deal of the field's output is driven by policy concerns and is limited to addressing government agendas (Silke, 2004d: 58). This characteristic is not at all surprising given that terrorism studies' origins lie in counter-insurgency studies, security studies, and neo-realist approaches to international relations at the height of the cold war (Burnett and Whyte, 2005: 11–13). In fact, the first major review of the field concluded that much of its early output appeared to be 'counterinsurgency masquerading as political science' (Schmid and Jongman, 1988: 182). More recently, the events of 11 September 2001 galvanised a whole new generation of scholars who were understandably eager to offer their skills in the cause of preventing further such attacks and 'solving' the terrorism 'problem'. They therefore had little reason to question the dominant orientation of the field towards assisting state security or the underlying assumptions this necessarily entails.

The desire to assist governments in their efforts to control the destructive effects of non-state terrorism is not necessarily problematic in and of itself; nor does it imply any bad faith on the part of individual scholars (Horgan and Boyle, 2008). In fact, the prevention of violence against civilians is a highly laudable aspiration. However, when virtually the entire academic field collectively adopts state priorities and aims, and when it tailors its research towards assisting state agencies in fighting terrorism (as defined by state institutions), it means that terrorism studies functions ideologically as an intellectual arm of the state and is aligned with its broader hegemonic project.

The field's problem-solving, state-oriented and therefore ideological character is also illustrated by the way in which the field's 'knowledge' functions to delegitimise any kind of non-state violence while simultaneously reifying and legitimising the state's employment of violence; and the way it constructs terrorism as a social problem to be solved by the state but never as a problem *of* state violence itself. From this viewpoint, the silence regarding state terrorism within the discourse (Jackson, 2008b), and in particular the argument of many terrorism studies scholars that state actions should not be defined as 'terrorism', actually functions to furnish states with an authoritative academic justification for using what may actually be terroristic forms of violence against their opponents and citizens. In effect, it provides them with greater leeway when applying terror-based forms of violence against civilians, a leeway exploited by a great many states who intimidate groups and individuals with the application of massive and disproportionate state violence. In other words, by occluding and obscuring the very possibility of state terrorism, and as a field with academic and political authority, the discourse of terrorism studies can be considered part of the conditions that actually make state terrorism possible.

Furthermore, the discourse is deeply ideological in the way in which its core assumptions, narratives, and knowledge-producing practices function to legitimise existing power structures and particular hegemonic political practices in society. For instance, the primary focus on the 'problem' of non-state terrorism functions to distract from and deny the long history of Western involvement in terrorism (see Blakeley, forthcoming), thereby constructing Western foreign policy as essentially benign – rather than aimed primarily at reifying existing structures of power and domination in the international system, for example. That is, by deflecting criticism of particular Western policies, the discourse works to maintain the potentially dangerous myth – the accepted common sense among Western scholars and Western publics – of Western exceptionalism. This sense of exceptionalism in turn permits Western states and their allies to pursue a range of discrete and often illiberal political projects and partisan interests aimed at maintaining dominance in a hegemonic liberal international order. Specifically, by reinforcing the dominant 'knowledge' that non-state terrorism is a much greater security threat than state terrorism and by obscuring the ways in which counterterrorism itself can morph into state terrorism (see Jackson, forthcoming), the discourse functions to legitimise the current global war on terror and its associated policies of military intervention and regime change, extraordinary rendition, military expansion to new regions, military assistance programmes (often to repressive regimes), the imposition of sanctions, the isolation of oppositional political movements, and the like (see, among many others, Stokes and Raphael, forthcoming; El Fadl, 2002; Mahajan, 2002, 2003; Callinicos, 2003). More directly, the discourse provides legitimacy to broader counter-insurgency or counterterrorism programmes in strategic regions where the actual underlying aims clearly reside in the maintenance of a particular political-economic order – such as is occurring in Colombia at the present time (see Stokes, 2006).

At the domestic level, the dominant terrorism discourse can and has been used by political elites to justify and promote a whole range of political projects, such as: expanding and strengthening the institutions of national security and the military-industrial complex; the construction of extensive surveillance and social control systems; the normalisation of security procedures across all areas of social life; expanding the powers and jurisdiction of state security agencies and the executive branch, in large part by normalising a state of exception; controlling wider social and political dissent, restricting human rights, and setting the parameters for acceptable public debate; and altering the legal system – among others (see, among many others, Mueller, 2006; Lustick, 2006; Cole, 2007, 2003; Jackson, 2007c; Scraton, 2002).

Lastly, we must note that powerful economic interests – particularly those linked to the security sector, such as private security firms, defence industries, and pharmaceutical companies, among others – all benefit materially and politically from the primary narratives of the terrorism studies discourse. For example, the accepted 'knowledge' that non-state terrorism poses a catastrophic threat to Western society has in part resulted in contracts worth many millions of dollars to private security companies for site security at airports and government buildings, while pharmaceutical companies have been contracted to provide millions of vaccines and decontamination material in case of bioterrorism (see Mueller, 2006). In other words, there are a clear set of identifiable political-economic and elite interests that are served by the discourse.

80   R. Jackson

In sum, it seems clear that the discourse functions to encourage the reification and extension of state hegemony both internationally and domestically, and directly serves a range of political and economic interests. Perhaps more importantly, the discourse reinforces the widely accepted belief in the instrumental rationality of violence as an effective tool of politics (Burke, 2008), particularly as it relates to counterterrorism. As such, it can be argued that the discourse and knowledge practices of terrorism studies function as a kind of disciplinary and hegemonic truth regime designed to reify existing structures of power and dominance. Despite the intentions of individual terrorism scholars therefore, who may believe that they are engaged in objective academic analysis of a clearly defined phenomenon, the broader discourse which they reproduce and legitimise actually serves distinctly political purposes and has clear ideological consequences for society.

Discourse and hegemony

From a certain perspective, the analysis above presents a genuine puzzle: how does a field based on a series of 'virulent myths', 'half-truths' and contested claims, and which is so obviously biased towards Western state priorities, maintain academic credibility and political influence over several decades? In large part, the answer lies in the position that the field occupies in the existing structures of power, and in its long-standing knowledge practices.

First, it can be argued that the core terrorism studies 'knowledge' persists and is continually reproduced because its nature and form reflect (and simultaneously construct) dominant values and existing cultural narratives. On the one hand, it provides a coherent and familiar discursive frame for internal policy debate; it confirms state perspectives and approaches and simplifies a set of complex challenges to an identifiable 'problem'. For the wider public, the narratives of the discourse construct a broad common sense understanding of terrorism and counterterrorism, or a 'grid of intelligibility' through which to interpret and make sense of events and actions. This is another of its key hegemonic or ideological effects, as this common sense 'knowledge' predisposes the public to accept and acquiesce to particular kinds of counterterrorism policies.

On the other hand, the terrorism studies discourse draws on a series of powerful cultural frames and existing discursive structures, making it ideal for the generation of public legitimacy and the construction of political boundaries (see Oliverio, 1997). For example, as Zulaika and Douglass's (1996) ground-breaking anthropological study demonstrated, the construction of the fanatical, dangerous terrorist reflects the 'wild man' figure of Western cultural imagination. Similarly, the field's construction of the threat posed by suicide bombers and WMD-terrorism taps into culturally defined taboos of suicide and the fear of poison, while the notion that Western states never commit terrorism but only respond to it reinforces the widespread belief in Western exceptionalism.

Second, the discourse maintains its dominance through a self-perpetuating set of knowledge-generating practices. For example, based on an examination of thirty-two prominent terrorism studies experts, Edna Reid describes the research process among these scholars as a closed, circular, and static system of information and investigation which tends to accept dominant 'myths' about terrorism without strong empirical investigation for long periods before empirical research disproves them (Reid, 1993: 28). The circular nature of the knowledge process can be further illustrated by noting how some terrorism scholars provide expert testimony to special commissions, such as the Bremer Commission and the 9/11 Commission, and then reference the commission reports in order to legitimise their own knowledge claims in later publications.[7] In a related process of exclusion, a recent analysis concluded that terrorism 'experts' who do not maintain a strong pro-Western bias in their work soon become marginalised in the field and are denied access to policymakers and major conferences (Ilardi, 2004: 222).

Lastly, the persistence and dominance of the core terrorism studies 'knowledge' is a consequence of the 'embedded' or 'organic' nature of many terrorism experts and scholars; that is, the extent to which terrorism scholars are directly linked to state institutions and sources of power in ways that make it difficult to distinguish between the state and academic spheres (see Herman and O'Sullivan, 1989; George, 1991a; Burnett and Whyte, 2005). Crucial here has been the influence of the RAND Corporation, a non-profit research foundation founded by the United States Air Force with deep ties to the American military and political establishments, as well as private security and military companies. Some RAND scholars have been influential in both constructing the accepted knowledge of the terrorism studies field and in communicating it to policymakers and the wider public for several decades now. Senior officials in several US administrations have held positions in RAND, and as with other foundations and think tanks, there is a revolving door of personnel between RAND and the state. For example, Condoleezza Rice and Donald Rumsfeld are both former RAND administrators (Burnett and Whyte, 2005: 8). Moreover, RAND scholars have been influential in establishing other influential terrorism research centres, such as the St Andrews Centre for Studies in Terrorism and Political Violence, and have been involved in the running of both *Terrorism and Political Violence* and *Studies in Conflict and Terrorism*. In fact, RAND scholars author a significant proportion of the articles published in these two popular journals (Silke, 2004c: 194).

In other words, it can be argued that the leading terrorism studies scholars now constitute an influential and exclusive 'epistemic community' – a network of 'specialists with a common world view about cause and effect relationships which relate to their domain of expertise, and common political values about the type of policies to which they should be applied' (Stone, 1996: 86). From a Gramscian perspective, the leading terrorism studies scholars can be understood as 'organic intellectuals' connected institutionally, financially and ideologically to the state. From this perspective, the state-centric orientation of the field and its continuing reproduction of the guiding myths is a natural and thoroughly unsurprising consequence of its position within society's existing power structure.

Conclusion

The analysis of the terrorism studies field presented in this chapter clearly has some important analytical and normative implications. In the first instance, it suggests that the field has a number of serious analytical weaknesses in terms of its broader ontological, epistemological, and methodological approaches, as well as its highly-restricted research focus, conformity in outlook, acceptance and reproduction of dubious 'knowledge', and obvious political bias towards Western states and interests. This state of affairs places major obstacles in the way of theoretical and empirical innovation, the articulation of new questions and approaches and the contestation of dominant knowledge claims. More prosaically, it is rather worrying that the field's 'knowledge' presently forms one of the bases of policy-making deliberations and public debate about how to respond to acts of terrorism.

Perhaps more importantly, an ethical-normative perspective suggests that terrorism studies is a largely (but not completely) co-opted field of research that is deeply enmeshed with the exercise of state power and the actual practices of counterterrorism. That is, it provides both a specific set of intellectual justifications for counterterrorist and security policies, and a broader academic legitimacy for the state.[8] This is disturbing, because it means that the field is in some small ways at least, complicit in some of the counterterrorism practices employed in the war on terrorism and in places like Colombia and Israel that are morally questionable, such as increased surveillance, profiling, shoot-to-kill policies, collective punishments, creeping restrictions on civil liberties, regime change, support for repressive governments, rendition, torture, and extrajudicial assassination.

In the end, the analysis presented here strongly suggests that it is time (again) for a more 'critical' approach to the study of political terrorism. More specifically, it suggests that there is an urgent need for further sustained review and reflection regarding the dominant knowledge and knowledge-generating practices of terrorism research, and the need to adopt an alternative set of ontological, epistemological, methodological, and ethical-normative commitments (see Jackson, Gunning and Breen Smyth, this volume). The open and determined adherence to these core commitments by all terrorism scholars would, I believe, go some way towards rectifying the key problems and challenges highlighted in this chapter.

Notes

1 An earlier version of this chapter was presented as a paper entitled, 'Research for Counterterrorism: Terrorism Studies and the Reproduction of State Hegemony', at the International Studies Association (ISA) 47th Annual Convention, 28 February–3 March 2007, Chicago, United States. I am grateful to my fellow editors, Marie Breen Smyth and Jeroen Gunning, for comments and suggestions.
2 For a related explanation of how the core field of terrorism studies is constituted and identified, see Raphael, this volume.
3 The following section is drawn largely from Jackson, 2007a.
4 An exact figure for the number of texts examined is not possible in this particular case. At the last count, 104 texts had been examined, but then several further texts

Knowledge, power and politics 83

were subsequently included in the analysis. The overall analysis continues in a continuous and iterative manner on an almost daily basis.
5 Although this term is becoming more contested in the broader field, leading scholars continue to employ it, new scholars frequently adopt it uncritically, and politicians and the media largely accept it as unproblematic. It therefore retains a great deal of purchase, despite a growing literature which criticises it – as I discuss below.
6 Narratives regarding the causes of terrorism are currently expanding at a tremendous rate and there is vigorous debate in the wider terrorism field about the main issues. The analysis in this section does not take account of these new developments, nor does it focus on the generally much more sophisticated literature originating from outside of the core terrorism studies field.
7 Examples of this process can be seen by examining the testimony and then subsequent publications of some of the scholars who testified to major US commissions such as the Bremer and 9/11 Commissions.
8 This is not to say that terrorism scholars never criticise state counterterrorism or debate the efficacy and morality of counterterrorism policies. However, for the most part, they do so from within the overarching discourse and the debates tend to remain limited to the tactical level, rather than questioning the foundational aspects of the discourse. In this case, disagreement can function ideologically as a means of legitimising the overall discourse through maintaining a myth of intellectual pluralism that in reality masks a level of ideological conformity.

Part II
Critical approaches to the study of political terrorism

5 Exploring a critical theory approach to terrorism studies

Harmonie Toros and Jeroen Gunning[1]

Introduction

Twenty years ago, Edward Said, the renowned Palestinian academic and political activist, lamented:

> I find the entire arsenal of words and phrases that derive from the concept of terrorism both inadequate and shameful. There are few ways of talking about terrorism now that are not corrupted by the propaganda war ... of the past decade, ... disqualified as instruments for conducting rational, secular inquiry into the causes of human violence. Is there some other way of apprehending what might additionally be involved when we now unthinkingly use the word 'terrorism'? Is there a style of thought and language that pretends neither to get past the word's embroiled semantic history, nor to restore it, cleansed and sparkling new, for further polemical use?
> (Said, 1988a: 53)

Can critical theory contribute to finding a way through the morass so aptly described by Said? In this chapter, we argue that a Frankfurt School-inspired critical theory approach can indeed provide a rich framework for thinking about terrorism and terrorism studies which can appeal well beyond the confines of those who describe themselves as critical theorists. In particular, we aim to show how such an approach offers a framework not just for critiquing and, importantly, engaging with traditional terrorism studies, but also for addressing precisely those shortcomings that have been identified in numerous internal critiques of the field: lack of self-reflexivity, lack of contextualisation, ahistoricity, statist bias, dearth of fieldwork, and so on (see also Gunning, 2007a).[2]

Critical approaches to terrorism – if 'critical' means, as per Robert Cox, to 'stand apart from the prevailing order of the world and ask how that order came about' (1986: 208) – are as old as the study of terrorism itself, with powerful challenges mounted by the likes of Said (1988a), Alexander George (1991b), Michael Gold-Biss (1994), and Joseba Zulaika and William Douglass (1996), among others. These critiques, however, have remained islands of resistance in what appears to be a sea of traditional writings on the topic – where 'traditional' is defined as taking 'the world as it finds it, with the prevailing social and power relationships and the institutions into which they are organised, as the given framework for action' (Cox, 1986: 208).[3] What is more, a majority of these critiques have been conducted from within a post-structuralist or post-modernist framework. Such scholarship has made an important contribution to the study of terrorism. However, as attempts are made to rally and strengthen critical approaches to terrorism, it is important to look at other potential sources of critical thinking.

One such source which has been largely overlooked – with the exception of recent contributions by Ken Booth (2008), Matt McDonald (2007; this volume), Harmonie Toros (forthcoming) and, more implicitly, Jeroen Gunning (2007a) – is the type of critical theory developed by the Frankfurt School and its various applications to the study of international politics and more particularly security studies. It is the aim of this chapter to examine what contribution taking a Frankfurt School-inspired critical theory (from now on, Critical Theory) approach to the study of terrorism can make.

Critical Theory is not monolithic. Its various proponents have disagreed over style and substance, and it has changed substantially over time (Wyn Jones, 1999; Booth, 2007: 43–45). This chapter will draw primarily on what has come to be known as the Welsh or Aberystwyth School of critical security studies (hereafter Welsh School) which has pioneered the application of Critical Theory to the study of security (see Booth, 1991, 1997, 2005, 2007; Wyn Jones, 1999). However, where relevant, it will also draw directly on the works of some of the key Critical Theory scholars who have influenced the development of the Welsh School, such as Max Horkheimer, Robert Cox, and Andrew Linklater, whose Habermasian dialogic approach offers a helpful counterpoint to Horkheimer's more materialist productionist approach – as well as on contemporary debates within critical international relations theory more broadly. We recognise that there are other key thinkers from among the Critical Theory family we could have engaged with (such as Theodor Adorno and Axel Honneth) or engaged more fully with (for example, Jürgen Habermas or Antonio Gramsci, who could be considered a distant relation of this 'family'; cf. Wyn Jones, 1999).

Our intent in this chapter is not to provide a comprehensive discussion of Critical Theory but to offer an initial exploration of how an approach inspired by Critical Theory can enhance the study of terrorism, opting for what Booth calls a 'pearl-fishing' approach – finding 'pearls of ideas that might be strung together' rather than a 'dogmatic identification with one system of thought' (2007: 39–40).

We hope to illustrate how applying insights from the Welsh School and other Critical Theory sources – internal contradictions notwithstanding – to the study of terrorism can offer an important alternative to both traditional and post-structuralist approaches to terrorism. It offers a powerful tool for the investigation and critique of the current dominant traditional approach. But it also offers a rich, theoretically-grounded framework through which an alternative conceptualisation of terrorism and a concrete research agenda emerges – thus marking a crucial difference from

Exploring a critical theory approach 89

post-structuralist work which has critiqued traditional studies but has largely failed to move beyond deconstructing existing discourses. It may therefore answer the question raised by Said and offer 'a style of thought and language that pretends neither to get past the word's embroiled semantic history, nor to restore it ... for further polemical use'.

We aim to examine what a Critical Theory approach to terrorism can offer, ontologically, epistemologically, and methodologically. This analysis shall be undertaken in two key moves put forward by Booth in the context of critical security studies (1997, 2007). The first of these is a process of *deepening*, of uncovering the ontological and ideological assumptions and interests behind terrorism studies, leading to a radical shift in how terrorism is to be conceived as contextually constituted, rather than a timeless, objective category, and with humanity, not the state, as the central unit to be preserved. The second move is that of *broadening*, or widening the research agenda beyond the field's current focus on spectacular terrorist violence (typically by non-state actors) to include state violence, other forms of (non-terrorist) violence, non-violence and the social and historical context within which these acts take place. These two crucial moves will bring us to the final section of the chapter examining how a Welsh School interpretation of Critical Theory can open the possibility for an emancipatory approach to terrorism and what that means for researchers in terms of praxis.

Deepening terrorism research

Theory is always from somewhere, for someone and for some purpose.

One of the core insights of Critical Theorists is the notion that science is not objective and value-neutral. Cox boiled this down to his celebrated phrase that 'theory is always *for* someone and *for* some purpose' (Cox, 1981: 128). Realism, for instance, with its dual claim that the state is the primary legitimate unit in international politics, and that the national interest should trump moral concerns, both reflects the interests of state elites and provides legitimacy for their policies – even when individual realist scholars are critical of particular policies (Wyn Jones, 1999: 94–102). Social science thus always has an ideological element, by functioning, often unconsciously, to conceal and serve the interests of those behind it (Cox, 1986: 247; Linklater, 1996: 283).

But Critical Theory points to a further, more fundamental, issue: namely, using Booth's succinct phrase, theory is not just *for* someone, *for* some purpose, it is also '*from* somewhere' (Booth, 2007: 150): that is, it is derived from a particular set of assumptions and values that are not universal but shaped by our particular context. What we choose to focus on, what we exclude, how we interpret data, and to what use we put them is influenced by our perceptions and ideological leanings, by the social processes we are part of, by the particular political and economic structures we inhabit, and the material and ideational interests that derive from them (Horkheimer, 1992: 195).

Thus, adopting a Critical Theory approach to the study of terrorism first of all means uncovering the ideological, conceptual and institutional underpinnings of terrorism studies.[4] Borrowing from Booth, this constitutes a 'deepening' of the concept of 'terrorism' (Booth, 1997: 111, 2007: 150–160; Wyn Jones, 1999: 102–103). Indeed, like security, terrorism is a derivative field of study that people approach through their understanding of politics (Booth, 1997, 2005: 13, 2008). We therefore need to examine 'the deeper assumptions about the nature of politics and the role of conflict in political life' (Wyn Jones, 1999: 102) in which studies of terrorism are rooted: what conceptions about the individual, communities, the state, and the international system drive particular studies; what conceptions about the efficacy of violence, the role of economics, the value of negotiations underpin them; whose interests they serve and what policies they enable.[5]

A contemporary illustration can be found in how many traditional terrorism scholars regard 'religious terrorism' as more violent, more lethal, and less ready to compromise, and somehow less comprehensible than ethnically-inspired terrorism (see for example B. Hoffman, 1998; Laqueur, 1999). Once one begins to 'drill down' (Booth, 2007: 155) it soon emerges that this understanding is not simply a function of the existence of particularly violent, religiously-inspired political groups. There are, after all, many examples of religiously-inspired groups which are either no more violent or less pragmatic than their secular or ethnic counterparts (if one can make such a distinction, given that religion and ethnicity often overlap) – or eschew violence altogether. Indeed, deepening our understanding of 'religious terrorism' would reveal that such an interpretation has an obvious utility for legitimising certain state policies (theory being '*for* someone' and '*for* some purpose'). For example, labelling Hamas as religious terrorists – and therefore, by implication, as purely interested in an other-worldly order and beyond the pale of reason – has arguably served to justify a refusal by Western states and Israel to engage in talks and move beyond violent counterterrorism measures which curb civil and political freedoms. It has also served to downplay Hamas's nationalistic or indeed its human rights-based claims, privileging religious motivation over all other explanations.

This conception is also *from* somewhere, and indeed can be traced back to the prevalence of a certain notion of 'religion' in the Western social sciences (Gunning, 2007c: 10–13). According to this notion – which has its roots in particular intellectual and political processes in Europe when religion came to be defined in opposition to science and rational politics and was institutionally relegated to the private realm – religion is a set of private beliefs that should be kept from the public realm (Asad, 1993; Salvatore, 1997: 29–32). When applied to, for instance, contemporary Islamist groups, the result is, as John Esposito observed, that 'the modern notion of religion as a system of personal belief makes an Islam (or any world religion...) that is comprehensive in scope, in which religion is integral to politics and society, 'abnormal' ... and nonsensical. Thus Islam becomes incomprehensible, irrational, extremist, threatening' (1999: 257–258). This perception is of course heightened if (some of) the groups studied are engaged in high-profile violence against Western targets.

Accepting that theory and knowledge are always rooted in their historical context and serve particular interests clearly places Critical Theorists in direct opposition to the traditional realist position that politics can and must be studied from a neutral objective standpoint. Indeed, it not only questions the very possibility of situating oneself outside the social world, but also asks the fundamental question of who benefits from a theory that advocates an objective neutral standpoint. Failure to reflect on the historicity, constructedness and institutional interests of social science has the effect of upholding and reifying the status quo (Wyn Jones, 1999: 131–132; Horkheimer, 1992; Cox, 1986). By claiming to be objective, traditional theory obscures the power relations, partisan interests, and context-specific perspectives that underpin its conceptual framework and methodology. Existing power structures are posited as natural, legitimate, and immutable (Linklater, 2001: 26), while scientific findings are presented as 'transcend[ing] history' and 'universally valid' (Cox, 1986: 247). The result is the reproduction of the status quo and its 'asymmetries of power, wealth, and opportunity' (Linklater, 2001: 26; see also Horkheimer, 1992: 196–197, 204–206; Wyn Jones, 1999: 19–20). Or, as Sara Roy noted in the concrete context of studying the Israeli–Palestinian conflict, because objectivity '[aims] to create balance or equity where none in fact exists', the result is the 'displacing [of] any kind of sustained attention to [local] realities and their damaging impact' and a 'political gamesmanship where the stronger party … dominates' (Roy, 2007: xv).

Turning specifically to the study of terrorism, mainstream terrorism research has overall adopted a traditional or 'problem-solving' approach, taking 'the world as it finds it'(Cox, 1986: 208; for application to terrorism studies, see Gunning, 2007a). By failing to question existing power structures and its own indebtedness to these structures, traditional terrorism studies has essentially served to sustain the status quo, reducing politics to the management of social order without much thought for emancipation – internal critics and dissenters notwithstanding. Its purpose has been essentially conservative and conformist, and critiques from within have typically focused on specific policies, rather than concerning themselves with how existing power structures came about and how they have helped to shape both the problem and prevailing knowledge about it (for a detailed critique, see the Part I in this volume).

In methodological terms, the starting point for a Critical Theory-inspired approach to terrorism should thus begin with a 'first-order critique' (Jackson, 2007a; see also Milliken, 1999) of traditional terrorism's core claims and normative values, comparing the claims made regarding values or facts against the evidence, on traditional theory's own terms and norms (see also Hutchings, 2001: 88; Wyn Jones, 1999: 160–161). Following the Welsh School, the task here is to challenge 'the prevailing hegemonic security discourse' as it applies to terrorism, and to question the views that 'serve to legitimate, and hence reproduce, the prevailing world order' with the help of 'expert knowledge' (Wyn Jones, 1999: 160). Is terrorism indeed the threat that it is portrayed as being? Is it always carried out by non-state actors or do states, including liberal democratic ones, at times engage in similar practices? Do states necessarily increase the security of their citizens and, more broadly, of human beings? Do particular counterterrorism strategies, for instance deterrence and collective punishment, indeed enhance security, and if so, whose and at what cost to others? Do negotiations necessarily encourage further terrorism by legitimising those who turn to terrorism?

Deepening thus leads us to engage with the 'what and whom theory is for' question and from where it emanates, ultimately bringing us to reject the notion of an idealised objective stance. But it does not stop here. For the next crucial (and more daunting) step is to go beyond critique, and following Hutchings, '[develop] new conceptual frameworks' and 'offer alternative explanations' (Hutchings, 2001: 88–89).[6]

Minimal foundationalism: retaining a category of violence

The development of an alternative research programme is facilitated by the fact that, unlike post-structuralism, (Horkheimerian) Critical Theory maintains what can be called a self-reflexive minimal foundationalism (M. Hoffman, 1991; Smith, 1996; Price & Reus-Smit, 1998). Although Critical Theory rejects the positivist notion of timeless categories and laws, it does not reject the notion of meticulously delineated 'concepts' or 'evidence' within the context of specific social and historical periods (Cox, 1986: 247; see also Horkheimer, 1992: 201). Nor does it exclusively focus on discursive representations and practices, as many post-structuralist scholars do (Devetak, 2005a). Rather than collapsing the ontological distinction between object and subject, it maintains it, while acknowledging that the two shape each other in a dialectical, never-ceasing dynamic (Horkheimer, 1992: 201, 226–230).

Similarly, (Horkheimerian) Critical Theory does not reject the notion of 'regularities' in human activity (what positivists would call laws) or the usefulness of the positivist approach in establishing these.[7] Again following Cox, '[r]egularities in human activities may indeed be observed within particular eras, and thus the positivist approach can be fruitful within defined historical limits, though not with the universal pretensions it aspires to' (Cox, 1986: 244; see also Horkheimer, 1992: 194, 208, 226–230). This type of Critical Theory approach does not reject problem-solving or traditional theory as such, but rather recognises its importance in this particular phase of human history and incorporates it while accepting its understandings as contingent on socio-historical context (Cox, 1986: 209; Horkheimer, 1992: 194, 205, 229; Booth, 2005: 10–11). Crucially, this should serve as a bridge between critical and traditional scholarship.

One consequence of this is that, in contrast to post-structuralist studies, a Critical Theory approach does not necessarily limit us to examining the 'discourse of terrorism' – important though that is – but permits the study of a form of violence that can be called 'terrorism'. It can accept that there is a category of violence formed by its repetition, to be understood within a particular socio-historical context which could, currently, be loosely described as: a violent means aimed at

Exploring a critical theory approach 93

triggering political change by affecting a larger audience than its immediate target, and which is broadly deemed illegitimate (for example by targeting what are perceived to be non-combatants). This category is not immutable and evolves along with social and historical processes. For instance, in the case of non-state actors targeting non-combatant citizens, it only makes sense as a category if those targeted distinguish between combatants and non-combatants and believe the latter to be illegitimate targets, whose protection is the state's duty and whose death is therefore not just fear-inducing but seen as de-legitimising the state (and eliciting escalating repressive responses). Thus, a Critical Theory approach, by looking beyond the 'discourse of terrorism' and studying this category of political violence that kills and maims thousands the world over, can also engage traditional scholars on their own terms, since it does not reject the category of 'terrorist violence' wholesale.

However, crucially, Critical Theory incorporates traditional theory *critically* and self-reflexively. If, following Horkheimer, Critical Theory should be 'suspicious of the very categories of better, useful, appropriate, productive, and valuable, as these are understood in the present order, and refuses to take them as nonscientific presuppositions about which one can do nothing' (Horkheimer 1992: 207), a Critical Theory approach to terrorism must always remain suspicious of the very terms it uses, historicise and deconstruct them, and uncover the interests they serve. Far from simply replacing one form of essentialism with another, it thus steers a way between positivism and post-structuralism, retaining categories of regularity while remaining aware of their contingency and political effect, and thus constantly seeking to interrogate and destabilise them. This is particularly pertinent in the case of terrorism studies where whether an organisation is labelled 'terrorist' is deeply dependent on political interests, and rigid us/them distinctions hinder both understanding and resolution (see Bhatia, 2005; Toros, 2008a). It also has serious consequences for the use of databases or comparative studies which uncritically group together incidents labelled as 'terrorist'.

Beyond state-centrism: from national security to securing humans

Examining the categories and regularities that are put forward as natural and immutable by traditional terrorism research crucially entails a questioning of the status quo and, in particular, its naturalised referent object: the state. For Booth, this is indeed one of the key steps of deepening security, one which undermines the state-centrism so far dominating security (and terrorism) studies.

Welsh School scholars make a powerful argument for rejecting the state as the ultimate object to be secured, given the state's temporal nature and its flawed record in providing security for those who are arguably the one constant in politics: human beings.[8] Rather, they argue that 'individual humans are the ultimate referent' (Booth, 1991: 319) – understood not as the (conceptually) atomistic, self-interest-maximising individual familiar from liberal perspectives, but as embedded, part of and shaped by social contexts and collectivities such as class, gender, states, ethnic, and/or cultural groups (Wyn Jones, 1999: 114–116). Because of this recognition of the individual's embeddedness, while the human being remains the ultimate referent object, in 'practice, the relevant referent will probably be chosen depending on the problem being investigated' (Booth, 2007: 186). Gender may be the referent for a study of Tamil female suicide bombers, while European Union member states could be the referent for a study of international cooperation in counterterrorism intelligence.

It is important to stress that this is not to say that a Critical Theory approach to terrorism studies rejects the state a priori as a (potentially) legitimate entity for providing security. The difference with traditional approaches is that the state is not automatically taken as the natural unit to provide security and thus to secure; rather it is judged on how well it provides security – in the first instance to its citizens, but ultimately in the context of humanity at large (following the cosmopolitan turn in international Critical Theory, see Linklater, 2005a).

A Critical Theory approach to terrorism would similarly scrutinise non-state actors in terms of their contribution to improving the security of humans. Non-state actors, particularly those involved in nationalist projects, display many of the same characteristics as state actors in their pursuit of state power, and thus their violence at times resembles state violence. The left-wing FARC in Colombia and the separatist Kurdish PKK (Kurdistan Workers' Party) in Turkey, for example, have both been accused of severe human rights violations against civilians who are often at the mercy of both state and non-state violence (Chernick, 2007; Ergil, 2007). Thus, the shift from the security of the state to that of human beings means that a Critical Theory approach has a normative framework from which to critique both state and non-state actors on the basis of whether they contribute to the security and freedom of human beings and end their suffering (see also Linklater, 2007).

A central task of a Critical Theory-inspired terrorism studies is thus to 'denaturalise' both the state and its opposition and to explore how both may have contributed to the terrorist threat. This would help overcome the state-centric bias that has often marred the study of terrorism, breaking down us/them and terrorism/counterterrorism dichotomies. Violent counterterrorism would no longer *necessarily* be viewed as a legitimate response to the violence of an *inevitably* illegitimate opposition, allowing the study of terrorism to move beyond what seems at times a 'how to' guide for states engaged in counterterrorism (Booth, 2007: 404). Crucially, it would also act as a safeguard against the automatic legitimation or glorification of opposition violence simply because it is in opposition, since the emancipation of human beings, rather than the success of a state or counter-state project, is the normative benchmark. Such a critique involves, as we shall examine more closely later, a meticulous analysis of the socio-historic context within which terrorism emerged.

Drilling down in the deepening move is thus like discovering a continent of ice below the tip of an iceberg. It means taking the neat, above-surface picture of terrorism offered by much traditional research and uncovering not only layers upon layers of ice under the water, but also the sources of water that feed the iceberg and help it remain afloat. It enables us to see the ideological as well as social and historical underpinnings that show that there is no such thing as a value-free, historically unbound 'terrorism', let alone an 'objective' study thereof. It nonetheless allows us to retain categories and properties – although always historically bound, value-laden, and politically implicated – allowing for the study of a particular category of political violence. Finally, it makes us question the ultimate referent of our work, challenging the state-centrism that has dominated the field of terrorism studies so far, rejecting the state as the *sole* referent object in favour of multiple referents ultimately grounded in the constant of humanity. Each of these moves calls in turn for a broadening of terrorism research, to which we now turn.

Broadening terrorism research

Incorporating state violence, counterterrorism and other forms of violence

For security studies, Wyn Jones used the term 'broadening' to denote 'incorporating nonmilitary issues onto the security agenda' (Wyn Jones, 1999: 103–104). Applied to the study of terrorism, this move would first mean broadening what can be considered 'terrorist'. Here, rather than the exclusion of non-military matters from the agenda (to which we will turn in the next section), at issue is the exclusion of the state (and other potential actors) as perpetrator of terrorist acts. From a Welsh School standpoint, it is possible to argue that following the deepening move which has unseated the state as ultimate object to be secured and replaced it with the human being, any violent act aimed at triggering political change by affecting a larger audience than its immediate target, which is broadly deemed illegitimate, should be understood as terrorist, whether carried out by an individual, a non-state group, a state or indeed an interstate organization (such as NATO, the African Union or ASEAN, the Association of Southeast Asian Nations).

Thus, broadening first involves challenging the state-centric notion that terrorism is only or primarily the prerogative of non-state actors used against states (for two prominent examples, see B. Hoffman, 1998; Laqueur, 1999) and acknowledging that terrorism, as a tactic, can be and has been extensively used by state actors (Sluka, 2000a; Stohl, 1988; Blakely, 2007a, 2008; Jackson, 2007g). But that is not all. For, since counterterrorism also often threatens the well-being of humans, replacing the state with human beings as ultimate referent means that scholars are also pushed to broaden the study of terrorism to include violent counterterrorism responses. Equally important, though often overlooked, are forms of structural violence, which institutionalise inequality (whether carried out by state or non-state actors) (Galtung, 1969), or the interplay between political violence and domestic violence which is similarly largely under-studied (McWilliams and McKiernan, 1993). Thus, the broadening move goes beyond the increasingly recognised argument that terrorism research needs to study state terrorism (see Blakeley, 2007a, 2008; Raphael, this volume).

We are not suggesting that terrorism, counterterrorism, and structural violence are to be equated, but rather that the different types of violence cannot be seen as separate and should be studied together. This holistic approach understands terrorism as a relational form of violence, one that cannot and should not be extracted from the other forms of violence that almost invariably precede, surround, and follow it, as well as from the equally crucial political, social, and economic context in which it occurs.

Putting terrorism in its place: the importance of context

Because, within a Critical Theory framework, 'facts cannot be separated from their social genesis; they are social and historical products' (M. Hoffman, 1987: 233), terrorism cannot be separated from its context, making the study of context central to any Critical Theory-inspired study of terrorism. Apart from giving scholars a greater understanding of the phenomenon, in terms of how the violence became possible, what impact it had on society, how it relates to other social practices, and the like, replacing context at the heart of the enquiry has several crucial repercussions.

First, context places terrorism in its temporal historical location, restoring a past and a future to terrorism. Traditional approaches to terrorism tend to engage with the group (usually non-state) only when they begin to perpetrate violence, ignoring the often long previous life of the movement. Thus, the PKK in Turkey is often only studied after it turned to armed struggle in 1984, ignoring its formative non-violent beginnings (from 1978 onwards), not to mention decades of Kurdish activism and revolts against incorporation into the Turkish republic. Similarly, groups engaged in terrorist violence drop off the map of terrorism scholars (along with that of the media and political actors) when they stop using terrorism. A classic example are the Italian Red Brigades, whose activities have been widely studied using their disbandment in the late 1980s as cut-off point. A sudden interest in what happened to the insurgents and their supporters emerged only in 1999, when the 'New-Red Brigades' assassinated a government adviser. Thus, putting context – and its corollary, time – at the centre of the study of terrorism means closely examining what preceded the violence and what succeeded it.

Second, an emphasis on context serves to de-exceptionalise terrorism and re-embed it within the wider social practices of which it forms but a part. In this sense, it resembles the move within Welsh School critical security studies to include 'non-military issues on the security agenda'. It links the study of (non-state) terrorism to an analysis of other forms of protest and contentious politics, whether violent or not. It encourages researchers to analyse acts of state terrorism in the context of other forms of repression and social control. It places acts that are labelled terrorist within the broader context of social practices, enabling researchers to see perpetrators of terrorism as part of a wider social movement (even if the links are tenuous), influenced by societal dynamics and broader intellectual debates, and moving in and out of terrorism (cf. also Gunning, this volume, 2007a: 378–379).

Third, a focus on context crucially restores to actors their multiple identities. The IRA, for example, cannot be merely understood as a 'terrorist group' once engaged in a battle with the British state. It also existed/exists at a community level within Ireland, in competition with other social movements and political parties, engaged in both violent and non-violent activities, and it existed at an international level with links to the Irish Diaspora in the United States and elsewhere, international social movements (only some of which employed what have been labelled terrorist tactics), and states (including, but not exclusively, so-called 'rogue states' such as Libya). All these elements constituted the IRA, and to regard it merely as a 'terrorist actor' fighting the state reduces our understanding of the group. Similarly, someone fighting on behalf of the Moro Islamic Liberation Front (MILF) in Mindanao is not simply an insurgent but often also a farmer, embedded in a local community. Or he may be a local official and thus technically accountable to the Philippine government, the MILF's opponent, or have fought for other insurgent groups, depending on their strength in his area (Toros, 2008b).

Re-embedding acts of terrorism and those who perpetrate them in their temporal context discredits the absolutism and essentialism of the commonly used phrase 'once a terrorist, always a terrorist'. Re-embedding them in their social context, moreover, discredits the use of the label 'terrorist' to describe groups or human beings altogether – leading us, the authors, to reserve the term strictly for describing specific acts. Labelling a group or person as 'terrorist' limits our understanding of them as *only* the perpetrators of terrorist acts, erasing their other identities, their political motivations and goals, their non-terrorist activities, and the possibility of transformation (Bhatia, 2005; Gunning, 2007a, this volume; Toros, 2008a, 2008b, forthcoming).

Fourth, an emphasis on context also allows for the recognition that terrorist tactics evolve. Terrorism has indeed mutated even if one merely takes into consideration its contemporary form, just as communities, the state, and the international system have. The strict hierarchical organisations of the 1960s continue to exist, but have been flanked by lone bombers such as Timothy McVeigh and more horizontal networks such as al-Qaeda. The heavier emphasis on guerrilla tactics and rural bases of the 1950s and 1960s has been superseded by a greater emphasis on urban targets, notwithstanding the continued existence of rural guerrilla dynamics in Sri Lanka and Colombia, for instance. Rather than having to create new categories, such as the heavily criticised notion of 'new terrorism', placing terrorism within its context allows for a framework which recognises that terrorism and its practitioners change along with other social processes, political structures, and technologies.

Finally, a focus on context pushes the scholar to move beyond traditional theory's notion of the atomised individual and its corollary, the rational choice actor, to a more holistic and dynamic model of embedded individuals, which recognises how individuals both shape and are shaped by larger communities, social processes, and group dynamics, economic and political structures, and ideologies (see also Gunning, this volume). This move mirrors Kratochwil's call, in the context of critical international relations theory, for a shift from the notion of *homo economicus* to *homo sociologicus* (Kratochwil, 2007: 44–45). This involves a move away from the economistic, self-centred, instrumental rationality – which, though dominant in traditional social science is but one, historically and culturally specific type of rationality – to a framework which recognises alternative types of rationality, such as altruistic or end-oriented rationalities (cf. Ferree, 1992).

Beyond a 'fetishization of parts': toward interdisciplinarity

A corollary of broadening the study of terrorism to include context is the need for it to break out of the isolation that academic specialisation imposes on us. Traditional theory, following Horkheimer, 'speaks not of what theory means in human life, but only of what it means in the isolated sphere in which for historical reasons it comes into existence' (Horkheimer, 1992: 197). This leads to what Wyn Jones has dubbed a 'fetishization of parts' (Wyn Jones, 1999: 22) and has, exceptions notwithstanding, resulted in a separation of the study of terrorism from that of social movements, international relations, and even more surprisingly, of conflict theory. Critical Theory urges us to reverse this trend by advocating 'the construction of a larger picture of the whole of which the initially contemplated part is just one component, and seeks to understand the processes of change in which both parts and whole are involved' (Cox, 1986: 209).

For the study of terrorism this means examining contemporary terrorism as embedded in other processes, including, for example, democratisation, modernisation, globalisation, the increasing challenge by non-state actors to the nation-state, and the deepening North–South divide and its related migrations (see also Linklater, 2005a, 2007). This means embedding terrorism studies in developments in cognate theories, such as democratisation studies, social movement theory, social psychology, conflict theory, or migration studies (Gunning, 2007a, 2007c; Toros, forthcoming; Egerton, forthcoming). It also means that studying terrorism can tell us something about these broader processes, and vice versa. How have the ideational and structural developments underpinning the emergence of modern states and the international system contributed to making terrorist tactics attractive (O'Sullivan, 1986), and what do the emergence of the latter say about the modern state and the international system? What has made the rise of loosely connected networks such as al-Qaeda possible and what does this tell us about transnationalism, the transformation of global identities, the nature of modernity and post-modernity, changing social forces, and the like? What does the evolution of the Italian Red Brigades, ETA, or Hamas say about the processes of state-building and modernisation?

At heart, this is a call for, at least initially, more interdisciplinarity, just as the Institute for Social Research in Frankfurt under Horkheimer expanded to become profoundly interdisciplinary (with the aim of eventually breaking down barriers between disciplines; see Wyn Jones, 1999: 22–23). While heeding Booth's warning of the dangers of a lowest-common-denominator approach to interdisciplinarity (Booth, 2008: 70), Critical Theory offers both a clarion call and a ready framework for engaging with cognate disciplines and gathering fragmentary insights, particularly from those who may be wary of traditional terrorism studies' perceived political bias and lack of self-reflexivity and theoretical rigour (see also Gunning, 2007a, 2007b).

Thus, a broadened understanding of terrorism – one which includes a focus on state terrorism, counterterrorism, and structural violence; re-embeds terrorism within the social practices (violent and non-violent) which precede, surround and succeed the 'terrorist' act; and restores multiple identities to groups and (socially-embedded) individuals – confronts scholars with the whole breadth of that submerged iceberg discovered through the deepening move. It confronts us with the need to move past the current obsession with the violent, spectacular act itself – which risks exoticising the act (Breen Smyth, 2008c) – to examine that violence as part of the processes that move and transform social reality more broadly. It is arguably a far more complex and confusing task than that which traditional terrorism scholars have concentrated on thus far, as it asks us to go outside our disciplines to confront an intricate web of social, economic, and political relations which constitute this broader understanding of terrorism. More than that, it requires a change in our relationship with the phenomenon itself. For, by embedding our inquiries in a network of social and political relations of which we ourselves are a part, terrorism becomes less 'othered' as the ways in which we are more or less implicated in it become more manifest.

Reconstruction and transformative potential

An emancipatory, normative framework

We have so far examined the implications of the Welsh School's call for deepening and broadening the study of terrorism. But the *sine qua non* of Critical Theory is emancipation. '[C]ritical theory', following Wyn Jones, 'stands and falls by the possibility that emancipatory potential exists. Epistemologically, it is only this possibility that gives critical theory coherence and, indeed, purpose' (Wyn Jones, 1999: 56). A concern for emancipation and Critical Theory's role in bringing it about is one of the few things that unite the disparate elements of the Frankfurt School.[9] Bringing us back full circle, 'it is critical theory's commitment to emancipation – understood as the development of possibilities for a better life already immanent within the present – that provides its point of critique of the prevailing order' (Wyn Jones, 1999: 28). The potential of, and necessity for, emancipation is what drives Critical Theory's critique of the notion of a (broadly) immutable status quo so dominant in traditional terrorism studies.[10] Furthermore, a commitment to emancipation is what distinguishes self-reflexive traditional theory from Critical Theory (Horkheimer, 1992: 228–229, 233; Wyn Jones, 1999: 154).

But what is meant by emancipation?[11] Horkheimer envisaged Critical Theory's goal as humanity's emancipation from slavery (Horkheimer, 1992), while Booth defines emancipation as 'the theory and practice of inventing humanity, with a view of freeing people, as individuals and collectivities, from contingent and structural oppressions' (Booth, 2005: 181). Emancipation, within a Critical Theory framework, however, is not about utopian goals out of humanity's reach, but must rather be grounded in feasible alternatives that grow out of the here and now – that is, the immanent. It is as critical of idealistic 'improbable alternatives' as it is of 'the existing order' (Cox, 1986: 210). It achieves this through immanent critique, by seeking within society the sources of emancipation and change rather than trying to find them in an extraneous utopia. Thus, contradictions are sought in the existing order, in the fissures through which the possibility of transformation transpires (Cox, 1986).[12]

Finding the source of emancipation in the context of terrorism is not easy. Who are the 'oppressed and marginalized' that Critical Theory must be partisan to (Wyn Jones, 1999)? Is it those killed and scarred by terrorist violence, those maimed and tortured by counterterrorism, those who resort to violence because they believe they have no 'feasible alternative', or those who, on the contrary, continue to shun terrorist violence despite oppression and tyranny? On what basis can one make such a judgement? Can such a judgement be made at all? We argue that such a choice does not need to be made – one does not have to choose between those victimised by one side and those victimised by the other. This can be done by understanding emancipation as emancipation for all, from all forms of violence: direct, structural, or cultural, state or non-state; or alternatively, as the creation of those political, social and economic conditions under which political goals can be legitimately and effectively pursued without recourse to terrorism.

Making the notion of emancipation central to the study of terrorism introduces an explicit normative commitment. Andrew Linklater summed this up, combining Horkheimer's productivist focus on class with Habermas's subsequent communicative turn which emphasises the importance of dialogue and creating cross-national speech communities:

> To increase the spheres of social interaction that are *governed by dialogue and consent rather than power and force* [emancipation from direct violence]; to expand the number of human beings who have *access to a speech community that has the potential to become universal* [lending voice to the voiceless]; and to create the socioeconomic preconditions of effective, as opposed to nominal, involvement for all members of that community [emancipation from structural violence and structures of inequality].
> (Linklater, 2001: 31; emphases and brackets added)

One could object to this particular summary, although it has the advantage of combining a commitment to emancipation from violence in all its forms as well as structures of inequality – rather than simply a condemnation of non-state violence without consideration of state violence and structures of inequality. It also simultaneously highlights the importance of dialogue, political participation and being heard – without, crucially, ignoring the need for concrete structural economic and political changes to make dialogue more symmetric and egalitarian (Linklater, 2001: 30; see also Wyn Jones, 1999: 75–76). But whichever definition one settles on, a Critical Theory approach inherently involves a commitment to a particular normative agenda. Making this explicit is important, both for clarifying the normative framework against which existing theories and practices are inevitably judged, and for the research to become more transparent.

A second issue is that from a Critical Theory perspective the means for achieving emancipation are just as, if not more, important than the goals pursued. Terrorism itself has been understood by its practitioners as a means of emancipation from oppression (also Gunning, 2007a: 386). However, if emancipation is not only an endpoint but mainly a process, one cannot, as Booth and Wyn Jones convincingly argue, separate the means from the end. Rather, '[w]hat is required ... is a model of analysis that recognizes ... that ends and means are not somehow casually related but are mutually implicated' (Wyn Jones, 1999: 131–132; see also Booth, 2005: 273). Critical Theory, after all, is at heart a critique of the dominance of instrumental reason in traditional theory, which places the consideration of ends outside the realm of investigation and distinguishes sharply between fact and value. This is precisely what underpins realism's claim that politics is amoral and liberalism's claim that ends should be a private concern.

Against this dualism, Booth argues for the adoption of a Gandhian non-dualistic vision, 'fusing ends and means in a manner whereby one's ideals are evident in how one acts, not only in what one hopes to achieve' (Booth, 2005: 273). Such a framework not only turns the notion of 'emancipatory terrorism' into a 'contradiction in terms' (Booth, 2008), but challenges the legitimacy of violent (counter)terrorism, repression, human rights violations, structural violence, and the like.

At the same time, where terrorism has been embarked upon as a means of emancipation, whether from oppression or to further emancipatory projects, the emancipatory impulse behind the violence should be recognised by Critical Theory-inspired scholars, just as the immanent possibilities for transformation among those engaged in terrorism, state or non-state, should be actively sought for. Here it is vital to move beyond the often static framework of traditional scholars and consider the possibilities for transformation of people within organisations engaged in terrorism (Gunning, 2004, 2007c; Toros, forthcoming). From such a perspective, arguably one of the tragedies of the Israeli–Palestinian conflict was the assassination of Ismail Abu Shannab, one of Hamas's leaders in Gaza, who had been one of the central forces behind the articulation of an alternative paradigm within Hamas which could eventually accommodate a two-state solution (Gunning, 2007c: 236–237, 2008).

Similarly, a Critical Theory-inspired scholar cannot write off a government organisation as beyond reform, simply on the basis that it is currently engaged in anti-emancipatory practices and should, instead, actively cultivate alliances with those who are working towards transformation from within. One example can be found in the work of Robert Lambert, the now-retired head of the London Metropolitan Police's Muslim Contact Unit, who worked tirelessly to engage Islamic groups in the UK, some of them widely viewed as radical. Another is that of British intelligence officers who pushed for contacts between top IRA officials and the British government in the 1980s, eventually leading to the 1998 Good Friday Agreement (Mallie and McKittrick, 2001; Powell, 2008); or the call by the Northern Ireland Head of Counterterrorism, Peter Sheridan, for negotiations with dissident Republicans as a means to bring their violence to an end (Breen Smyth, 2008d).

What emancipation actually entails can only be truly engaged with when studying specific cases. Although discussing it in the abstract is necessary to 'clarify what the broad issues in question are', it is only 'when specific, historical examples are addressed that the discussion of emancipation can proceed to the consideration of particular institutions and forms of life' (Wyn Jones, 1999: 121). This introduces a potential tension between the universal claims of an emancipatory perspective and local contextualised claims. Although we, the authors, may condemn violence in a theoretical sense, we recognise that for someone embedded in a particular context, whether it is that of the myriad Israeli counterterrorism organisations, or the rural hinterland of the Colombian FARC, violence may seem contextually legitimate as the most compelling means to increase the security of their community. Indeed, we ourselves might have adopted a very different perspective had we grown up in a Palestinian refugee camp, in an Israeli settlement, or in the Falls or Shankill roads of Belfast (see also Booth, 2008). Without such an appreciation of context, it would indeed be impossible to understand, for instance, the popularity of Palestinian suicide bombers at the height of the al-Aqsa Intifada (Gunning, 2007c: 216–220). How, then, can a Critical Theory-inspired terrorism studies ground its claims regarding what constitutes emancipation in a particular context convincingly – particularly when faced with situations where real people are suffering and political violence appears to offer a way out?

The standard response is that Critical Theorists must work from within the fissures of existing local practices, which, after all, is the meaning of immanent critique. However, that answer may also belie the possibility that what ends up being advocated as emancipatory has more to do with the perspective of the scholar than with the reality or potentialities on the ground. A commitment to ending political violence in a particular context[13] may encourage critical scholars to, for example, support the track-three peace initiatives by Israeli and Palestinian technocrats and academics without a real power base. In so doing, they may unwittingly contribute to perpetuating violence by being too divorced from the reality ordinary people on the ground experience, and by ignoring the militants and power-brokers on both sides who need to be brought on board to end the violence.

This is precisely why post-structuralists condemn Critical Theory for imposing their own totalising project on those they seek to emancipate (Hutchings, 2001: 90; Alker, 2005: 202; Linklater, 2001: 30–31, 42–43). More broadly, a Critical Theory understanding of terrorism needs to recognise, following Linklater, 'that some forms of [emancipatory] universalism have wished to submerge or extinguish the difference of the other', and thus must be 'explicitly concerned not only with tolerating difference but with enlarging human diversity' (Linklater, 2001: 43, see also 2005b). It is not clear whether a Critical Theory approach to terrorism can both 'enlarge human diversity' and promote emancipation from political violence if the diversity in question revolves around precisely the use of political violence (see also Gunning, 2007b: 241–242). This becomes particularly problematic in situations where non-violent political methods of affecting change are believed by participants to be ineffectual because of a severe power asymmetry. Delegitimising violence may in such instances make the individuals and communities one seeks to secure less secure, unless a credible alternative is found that is not just morally attractive but practically feasible – a tall order when power asymmetries are deeply entrenched, and those advocating non-violent solutions lack any concrete power base.

Here, more than anywhere, a critical approach to terrorism must heed Horkheimer's admonition to think constructively, beyond empirical verification (Horkheimer, 1992: 221). In the case of terrorism, this may involve a concerted effort to rethink human interaction and social structures from the roots up, even though this introduces a utopian element in the critical project – what Booth calls 'utopian realism' (2005: 273) or, more recently, 'emancipatory realism' (Booth, 2007). Whether or not this is the way forward, Linklater's advice to 'enlarge human diversity' and, by extension, to remain deeply aware of the cultural-historic limitations of our own thinking, is supremely important if we are to avoid imposing our own framework, particularly if this contributes to creating the conditions for a violent response. Critical Theory, Linklater reminds us, 'is not a form of "moral rigorism" which applies universalisable principles in a mechanical fashion with no regard for personal need and social context'. Rather, '[t]rue dialogue ... requires genuine engagement with the different and possibly alien standpoint taken by the "other"' (Linklater, 1996: 291)[14] – although always within the framework of a common humanity. This, inter alia, applies as much to dialogue with those engaged in violence, as to dialogue with those who study terrorism differently, whether from a traditional or a post-structuralist perspective.

One of the charges against Critical Theory is that its main proponents have been deeply Eurocentric (Wyn Jones, 1999: 127), contaminating not only the notion of emancipation but also its perceptions of the individual, religion, the community, and the like. John Hobson similarly charges Cox and the neo-Gramscian school in international politics, one of the sources of Welsh School Critical Theory, with 'subliminal Eurocentrism' (Hobson, 2007: 95–99). Because terrorism occurs in conflicts where both Westernisation and Western double standards are cited as causes, one central task of a Critical Theory-inspired terrorism studies is thus to 'reveal the post-racist contradictions and double standards that [Western discourse] consciously and subconsciously smoothes over' (Hobson, 2007: 116). This can be done by holding Western discourses and practices – including those of Critical Theorists – up to their own proclaimed standards following the type of immanent critiques outlined above.

But it also involves the far more difficult task of '[a]ccepting the Other in the Self and recognising that the Self is therefore hybrid' (Hobson, 2007: 113) – particularly challenging if 'the Other' is engaged in terrorism against 'us', or calls into question 'our' conception of what it is to be human (by, for instance, according religion a more central place, or by discriminating on the basis of gender). For this to be possible, any form of 'subliminal Eurocentrism' which, among other things, denies non-Westerners agency (Hobson, 2007: 97), must be addressed. It also means subjecting the secular Enlightenment values on which Critical Theory is built to the scrutiny of dialogue with 'others', rather than holding up these values as somehow a priori, and reflecting on whether any of these have contributed to the phenomenon of terrorism. Here Butler's notions of a 'not-yet arrived universality' and the need for the 'labor of translation' may provide a useful roadmap (Butler, 1996: 46–49, 52).

Thus, although emancipation must be a central component of a Critical Theory approach to terrorism, its application to terrorist violence cannot be reduced to a simple condemnation of such violence. It needs to tackle the difficult questions of why such violence emerged, how it is linked to other forms of violence, and how emancipation from these different forms of violence marring a specific context can be achieved. It also needs to acknowledge the potentially emancipatory objectives of violent actors, without discrediting the often arduous and less public struggle of non-violent actors. Most of all, critical theorists armed with 'good' (emancipatory) intentions must beware of imposing totalising projects that may further subjugate rather than emancipate. As a process, any emancipatory framework must thus be constantly reviewed, questioned, and challenged.

Praxis: lending a voice to the voiceless, locating possibilities for transformation, engaging policy-makers and suspect communities

The final challenge of Critical Theory lies in the notion that (research) practice and theory cannot be separated, but are mutually implicated. The critical theorist is, indeed, at the heart of the Critical Theory project, forcing us scholars to take responsibility for our role in the constant (re)construction of what is knowledge and as potential promoters of emancipatory change. Though the Frankfurt School emphasises this point in theory, none of its main proponents provides a clear roadmap as to how praxis – the transformation of the world by putting theory into practice – is to be done (Wyn Jones, 1999: 151–153). This is where Gramsci and his concept of 'organic intellectuals' comes into its own. Building on Gramsci, Wyn Jones argues that

> [o]rganic intellectuals have a crucial role to play in this process by helping to undermine the "natural," the "commonsense", internalized nature of the status quo. This in turn helps create political space within which alternative conceptions of politics can be developed and new historic blocs created
> (Wyn Jones, 1999: 160)

Since these emancipatory alternative conceptions are not based in abstract utopias but in feasible alternatives, it is our duty as scholars and activists to search for these feasible alternatives and promote them. Research should thus be policy relevant, no doubt, but should also look past the spheres of government (Gunning, 2007a, 2007b; Booth, 2008). In line with the shift from taking the state as ultimate referent to secure to focusing on the security of human beings, research should engage not just policymakers but also 'policy-takers' (Neufeld, 2001) and, in particular, in the context of terrorism, those considered by the state as 'suspect communities' (Hillyard, 1993; see also Gunning, 2007a: 388–389). Most of all, research 'must be particularly attuned to listen to what is not being said, and to interpret the hopes and fears and interests of those sectors of society that are silent, if not actually silenced' (Booth, 2008: 68) – or without an arena in which to speak.

This arguably requires scholars, where possible, to engage in field research so as to personally access people on the ground – as those who are silent or silenced cannot, by definition, be heard from a distance. This is particularly pertinent in societies that rely heavily on oral communication, a feature which is especially prominent in societies under occupation and among underground organisations (see also Gunning, 2007c: 20–21). With regard to the study of terrorism, this means engaging with the victims of terrorism, the victims of counterterrorism, as well as the perpetrators of terrorism and counterterrorism. Such direct engagement through fieldwork is both encouraged by Linklater's Habermasian call for dialogue and by Cox's admonition to, above all, 'not base theory on theory but rather on changing practice and empirical-historical study, which are a proving ground for concepts and hypotheses' (Cox, 1986: 206; see also Breen Smyth, this volume).

Fieldwork is central to increasing our understanding of local practices and meanings. Without being on the ground, talking to local actors, observing community practices, it is difficult to decipher local dynamics and succeed in grasping the local meaning of an act (Toros, 2008b). One should not stop there, of course, since a critical approach forces one to stand back from existing power structures. The danger of 'going native' is always present – although empathy, from a Critical Theory perspective which recognizes that all subjects have their subjective standpoints, is not so anathema as it may be for traditional theorists intent on maintaining their neutral, objective stance. Furthermore, as Booth points out, fieldwork is not the only way to acquire such understanding as that would at a stroke render historians obsolete (Booth, 2008). When faced with the apparent impossibility of fieldwork – be it due to security, ethical or other concerns (see Breen Smyth, this volume) – students of terrorism can always find other ways of conducting their research. However, we would argue that a Critical Theory approach, with its emphasis on context and lending a voice to the voiceless, means that scholars need to think very seriously about carrying out fieldwork, particularly given how little traditional studies have fathomed local context (Gunning, 2007a).

Field research is also encouraged by the notion that we, as scholars, can be a locus for emancipation by being part of the emergence of counter-hegemonic discourses and communities seeking to transform existing hegemonic discourses and structures, whether state or non-state. Participative action research which entails the engagement of the 'researched' in the research process by creating research partnerships with activists within 'suspect communities', is one way forward (Breen Smyth, 2004). But so is the creation of emancipatory partnerships with traditional security communities, to facilitate immanent change. Although both paths bring with them dangers in terms of co-option and the re-emergence of instrumental rationality as the dominant form of reasoning (see Gunning, 2007b: 240–241), the praxeological imperative inherent in Critical Theory does not, on our reading, allow us the luxury of non-engagement. Moreover, there are instances where organic critical scholars have successfully engaged with existing power structures and helped to transform existing practices. The *Human Development Reports*, the UN's 'Women, Peace, and Security' resolution, and the spread of the notion of 'common security' towards the end of the cold war are cases in point – although all are 'works-in-progress' (Murphy, 2007: 127–130; Wyn Jones, 1999: 156–158; Basu, 2008).

More fundamentally, praxis should be informed by the Critical Theory insight that subject and object are mutually implicated, and that research affects both (Whitworth, 2001; Breen Smyth, 2005). Thus, who we are, what motivates us, the way we interact with those we interview, the types of questions we ask and the way we handle our and our interviewees' emotions, profoundly affect research. Similarly, what types of knowledge we create and spread, and how these affect those we study through the way they influence policies and public opinion, should be a central praxeological concern. This is particularly pertinent to terrorism studies given that who or what is called terrorist or suspect has very serious real-life implications. Thus, contrary to the more positivist among traditional scholars, who maintain an artificial separation between their research and the political, the aim of Critical Theory scholars is to understand *our* role in existing power structures and explicitly use this understanding to work towards transforming the status quo in an emancipatory direction.[15]

Conclusion

We have shown various ways in which Critical Theory offers a rich, theoretically-grounded framework for conceptualising and studying terrorism. It provides both a way to critique existing terrorism studies, and a call for providing new conceptual frameworks, new explanations, and new foci of study. In the words of Booth, it offers an ontology, an epistemology, and an orientation toward praxis (Booth, 2005).

Ontologically, it rejects the notion of an objective social science as a hegemonic project to sustain the status quo and calls for exposing the ideological assumptions and material interests behind social science. It alerts us to the historicity of the status quo, the inevitability of transformation, and the need to consider the status quo's implication in creating the conditions out of which terrorism has emerged. It simultaneously provides a minimal foundationalist position which avoids 'throwing the baby out with the bathwater' (Gunning, 2007b), and enables us to study both the political usages of the discourse of 'terrorism' and a historically contextualised form of violence. By replacing the state with human beings as the ultimate referent to be secured, the normative moorings of research are fundamentally changed, making human emancipation and an end to avoidable human suffering the central concern of any research enterprise.

Epistemologically, a Critical Theory approach encourages us to broaden the focus of terrorism research to include both state and non-state terrorism, counterterrorism, and structural violence. It encourages us to place context at the heart of the investigation, restoring a past and a future to terrorism, allowing the concept to evolve along with the world, and embedding (counter)terrorism within its wider socio-historical context of social movements, political, societal and economic structures, non-violent social practices, and the like. Rejecting traditional theory's 'fetishization of parts', it embeds terrorism in broader social and political theory through a call for greater interdisciplinarity and re-linking terrorism to the broader social processes of which it is part.

Finally, in its orientation toward praxis, it vindicates a normative emancipatory commitment which can be understood in this context as the aim of transforming terrorist violence – not by any means, but through means that are compatible with the ridding of direct, structural, and cultural violence. As part of this praxeological dimension, a Critical Theory approach calls for engaging the silenced and the suffering (though not without critical distancing), sustaining counter-hegemonic discourses and communities, and working with both suspect communities and policy-makers contributing to the transformation of both (and expecting to be transformed oneself in the process). Underpinning this orientation is a notion of emancipation as process, involving genuine dialogue with those considered 'other' – including members of organisations involved in violence (whether state or non-state) – rather than as predetermined endpoint. It demands that we seek the fissures and contradictions through which counter-hegemonic discourses emerge and that we engage with victims, perpetrators, policymakers, and policy-takers to articulate, and contribute towards, the emergence of emancipatory alternatives. Most fundamentally, it demands the recognition of a common humanity – one in which we are all capable of violence and pain, but also, crucially, of imagining a better future.

Notes

1. The authors wish to thank Ken Booth, Andrew Linklater, Nick Rengger, Richard Wyn Jones, Richard Jackson, Marie Breen Smyth, and Frazer Egerton for their comments on earlier drafts.
2. We will not examine in detail who constitutes 'traditional' terrorism, on what grounds it has been critiqued, or signs of immanent transformation within the field. For an overview, see the first section of this book and Gunning, 2007a. For a definition of 'traditional', see the following paragraph.
3. We here adopt Mark Hoffman's suggestion that Cox's 'problem-solving theory' is what Max Horkheimer originally labelled 'traditional theory' (M. Hoffman, 1987).
4. In this, it overlaps closely with post-structuralist critiques.

5 For examples of this type of research, see Jackson, 2005; George, 1991b; Burnett and Whyte, 2005.
6 The third part of Hutchings' agenda ('study marginalised phenomena') is discussed in the sections on broadening and praxis.
7 Here the distinction advocated by Booth between naturalism and positivism is particularly useful (Booth, 2007: 193–194).
8 Wyn Jones calls this move 'extending' rather than 'deepening' (Wyn Jones, 1999: 103–104).
9 Even in the very pessimistic *Dialectic of Enlightenment*, Adorno and Horkheimer maintain a notion of emancipation, albeit one based on an essentially unachievable new relationship between humanity and nature (Wyn Jones, 1999: 38–39).
10 This is not to say that traditional scholars are not committed to the arguably emancipatory goal of ending terrorism. The distinction is that they broadly support the existing political order and are less willing to investigate how it is implicated in the 'problem' of terrorism, thus rendering the goal of ending terrorism more utopian and less immanent (at least from a critical standpoint).
11 For a different and more extensive discussion of emancipation and terrorism, see McDonald's chapter in this volume.
12 There is an ongoing debate on the actual 'grounding' of emancipation in critical theory (Wyn Jones, 1999). However, as Wyn Jones points out, this debate does not prevent scholars from seeking emancipation in specific empirical examples.
13 This is not to be confused with pacifism, although the two positions can overlap.
14 This view is contested by several authors (cf. Shapcott, 2001), who argue that Habermas's dialogue requires acceptance of a post-conventional morality, thus possibly excluding precisely those actors a Critical Theory approach to terrorism would want to engage with.
15 As Wyn Jones notes regarding security studies, not all traditional scholars accept this positivist separation between theory and politics; some – the 'organic intellectuals' of the 'ruling strata' – use their position explicitly to buttress the status quo (Wyn Jones, 1999: 154). Commitment to emancipation is what distinguishes the 'critical' from the 'status quo' organic intellectual.

6 Emancipation and critical terrorism studies

Matt McDonald

Introduction[1]

This chapter addresses the question of what a 'critical terrorism studies' research agenda defined in terms of a concern with emancipation might look like. For some, the role of emancipatory concerns is self-evidently central, given the association of 'critical' with the critical theory of the Frankfurt School. For others, defining 'critical terrorism studies' in terms of a concern with the promotion or realisation of emancipation is problematic, excluding some who would support a move away from traditional/orthodox approaches to the study of terror but stop short of defining their research in emancipatory terms. Most obviously, the traditional post-structural objection to emancipation has been that as a modernist, cosmopolitan political agenda (particularly one with philosophical linkages to Marx and invoked historically to justify violent action to 'free' others), the grand narrative of emancipation risks creating new forms of violence and exclusion in the process of removing others. Such an account would be closer to embracing a definition of 'critical terrorism studies' closer in orientation to Robert Cox's (1981: 129–130) definition of critical theory as a broad orientation that encourages questions about how the world came to be constituted as it is and whose interests these arrangements serve. In international relations and security studies, the distinction between this broader definition and a more explicit concern with emancipation is evident in Chris Brown's (1994) elaboration of the differences between upper case and lower case Critical Theory/critical theory, and in the different definitions of critical security studies elaborated by Keith Krause and Michael Williams (1997b) on the one hand and Ken Booth (1991, 1997) and Richard Wyn Jones (1999) on the other.

These differences are not unimportant and the objections raised by those with normative concerns about emancipation are crucial in recognising, following Foucault, the dangers inherent in any attempt to articulate a vision for a 'better' world. But should these concerns lead to a rejection of the emancipatory project as a whole? I would argue here that they should instead encourage a reflexiveness about the opportunities and limitations of political analysis informed by emancipation, but should not lead us to reject the philosophical foundations, core ethical commitments, and tools of emancipatory critical theory. More specifically, I suggest that defining 'critical terrorism studies' in terms of a concern with emancipation may prove useful both in guiding the types of questions we might ask and particularly in providing 'philosophical anchorage' (Booth, 1999: 43) for an emphasis on those whose voices and interests are marginalised or excluded from traditional accounts of 'terrorism' and responses to it (see also Gunning, 2007a).

There are of course a range of different ways of understanding and approaching emancipation. Important distinctions were evident within the Frankfurt School itself, most prominently on the question of the prospects and sites for realising emancipation. Horkheimer (1972), for example, while sceptical of Marx's emphasis on the proletariat as the key agent of emancipation and increasingly on the possibility for realising emancipation at all, like Marx focused on the means of production as the central site for achieving emancipation and defined emancipation in terms of the removal of material restraints imposed by nature. Habermas (1984), meanwhile, defined communication as the key site for realising emancipatory change, emphasising the importance of the expansion of realms of open dialogue. Further differences are evident in later articulations of emancipation and the prospects for its realisation by theorists working within the Frankfurt School tradition. Axel Honneth (1995) positions recognition of identity as the focal point for emancipation and emancipatory potential, while Andrew Linklater (1998) suggests the possibility of expanding Habermas's communicative ethics to the realm of global community.[2]

It is clearly beyond the scope of this chapter to outline how these multiple understandings of emancipation and the sites for its realisation might inform an academic engagement with 'terrorism'. Such a task is made even more difficult by the fact that there are multiple ways of defining and approaching 'terrorism', and particular definitions of emancipation encourage particular types of research programmes or agenda. As such, in this chapter I will narrow the analysis in three ways. First, while endorsing a broad definition of emancipation as the process of removing unnecessary structural restraints, I will focus in this chapter on the expansion of dialogic community – 'advances in non-repressive deliberation' (Apel in Linklater, 2005b: 120–121) – as the key site for the realisation of emancipatory change. Such an approach enables a retained concern on material inequality and deprivation – clearly relevant to questions of 'terror' and 'counterterror' – while focusing our attention on the central questions of whose voices are heard in defining 'terrorism' and responses to it, and what prospects exist for the expansion of dialogue and deliberation.

Second, and following from the above, I focus here on 'terrorism' in its political usage rather than on an abstract definition of the concept. Specifically, I focus on those struggles, dynamics and actions that have been constructed as 'terrorist' in particular contexts. While at a superficial level such an approach might seem to reify the position of the political elite and traditional analysts in defining what counts as 'terrorism', I suggest that coming to terms with the political power of the label itself requires attention to dominant discourses of it. And perhaps more importantly, possibilities for emancipatory change can be located precisely in the tensions at the heart of these dominant articulations of 'terrorism' and 'counterterrorism'.

Finally, I narrow the scope of this analysis by suggesting the possibility of developing an emancipatory 'critical terrorism studies' informed by the emancipatory 'critical security studies' of the 'Welsh School'. At the least, the Welsh School's attempt to develop an emancipatory framework for the broader study of security has much to tell us about the challenges and possibilities for advancing emancipation in the context of an approach to the study of terrorism.

This paper is divided into two parts. The first part outlines the Welsh School critical security studies research agenda in order to identify possible contributions to the study of 'terrorism', noting how emancipation is defined in this approach before outlining how it is understood in this paper. The second part outlines what such an emancipatory 'critical terrorism studies' might look like, focusing on a series of key questions that such an approach might encourage in the context of the post-2001 'war on terror'. I conclude by suggesting that, while not without its dangers or limitations, a reflexive commitment to emancipation as the removal of unnecessary structural constraints through a process of freeing up space for dialogue provides a basis for both analytically important and normatively progressive research on 'terrorism' in international politics.

Critical terrorism studies, critical security studies, and emancipation

The (explicit) association of emancipation with the study of international security has been relatively recent and has been advanced most prominently by the so-called 'Welsh School' of critical security studies. Associated with the work of Ken Booth (1991, 1997, 1999, 2005, 2007) and Richard Wyn Jones (1999, 2005) at Aberystwyth University, the Welsh School research agenda emerged out of post-cold war debates about the meaning of security. More accurately, debates about security that developed in the later years of the cold war tended to focus on the content of security rather than its meaning: on which issues should or should not be included on states' security agendas. While welcoming the attempt to orient security away from the traditional exclusive concern with the state, militaries, and conflict, Booth and others pointed to a central but surprisingly neglected question: 'whose security?'. Booth (1991) suggested that it made sense to think of states as (possible) agents rather than referents of security – as means rather than ends – and to orient the study of security away from preserving the territory of the state and towards redressing the suffering of the most vulnerable people in global politics. In doing so, he suggested that security should ultimately be defined as emancipation.

The key points to note here are that security is oriented towards people rather than states; that the study of security is at its heart a normative exercise; and that the role of the theorist of security should be to identify, help develop an understanding of, and attempt to redress instances of political repression or structural violence. There is much about these core commitments – and the Welsh School framework generally – that could usefully inform the developing 'critical terrorism studies' research agenda. 'Critical terrorism studies' could certainly be defined in such a way as to emphasise the normative role of theorising; the centrality of 'emancipation' as philosophical anchorage; the ultimate emphasis of analysis on the most vulnerable people rather than states; and the central praxeological goal of locating possibilities for emancipatory change in particular contexts. In pointing to the utility of the Welsh School framework here, I begin by outlining how 'emancipation' is defined within this approach. I then point to the Welsh School's attempt to locate emancipation within a cosmopolitan ethical framework emphasising global community, before exploring the centrality of immanent critique as a means for locating possibilities for emancipatory change in contemporary political practice.

In his earliest statements on the security-emancipation relationship, Ken Booth (1991: 319) defined emancipation as 'freeing people from those constraints that stop them carrying out what they would freely choose to do'. This broad definition can and should be viewed as an initial statement, with subsequent iterations (Booth, 1999: 43–46, 2005: 181–182) focusing on the multiple functions of emancipation within the critical security framework (as 'philosophical anchorage', 'strategic process', and 'a guide for tactical goal setting') and increasingly emphasising the need to define emancipation in procedural and dialectical terms. In his most recent attempt to define emancipation, Booth (2007: 112) conceptualized it as follows:

> As a discourse of politics, emancipation seeks the securing of people from those oppressions that would stop them from carrying out what they would freely choose to do, compatible with the freedom of others. It provides a three-fold framework for politics: a philosophical anchorage for knowledge, a theory of progress for society, and a practice of resistance against oppression. Emancipation is the philosophy, theory, and politics of inventing humanity.

This broad definition ultimately stops short of providing a clear idea of what emancipation looks like in practice or how it might inform our analyses of empirical contexts. This lack of definitional precision is justified on the basis that emancipation is better conceived as process than endpoint and that it is better understood in terms of the specificity of particular struggles and dynamics in world politics than in purely abstract terms (Booth, 1999: 41–46, 2005: 182). On the production-dialogue distinction within critical theory noted earlier, the Welsh School approach attempts to incorporate both into its definition of emancipation, suggesting the need to amplify the voices of marginalised actors to speak security as a means for altering material structures of oppression.[3] Further, changes in material distribution of power and resources are conceived as central to the task of enabling an appropriate dialogic community to emerge.

As such, the Welsh School conception of emancipation suggests the possibility of a focus on the process through which both marginalised voices can be

Emancipation and critical terrorism studies 113

empowered and heard, and the material conditions of their marginalisation redressed. While retaining a concern with material inequality and deprivation as a crucial dimension of emancipation, in this chapter I focus in particular on possibilities for emancipatory change through 'advances in nonrepressive deliberation' (Apel in Linklater, 2005b: 120–121). This, I would suggest, is especially relevant to 'critical terrorism studies' both analytically and normatively. The centrality of 'discourses' of 'terrorism' and 'counterterror' to the dynamics of this form of political violence certainly underscores the importance of a focus on communicative action. And closely related to this, the process of freeing up space for alternative voices to be heard is seen here as central to the means through which political violence – whether defined as 'terrorist' or not – is least likely to be pursued.

The ethical foundation of emancipation is radically cosmopolitan. Indeed, for the Welsh School the development of its security framework was based upon Booth's (1991) critique of the limits of communitarian approaches that privileged states as ethical containers and providers for their citizens. Wyn Jones (1999: 159), meanwhile, has suggested that 'critical security studies is for the voiceless, the unrepresented, the powerless, and its purpose is their emancipation'. Such a concern entails a shift of focus in security politics away from states and elites and towards those most at risk from the effects of a wider range of practices and least able to have their own voices heard. This is given its fullest philosophical statement in Andrew Linklater's (1998) discussion of possibilities for global citizenship, which he subsequently (2005b) relates to the critical security studies project in drawing linkages between security and global community. At all these levels, the cosmopolitan ethic at the heart of emancipation questions ultimately rejects the moral primacy of states, encouraging instead a focus on the ways in which relatively arbitrary definitions of 'national security', for example, work to exclude the rights and needs of the most vulnerable. As will be noted, these questions of vulnerability are central to making sense of 'terrorism' and how we might respond to it.

The final point to note in illustrating the potential benefits of drawing on the Welsh School research agenda for 'critical terrorism studies' concerns its method, itself informed by a particular conception of the role of analysts (see Booth, 1997: 115, 2008: 67). In seeking to locate possibilities for emancipatory change in particular contexts, working from a commitment to developing security praxis, Welsh School theorists emphasise the central critical theoretical tool of immanent critique. Immanent critique is defined here as a dialectical method of inquiry that engages with the core commitments of particular discourses, ideologies, or institutional arrangements on their own terms, in the process locating possibilities for radical change within a particular existing order. This has two intimately related but distinct components. The first is the praxeological focus on pointing to possibilities for change *within* particular contexts. This is particularly prominent in Booth's (2007: 250) suggestion that 'immanent critique involves identifying those features within concrete situations (such as positive dynamics, agents, key struggles) that have emancipatory possibilities, and then working through the politics (tactics and strategies) to strengthen them.' As such, the goal of the theorist is that of identifying, empowering, and amplifying silenced voices in particular contexts rather than articulating one's own vision to be imposed externally. As Richard Wyn Jones (1999: 76–78) suggests, the focus through immanent critique should be on 'concrete utopias': realisable visions of emancipatory orders grounded within those contexts themselves. The central focus on immanent critique as a form of praxis might inform the location of possibilities for the resolution of conflicts that give rise to or are characterised by 'terrorism'. Indeed, such an approach has been applied to conflict in the Middle East (Bilgin, 2005) and in Northern Ireland (Ruane and Todd, 2005).

The second component of immanent critique addressed here is the analytical focus on fissures, tensions, and inconsistencies within discourses, ideologies, and institutional arrangements. This dimension is less prominent in Welsh School accounts of immanent critique although, of course, the basis of the critique of traditional theories and practices of security as a whole is that these approaches fail to live up to their own commitments. For Booth, the reality of poverty, starvation, disease, human rights violations, and refugee flows suggests that those actors who have justified their existence of the basis of providing security (states and their leaders) are not actually 'doing the job' they had committed themselves to for their populations (see also Fierke, 2007: 190–193). Applied to the study of 'terrorism', such an approach might be used to interrogate the extent to which the commitments of 'counterterrorism' discourses (for example, ridding a country/the world of 'terrorism') are being realised through the practices that they are invoked to justify (such as military campaigns) (see Fierke, 2007: 167–185; Krebs and Lobasz, 2007: 450–451). Locating disjunctures here potentially provides a basis for radical change in dominant means of engaging with the threat posed by 'terrorism', a point I will return to later.

An emancipatory critical terrorism studies: key questions

While the above suggests the possibility of developing a 'critical terrorism studies' research agenda informed by the Welsh School critical security studies framework, it leaves open the matter of what types of questions and research programmes might be undertaken. This section briefly suggests a series of key issues for a 'critical terrorism studies' defined in such terms, focusing especially on the post-2001 'war on terror'.

An initial question suggested by an emancipatory approach to 'critical terrorism studies' might be: whose voices are marginalised or silenced and whose are empowered in defining 'terrorism' and responses to it in particular contexts? Indeed, this question might be usefully split into three for our purposes: who defines 'terrorism'?; who defines 'terrorists'?; and who defines the dominant response to the 'terrorist threat'? These questions build on the core Welsh School concern with 'whose security' is prioritised and how the voices of the marginalised might be amplified. They also suggest themselves from the focus here on the diffusion of power to speak and the opening up of space for non-repressive dialogue. Understood in such terms, the imperative becomes one of recognising how current spaces for dialogue are constructed or limited; exploring how dominant definitions of key concepts and practical responses have *become* dominant; and locating silenced and marginalised articulations of 'terrorism' and responses to it.

Various authors have engaged with the question of how 'terrorism' itself is defined in particular institutional contexts; who is privileged in defining it; and whose ends are served by those definitions (Blakely, 2007a; Tilly, 2004; Jackson, 2007a). This question is important because of the ways in which the label 'terrorism' works as a powerful political signifier, serving to delegitimise certain forms of action and the actors undertaking them. Norris *et al.* (2003: 9) suggest that definitions of 'terrorism' in established democracies are likely to favour violence perpetrated by non-state actors against the state, in part because of the interests of government in delegitimising the actions of others and re-inscribing the rights of states to act violently themselves. They further suggest that such a definition is dominant within the research communities of such states, not least because researchers seek, or are reliant upon, government funding for research activity.[4] If the invocation of 'terrorism' itself serves to legitimise the use of force (in response or pre-emptively), in turn creating conditions for counter-violence, then asking fundamental questions about whose voices are marginalised or empowered in defining 'terrorism' opens up space for reflecting upon how violence itself becomes possible.[5]

The concern with who defines 'terrorism' of course maps closely on to the question of who defines 'terrorists'? While definitions of 'terrorism' enable and constrain particular types of practices at a general level of legitimation, the capacity to label a group as a 'terrorist' group often carries with it particular (often legal) implications. The 'war on terror' provides a range of such examples. Jenny Hocking (2004) points to the ways in which post-2001 anti-terror legislation in Australia allowed the Attorney General to label and ban particular groups as 'terrorist' groups and to detain their members without trial. The Chinese government, meanwhile, was successful in convincing the US administration to reverse previous policy and label a Uighur separatist group (ETIM) in north-west China as a 'terrorist' organisation in an apparent quid pro quo for Chinese participation in the 'war on terror'. The US government's decision was consistently invoked by Chinese officials in justifying both military action against that group and the sentencing to death of dozens of its members (Foot, 2005: 422–423). Such policy and political implications have historical antecedents, not least in the decision of Western governments to accept the South African government's labelling of the ANC (African National Congress) as a 'terrorist' organisation during apartheid. At all these levels, the capacity for certain voices to define who 'terrorists' are has important and often direct political implications. There are certainly genuine concerns here that the labelling of 'terrorists' either constitutes a legitimation strategy for suppressing political dissent or serves to narrow the boundaries for political deliberation and debate. An emancipatory framework would conceptualise the latter – and the general post-2001 tendency to limit 'inflammatory' or 'unpatriotic' forms of speech – as a danger in itself rather than as a means for redressing the threat of 'terrorism' (Burke, 2008: 43; Booth, 2007: 261–264).

Finally, a crucial question about which voices dominate and which are marginalised is: who defines responses to 'terrorism'? Of course, political elites within states are again central to which actions are enabled or marginalised. Not only are governments in a strong position to pass domestic 'counterterrorism' legislation or enable military action, for example, they are also in a particularly strong position when it comes to framing or representing the severity of a threat or the way a particular situation should be interpreted in the broader population. In the United States, the administration's use of the term 'war' was central to creating a particular image of the September 11 attacks and creating a context in which military action and invasion became possible in response (Jackson, 2005).

Part of this equation is also the question of how other voices are marginalised or silenced in attempting to influence the nature of a response to the threat of 'terrorism'. If 'security' is a site of contestation over what our core values are, from whom we need to be protected, and how we should act to preserve or advance those values, it becomes crucial to reflect on why some articulations win out over others. Those articulating (particularly radical) alternatives are often themselves marginalised from policy debates and presented as unconcerned about 'national security' or even 'traitors', for example. This is sometimes evident in government denigration of political opponents (see M. McDonald, 2005: 311–313), but also in the way a range of other actors marginalise opposition. Again, in the United States, mainstream media sources broadly endorsed the government's representation of September 11 and its responses to it, narrowing the scope for political opposition (Croft, 2006; Norris *et al.*, 2003: 12–16). More directly, the influential American Council of Trustees and Alumni published a paper in 2002 titled 'Defending Civilisation: How our Universities are Failing America and What Can be Done About it' (Martin and Neal, 2002). The paper detailed a list of American academics who were calling for a re-examination of American foreign policy in light of the September 11 attacks, and suggested that such academics should show (patriotic) solidarity with the majority of fellow citizens on questions regarding the appropriate response to 'terrorism'. Such representations are directly in opposition to the emancipatory impulse of creating situations of open dialogue and debate. An emancipatory approach would entail locating solidarist, non-violent, and inclusive approaches to problems of political violence precisely within the voices marginalised and silenced in reactionary mainstream and elite accounts. Such an approach would also be relevant to the ways in which moderate voices on all sides of violent conflict can become marginalised, and a broader conflict captured by those militant voices engaged in 'terrorist' violence claiming to speak for a particular community.[6]

Following from the above, a second question for a 'critical terrorism studies' defined in terms of a concern with emancipation and building on the Welsh School framework might be: what are (immanent) possibilities for emancipatory change in the context of contemporary practices of 'terrorism' and 'counterterrorism'? As noted, tensions and inconsistencies are central here and various elements of the 'war on terror' suggest themselves readily as tensions of significant proportions. First, we might explore the extent to which the 'war on terror' is self-defeating in rendering participating states' populations more vulnerable to 'terrorist' attack. This form of critique is becoming so prominent that it has recently been expressed by law enforcement and intelligence agencies, particularly in participant states in the Iraq war (see BBC, 2005; Burke, 2008; Dodd, 2006). This suggests tensions at the heart of practices justified on the basis of *redressing* the threat of 'terrorism', and as such also suggests possibilities for a movement away from the use of violence to respond to violence.

Another central tension or inconsistency that provides possibilities for emancipatory change concerns the role of liberal, democratic values in responses to 'terrorism'. While political leaders engaged in 'counterterrorism' often express a rhetorical commitment to the defence of democracy and liberal values *from* terrorism, they have also frequently participated in actions that serve to undermine democratic institutions and values. Such a critique is again particularly applicable to the 'war on terror' which has seen participant states pursuing restrictive 'anti-terror' legislation, for example, or engaged in illiberal and illegal detention practices such as extraordinary rendition flights, the use of torture, and the long-term incarceration of 'enemy combatants' at facilities such as Camp X-Ray in Guantanamo Bay. There are, of course, a range of legal and ethical concerns associated with such practices, not least when viewed within a liberal ethical framework (Bellamy, 2006). The demand to meet standards set by political leaders themselves (such as the protection of liberal democratic values) is an important basis for bringing about (emancipatory) change. Adam Roberts (2005) has also suggested in this context that aside from the obvious moral concerns with such illiberal practices, historically successful campaigns to resolve conflicts characterised by the use of 'terror' have generally avoided suspending liberal democratic values and have instead utilised open deliberative mechanisms. Indeed, Anthony Burke (2008: 40–41) endorses non-violent responses to 'terrorism' as much because of their strategic effectiveness as their normative preferability. Here, emancipatory change becomes simultaneously ethically desirable and politically efficacious.

Finally, the idea of the global promotion of liberal democracy and freedom through the 'war on terror' could be (and indeed has been) contrasted with the willingness of the United States and its allies to cooperate with illiberal regimes in the fight against terrorism, to the point of sanctioning the repression of domestic dissident groups in cooperative states. Previous examples of cooperation with the regimes of China and Pakistan suggest themselves here, as does cooperation with states such as Russia and Malaysia (to name a few). Again, there is a core tension between a stated concern with the protection or promotion of democracy on the one hand and the support for political regimes simply not in the business of democracy on the other. This has certainly made life more difficult for a range of dissident political groups in these states either through direct support for governmental 'anti-terror' practices or the removal of pressure on these regimes from powerful external actors (see Foot, 2005; Herring, 2008).

Nevertheless, this tension does provide possibilities for critique and change, evident in increasing pressure on the Bush administration from Congress to develop or keep in place limits on military cooperation with non-democratic regimes, for example (Pessin, 2005).

Together, these forms of immanent critique provide a basis for fundamentally destabilising the dominant discourses of 'counterterror' that legitimise and increase the likelihood of violence. More fundamentally, as a form of praxis, immanent critique is based on the commitment to the idea that there are always voices articulating alternatives in any context, no matter how unpromising. The task of the critical theorist then becomes one of amplifying these voices. As it applies to the study of 'terrorism' here, locating possibilities for emancipation extends beyond a recognition of tensions and inconsistencies to an examination of the range of ways in which different actors contest dominant accounts of 'terrorism' and 'counterterrorism', articulate more inclusive and cosmopolitan visions of community, and suggest alternatives to violence. Non-governmental organisations and minor political parties regularly articulate such alternatives. Both domestic and international human rights NGOs have highlighted illiberal practices and precisely drawn attention to the contradictions inherent in governments' anti-terror campaigns.[7] And in conflict situations themselves, grassroots movements and moderate voices on both sides of conflicts have articulated alternatives to violence, often in cooperation with like-minded groups and individuals on the 'other side' (see Maoz, 2004). Pointing to and amplifying these voices is central to an emancipatory praxis concerned with opening up possibilities for non-repressive communication.

A third question, following from the global cosmopolitan ethical framework elaborated by the Welsh School and evident in broader critical theory, might be: who are the most vulnerable? Rather than working with the usually unquestioned assumption of the need to prioritise the interests of a particular vision and membership of the nation-state, an emancipatory approach necessitates attention to the question of which people are most at risk from 'terrorism' and responses to it in international politics? Of course, the most obvious place to start in this context are those non-combatant civilians killed through 'terrorist' violence and counter-violence. Depending of course on how 'terrorism' is defined, we might identify here the 37,000 killed in conflict between the Kurdish separatist group the PKK and the Turkish government in the 1980s; the 5,000 killed in the second Intifada in Israel-Palestine from 2000 until mid 2007; or the 3,700 killed in conflict relating to 'The Troubles' in Northern Ireland from the late 1960s. But what is it that ties these casualties together in terms of making sense of vulnerability? Here, we might suggest that such people have in part been rendered vulnerable by those claiming to be acting in their name. While there are clearly choices about how others respond to even the most shocking acts of violence, the violence that groups such as the IRA or the Turkish government employed, encouraged, and endorsed in the names of their constituents, both directly took lives and indirectly contributed to a context in which violent responses (again involving the loss of life) became possible. The most vulnerable here might be viewed as those 'acted for'. Various attempts to contest such claims, evident in the 'not in our name' slogans of the anti-Iraq war movement, can be viewed as attempts to reclaim political agency and contest the rights of leaders to justify violence in the name of constituents. They also arguably evoke the recognition of ethical responsibility towards those outside the state, including most prominently in the above example to potential victims of violence in Iraq, at least 85,000 of whom would be killed from the start of Operation Enduring Freedom in 2003 to mid 2008 (www.iraqbodycount.org).

In the context of 'counterterror' campaigns, some of the other particularly vulnerable groups include those political dissidents conflated with 'terrorists' (noted earlier) or others such as 'suspect communities' whose marginalisation or oppression is in part justified on the basis of the 'terrorist threat'. Perhaps the most prominent example here are refugees and asylum seekers, among the most vulnerable people in the world. In states such as Australia, hard-line approaches to asylum seekers have been justified on the basis of the 'terrorist' threat, to the point of suggesting that asylum seekers may be 'terrorists' seeking to gain entry to the country (M. McDonald, 2005: 305–308). Another prominent example here is that of those Palestinians who have lost their homes and livelihoods as a result of Israel's security barrier (Falah, 2004), defined as a measure to reduce the threat of 'terrorism'. The most vulnerable may also include victims of opportunity costs: those who have been put most at risk by the changing set of priorities and commitments entailed through the pursuit of the 'war on terror' itself. In this context, we might talk about impoverished populations in the third world, where humanitarian aid from participant states in the 'war on terror' has either been reduced or redirected towards more overtly strategic objectives (Reuters, 2004). A more direct example is that of the US response to Hurricane Katrina in 2005 which was undermined by the presence of National Guard forces in Iraq. Stephen Zunes (2005) locates the slow nature of the government's response in its broader and changed security priorities. A focus on vulnerability in this sense – those most at risk from shifting political priorities associated with the 'war on terror' – reminds us of the continued central role of historical materialist concerns with inequality and deprivation in the emancipatory project (see Herring, 2008).

This set of people and groups – those drawn into conflict by violent action carried out in their name, those conflated with 'terrorists', and the victims of opportunity costs – are ultimately those most at risk from 'terrorism' and responses to it. An emancipatory approach would entail drawing attention to and prioritising the needs and concerns of these most vulnerable, contesting in the process the moral relevance of state boundaries and the legitimacy of violent action carried out in the name of the 'nation'.

A fourth and final question suggested here is: what would emancipation look like in the context of approaches to and practices of 'terrorism' and 'counterterrorism' in international politics? This type of question is central for the Welsh School given the commitment to develop practically engaged and grounded theory (Booth, 1997, 2008). At some level, this can be viewed as a pre-emptive response to one of the most prominent critiques of critical theory: that the conditions for the realisation of emancipation (such as Habermas's 'ideal speech situation') are utopian and almost impossible to recognise analytically much less imagine in practice. This criticism becomes less devastating if emancipation is conceived as 'a (strategic) process of freeing up' rather than 'a condition of being freed'. Viewed in such terms, and defined by Wyn Jones (1999: 76–78) as a concern with locating and outlining 'concrete utopias', it is easier to address questions about what emancipation might look like in contemporary contexts. Here, analyses might locate emancipatory practices in the increasing role of (previously marginalised) moderate voices and political representation of dissident groups and its relationship to diminishing frequency of 'terrorist' and 'counterterrorist' violence (see Burke, 2008: 47). Such processes have been evident in changing relationships between the Turkish government and Kurdish population in Turkey, and more recently between government and separatist groups in the Indonesian province of Aceh. In both cases, movements towards increased political representation and peace have been intimately related. Recognising such processes as emancipatory and asking how they came about and how applicable they might be to other contexts must be central to an emancipatory 'critical terrorism studies' agenda concerned with escaping the zero-sum logic of security that legitimises – and arguably encourages – violence.

One example of the myriad NGOs addressing the Arab-Israeli conflict is particularly illustrative of emancipatory practices and approaches at work in contemporary contexts often taken as paradigmatic of 'terrorism' and 'counterterrorism'. The American-based international NGO, 'A Different Future' (ADF), defines its remit as that of drawing attention to moderate voices advocating nonviolence and pursuing cooperative approaches to conflict. Specifically, it suggests that its role is that of:

> helping moderate majorities reclaim the public idea space and regain control over the policy agenda that will determine our collective futures. ADF uses communications experts to amplify the voices of Israelis and Palestinians who work together. We create new collective voices of Jewish, Christian and Muslim religious leadership, locally, nationally and internationally. If enabled, these voices can contain the violence that originates within their cultures more effectively than force from without.[8]
>
> (A Different Future, no date)

The commitments articulated here are emancipatory. This project is concerned with amplifying voices silenced by dominant discourses advocating violence; it is committed to opening up space for political dialogue and debate to a wider range of voices; it recognises the importance of locating possibilities for change within particular contexts rather than imposing them from outside; and it is ultimately suggestive of shared membership in a global community. This example suggests that rather than constituting an abstract idea never likely to be found in political practice, emancipation is in fact practised and advanced in a range of

Emancipation and critical terrorism studies 121

sites, albeit often those hidden from traditional accounts of international relations, security, and 'terrorism'. And to return to the understanding of emancipation endorsed here, such a commitment to opening up dialogic space for a wider range of voices to be heard is central to redressing the structures of inequality and deprivation that both constitute forms of violence and provide conditions in which the specific use of force is more likely to occur (see Herring, 2008).

Of course, a range of other questions suggest themselves beyond the four I have identified as arising from a central concern with emancipation. In the questions noted – and examples cited of those working with such questions – it is also important to note that analysts may not self-identify as working within an emancipatory critical theoretical tradition. As Richard Wyn Jones (2005: 216) has argued persuasively, however, it is difficult to develop critiques of the status quo that are not at some level informed by an emancipatory impulse. Viewed in this light emancipation can certainly be conceived of as a common concern of those engaging in 'small c' critical approaches to the study of 'terrorism' or indeed global security politics. For many in this context, emancipation may be best advanced through the freeing up of space to think, speak, and write differently about what 'terrorism' means, how it might be studied, and how to make sense of effective responses to it.

Emancipation: dangers and possibilities

Positioning emancipation as central to the study of 'terrorism' is not without its dangers and certainly not without its critics. Emancipation is without doubt both universalist and utopian. Critics of the former – particularly those working in the post-structural tradition – express concerns about the dangers of forcing others to be free, denying the legitimacy of difference, and imposing values that are ultimately Western in philosophical origin. In global politics generally, such concerns developed from the twentieth century experience of violent Marxist revolution, justified on the basis of a particular conception of emancipation. In a more contemporary setting, such concerns might seem relevant to President Bush's use of the language of 'emancipation' to justify military intervention in Afghanistan and Iraq as part of the 'war on terror'. At this level, advancing the normative imperative of emancipation arguably risks contributing to the possibility of its invocation as intellectual ballast for violent crusades involving the 'enforcement' of freedom.

But rather than illustrating the inherent problems of emancipation as a guiding normative principle, it may well be that precisely the internal tensions and contradictions of practices carried out in the name of 'emancipation' (the tens of thousands of dead among those 'liberated' in the case of Iraq, for example) provide the basis for immanent critique and *genuine* emancipatory change. Genuine emancipation cannot, as Booth (2008: 77) has suggested, be achieved at the expense of others (except those who benefit from oppression), while the reliance on violent means to eliminate the 'terrorist' threat will ultimately ensure that the stated ends sought will not be those realised. Emancipation is certainly universalist, but for

Booth the commitment to the removal of unnecessary structural constraints and the democratisation of the public sphere is one that is given meaning in particular historical, political, and social settings. And in response to criticisms of his universalism, Booth (2005: 181) is (typically) blunt in suggesting that 'relativist thinking is calculated to replicate only a dismal and impoverished world', further arguing that 'what matters is not where ideas come from but how well they travel'.

On the question of utopianism, the Welsh School approach has been viewed as dangerous from opposite directions. The more common criticism of critical theory, expressed by Mark Neufeld (2004), is the danger of building a theory based on the need to realise an ideal speech situation or reach some endpoint of emancipation. In response, Welsh School proponents have been at pains to develop grounded and strategic approaches to emancipation, captured in the method of immanent critique and the goal of realising 'concrete utopias' (Wyn Jones, 2005). But here, others have implied that such a commitment to 'groundedness' risks either collapsing the theory back into traditional, problem-solving theory (Rengger, 2001), or eschews a concern with transcendental critique – forms of critique which seek to 'imagine' alternatives in situations that are least conducive to progressive change (Burke, 2007a; Lee Koo, 2007). These perceived dangers or weaknesses raise important questions and will always be difficult to fully resolve given the desire of emancipatory critical theorists to reclaim politics as ethics and develop a practical philosophy for societal change (M. Hoffman, 1987: 234). A response would nevertheless emphasise the central task for theorists to engage reflexively with hard cases of contemporary political practice, and suggest that regardless of how unpromising a context appears to be, there are *always* immanent possibilities for emancipation.

This chapter has pointed to the possibility for and benefits of building a 'critical terrorism studies' on the basis of a normative concern with emancipation, one informed by the insights and framework of the Welsh School of critical security studies. I have suggested in particular that central to realising emancipation is the opening up of discursive space. As applied to the 'war on terror', this approach would involve recognising the central importance of empowering those moderate voices on both sides marginalised in the 'war on terror' itself: often those voices most vulnerable to violence and the changing political priorities associated with it. It would also point to the narrowing of space for debate – a feature of the politics of the 'war on terror' – as a danger in itself and as fundamentally inconsistent with redressing the threat of 'terrorism'.

While the (forcible) application of particular versions of emancipation may be troubling, and while the task of engaging in practical philosophy for emancipatory ends is both complex and difficult, a 'critical terrorism studies' defined in emancipatory terms has a great deal of analytical and normative promise. The questions encouraged by adopting an emancipatory approach are crucial to developing a sophisticated and reflexive understanding of 'terrorist' violence and counter-violence, one informed by a set of core ethical commitments to the most vulnerable.

Emancipation and critical terrorism studies 123

Notes

1 For their insightful comments on an earlier version of this chapter, I would like to thank James Brassett, Chris Browning, Tony Burke, Mark Fowle, Kath Gleeson, Jack Holland and, of course, the editors.
2 On the above distinctions, particularly as they apply to IR/security studies, see Devetak (2005); and Wyn Jones (1999).
3 Though Booth (2008) and Wyn Jones (1999) arguably emphasise the material dimensions of emancipation while Linklater's (2005) account of emancipatory change prioritises the expansion of dialogic communities.
4 Of course, government funding does not preclude critical research on 'terror' and responses to it, as Weinberg and Eubank (2008) argue.
5 Such a concern need not be restricted to approaches working explicitly with a notion of emancipation. Indeed, it is suggestive of genealogical approaches that seek to trace how a particular meaning of 'terrorism' has become dominant.
6 This is arguably relevant to Bin Laden's representation of the 'Islamic community' in the context of the 'war on terror' (see O'Hagan, 2004). On the relationship between the role of moderate voices and the likelihood of violence more generally, the International Crisis Group (2007) suggests that the increasing threat posed by radical militant terrorism in Pakistan is linked to President Musharraf's marginalisation of moderate voices within Pakistan.
7 Amnesty International, for example, has highlighted the ways in which practices in the 'war on terror' have contravened states' commitments to uphold the UN Declaration on Human Rights, and suggested that when 'governments use torture and other ill-treatment, they resort to the tactics of terror'.
8 www.adifferentfuture.org. This goal shares much with that of another US-based international NGO, OneVoice, which 'aims to amplify the voice of the overwhelming but heretofore silent majority of moderates who wish for peace and prosperity, empowering them to demand accountability from elected representatives.' (www.onemillionvoices.org).

7 Middle East area studies and terrorism studies
Establishing links via a critical approach

Katerina Dalacoura

Introduction

The questions raised by 'critical terrorism studies' are nowhere more poignant and pertinent than in the context of Middle East area studies. The emotive debate around the 'T' word is at its most shrill in the region, and its usage is at its most flippant and polemical. The foreign and security policies of Israel and Iran, the activities of Hamas and Hezbollah, the 'war on terror' waged by the United States following the attacks of 9/11, and the activities and statements of al-Qaeda and its various franchises in the Maghreb, Mesopotamia, and the Arabian Peninsula; all of the above are hotly contested, with each side in the various intermeshed disputes claiming moral righteousness and accusing the other of being a 'terrorist'.

But if terrorist actors operating *from* and *in* the Middle East currently occupy the greatest attention in public debate and commentary in Western and Middle Eastern contexts, intellectual intercourse between terrorism studies and Middle East area studies is problematic, and for those who attempt it, disturbing. This is mainly because the two fields are so incongruent. On the one hand, terrorism specialists who deal with Middle East terrorist actors often do so in a superficial manner, ignoring the specificities and realities of the region or assuming that the causes of their actions can be reduced to 'religion'. On the other hand, Middle East area studies, suffering from an isolationist tendency which tends to afflict all area studies, rarely make use of the wider perspectives and conceptual tools that terrorism studies can offer, thereby reinforcing the perception that terrorism in the Middle East is a unique phenomenon. Furthermore, as both terrorism and Middle Eastern studies tend to be under-theorised (Gerges, 1991; Teti, 2007), conceptual linkages between the two fields are rendered quite weak.

This chapter attempts to bridge the gap between Middle East area studies and terrorism studies. Using empirical material, it draws on those methodologies and approaches within Middle East area studies which in my view contribute towards making the study of terrorism less simplistic, politically biased, and de-contextualised. These are contested of course, but they include at a very minimum: a focus on the historical background knowledge of the region; an emphasis on the common characteristics of the region but also on individual societies as discrete entities; an attunement to local social and cultural particularities, including but not exclusively through the knowledge of local languages; and – as is the case with all area studies – an interdisciplinary approach. More particularly, the analysis here draws on a strong methodological tradition in Middle East area studies which allows indigenous voices to be heard and interacts with the subject of its enquiry, as opposed to dominating or controlling it through the construction of knowledge. Thus armed with these methodologies and approaches, and using particular case studies, the chapter seeks to provide substance to an emerging – and still very contested – field of 'critical terrorism studies', in contradistinction to a traditional/conventional discussion of the terrorism phenomenon. It also, in turn, considers what a 'critical terrorism studies' can offer to Middle East area studies and how it can enrich it.

This is not the place to revisit the theoretical ground of what a 'critical turn' in terrorism studies consists of, or how it challenges a traditional/conventional understanding of terrorism, given that this has been so widely covered in other chapters in this volume. However, a brief statement of the approach to critical terrorism studies used in this chapter is in order. A fundamental premise uniting the many variants of critical theory is that knowledge is constituted by human interests and that social science theories, far from being neutral, are embedded in social and political life. Within the boundaries of our specific subject, 'terrorism', a critical approach points to the dominant role of the state in 'framing' the problem. States have always resisted applying the description 'terrorist' to themselves, but are keen to use it on their opponents: terrorism has multiple uses in what critical theorists would call the 'hegemonic project' of states. But non-state actors also have hegemonic projects and employ terrorism, as act and speech act, to facilitate their realisation. Instead of taking a given situation at face value and then proceeding to 'solve a problem', a critical approach to terrorism studies encourages us to highlight the historical *context* in which political actors operate.

States and the 'terrorist' label

A number of traditional/conventional terrorism authors do acknowledge that states can be perpetrators of terrorism, either directly or as 'sponsors' of terrorist acts (see Wilkinson, 1984; see also Jackson, 2008b). However, there has been little detailed exploration of this phenomenon, resulting in the skewed perception that states can be excluded from consideration when studying the phenomenon of terrorism.[1] In traditional/conventional terrorism studies, 'terrorist' more often than not continues to refer exclusively to non-state actors, 'upstarts' who challenge the state or more generally the status quo. There are problems with this assumption. For the purposes of this chapter, terrorism is defined as

> a political act, ordinarily committed by an organized group, involving the intentional killing or other severe harming of non-combatants or the threat of

the same or the intentional severe damage to the property of non-combatants or the threat of the same.

(Coady, 1985: 52)

If a state intentionally kills or harms non-combatants or destroys their property, and does so with political purpose, why should it not be described as terrorist?

The contribution of area studies, and Middle East studies in particular, to the debate on the state-centredness of traditional/conventional terrorism studies is potentially enormous. The Middle East as a region is persistently associated with the terrorism phenomenon, not least by the world media. But the association, more often than not, is between terrorism and non-state actors, with states and governments remaining on the margins of the discussion, except when counter-terrorism is concerned. However, the meticulous and careful study of specific government policies and the use of case studies from the Middle East can reveal the dominance of state interests in the production of terrorism knowledge and the terrorism discourse.

An important first case which can illustrate the various aspects of the debate on the state-centredness of traditional/conventional terrorism studies is Israel's policies in the Occupied Palestinian Territories. These policies have been criticised for intentionally aiming at non-combatants in targeted assassinations,[2] and also frequently resulting in the death of bystanders (Amnesty International, 2003). The application of collective punishments, such as the demolition of the houses of suicide bombers (Amnesty International, 2002), can also be described as serving to instill fear in the civilian population through destroying property and also, at times, the lives of the bombers' families. Israel has also been castigated for the indiscriminate use of firepower against the Palestinian Occupied Territories and during the war of summer 2006 with Hezbollah in Lebanon (Human Rights Watch, 2006a, 2007b).

In a second example, the actions of the United States in Iraq since 2003, but also elsewhere in the Middle East, are described by critics as involving the intentional killing or harming of non-combatants and of their property.[3] Criticism of the US invasion of Iraq in 2003 often refers to the tremendous cost to its civilian population. To describe this as terrorism is more emotive than accurate, however, given that whatever the responsibility of the Bush administration in initiating the 2003 war in Iraq, the killing of civilians by US forces is not deliberate policy and, although it undoubtedly occurs, is punishable and sometimes punished by US law. Nevertheless, US and UK forces in Iraq have also been accused more accurately of human rights violations against Iraqi civilians, including unlawful killings (Amnesty International, 2007). Additionally, the infamous pictures of abuse in Abu Ghraib prison have thrown oil on the proverbial fire. Furthermore, the United States is accused of being engaged in terrorism in the Middle East by association, because of its material and political support of Israeli[4] and some Arab policies.

Middle East states can also be criticised for being terrorist actors because of how they treat their own civilian populations. Algeria is a prominent example.

During the civil war which erupted after a military coup averted the imminent Islamic Salvation Front (FIS) victory in the legislative elections of January 1992, regime measures against the Islamists were spearheaded by the 'eradicator' factions within the army, who opposed dialogue and believed that the Islamist challenge must be eliminated by force of arms. In its battle against Islamist insurgency in the 1990s, the Algerian state, and specifically the Algerian army, used many similar methods to those of the armed Islamist terrorist groups (to the point of employing hooded commandoes, nicknamed 'ninjas', who engaged in summary executions of non-combatants) (Pierre and Quandt, 1995: 131). They perpetrated a policy of torture and extra-judicial executions, 'disappearances', mass arrests, and arbitrary detention (Hafez, 2004: 46). The Algerian government was also accused of complicity in some of the most vicious Islamist violence, or at least of turning a blind eye to massacres while they were being carried out. The publication in France of Habib Souaïdia's book, *The Dirty War*, strengthened allegations that the army took part in civilian massacres, sometimes disguised as Islamists, in order to fire popular revulsion against them (Souaïdia, 2001). Here again it may be difficult to disentangle fact from rumour. For example, country specialist Hugh Roberts has argued that what appeared to have been deliberate army complicity to Islamist massacres was more probably due to a temporary paralysis in the army's command structure (Middle East Report, 1998). Nevertheless, the use of terrorising methods by the Algerian army against the Algerian population is indisputable.

The Egyptian state employed similarly brutal methods to crush extremist Islamist groups from the 1980s onwards, and especially between 1992 and 1998. Government forces did not hesitate to kill Islamist leaders publicly, the prime example being the assassination of Ala Muhyi al-Din, the official spokesman of the Gamaa, in 1990.[5] Whole communities, particularly in Upper Egypt but also within the poorer parts of Cairo, suffered from repression and violence by the Egyptian state. After the extremists declared an 'Islamic Republic' in Imbaba, a slum area in central Cairo, the government sent in 16,000 soldiers to 'liberate' it. Thousands were arrested in an indiscriminate fashion and thrown into prison without trial where torture was widely and routinely used. Supporters, families of the suspects, and anyone displaying outward signs of religiosity were targeted. The state used 'hostage-taking', whereby the relatives, especially the wives of militants, were detained until the latter gave themselves up. The number of death sentences and executions reached unprecedented levels (Hafez, 2003: 84–88).[6]

It is evident from the above discussion that the debate on state responsibility in planning and carrying out acts which can be described as 'terrorist' is ongoing. It is not the place here to arrive at the establishment of clear criteria to answer the question 'should the label "terrorist" be applied to states?' Instead, this section used cases from the Middle East to highlight that considerable ambiguity surrounds state actions and that the description or definition of these actions is contestable and politicised. Ultimately, the important contribution of Middle East area studies to this debate is to disentangle facts from emotions and polemics.

Religion and terrorism

Contemporary studies have increasingly focused on religion, and Islam in particular, as a cause of the 'new terrorism'. Bruce Hoffman's statement is typical of this trend: 'the religious imperative for terrorism is the most important defining characteristic of terrorist activity today'. What is more, he argues that terrorism motivated by religion uses different means from secular terrorism and is more destructive (B. Hoffman, 2006: 82–83). Jessica Stern similarly emphasises 'religion' as a cause of terrorism (Stern, 2003), and Marc Sageman's book on global jihadism begins with an analysis of 'Islam' and its concepts (Sageman, 2004).[7]

Area specialists who appreciate the local context and the specific historical circumstances of radical Islamist movements are best positioned to counter the idea that religion *as such* leads individuals or groups to take up terrorism. Although there is no unanimity on these issues within Middle East area studies, the field contains a strong tradition which, first, points to secular political objectives and ideologies which lie behind religious imagery and discourse. Second, it investigates the subtle overlap between ideational and material factors in explaining the causes of Islamism. Finally, Middle East area studies allows for the possibility that Islam's (and Islamism's) various interpretations are determined by secular social, political, and economic factors.[8] According to this approach the reasons why the most extreme variant of Islamism opts for violent methods should not primarily or exclusively be sought in the precepts of the Islamic religion.

There are no better cases to illustrate this controversy than Hamas and Hezbollah, both considered archetypical purveyors of 'religious terrorism'. The debate over whether Hamas should be described as a terrorist entity is ongoing. The US placed Hamas on the list of Foreign Terrorist Organizations in 1997,[9] Israel consistently and exclusively represents Hamas as a terrorist organisation,[10] and the European Union also placed the movement on the list of terrorist organisations in 2003.[11] Hamas and its supporters, on the other hand, describe themselves as a legitimate armed resistance movement struggling for Palestinian liberation.[12] They justify the use of terrorist methods such as suicide bombings (also used in the post-2000 second Intifada, one must recall, by the armed wing of the non-Islamist al-Aqsa Martyrs' Brigades) using three arguments.[13] First, that the objective of liberating Palestine would be unattainable given Israel's overwhelming power, unless terrorist means were used. Second, it presents its violent acts as reciprocal to Israel's targeting of civilians.[14] Third, Hamas argues that because all Israelis have to serve in the army, the distinction between combatants and non-combatants dissolves in Israeli society (Bloom, 2006: 39). Hamas is also at pains to differentiate itself from groups such as al-Qaeda by arguing that the type and purpose of its political violence is of a different category (Usher, 2005: 3).

The controversy over whether Hamas is a terrorist entity is interesting in itself, but is also highly relevant to the debate on religion and terrorism. In contrast to those who argue that Hamas's violence flows from an uncompromising religious rationale (B. Hoffman, 2006: 92), Hamas's own justification demonstrates an instrumental understanding of terrorist violence, and one that is, furthermore, focused on defending the Palestinian nation. The shift away from 'religion' as an explanation for Hamas's actions is further reinforced if we look at the movement in its totality, instead of seeing it as a single-purpose monolith (see Gunning, this volume). Hamas's use of terrorist methods falls within its wider use of guerrilla tactics.[15] Apart from its association with violence, Hamas is a social movement and a political party which won a clear majority in national legislative elections in January 2006, and which has displayed the ability to pragmatically adapt its ideology and goals to political circumstance (see Roy, 2003; Klein, 2007; Gunning, 2007c).

The example of Hezbollah can also serve as a useful illustration of the controversy on religion and terrorism. Although since the early 1990s Hezbollah's complicity in terrorist acts has been a matter of dispute, the movement can more firmly be linked to terrorist attacks in the early 1980s, in particular against US and French peacekeepers in October 1983; in Buenos Aires, Argentina, in 1992 and 1994; and (much more tenuously through a 'Saudi Hezbollah' group), to the Khobar Towers in Saudi Arabia in 1996. The controversial question of targeting civilians in the conflict with Israel is also relevant to Hezbollah's characterisation.[16]

In justifying its acts and even its very existence, Hezbollah uses a religious discourse which is closely linked to the Shia Islamism emanating from the Islamic Republic of Iran. But, alongside that, it claims that it has been conducting a war of liberation against Israel's occupation of South Lebanon since the mid 1980s and depicts its violence against Israel as part of guerrilla warfare with the aim of resisting occupation (Harik, 2004: 2). Hezbollah's justification of violence is similar to that of Hamas, in that it is instrumental and focuses on the defense of the Lebanese and Arab nation against Israel. Furthermore, placing Hezbollah in its local context brings into the picture its multiple roles: provider of welfare and charity; political party; and protector of Shia interests within Lebanon's inter-sectarian system. Ultimately, an area studies perspective which focuses on the particular political Lebanese context, plus the regional connections of the movement, allows us to avoid reducing a complex set of motivations and discourses to 'religion'.

State hegemony and the terrorism discourse

Traditional/conventional terrorism studies is geared towards an 'objective' assessment of the terrorist threat and the effectiveness of counterterrorism methods in dealing with this threat, thereby reinforcing the image of the state as 'protector' of the public good. Although undeniably a threat to states (as well as to society), terrorism can also serve in buttressing their authority or, as critical theorists would put it, supporting their hegemonic projects. The Middle East offers countless examples of this process.

In the current political configuration of pro-Western versus anti-Western states and actors, which is one of the main fault-lines of Middle East regional politics, the term 'terrorism' has multiple uses. The United States – for which, more than any of its Western counterparts 'terrorism' is a foreign policy cornerstone – designates the 'axis' of its opponents, Iran, Syria, Sudan, and until recently Libya, as terrorist states or 'state sponsors of terrorism'. Being a 'state sponsor of terrorism' involves plotting attacks and dispatching agents to other countries (or indeed your own) to carry out killings or other violent attacks with a political motivation.

The arch-villains in the Middle East, according to successive US administrations, are Syria, and more notoriously still, Iran. Their alleged support of terrorism plays a key role in this characterisation. Since the Islamic Revolution of 1979, numerous acts of international terrorism have been attributed to Iran, including attacks in Saudi Arabia, Argentina, Germany, and Lebanon. According to the US State Department's Country Reports on Terrorism of 2007, 'Iran remained the most active state sponsor of terrorism', both through its support of Hezbollah and Palestinian terrorist groups (including Hamas) and because of its attempts to destabilise Iraq. Syria is suspected of the assassination of former Lebanese Prime Minister Rafiq Hariri in 2002 in Lebanon, and a number of other anti-Syrian journalists and politicians since then. It is designated as a 'state supporter of terrorism' because of its support of Hezbollah and a number of Palestinian terrorist groups (US Department of State, 2007: Chapter 3).

The description of Iran and Syria as 'state sponsors of terrorism' may have been valid in the past, but it has most recently come to depend on their support of Hamas and Hezbollah – and therefore the characterisation of groups such as Hamas and Hezbollah as terrorist organisations with all the problems that this simplification entails, as discussed above. If we remove Hamas and Hezbollah from the picture, the evidence that Iran and Syria are 'state sponsors of terrorism' is much less overwhelming. By the State Department's own admission, with the exception of Syria's suspected, though yet unproven, assassination of Hariri and the others, 'Syria has not been implicated directly in an act of terrorism since 1986' (US Department of State, 2007: Chapter 3). Iran expert Gary Sick argues that Iran stopped its policy of assassinations by 1993 and that its direct involvement in supporting terrorist groups has declined since the early days of the Revolution (Sick, 1998: 13, 15). Attacks such as those in Khobar, Saudi Arabia, in 1996 have been attributed to Iran (and its ally Hezbollah), but the evidence remains highly contested.

Terrorism is an absolutely vital concern for US foreign policy in the Middle East. It is fascinating to observe the prominent role cooperation, or lack thereof, on the terrorism issue has in determining a country's relationship with the United States and the aura which surrounds the issue. This was most evident in the case of Libya. Its 'renunciation' of terrorism in 2003, which led to its removal from the list of state sponsors of terrorism in June 2006, had a ritualistic air about it (US Department of State, 2007: Chapter 2). Sudan was for many years suspected of being a supporter of international terrorism. However, according to the US State Department, it has recently become a 'strong partner' of the United States in the 'war on terror' (US Department of State, 2007: Chapter 3).

Terrorism, therefore, has multiple uses in what critical theorists would describe as the United States' 'hegemonic project' in the Middle East, and plays a key role in the conflict between Western and anti-Western states. But its contribution to the hegemonic projects of Middle Eastern states in relation to their own societies is also crucially important, particularly in situations of internal conflict. Despite important exceptions, such as the Kurdistan Worker's Party (PKK) and the Mujahedin-e Khalq (MKO), to be discussed below, more often than not nowadays these conflicts pit states against radical Islamist challengers. In these contexts, regimes present themselves as the defenders of 'the people' or 'society' and its 'values' against a brutal enemy who does not hesitate to indiscriminately attack civilians.

The case of Algeria is instructive here once again. The Algerian regime tried hard to tar the Islamic Salvation Front (FIS) with the 'terrorist' brush from 1993–4 onwards; this was a key element of the 'eradicator' discourse discussed above.[17] In this, the regime was considerably successful. Its efforts and the polarisation of Algerian society more broadly after the civil war of the 1990s, meant that the whole Islamist movement, not just the extremists, has come to be associated with terrorism. Walking in the streets of Algiers in 2007 – long after a political process of amnesties, referenda and national reconciliation programmes were meant to have put the Algerian civil war to rest – a journalist friend would point to any passing (male) individual clad in a long white robe and beard and exclaim, half-jokingly: 'Terrorist!'

Tunisia offers another good example of the uses of the 'terrorism' label in the hegemonic project of states. President Zine el Abidine Ben Ali came to power in 1987. In the two to three years after assuming office, alarmed by the challenge that the Islamist al-Nahda movement appeared to pose to his rule, Ben Ali moved against it. The repression that the Islamists have suffered in Tunisia since then has been severe and is a measure of the profound authoritarianism of the regime. As Human Rights Watch put it: 'The government [of Tunisia] uses the threat of terrorism and religious extremism to crack down on peaceful dissent.' Furthermore, the 'Tunisian authorities claim that they have long been at the forefront of combating terrorism and extremism', even though not a single terrorist attack occurred in Tunisia between 1991 and 2002 (Human Rights Watch, 2007a). Ben Ali's government has used the fear of 'terrorism' extensively to legitimise its repressive practices. But the fact of the matter is that al-Nahda is one of the most moderate (though not necessarily liberal) Islamist movements in the region, and that its association with terrorism was weak and occurred only in the mid 1980s.[18] The more recent, sporadic terrorist activity in Tunisia in 2002 and 2006–7 has not been linked to al-Nahda.

Non-state actors and the hegemony of counter-hegemony

The previous section discussed how the terrorism discourse can buttress states' hegemonic control over society. But a Middle East area studies perspective which focuses on the politics of the region more widely and more deeply, and takes 'indigenous' discourses seriously, demonstrates that non-state actors are also involved in building hegemonic projects. It shows that in constructing counter-hegemonic discourses, Middle East state and non-state actors ironically also seek to build their own hegemonies.

Robert Cox describes as 'counter-hegemonic' those forces which can bring about fundamental changes in world order.[19] Similarly, 'counter hegemonic forces could be states, such as a coalition of Third World states which struggles to undo the dominance of "core" countries, or non-state actors such as classes, or new social movements' (Devetak, 1996: 160). In the current political configuration in the Middle East, an anti-Western cluster of states and non-state actors is forming around Iran and 'terrorism' plays an important role in their counter-hegemonic discourse against the West. In effect, this discourse describes the United States, those Western countries closely associated with it such as the United Kingdom, and their allies, primarily Israel, as *the* purveyors of terrorism in the region. The logic is simple, albeit flawed (as it rests on numbers, not the type of violence employed): they and their policies are the cause of the largest number of civilian deaths in the Middle East.[20]

Non-state actors also play a vital role in this formation of counter-hegemonic forces, and in doing so challenge their own regimes as well as their Western backers. Within a worldview defined by the pernicious yet increasingly widely accepted 'clash of civilizations' between 'Islam' and 'the West', many of these non-state actors are Islamist movements. In constructing their own Islamist anti-Western worldviews and discourses, these groups, moderate and extremist, also seek to extend hegemonic control over their supporters. Although the source of their hegemony is not a particular class, Islamist movements do garner support through a network of social services and institutions, for example, mosques, clinics, schools, and welfare provision in time of need. But ideas, reinforced through peer pressure and the need to conform, are also crucially important in constructing alternative Islamist social worlds. The image of a terroristic and terrorising West is vital in the construction of the 'Other' on which alternative Islamist worldviews vitally depend. The idea of clashing worlds is strengthened by juxtaposing the violence perpetrated by the West with the 'pure' act of opposing it. In this way, acts such as suicide bombings can be placed in a different category to terrorism and described as feats of resistance.

Examples of this process abound. In Palestine during the second Intifada, being a *shahid* (martyr) was an honor, evident in the admiration and respect bestowed on the families of suicide bombers. An even more relevant case is Hezbollah, already discussed above in a different context. Hezbollah views the world as divided into 'oppressors' and 'oppressed', an idea formulated by the ideologues of the Iranian Revolution and in particular, Imam Khomeini (Saad-Ghorayeb, 2002: 16). Terrorism is a centrepiece in this worldview. According to Hezbollah, 'Israel's successive invasions [of Lebanon], its occupation of Lebanese territory, its indiscriminate, and often surgical, bombardment of civilian areas, in addition to its unlawful detention or "kidnapping" of Lebanese civilians, render it a terrorist state'. On the other hand, Palestinian suicide attacks against Israeli civilians are not seen as terrorist acts but as legitimate self-defence in the face of Israeli oppression. In other words, 'Hizballah's conception of terrorism hinges on the essential goodness or badness of a cause' (Saad-Ghorayeb, 2002: 146).

If terrorism is instrumental in the formation of an 'anti-Western' counter-hegemonic discourse throughout the Middle East, it also has many uses in other confrontations in the region. One fascinating example here is the conflict between the Islamic Republic of Iran and the Mojahedin-e Khalq (MKO), a leftist-Islamist organisation that very quickly turned against the Iranian government after the Revolution of 1979. From its base in Iraq, the MKO waged military attacks against Iran in the course of the Iran–Iraq war of 1980–8. It has also perpetrated a campaign of bombings against civilian targets within Iran since that time. The Islamic Republic responded with widespread suppression of the movement. It accuses the MKO of being a terrorist organisation (and the US and many European governments agree with this description, even though the former in particular has extended political support to the group). The MKO makes similar accusations against the Iranian government. Its ideology is imbued with violence and rests on maintaining total control over its members' personal lives.[21] The struggle between the Islamic Republic and the MKO remains unabated until the present time and the role of terrorist violence is instrumental in what can be described as a conflict between two opposing, hegemonic *versus* counter-hegemonic, discourses (see Human Rights Watch, 2005).

'Problem-solving' in the study of terrorism

Terrorist activity can be a security or 'technical' issue to be resolved by counterterrorism experts. But, more often than not, it is a symptom of a wider social, economic, and political malaise as opposed to a problem to be 'solved'.[22] An area studies perspective enables us to historicise the activities of terrorist actors by placing them in their regional Middle East context. By asking questions about these actors' origins and evolution, their relationship with the societies in which they emerge, and the reasons why they may enjoy social and political support, an area studies perspective can help to properly assess the causes and impact of particular terrorist phenomena.

The Egyptian case, already mentioned above in a different context, demonstrates that if a state treats extremist groups which employ terrorist methods simply as a security challenge, it will be encouraged to use excessive violence. The Egyptian state's heavy-handed tactics – as a popular reaction to the growing cost of terrorism in the 1990s – may appeared to have 'solved' the problem, particularly after the ceasefire proclaimed by the Gamaa Islamiya, its main challenger, in 1997–8. But success came at tremendous cost to human rights which further delegitimised the regime (as the problem was to some degree 'exported' to Afghanistan). It has been argued that the resurfacing of the terrorism problem, in another form, in Egypt after 2004 – in the attacks against tourist centres in the Sinai Peninsula, for example – is one of the outcomes of these heavy-handed tactics, as well as the state's ignoring of the socio-economic, cultural, and political problems which are at the heart of Sinai's problems (International Crisis Group, 2007).

A second interesting case illustrating how treating a terrorist challenge primarily as a security issue is profoundly problematic is the Kurdistan Workers' Party (PKK) in Turkey. The war between the Turkish state and the PKK lasted from 1984 until the arrest of Abdullah Öcalan in 1999 and has been estimated to have cost 37,000 lives. The description of the conflict is very much contested. Supporters of the PKK in Turkey and outside describe the movement as one of national liberation. The Turkish state, and a large part of Turkish society however, describe the PKK as a terrorist organisation. This discrepancy harks back to the discussion above on the terrorism label and the question of national liberation movements, but is not the issue here. Whichever way the Turkish state describes the PKK, the choice of treating it primarily as a security problem has meant that its ability to deal with it effectively has been severely limited. Instead of prioritising the economic, social, and political problems of the south-east of Turkey (which is where the PKK movement emerged), or addressing the wider issues facing the Kurdish minority in Turkey, the Turkish state opted for a military solution to the PKK challenge. The result has been a familiar one: while the problem appeared for a while to have been eliminated, it resurfaced after 2004 to haunt Turkey once again (Barkey, 2007).

Finally, al-Qaeda provides a useful counter-point to this discussion.[23] It is more accurate to describe al-Qaeda as an ideological label, a state of mind, and a mobilisational outreach program (Gerges, 2005: 40) rather than a movement with a central command, a well-defined membership, or even a coherent set of objectives. Al-Qaeda now is less of an organisation and more of an order, in which a central base provides ideological guidance to semi-autonomous cells around the world (Khalaf and Fidler, 2007: 8). The dismantling of the al-Qaeda central control structure (if, indeed, it ever existed) means that small semi-autonomous local affiliates and factions may be inspired by al-Qaeda and carry its ideological label, but have little or no direct support from it. These various franchises and branches act independently and carry out less sophisticated (though not necessarily less lethal) attacks. The 2004 and 2005 bombings in Madrid and London may be cases in point (Khalaf and Fidler, 2007: 217–218). Various groups in Saudi Arabia, Iraq, Algeria, Indonesia, Uzbekistan, Libya, and Morocco may also have links.[24]

The 'franchising' of the al-Qaeda brand to various local organisations has benefited the original outfit, but also the local groups which have for various reasons found it useful to adopt the al-Qaeda label. It is appropriate and effective to treat such organisations, which are sometimes mere fringe factions, as security problems and dispel the myth that they form part of a formidable transnational network. A perspective from Middle East area studies helps to think about how aspects of the status quo, and in this instance the US-led 'war on terror', reinforces al-Qaeda, not only by rendering its rhetoric resonant with target audiences but also with providing a renewed focus to local movements, such as the GSPC in Algeria, which were otherwise starting to become defunct. In this, as in other instances, the perspective from the region – 'from below', so to speak – is a useful corrective to the view that terrorism is a 'global' phenomenon requiring 'global' solutions.

Conclusion

This chapter has highlighted some possible contributions of Middle East area studies to terrorism studies using a critical approach. First, it has sought to demonstrate how a Middle East area studies perspective can add to the debate on the state-centredness of traditional/conventional terrorism studies. Case studies from the Middle East were used to show that state actions can be described or defined as 'terrorist', although no final answer was offered about the appropriateness of doing so. Second, the chapter employed an area studies methodology – which focuses on the local historical and political realities of Islamist movements – to question the idea that 'religion' as such is the cause of terrorist violence. Third, the chapter used a Middle East area studies perspective to show that terrorism and the terrorism discourse can be used in the construction of the hegemonic projects of states. But it also argued, fourth, that the terrorism discourse has its uses in the building up of the counter-hegemonic projects of state and non-state actors and that 'counter-hegemony' also involves the building of alternative hegemonic projects. Fifth and finally, a Middle East area studies perspective was used to indicate that the focus of traditional/conventional studies on terrorism as a security problem that can be 'solved' by the proper counterterrorism methods often (though not always) misses the point of what terrorism exactly represents.

But what, in turn, can critical terrorism studies offer Middle East area studies? The ultimate, practical objective of critical terrorism studies – as is the case with all variants of critical theory – is emancipation (albeit often an ill-defined one), and the point of revealing the interests which underpin a particular order is to change that order. A critical terrorism studies perspective therefore can offer Middle East area studies a series of tools for engaging with questions of terrorism without accepting dominant discourses at face value. By contrast to the 'embedded' nature of a considerable part of the terrorism expertise, critical terrorism scholars would keep a distance from the structures of state power by highlighting how state interests shape existing knowledge about terrorism and contribute to shaping the conditions which increase terrorism's appeal. Critical theorists would also question the world views constructed by non-state actors who also often use the terrorism concept to discourage dissent. Finally, as in cases of conflict resolution, critical theorists could attempt to achieve conciliation not by 'banging heads', but by bringing to light the interests which underlie opposing sides' seemingly irreconcilable positions (see for example, Miall *et al.*, 1999; Jones, 1999).

The role of critical scholarship and critical terrorism studies in relation to both state and non-state actors is particularly important in the Middle East where pressures to conform resulting from a sense of siege and the heavy hand of censorship and self-censorship often preclude the questioning of established wisdom and stifle vigorous debate. It is also important in a region where, even more than in the West, an ever-increasing number of anti-terrorism laws and measures profess to protect citizens' safety and security, but in reality often serve to further undermine their civil and political rights.

What recommendations for a future research agenda can we derive by establishing links between Middle East area studies and terrorism studies via a critical approach? A focus on the Middle East as a region, as opposed to Islam as a religion, will weaken the current emphasis on 'religion' and 'Islam' in particular as the cause of terrorism. The history of terrorism in the Middle East is a long one and in many ways, Islamist militant organisations follow in the traditions of and sit alongside secular terrorist groups such as (formerly) the PLO, the PKK, and the al-Aqsa Martyrs' Brigades. It is important to situate the so-called 'new terrorism' within this context. A future research agenda will combine the global perspective of terrorism experts with the local, regional knowledge of Middle East area studies. Doing so while using a critical approach shifts the focus away from 'counterterrorism' or 'security' narrowly defined, to 'emancipation' and 'human security'.

Notes

1 On this debate, see the contrasting positions of Horgan and Boyle, 2008, Weinberg and Eubank, 2008, and Blakely, 2008.
2 International law is clear on the point that Israeli assassinations target non-combatants. Amnesty International draws on the Fourth Geneva Convention and the Additional Protocols to assert the following point:

> Palestinians engaged in armed attacks against civilians or in clashes with Israeli forces are not combatants. They are civilians who lose their protected status for the duration of the armed engagement. They cannot be killed at any time other than while they are posing an imminent threat to lives. Proof or suspicion that a person participated in an armed attack at an earlier point does not justify, under international law, targeting them for death later on. Those who are not posing an imminent threat to lives may not be assassinated as punishment or as a preventive measure
>
> (Amnesty International, 2003: 4)

3 The leading exponent of this view is Noam Chomsky, although his focus is not solely the Middle East (see for example, Chomsky, 2001, 2006).
4 Note that the US State Department includes assassinations under its definition of 'terrorist activity', but does not apply this to Israel (see: www.state.gov/s/ct/rls/fs/37191.htm).
5 Interview with Diaa Rashwan, Al Ahram Center for Political and Strategic Studies, Cairo, 1 November 2007.
6 The annual reports and various statements of the Egyptian Organization of Human Rights also graphically describe the state's heavy-handed tactics (see www.eohr.org/).
7 See especially Chapter 1 on 'The Origins of the Jihad'.
8 While situated in the field of International Relations, as opposed to Middle East area studies, this approach informs Dalacoura, 2003.
9 For the relevant information, see: www.state.gov/s/ct/rls/fs/37191.htm.
10 See for example the website of the Israeli Ministry of Foreign Affairs at: www.mfa.gov.il/MFA; and the Israeli Embassy at: http://london.mfa.gov.il/mfm/web/main/missionhome.asp?MissionID=34&.

Middle East studies and terrorism studies 137

11 This trend also has important political consequences. While the European Union placed only the Qassam Brigades on its list of terrorist organisations in 2002, it placed the movement as a whole on it in 2003 (see: www.statewatch.org/news/ 2004/apr/03terrlists.htm. Note that the EU created the list after the 11 September 2001 attacks).
12 'Armed resistance' can be contrasted to 'revolutionary violence', which is how international terrorism was dubbed in Palestinian discourse in the 1970s (Sayigh, 1997: 210).
13 Academic discourse which is partial to Hamas also reflects that (see, for example, Tamimi, 2007).
14 Interview with Khaled Dwaib, PLC Member (Hamas), Bethlehem, 26 October 2007. Khaled Dwaib denied that Hamas had a strategy of targeting civilians and argued that they had been forced to do so from the mid 1990s because of the great difference in the ratio of Palestinians and Israelis killed and in retaliation for Israeli actions. These points were put to me by Hamas supporters on many occasions.
15 Israel does not distinguish between attacks against Israeli civilians and soldiers, describing both as terrorist acts (see, for example: www.mfa.gov.il/MFA/ Terrorism-+Obstacle+to+Peace/Palestinian+terror+before+2000/Fatal+Terrorist
+Attacks+in+Israel+Since+the+DOP+-S.htm). But if we accept Hamas's argument that it is at war with Israel, then the targeting of cities like Sderot using Qassam rockets can be described as violations of the principle of discrimination, not terrorism.
16 This is a complex issue. Hezbollah and Israel worked out tacit understandings to reciprocally avoid targeting civilians. In the 1990s, the two sides stuck to these 'rules of the game' whereby Israel would not attack civilian targets in Lebanon and Hezbollah would focus its actions on the Security Zone in South Lebanon (Norton, 2007: 83–84). Hezbollah's 'self-martyrdom missions' (suicide bombings) targeted, for the most part, Israeli officials and soldiers or Israeli allies in Lebanon which were, according to Hezbollah, legitimate resistance targets. The debate flared up once again during the war of summer 2006. Hezbollah placed weapons or ammunition inside civilian homes or villages, as well as sometimes firing rockets from densely populated areas, triggering deadly Israeli counter-strikes. However, while failing to take precautions to protect civilians, Human Rights Watch found that in very few cases were civilians intentionally used by Hezbollah as 'shields' from attack (Human Rights Watch, 2006b).
17 Email communication with Hugh Roberts, Algeria and political Islam expert, 28 November 2007.
18 The leader of al-Nahda, Rachid Ghannouchi, exiled in London since 1989, has won libel cases against newspapers labelling him a terrorist on a number of occasions (see: www.carter-ruck.com/Newsletters/2003–2004-Ghannouchi.html, accessed 7 December 2007).
19 E.H. Carr wrote of 'satisfied' and 'dissatisfied' powers (Carr, 1946: 105).
20 See, for example, the statement of Iranian Foreign Minister, Manouchehr Mottaki, on Islamic Republic News Agency (IRNA), 21 January 2008, available online at: http://www2.irna.ir/en/news/view/menu-236/0801212188213700.htm, accessed 25 February 2008.
21 A harrowing description of the impact of the movement's total ideological control over its members' lives and minds can be found in Banisadr, 2004.
22 The allusion here is to Robert Cox's statement of critical theory. According to critical theorists like Cox, 'problem-solving' theory is non-historical or a-historical, while critical theory questions any given situation with a view to changing it (Cox, 1996: 88–89).
23 Al-Qaeda is not, of course, an exclusively Middle East organisation, but it has sufficient roots and activities in the region to be considered in the context of a paper on the Middle East.
24 Some of this information is in Gerges, 2005: 247.

8 The contribution of anthropology to critical terrorism studies

Jeffrey A. Sluka

> The common links ... are the themes of terroristic massacre, cannibalism by imaginary dog-headed monsters, a political opportunism that makes your opponents virtuous or monstrous as a matter of convenience without regard for empirical facts of the case, and the principle that if the lack of shared moral values is so complete that the 'other' comes to be categorized as a wild animal, then every imaginable form of terrorist atrocity is not only attributed to the other side but becomes permissible for oneself. Indeed, counter terrorism becomes, in a bizarre sense, a religiously sanctioned duty
>
> (Leach, 1977: 36)

Introduction

This chapter considers what anthropology brings to the study of terrorism and how the discipline can help to facilitate a critical terrorism studies (CTS). I also seek to describe in general terms how social or cultural anthropology represents a cognate discipline which is very much in agreement with the basic principles, core commitments, and research agenda of CTS.[1]

The hallmark of anthropology is that it combines empirical methods with a cultural approach, and from this perspective considers 'terrorism' both as an empirical reality and as a cultural construct, belief system, or ideology. The discipline brings to critical terrorism studies what it brings to the study of human conflict in all its forms – a *cultural* perspective; extreme topical and theoretical eclecticism; a cross-culturally comparative and holistic perspective; an ethnographic approach based on long-term fieldwork and direct participant-observation in the community studied; a scientific commitment to both objectivity and getting as close as possible to the subjective, participants, or *emic* point of view; an appreciation of the impact of ethnocentrism and cultural relativity; and a humanist concern for ethics, the potentially negative affects research may have on those studied, and the 'Enlightenment vision' that research should be applied for the improvement of the human condition (Sluka, 1992). Along with fieldwork and ethnographic case studies of armed conflicts, anthropology also brings a long tradition of comparative theory building and analysis of conflict situations, and a well-developed reflexive tradition as a form of 'cultural critique'. The combination of these

The contribution of anthropology 139

paradigmatic elements creates the 'anthropological imagination' – a unique perspective not found in other disciplines – which has already contributed important critical analyses of terrorism and has much to offer CTS.

While anthropologists have not written a great deal about 'terrorism' per se, what they have contributed has been important and critical of official perspectives and definitions. Anthropologists have studied and written about both state terrorism – and we should never forget that this is by far the main form of terrorism – and the armed resistance by 'sub-state' groups which is usually defined in orthodox or pro-state terrorism studies as 'terrorism.' CTS calls for increased attention by scholars to state terrorism and the role of the state in the sponsorship of 'terrorism'; anthropologists have written ethnographic studies and comparative analyses of the dynamics of state domination and terror (see Robben, 2005; Sluka, 2000a; and Suarez-Orozco 1987, 1990, 1992). The only anthropologist listed by Herman and O'Sullivan (1989) in their study of the leading publicly recognised 'terrorism experts' is E.V. Walter (1969) who wrote a classic ethnographic study of despotic rule in some African kingdoms, particularly that of the famous Zulu King Shaka.

Anthropologists working in 'high conflict' areas have studied violence, terror, and resistance, and written detailed ethnographies of armed indigenous, ethnonational, and religio-national movements frequently described as 'terrorists,' and all of these studies have been critical of the characterisation of this violence – which includes most of the armed conflicts in the world today – as 'terrorism' rather than more accurate terms such as war, insurgency, or 'resistance' (see Zulaika, 1988; Sluka, 1989; Feldman, 1991; Nordstrom and Martin, 1992; and Mahmood, 1996).[2] The empirical reality of the contemporary armed popular movements we have studied has simply not fitted with the 'terrorism' image presented by governments and the mainstream media. In general, anthropologists who have studied and written about terrorism have found that the perspectives produced by governments and their academic and media supporters in what Herman and O'Sullivan (1989) describe as 'the terrorism industry,' and much of what passes for orthodox 'terrorism studies,' is often unreliable, invalid, biased, and propagandistic, and simply does not fit the grounded reality of the political violence we have studied.

Anthropologists bring an evolutionary perspective to the consideration of terrorism and know that terrorism, as a coercive strategy of political intimidation or fear, is as old as the state and civilisation – in fact, we would argue that terrorism is fundamentally a product of social inequality and state politics. The first states emerged approximately 5,500 years ago, and political anthropologists believe that 'terrorism' in the modern sense as a political weapon to support elite rule or to resist it was unknown in bands, tribes, and chiefdoms, that is, for approximately 99 per cent of human history. That 'terrorism' is a dependent variable in the state equation of social inequality and stratification, rather than the independent variable most elites, governments, and orthodox terrorism studies experts treat it as, is one of the most significant critical perspectives anthropology brings to the debate (see, for example, Berreman, 1980; Bodley, 1990, 1995).

More than any other social science, anthropologists have observed and studied state terrorism and popular resistance at the grass roots level, particularly in the Third World, and along with an evolutionary perspective, we have brought at least four other important perspectives to the debate on terrorism. First, as mentioned above, anthropologists have written detailed critical ethnographies of popular armed resistance movements described as 'terrorists.' Second, anthropologists are more aware than most of the fact that, historically, all the indigenous and other 'nation peoples' who have resisted state conquest and domination have been denounced and vilified by those states as inhuman 'savages'. There is a clear correspondence between the former imperialist ideology of the 'savage' other and the contemporary one of the 'terrorist' other. Third, anthropologists have applied our core concept – culture – to the debate, developing new conceptual models of state terrorism and 'cultures of terror' where fear becomes a 'normal' or everyday part of peoples way of life (Taussig, 1984; Green, 1995). Lastly, anthropologists have engaged in critical cultural deconstruction of the *idea* of terrorism and how it is employed in society today (Zulaika and Douglass, 1996).

Critical terrorism studies and anthropology

As Richard Jackson has observed, the emerging field of critical terrorism studies (CTS) is broadly defined by a sceptical attitude towards state-centred understandings of terrorism and is founded on the growing number of compelling critiques of the rapidly expanding literature on terrorism and of 'orthodox' approaches to terrorism 'knowledge' – particularly its strong institutional links with state security projects and its prophylactic or 'problem-solving' orientation. Jackson identifies the core epistemological, ontological, and ethical commitments of CTS as including:

1 an appreciation of the politically constructed nature of terrorism knowledge;
2 an awareness of the inherent ontological instability of the 'terrorism' category;
3 a commitment to critical reflexivity regarding the uses to which research findings are put;
4 a set of well-defined research ethics; and
5 a commitment to an emancipatory political praxis.

(2007e: 244)

The aim of CTS 'is to destabilise dominant interpretations and demonstrate the inherently contested and political nature of the discourse – to reveal the politics behind seemingly neutral knowledge' (2007e: 247).

Several of the core concepts and commitments of CTS have a particular resonance/relevance for anthropologists. First, both CTS and anthropology are characterised by a general scepticism about, and strong reticence towards employing, the 'terrorism' label because in practice this 'has always been a pejorative rather than an analytical term' and its use has most often represented a powerful form of 'felon-setting' or negative labelling that 'implies a political judgment about the legitimacy of actors and their actions' (Jackson, 2007e: 247). Anthropologists agree with CTS advocates that 'one of the most fundamental problems is that the central concept of the field – "terrorism" – remains essentially contested; in practice, its use is always highly subjective and politically stigmatising' (Jackson, 2007h: 225). Second, anthropologists strongly agree with the CTS perspective that in employing the concept of 'terrorism' there is no escaping the ethical and political content of the subject because terrorism studies 'actually provides an authoritative judgement about who may legitimately be killed, tortured, rendered or incarcerated by the state in the name of counterterrorism' (Jackson, 2007e: 249). Third, anthropologists who have written about terrorism and reviewed orthodox terrorism studies literature, have, like CTS advocates, come to the conclusion that much terrorism research 'lacks rigorous theories and concepts, is based primarily on secondary information, lacks historical context and is heavily biased towards Western and state-centric perspectives' (Jackson, 2007h: 225).

Marie Breen Smyth has also identified key elements of the CTS perspective which anthropologists would strongly agree with, including that 'the state-centrism of orthodox "terrorism studies" ignores the roots or causes of terrorism and the contribution the state makes to creating the conditions in which 'terrorist' action by non-state actors occurs.' Breen Smyth also notes that orthodox terrorism studies is characterised by an 'aura of moral certainty.' Terrorism has always been viewed in moral terms, with a strong tendency to characterise 'terrorists' as 'evil': 'This discourse of "evil" is antithetical to scientific inquiry; yet to produce nuanced explanations for the motivation of "terrorists" is to risk being named as an apologist for them' (Breen Smyth, 2007: 261). Finally, Breen Smyth observes that one of the key ideas about terrorism found in the critical approach is the observation that

> there is a symbiotic relationship between "terrorism" and counter-"terrorism" – that counter-"terrorist" interventions by the state, which are primarily of a military and security nature, tend to escalate rather than alleviate levels of perceived threat, actual violence and alienation of the base population.
>
> (2007: 265)

Breen Smyth notes that there is little 'systematic evidence to support this assertion,' but a good deal of such evidence is already found in ethnographic studies produced by anthropologists, which are outlined in the following section of this chapter. Breen Smyth also argues for the need 'for expansion beyond the state-centric orientation of contemporary research' and that it is imperative that academics 'undertake "othercentric" research which sheds light on the experience of "suspect" communities, with a focus on the subjectivity and lived experience of the "other"' (2007: 266). This is, of course, precisely the greatest strength and contribution of cultural anthropology in general.

Finally, if we mean by 'emancipation' 'freedom from fear and the threat of both terrorism and counterterrorism, achieved by methods other than violence and repression' (Breen Smyth, 2007: 264), then anthropology shares with CTS a strong commitment to an 'applied' emancipatory ethos and political praxis. The following sections identify and illustrate some critical anthropological perspectives on 'terrorism' and 'terrorism studies' that illustrate these significant shared perspectives between the discipline and CTS.

Terrorists or freedom fighters?

My first book, based on my PhD fieldwork, was an ethnographic study of popular support for the Irish Republican Army (IRA) and Irish National Liberation Army (INLA) in Divis Flats, a Catholic-nationalist ghetto on the Falls Road in Belfast, Northern Ireland (Sluka, 1989). In the late 1970s and early 1980s when I was a postgraduate student, the modern idea of 'terrorism' first emerged as an ideological weapon of the New Right driven by the Reagan and Thatcher regimes who, following the Israeli lead in employing the 'terrorism' label against Palestinian militants, adopted the idea of 'terrorism' and 'counterterrorism' as their dominant foreign affairs focus. In the US, the Reagan administration came to office declaring they would dedicate themselves to eliminating the plague of 'international terrorism'. Their public relations system then constructed the myth of the 'international terrorist network/conspiracy' and a series of appropriate demons – an 'Axis of Evil' including Qaddafi, the PLO, the Sandinistas, Castro, and so on – was presented to the public as Soviet clients. In the UK, Thatcher adopted a propaganda policy of 'criminalisation' as a counter-insurgency weapon to fight the IRA, under which the war in Northern Ireland was officially defined as 'terrorism,' and the British government claimed that the Republican guerrillas were 'criminals' and 'terrorists' with no legitimate political aims and little popular support, who survived only by terrorising their own community. These examples were then followed by every other state in the world fighting insurgents, particularly Spain in their war against the Basque ETA and various Latin American regimes in their numerous wars with left-wing insurgents.

At that time, as a direct academic response to the development of these American and British policies and largely in support of them, 'terrorism studies' first began to emerge. In reading this developing literature prior to my fieldwork in Belfast, I found that the IRA was invariably identified as one of the leading 'terrorist' groups in the world. As a student of political violence and social conflict this intrigued me, because it was clear that there was great public debate about this issue and that most Catholics in Northern Ireland and millions of Irish-Americans and others around the world were convinced that the IRA were 'freedom fighters' or a legitimate armed national liberation group.

Thus, I set out in my research to empirically test the British state's claim that the IRA and INLA were illegitimate 'terrorists' and the guerrillas' opposite assertion that they were legitimate 'freedom fighters.' I lived in the lower Falls Road community for nearly a year and conducted fieldwork based primarily on participant-observation and interviews with seventy-six families or households. These ethnographic methods allowed me to gain the 'rapport' – that is, the acceptance

The contribution of anthropology 143

and trust – of people so that they would feel free to speak openly and honestly about this potentially dangerous topic.[3] In my analysis, I applied the 'hearts and minds' theory of insurgent conflicts which emerged in the 1960s and 1970s from analysis of the Vietnam and other ongoing imperial wars, and found essentially that:

1. the IRA and INLA were not 'terrorist' groups but rather armed ethno-nationalist guerrilla or resistance organisations;
2. that they had a great deal of popular support in this community;
3. that they did not terrorise their own people; and
4. that their primary recruiting tool and legitimising agent was the state terrorism of the brutal 'dirty war' counter-insurgency tactics employed by the British army and paramilitary police in Northern Ireland.

I concluded that the IRA and INLA could not be defined as 'terrorists' because they did not fit the objective definition. They did not *purposely* inflict civilian casualties, which is the primary definition of terrorism.[4] They had well-elaborated, though imperfect, bomb-warning systems which worked fairly effectively to minimize civilian casualties, they had internal codes of conduct which specifically prohibited targeting innocent civilians and provided for sanctions against 'Volunteers' – as they termed themselves – who violated this ethic, and in their violence they were statistically the *most* discriminate of the three parties to the war – the Republican guerrillas, the British Security Forces, and the Loyalist 'paramilitaries', as Table 8.1 shows.

By the objective definition of terrorism specifically as violence aimed at civilians in order to create fear for political purposes, only the Loyalist death squads in Northern Ireland, over 90 per cent of whose victims had been randomly selected for sectarian assassination based solely on their ethno-religious identity, actually fitted that definition – yet, ironically, they were almost never referred to as 'terrorists' (Sluka, 2000b).

I concluded my ethnography on popular support for the IRA and INLA by arguing that while counter-insurgency and counterterrorism had become something of a politico-military science redefined as 'terrorism studies,' the social science and political theory of many so-called 'terrorism experts' was frankly dismal. I identified at least four major weaknesses often found in the work of counter-insurgency specialists and the orthodox literature on terrorism.

Table 8.1 Percentage of deaths of civilians in Northern Ireland, 1969–88

	Security Forces	Nationalist Guerrillas	Loyalist Paramilitaries
Civilian deaths as a percentage by this agency	54.6	37.3	90.5

Source: Irish Information Partnership, cited in Weitzer, 1990.[5] See also Fay *et al.* 1999.

First, a near total failure to arrive at empirical conclusions derived from primary or first-hand research with the militants they define as 'terrorists' or in the communities that support them, and a corresponding failure or refusal to look at the question from the participants point of view. These people's views are rarely sought, and little effort is made to arrive at an empirical understanding of why they engage in or support political violence against the state.

Second, their analyses and conclusions are based almost solely on mostly secondary information and interpretations provided by governments, intelligence agencies, and security forces actively involved in fighting the 'terrorists' (see, also, Ranstorp and Raphael in this volume). This is not objective social science, because no effort is made to establish the validity or verify the reliability of these mostly secondary data and interpretations received from 'official' sources which it would be naïve or biased to accept at face value as objective and reliable.

Third, they tend strongly to view the civilian populations which militants come from as being passive, ignorant, and manipulable, and as either 'terrorised' dupes or 'terrorist supporters'. This preconceived notion shapes their fundamental approach, and yet no more attempt is made to establish its validity than is made to establish that of data and interpretations received from 'official' sources actively involved in counter-insurgency or counterterrorism.

Fourth, not only do they generally approach their work from the perspective of those combating militants, there is nearly always an implicit moral assumption or judgement, which reveals a state-centric bias, that states combating political militants they define as 'terrorists' are inherently legitimate and moral (the 'good guys'), and the militants inherently illegitimate and immoral (evil, the 'bad guys'). There is rarely any suggestion that governments and security forces may be just as illegitimate, Machiavellian, cynical, and immoral in their use of violence, force, and terror as they generally presume the militants are, or that the violence of the militants is, from their perspective and usually an objective one as well, a reaction and form of resistance to their experiences of state terror, oppression, and injustice, which are among the root causes of anti-state terrorism.

Dehumanisation and sacralisation in anti-terrorism rhetoric

At least one political anthropologist – Sir Edmund Leach – was among the very first academics brave enough to criticise the emergence of the propaganda use of the idea of terrorism. In a lecture presented in 1977, he observed that the ideology of anti-terrorism included two dangerous elements – *dehumanisation* and *sacralisation.* Leach observed that the dehumanisation of other people who do not conform to our values is a tragic but common occurrence, and warned that this was an aspect of labelling people as 'terrorists.' The label implies that they are somehow fundamentally different from us and are not as good or as human as we are. Leach was sensitive to the political opportunism that often goes along with such exercises in dehumanisation. He made the essentially mimetic argument (cf. Girard, 1982), which Michael Taussig (1984,

1987, 1992) has also applied to the historical labelling of native peoples as 'savages,' that if those labelled as 'terrorists' are defined as less than human, then every form of terror attributed to them becomes not only permissible but defined as noble when we do it to them. Taussig has shown how the myth propagated by colonising Europeans of the putative 'savagery' of native peoples was hugely exaggerated and used to rationalise and justify their own massive, frequently genocidal, violence against the natives. It appears that this same sort of mythology is extant with respect to the current 'war on terrorism,' where it serves a similar function. Today, 'terrorists' represent the latest incarnation in our culture of the violent, subhuman, evil, 'savage' other against whom we are prepared to employ 'good violence' – which now includes *terrorism* such as torture, 'extraordinary rendition', detention without trial, and the killing of civilians.

This leads to Leach's second point, his warning that counterterrorism can become a religiously sanctioned moral duty and take on sacred aspects as a type of 'holy war' between the forces of Good and Evil. Anti-terrorism, like anti-communism, which preceded it as the cornerstone of US and British foreign policy, is generally presented as a higher moral imperative. Terrorism, which is structurally the same thing as 'subversion' and 'communism' in right-wing ideology, is presented as not only a physical threat but also a metaphysical *evil* that must be destroyed in a permanent global holy war in which the defenders of good, democracy, and civilisation have a sacred duty to confront and defeat the proponents of evil/communism/terrorism. Perhaps the best example of the inclusion of sacred elements in anti-terrorist rhetoric is found in Israel, where some members of the government and military unquestioningly believe that they have a sacred duty to defeat 'terrorism' in order to protect and preserve the Zionist state. Herman (1982) notes that there is often a simplistic duality in this model between good and evil, light and darkness, democracy and communism (and/or terrorism), and this duality has a tendency to take on sacred aspects, becoming in some respects a 'holy war' against an insidious 'terrorist' enemy who comes in many subversive guises.

As Leach pointed out, not all crimes are sins, and not all sins are crimes; but some crimes *are* sins and Zulaika and Douglass observe: 'The crimes of Nazism and Stalinism fall into this category, and in current political discourse terrorism has emerged as the prototype of such sinful criminality against which the public reacts with the horror of taboo' (1996: 188). Terrorism and acts of political violence aimed at 'us' and our allies are viewed as sins against 'freedom and democracy' everywhere. This sacralisation of anti-terrorism is obviously not confined to colonial and authoritarian Third World regimes, as we see from Reagan's references in the 1980s to the former USSR and its allies as an 'Evil Empire' behind terrorism, and Bush's elaboration of this theme in his contemporary 'Axis of Evil' comments.

Leach wrote his critique of the political use or abuse of the idea of 'terrorism' more than thirty years ago, at the beginning of the emergence of anti-terrorism rhetoric as an ideological weapon of the New Right. He observed that:

> In the present situation of 1977 'we' are the respectable, law abiding, middle class citizens of the capitalist West. We see ourselves as threatened by 'others', that is by lawless terrorists of all kinds who do not accept our moral conventions, and the more hawkish among us not only advocate policies of counter terrorism but do so in a spirit of religious self-righteousness ... In our attitude towards the modern terrorists we tend to aspire to vengeance. We are inclined to preach crusades of reprisal against all those who engage in violent non-conformity. But vengeance is not a wholesome sentiment; it tends to fog one's sense of reality.
>
> (Leach, 1977: 36)

Leach finished with an important and humanising conclusion: 'However incomprehensible the acts of the terrorists may seem to be, our judges, our policemen, and our politicians must never be allowed to forget that terrorism is an activity of fellow human beings and not of dog-headed cannibals' (1977: 36).

Critical cultural deconstruction of terrorism

The most outstanding contemporary anthropological study of terrorism as a cultural phenomenon is Joseba Zulaika and William Douglass' superb critical deconstruction of the idea or what they identify as the *myth* of terrorism in their book, *Terror and Taboo: The Follies, Fables, and Faces of Terrorism* (1996). This is the first modern *cultural* analysis of the idea of terrorism itself, and how it is employed in American society. Zulaika and Douglass show how fear of terrorism is fuelled by vested interests – including academics, the media, filmmakers, and novel writers, but mainly a plethora of government agencies, right-wing think tanks, and the multi-billion dollar security industry, for their own political purposes. Zulaika and Douglass begin by observing that:

> We are baffled by the use and abuse of terrorism discourse; we voice our scepticism. After many years of writing on the issues of political violence, our misgivings about the intellectual and moral values of the concept of terrorism have only increased. ... It is the reality-making power of the discourse itself that most concerns us – its capacity to blend the media's sensational stories, old mythical stereotypes, and a burning sense of moral wrath. Once something that is called 'terrorism' – no matter how loosely it is defined – becomes established in the public mind, 'counterterrorism' is seemingly the prudent course of action. Indeed, at present there is a veritable counterterrorism industry that encompasses the media, the arts, academia, and, to be sure, the policy makers of most of the world's governments. There is now, in fact, an 'official' line acknowledging that terrorism poses a global threat to world security, which in turn justifies the expenditure of billions of dollars on counterterrorism measures.
>
> (Zulaika and Douglass, 1996: iv)

The contribution of anthropology 147

Zulaika and Douglass argue that terrorism as presented by the authorities and the media is, in effect, a fiction; they argue that 'regarding terrorism, the brandishing of stark facts goes hand in hand with great leaps in discursive fantasy' (1996: 4). It is not coincidental that this is the fundamental characteristic of propaganda, and they conclude that the hype about terrorism – the 'terrorism scare' – is essentially a powerful political myth with enormous consequences (cf. Mueller, 2006).

Along with Edward Said (1988a), Zulaika and Douglass conclude that the concept of terrorism is 'analytically far more of a hindrance than an aid to understanding political violence' (1996: 60): 'It is not simply that, like "Communist" or "fascist," the word "terrorist" is being abused; rather the word is itself an abuse, a banality that disguises reality while impoverishing language and thought by obliterating distinctions' (1996: 98). They ask a sceptical question – 'If all sorts of murders, kidnappings, threats, civil wars, government crimes, killings by secret or underground organizations, paramilitary executions, and so on, were simply called by those names without ever using the word "terrorism," would there be something missing in the description of the real world?' (1996: 102–103). Finally, they suggest that while there is a great deal of armed conflict and political violence in the world, the

> real issue concerns the wisdom of describing all (or many) of such events as the work of "terrorism." Does this concept better clarify the facts, or is it, as with so many other historical constructs, a hypostatized creation of learned and lay people alike that is a certain path to self-deception?
>
> (1996: 100)

In their analyses, Zulaika and Douglass argue that the concept of 'terrorism' is a cultural construction of a pervasive social phenomenon that, on closer inspection, is revealed to be mainly a social myth – an imaginary construct deeply embedded in the culture of our times. They postulate that the terrorism myth is an example of 'collective enchantment' comparable to other social myths that generated extraordinary historical stereotypes such as the Jewish conspiracy, the witch craze, the idea of 'race', and the Red Scare: 'Each, like "terrorism," resulted in a chimerical construction so steeped in imaginary fear and terror as to blur the distinction between fiction and reality' (1996: 183). Having defined terrorism as a cultural construct, Zulaika and Douglass observe that 'in the final analysis, cultural constructions [are] amenable to demythification' or critical cultural deconstruction (1996: 150), and in their book they effectively demythify the 'terrorism scare'.

Zulaika and Douglass' conclusion, written five years before the 9/11 terrorist attacks in the US, looks now, with hindsight, to have been prophetic:

> We have argued that the American quest for 'terrorism' has had a lot to do with a Beckettian theatre of the absurd as well as with the political manipulations of collective fantasies of ... savagery. It doesn't take an uncommon sagacity to perceive that the journalistic and academic fashionings of the

'thing' itself are flawed and self-deceptive. But, even if we have concentrated on showing the discursive basis of the culture of terrorism, there is a point in which the thing itself, no matter how reified or distorted or banal, becomes a structural reality and a historical force. It appears that 'terrorism' is fast becoming a dominant medium through which American society and domestic politics need to be interpreted ... Terrorism is now becoming a functional reality of American politics, an autonomous prime mover of enormous consequence affecting national policy and legislation. This is no longer mere phantasmagoria but rather an irreducible dimension of a political ideology that profoundly affects the material reality of American society. Terrorism has been 'naturalized' into a constant risk that is omnipresent out there, a sort of chaotic principle always ready to strike and create havoc, and against which society must now marshal all its resources in an unending struggle. Now that it has become a prime *raison d'état*, its perpetuation seems guaranteed.

(Zulaika and Douglass, 1996: 238)

Humanising the 'terrorists'

Anthropologists who have studied armed resistance movements are overrepresented among the few academics who have actually conducted first-hand research with militants defined by their powerful state enemies as 'terrorists' (see Zulaika, 1988; Sluka, 1989; Feldman, 1991; Mahmood, 1996). We have broken the taboo of never talking to terrorists, and by presenting their perspectives and experiences have tended strongly to humanise rather than dehumanise them. In anti-terrorism propaganda, 'terrorists' are presented as evil and inhuman cowards motivated by hatred, but research anthropologists have done with militants strongly refutes this.

A particularly important ethnographic study of militants frequently described as 'terrorists,' including a discussion of whether they are terrorists or freedom fighters, is Cynthia Mahmood's book *Fighting for Faith and Nation: Dialogues with Sikh Militants* (1996). Mahmood is a leading anthropological authority on militant forms of religious nationalism, particularly among Sikhs and Kashmiris. She found that the Sikh and Kashmiri fighters she interviewed were adamant that they were motivated by 'love' rather than hatred, and she found that the families of dead guerrillas and other members of their communities who knew them described them positively and as good people who were 'full of love'. We do not typically envision guerrilla fighters – yet alone 'terrorists' – as being motivated by love or any other positive values. But the philosopher Cicero declared that 'Of all the emotions there is none more violent than love. Love is a madness,' and the poet Pope asked, 'Is it, in Heav'n a crime to love too well?' Yeats wrote of the executed leaders of the 1916 Easter Rising in Ireland that 'They died of an excess of love,' and Che Guevara is famous for his statement that 'Let me say, with the risk of appearing ridiculous, that the true revolutionary is guided by strong feelings of love. It is impossible to think of an authentic revolutionary without this quality'.[6] In my research, when I once asked the leader of an Irish guerrilla group why some individuals became 'freedom fighters' when most did not, he said the ones who joined had 'the least tolerance for oppression and the greatest love for freedom'.

It is objectively clear, though perhaps disturbing to some, that those who have actually done research with militants described as 'terrorists' at first hand or face to face, have invariably found that they show no signs of being evil, crazy, or particularly motivated by hatred or envy. Looked at from *their* perspective, they are fighting for their nation and/or faith; they are primarily motivated by 'love' in the sense of patriotism and/or selfless commitment to the people and/or cause they believe they represent, and their actions are frequently extraordinarily – even suicidally – altruistic, brave, and objectively 'heroic'. While they typically come from environments where they, their families, and their communities have been the direct victims of extreme forms of injustice, oppression, and state terrorism, most are not particularly motivated by hatred, though it is an apparently natural human reaction for some who are oppressed to come to not only love freedom but hate their oppressors. This may seem obvious to some, but it needs to be said because the propaganda picture of terrorists is entirely the opposite of this reality.

Relativity, subjectivity, and terrorism

The obvious but important relativity that those labelled as 'terrorists' do not view themselves that way but rather as patriots, 'freedom fighters', and defenders of their people and values, is matched by the renowned subjectivity found in judgements about whether particular struggles represent terrorism or freedom fighting. Depending on the perspective taken, 'terrorists' have been characterised positively as heroes, patriots, and martyrs, and negatively as villains, criminals, fanatics, savages, and crazies. For most people, including academics, the definition depends on their point of view. To the English, Braveheart was a terrorist, and so were George Washington, the Minute Men, and the American patriots involved in the Boston Tea Party; Spartacus and Jesus would have been terrorists to the Romans; Custer to the Sioux and Cheyenne; Geronimo and Red Cloud to American settlers; Lawrence of Arabia to the Turks; Churchill to the people of Dresden; the Japanese to the residents of Nanking; French partisans to the Nazis; and Truman to the people of Hiroshima and Nagasaki. Virtually everyone extolled by anyone as a 'freedom fighter' has been simultaneously vilified as a 'terrorist' or the equivalent by the oppressors they struggled against – and even those who did not employ violence, such as Mahatma Ghandi and the Dalai Lama, have been condemned oxymoronically as 'pacifist terrorists'. The notorious subjectivity of the term 'terrorist' has always been recognised in the familiar cliché that 'one person's terrorist is another person's freedom fighter'. While legitimate resistance movements sometimes employ terror tactics, it is usually wrong to portray them as 'terrorists' rather than insurgents or freedom fighters.

150 J.A. Sluka

Political geographer Bernard Nietschmann (1987) has observed that oppressive states fighting internal wars against indigenous and other 'nation peoples' refer to this as 'counterterrorism' and all try to defeat the nation fighters and crush their civilian support by employing state terrorism or 'dirty war' tactics. There are many dozens of examples of the abuse of the epithet 'terrorism' by applying it to legitimate armed resistance movements, but just a few prominent contemporary examples include all of the major hot spots of political violence in the world today – including the Colombian government's claim that the FARC *guerrilleros* are 'terrorists', the Russian government's claim that Chechen rebels are 'terrorists', the Israeli government's claim that the PLO and Hamas are 'terrorists', the Chinese government's claim that Uigher and Tibetan activists are 'terrorists', the Indonesian government's claim that the Free Papua Movement (OPM) and Free Aceh Movement (GAM) are 'terrorists', the Sri Lanka government's claim that the Tamil Tigers (LTTE) are 'terrorists', the Spanish and French governments' claim that the Basque ETA are 'terrorists', the Burmese juntas' claim that ethnic rebels in the highlands are 'terrorists', the Indian government's claim that the indigenous rebels in Kashmir and other regions are 'terrorists', and the US and UK governments' claim that the insurgents in Iraq and Afghanistan are 'terrorists'. This is just the tip of the iceberg. Because in all these cases many well-informed people may be inclined to believe that the causes are just, these governments have tried to convince the world that their opponents are all 'terrorists', which implies that the solution need not involve political negotiation and concessions but merely a vicious 'counterterrorism' (really counter-insurgency) campaign.

Not surprisingly, since the 11 September 2001 terrorist attacks on the US, virtually every state confronting a popular insurgency or separatist movement has eagerly jumped on the 'war on terrorism' bandwagon, branding its domestic opponents as 'terrorists' and, as Whitbeck notes,

> at least implicitly, taking the position that, since no one dares to criticize the United States for doing whatever it deems necessary in its 'war on terrorism,' no one should criticize whatever they now do to suppress their own 'terrorists'.
> (2001: 2)

Critical perspectives as 'support for terrorism'

Zulaika and Douglass (1996: 62) observe that:

> It is one of the tenets of counterterrorism that any interaction with the terrorist 'Other' is violation of a taboo. Terrorists are kooks, crazies, demented, or at best misguided. Contact with them is polluting; dialogue is pointless since terrorists are, by definition, outside the pale of reason. Yet as anthropologists working in the field, we have lived many years in communities that have produced 'terrorists.' As a practical matter, we could not simply demonize and then shut them out of our awareness.

As a result of their research on the Basque ETA, they conclude 'the very act of writing an ethnography of political violence outside of conventional terrorism discourse can become in itself a major act of transgression of the policy of tabooing the violent actors' (1996: 62). Those anthropologists who in their pursuit of truth or understanding have done first-hand research with militants, have broken the taboo of never talking to 'terrorists', and beyond that they have dared to describe them, not as subhuman savages, but as fully human beings who are products of the oppressive political environments from which they come. Because they have 'put a human face on terrorism', these anthropologists have been criticised, threatened, and attacked. In particular, they have found themselves accused of being terrorists or sympathisers with them.

In a 1995 article titled 'The Anthropologist as Terrorist', Zulaika describes the consequences of his failed attempt to actually join the ETA in order to study them. The main point of this article was that simply for daring to try to enter into a face to face dialogue with them, and for writing a book about and thereby giving a public forum to 'terrorists', he was severely criticised, his ethics were questioned, and he was accused of being an 'academic terrorist'. Similarly, in her study of Sikh militants, Mahmood (1996: 272) records her experience that:

> No matter how vociferously we anthropologists of militancy assert our commitment to maintaining an ultimate intellectual distance from our research participants, we all suffer the accusation of partisanship from their enemies. This response is to be expected. Less understandable is the common sceptical reaction from the general public and indeed the world of scholarship, which often goes beyond the charge of one-sidedness. We are accused of creating a pornography of violence, of providing an 'aesthetic alibi' to terrorists, even of *being* terrorists. Having transgressed the taboo of never talking to 'terrorists,' of never putting a face on the acts of violence we find so easily revolting on the evening news, we find ourselves contaminated and in some ways stigmatized by what we study.

For those ideologically dedicated to counterterrorism, academics and universities, with their traditions of independence, objectivity, and dedication to pursuing knowledge and truth, have long been viewed as essentially dangerous and at least potentially, if not actively, subversive. In 1981, while I was doing fieldwork in Belfast, a leading counterterrorism expert – Paul Wilkinson – suggested in an article presenting proposals for government responses to terrorism that they

> must effectively counter the barrage of terrorist propaganda bases that are active in our communities. ... There are ... certain danger spots within the university systems ... we should know, and most of us can identify very easily if we do not know already, those university departments and those *individuals* in departments who are carrying out tasks for terrorist organizations as propagandists, as agents, and as recruiters. And they are the *key* initial point of entry for most active terrorists. ... In democracies our

government and intelligence agencies should make a priority of examining the development of university bases of recruitment by the terrorist organizations operating in their region. And they should have close liaison with the academic authorities known to be sympathetic to the task of protecting free societies in order to elicit their cooperation in avoiding recruiting to university staff people who are likely to act as terrorist agents and propagandists ... Thus, part of the war against terrorism has to be fought out in the seminar and lecture rooms of the universities of the Western world; it is literally a struggle for the souls of the young.

(Wilkinson, 1981: 166–168. Emphasis in original)

Wilkinson is a leading figure in orthodox 'terrorism studies' and the pro-state 'terrorism industry' and, in light of the discussion of sacralisation in antiterrorism rhetoric discussed above, it is worth noting the sacred allusion he makes to the 'war against terrorism' as a struggle for souls.

While this threat to academic freedom and objectivity is not new, it has emerged with new vigour as a result of President Bush's 'war on terrorism' response to 9/11. In November 2001, the American Council of Trustees and Alumni (ACTA), a well-financed conservative group devoted to curbing liberal tendencies on campuses, issued its first blacklist of professors it considered insufficiently 'patriotic' and something akin to traitors in times of war for daring to challenge the President's policies. They issued a list of the names of academics along with 117 statements they made in public forums or classes, which questioned aspects of the Bush administration's 'war on terrorism.' They claimed that 'University faculty have been the weak link in America's response to the attack,' and asked alumni to bring their (presumed) displeasure about these views to the attention of university administrations in an effort to shut them up or get them fired (Sherwin, 2002). Recently, critical observers have described these and other contemporary blatant attempts by the Right in the US to use 9/11 as a pretext for curbing political dissent in academia as the 'New McCarthyism', and they have warned that the climate for academic freedom and intellectual dissent is 'worse today than at any other time in the last fifty years' (Schueller and Dawson, 2007: 11; see also Gold-Wartofsky, 2008 and Breen Smyth in this volume).

Conclusion

At some point (which is not yet near enough) the machinery for pushing the terrorist scare will stand exposed for the political and intellectual scandal that it is ... For the present, however, the wall-to-wall nonsense about terrorism can inflict grave damage.

(Said, 1988b: 150)

The greatest threat to world peace today is clearly 'terrorism' – not the behaviour to which the word is applied but the word itself. For years, people have recited the truisms that 'one man's terrorist is another man's freedom fighter' and that 'terrorism, like beauty, is in the eye of the beholder.' However, with the world's sole superpower declaring an open-ended, worldwide 'war on terrorism,' the notorious subjectivity of this word is no longer a joke. It is no accident there is no agreed definition of 'terrorism,' since the word is so subjective as to be devoid of meaning. At the same time, the word is extremely dangerous, because people tend to believe that it does have meaning and to use and abuse the word by applying it to whatever they hate as a way of avoiding rational thought and discussion and, frequently, excusing their own illegal and immoral behaviour.

(Whitbeck, 2001)

Anthropologists have made, and can continue to make, a major contribution to CTS and our understanding of terrorism by studying it both as an empirical reality and a political and cultural construction, and by exposing the concept to critical scrutiny and demonstrating the many political, social, and cultural complexities underlying what is often simply telescoped by authorities and the media into faceless, evil, irrational 'terrorism'. Some critics, including Edward Said and Amnesty International, have argued that the idea of 'terrorism' is so subjective and so overwhelmingly employed as an epithet or term of abuse that it has no intrinsic meaning, and is so dangerous and harmful in its application by state agencies that it should be abandoned entirely. While there is a strong argument for this, the practice of terrorism, particularly by state governments, is so real and fateful in the lives of hundreds of millions of people, and the politics of fear has become so predominant a reality of our times, there remains a compelling need to study how fear is constructed and employed as a weapon of political control, intimidation, and coercion.

The empirical or referential root of terrorism is 'terror', which is a subjective psychological experience characterised by intense, overpowering fear. In contrast to simple fear, terror implies a prolonged experience of psychic intimidation resulting not only from a perception of an immediate threat to personal well-being, but from the expectation or apprehension that the threat will continue indefinitely into the future. To 'terrorise' means to act with the intention of producing a state of terror, of creating fear, or of overcoming with fear – that is, to seek to dominate or coerce by intimidation. Despite ongoing debate about the definition of 'terrorism', the objective, valid, and reliable definition has, in fact, been established since the 1970s, when it was originally defined as the direct use of violence against civilians to inspire fear for political purposes – a form of political intimidation and control of individuals, groups, communities, and populations. Thus, the *scientific* definition of terrorism is that it is 'the policy of using acts inspiring great fear as a method of ruling or of conducting political opposition' (cited in Nagangast, 1994: 114), and it is essential that we understand the political and cultural dynamics of how this actually works.

Anthropologists stress that people do not act on the basis of what is true 'in reality', they act on the basis of what they *believe* to be true. Thus, their beliefs – even those that are fantastical – have real effects or consequences. Just as

Ashley Montagu (1997) has demonstrated that the reality of human biological diversity is mythologised as 'race', similarly, the reality of a world marked by ever increasing political violence and declining human rights, is now being mythologised and dichotomised as either 'terrorism' or 'anti-terrorism' (President Bush's 'for us or against us'). Just as 'races' do not exist in reality, but classifications of humankind do, so too terrorism, at least as presented by elites, the mainstream media, and much of orthodox terrorism studies is unreal, but the classification of this political violence as 'terrorism' has real and fateful results. Thus, it seems to political anthropologists that the belief in 'terrorism' is rapidly emerging as humankind's most dangerous contemporary myth. Anthropology and critical terrorism studies stand on common ground in the conviction that this myth requires critical deconstruction and active 'demythification.'

For the future research agenda of CTS, the inclusion of an anthropological perspective encourages critical scholars of 'terrorism' to:

- Not view the state as the sole legitimate referent and to look beyond state-centric perspectives and security notions.
- Put primary emphasis on the main form of terrorism – *state terrorism*.
- Consider wider notions of how 'terrorism' and 'counterterrorism' affect not only state security but the security of *everyone*.
- Conduct research into the dynamics of violence between states and anti-state militants, and particularly the way in which repressive state policies produce oppositional political violence.
- Include in their analysis concepts such as social justice, inequality, structural violence, culture and discrimination.
- Historicise and contextualise conflicts by looking at the evolution of violence and the relationship between violence, social movements, and the state.
- Look at the relationship between human rights and terrorism.
- Analyse how 'terrorism' discourse is used both by states as a powerful form of propaganda and 'manufacturing consent' for government policies, and by anti-state forces to discredit elites and undermine the state.
- Consider the dynamics of how the idea of 'terrorism' is culturally constructed in the popular imagination.
- Analyse the social and political dynamics of fear as a political weapon.
- Move away from paradigms that prima facie accept the eradication of non-state actors through military means ('counterterrorism').
- Use ethnographic methods and interviews and break down us/them dichotomies.
- Engage with their 'research subjects' at a human level with the purpose of 'humanising the other'.

In 1933, in the context of the 'Great Depression', US President Franklin Delano Roosevelt famously warned that 'The only thing we have to fear is fear itself – nameless, unreasoning, unjustified terror which paralyzes needed efforts to convert retreat into advance'. Eight years later, in the context of another great crisis – the Second World War and the threat of global totalitarianism – he asserted that we should seek to build a better world founded upon four essential human freedoms, of speech, of worship, from extreme poverty, and from fear. Those freedoms matched America's Constitutional principles and provided one of the main foundations for the establishment of the United Nations at the end of the war. Roosevelt asserted that 'Freedom means the supremacy of human rights everywhere. Our support goes to those who struggle to gain those rights or keep them ... To that high concept there can be no end save victory.' With respect to the current hysteria with regard to terrorism, anthropologists are united with other practitioners of critical terrorism studies by shared commitment to the 'high concept' that freedom – including emancipation from the fear of terrorism and counterterrorism – means the supremacy of human rights everywhere.

Notes

1 For elaboration on the theme of anthropology and CTS, see Sluka, 2008.
2 One of the major flaws in the anti-terrorism literature is the confusion of, or failure to distinguish between, insurgency and guerrilla warfare on the one hand, and terrorism per se on the other.
3 Under draconian British 'anti-terrorism' legislation it was illegal to support a 'terrorist organisation,' and those suspected of such support were likely to be raided, harassed, and/or detained and interrogated by the Security Forces – that is, subjected to state terrorism.
4 In modern wars, all armies kill many innocent civilians. That is why it is sometimes asserted, for example by Howard Zinn (2002), that war *is* terrorism. But if we want to distinguish 'terrorism' from war in general, the core or defining characteristic is the intentional targeting of innocent civilians in order to generate fear for political purposes.
5 This is for the period 1969–88, and does not include the last years of the conflict up to 1994, during which Loyalist violence surged and surpassed Nationalist violence as the major source of political violence in Northern Ireland.
6 Cicero (106 BC–43 BC) quoted in L.R. Franzini and J.M. Grossberg's *Eccentric and Bizarre Behaviors*, 1995, New York: John Wiley and Sons, p. 5; Pope quote from 'Elegy to the Memory of an Unfortunate Lady' (1717); Yeats quote from 'Easter, 1916'; Guevara quote from *Man and Socialism in Cuba* (1965).

9 Social movement theory and the study of terrorism

Jeroen Gunning[1]

Introduction

Much of terrorism research concerns aspects of what in sociological circles are called 'social movements'. Granted, terrorism scholars more often focus on smaller-scale, underground organisations engaged in violence rather than the generally non-violent, broad-based movements that tend to populate social movement studies. But the organisations that terrorism scholars study are not only typically part of broader social movements but are affected by similar opportunities and constraints, and profoundly shaped by their interaction with these broader movements and their detractors. An increasing number of social movement theorists have begun to apply their framework to the study of political violence. However, within terrorism studies, social movement theory has remained, until recently, largely under-used. In this chapter, I will argue that social movement theory is an appropriate tool to study 'terrorist organisations' – which for reasons to be discussed shortly, I shall refer to as 'militant organisations' – and, crucially, that it can make a major contribution to overcoming some of the weaknesses of terrorism research.

Social movement theory (SMT) has been developed to study social movements, defined here as a collection of '(1) informal networks, based (2) on shared beliefs and solidarity, which mobilize about (3) conflictual issues, through (4) the frequent use of various forms of protest' (della Porta and Diani, 1999: 16). Though its focus has predominantly been on movements employing civil disobedience tactics, throughout, and increasingly since the late 1980s, some of its practitioners have applied this framework to study political violence (e.g. Gurr, 1970; Gamson, 1975; Tilly, 1978, 1979; della Porta and Tarrow, 1986; Haines, 1988; della Porta, 1992a, 1995b; Hafez, 2003; Wiktorowicz, 2004a; Bergesen *et al.*, 2007).

However, SMT has so far only made modest inroads into the field of terrorism studies. A keyword search within what have been considered the two core terrorism studies journals (*Terrorism and Political Violence* and *Studies in Conflict and Terrorism*; see Silke, 2004c) returns only one out of 1,569 articles with the phrase 'social movement theory'. The term 'social movement' appears in a further five articles. A search under the subject heading 'social movements' delivers only seventeen articles, including those already mentioned; and only seven of these actually employ SMT theory to study political violence.[2] By comparison, a general search of the IBSS (International Bibliography of the Social Sciences) database for the terms 'terrorism' and 'terrorist' under the 'social movements' heading yields eighty-one articles. Since much terrorism research is not published in the two core 'terrorism journals', these findings are far from conclusive. They do, however, suggest that SMT is still relatively marginal within the traditional terrorism research community.

While the earliest of the terrorism journals' articles appeared in 1993, the bulk are dated from 2000 or after, suggesting that SMT is building momentum within the field. Some only use SMT sparingly to frame their research (Wiktorowicz, 2006; Parker, 2007), while others use it extensively (Alimi, 2006; Araj, 2008). But none of the cited articles systematically discuss the benefits of employing an SMT framework for studying terrorism. Some meta-theoretical discussions have been conducted by social movement theorists with an interest in political violence (della Porta, 1992a, 1995b, 2008; Hafez, 2003; Wiktorowicz, 2004a). This chapter is an attempt to do this within the terrorism studies literature (see also Chandler, 2005).

A discussion of SMT is particularly pertinent to the 'critical terrorism studies' project of which this book is a part (see Introduction) – although it has a much broader application and is relevant for all terrorism research. While SMT contains aspects that are positivist or 'problem-solving' (Cox, 1981), it is – at least since the 1960s – broadly 'critical' in the Coxian sense of standing back from the status quo to consider how its structures came about and affected movement outcomes. In addition, some of the main 'schools' within SMT are indebted to Marxian or post-structuralist approaches (Garner, 1997).

Whether or not it is 'critical' in this sense, employing an SMT perspective can serve to accelerate the 'critical turn' in terrorism studies by providing a conceptual framework that directly addresses some of the key concerns raised by critiques of orthodox terrorism studies. Seeing militant organisations as part of a wider social movement, with a history and interacting with political actors and structures, helps to counter the ahistoricity and lack of context that terrorism research has often been accused of (Silke, 2004c: 207–209; Crelinsten, 1997: 4–6; Ranstorp, 2006b: 7; della Porta, 1995b: 5–7). A focus on state practices and their effect on oppositional movements, found among some schools of SMT, similarly addresses the critique that terrorism research has too often ignored the role of the state in contributing to the development of a terrorist response (George, 1991b; della Porta, 1995b; Araj, 2008).

Adopting an SMT perspective can serve to challenge many of the underlying assumptions of much traditional terrorism research. Among other things, it can de-exceptionalise terrorism by conceptualising it as part of a wider, evolving spectrum of movement tactics, thereby broadening the research focus as well as challenging its ideological underpinnings. It can denaturalise the state by making human as opposed to state actors the primary unit of moral value. And it can destabilise the sharp dichotomy drawn by statist accounts between a presumed legitimate state and supposedly inherently illegitimate terrorist opponents. As such, the adoption of an SMT framework can resemble the critical move in security studies, as conceptualised by Welsh School Critical Security Studies (Toros and Gunning, this volume): it can 'deepen' the field by challenging the assumptions underlying research frameworks, and 'broaden' it by incorporating a wider set of issues into the research (Booth, 2007: 150–172; Wyn Jones, 1999: 102–104).

I start with a brief overview of SMT and its relevance for studying organisations engaged in terrorist tactics. I then explore how adopting an SMT framework can 'broaden' the focus of terrorism research, starting with a discussion of how it places violence in its social and temporal context, and how it can help to move beyond the single-level analysis that terrorism research has been accused of (della Porta, 1995b: 5–7; Hafez, 2003: 17–19). I illustrate this with a discussion of how SMT scholars have combined a rational choice analysis of interests with an emphasis on ideas and values, and how these can be linked to wider structural changes. I then discuss how an SMT framework can serve to bring two understudied areas into sharper focus: the impact of state practices on terrorist tactics and the effect of internal group dynamics.

I end with two reflections on how an SMT framework can help to 'deepen' terrorism research. I first show how it can aid in overcoming the 'Orientalist' bias that haunts aspects of terrorism research, particularly on militant Islamist organisations (Jackson, 2007a: 399–400; Wolff, 1998: 43–46; Wiktorowicz, 2004b: 3). I then argue that an SMT framework can increase terrorism research's self-reflexivity and theoretical rigour, the relative absence of which numerous scholars have lamented upon (Silke, 2004c: 207–210; della Porta, 1995b: 5–7; Weinberg and Richardson, 2004: 138; Ranstorp, this volume).

A brief overview of social movement theory

Social movement theory is neither homogeneous, nor a theory in the strictest sense of the word. It contains a broad set of analytical frameworks for exploring social movement dynamics. In its earlier incarnations, attitudes resembled those found among some early terrorism scholars: mass movements were explained by psychological deviance, systemic strain (such as inequality), or both. One of the most influential models to emerge from this phase was Ted Gurr's *relative deprivation model* (1970), which held that violent rebellion was driven by frustration with systemic inequalities.

Resource mobilisation perspectives emerged as a critique of sociopsychological explanations, arguing that neither structural strain nor psychological characteristics explained why movements emerged in certain contexts and not others. Instead, movements were proposed to be a function of the existence of dense social networks and access to resources, elites, and innovative mobilisatory and movement tactics.[3] Following the turn towards rational choice and organisational behaviour models in the social sciences, movement activists were reconceptualised as rational choice actors, rather than psychological deviants (for which there was no evidence), and a distinction was introduced between the wider, unstructured movement, and the structured social movement organisations within it. Researchers began to focus on the impact of organisational structure, mobilisation tactics, and intra-movement competition for resources, members, and the sympathy of bystander audiences on movement outcomes (cf. Zald and Ash, 1966; McCarthy and Zald, 1977; A. Morris, 1981, 1984; C. Jenkins, 1983).

The *political process model* critiqued both the socio-psychological and *resource mobilisation* frameworks, on the grounds that neither structural strain nor the availability of networks and resources were sufficient to explain movement emergence or indeed the specific form a movement took. Movements, according to this model, are both a function of pre-existing networks and resources, and develop in interaction with the existing political system, state practices towards opposition, elite alliances, and prevailing socio-economic conditions – in short, the prevailing 'political opportunity structure'. In addition, inspired by the re-emergence of Marxian perspectives in the social sciences, *political process* theorists emphasised the importance of ideology, and in particular the role of 'cognitive liberation' – a shift from seeing inequalities as inevitable to regarding them as remediable through a re-evaluation of existing conditions, opportunities, and resources (cf. McAdam, 1982; Tilly, 1984; Kitschelt, 1986; Kriesi, 1989; Costain, 1992).

Two further models emerged in response to the 'cultural turn' in the social sciences. First, *framing theory* kept *resource mobilisation* theorists' focus on micro-mobilisation but shifted its concentration to how opportunities, identities, and action repertoires were framed. According to this model, too little attention had been paid to the role of framing in micro-mobilisation dynamics, and in particular, how movement entrepreneurs reinterpreted, bridged, amplified, or extended existing ideologies, cultural 'master frames', and life experiences to mobilise activists and bystander publics (cf. Snow *et al.*, 1986; Gamson and Meyer, 1996; Benford and Snow, 2000).

Second, *new social movement theory* had more affinity with the *political process* model with its dual focus on long-term socio-economic and political changes and ideology. However, it differed from the latter in its emphasis on culture, emotions, and identity – which it believed earlier SMT models had overlooked – and also by largely ignoring the impact of organisational dynamics on movement outcomes. Its focus was also narrower, concentrating on what it called 'new social movements' – movements in post-industrial societies which were characterised by less hierarchy, less class-focus, and more emphasis on identity and life-style than earlier movements (cf. Cohen, 1985; Melucci, 1985; Laraña *et al.*, 1994; Kriesi *et al.*, 1995). More broadly, a number of scholars across the field began to bring emotions into the equation, drawing on social psychology (cf. Gamson, 1992; Jasper, 1998; Goodwin *et al.*, 2000, 2001).

The SMT framework adopted in this chapter is a synthesis of these models (cf. McAdam *et al.*, 1996b). Such a synthesis is made possible by the fact that the different models both overlap – for example, both the *political process* and *new social movement* models focus on long-term socio-economic changes, while *resource mobilisation*, *framing*, and *political process* theorists all highlight the centrality of micro-mobilisation tactics – and complement each other. *New social movement* theory's focus on culture and identity, for instance, or the *political process* model's emphasis on state practices, fills significant gaps in the other models. Moreover, such a synthesis allows us to analyse the interaction

160   J. Gunning

between different factors, for example, how state practices towards a movement or its organisational structure affects the movement's framing and behaviour.

The relevance of SMT to the study of terrorism

The movements studied by post-1960s SMT scholars have typically been broad-based, non-violent movements. Though many had 'radical flanks' (Barkan quoted in McAdam *et al.*, 1996b: 14), the focus has usually been the non-violent parts of these movements. In sharp contrast, terrorism scholars have typically focused on smaller militant organisations, often operating underground and thus subject to different dynamics. A small, underground organisation bent on evading discovery is more likely to emphasise ideological purity and exclusivity, while a broad-based organisation intent on expanding its support base is more likely to focus on proselytisation and inclusivity (della Porta, 1995b: 20; see also Hafez, 2003, 2004).

However, though movement dynamics may differ, the categories SMT uses to analyse social movements are as relevant to violent as to non-violent organisations (see also della Porta, 1995b: 22). Like their larger, legalised counterparts, militant organisations are dependent on resources, micro-recruitment, and finding compelling ideological justifications. Like their non-militant counterparts, they are affected by the prevailing political system, state practices, socio-economic changes, and wider ideological trends.

Militant organisations, moreover, are typically part of larger social movements. Militants often begin as activists in a wider social movement and move towards militancy as a result of dynamics within this wider movement and its external context. The Italian Red Brigades, the Provisional IRA, and Hamas, for instance, all emerged out of broader social movements and were shaped by the organisational and ideological legacies of these movements and their interactions with the state and ideological rivals (see below). The boundaries between militant and non-militant organisations are often fluid, and militants and non-militants usually regard each other as part of the same social movement sector, whether they label each other as heroes or 'comrades [gone] wrong' (della Porta, 1995b: 12).

In addition, many contemporary organisations involved in terrorist tactics exhibit typical 'new social movement' traits. Out of the eight features listed by Johnston *et al.* as defining new social movements (1994: 6–9), in only two do militant organisations typically differ significantly: they do not 'employ new [radical] mobilization patterns characterized by non-violence and civil disobedience', and they do not necessarily 'exhibit a pluralism of ideas and values' with a commitment to 'institutional reforms that enlarge ... members' participation in decision making' (although some, like Hamas, do display a commitment to the latter; see Gunning, 2007c). They do, however, typically 'transcend class structure'; 'involve the emergence of new or formerly weak dimensions of identity'; blur the relationship between individual and collective; involve changes in 'personal and intimate aspects of human life'; are often, in part, a response to a 'credibility crisis of the conventional channels for [political] participation'; and, in contrast to the 'centralized bureaucracies of traditional mass parties', tend to be 'segmented, diffuse, and decentralized' (although this holds less for the larger, nationalist liberation-type organisations).

Broadening terrorism research

Putting the context back into violence

One of the key contributions SMT can make to terrorism research is to relocate violence within its social context and encourage investigation into the interactions between militant organisations, the larger social movement of which they form a part, and the society and political system more broadly. Militant organisations are usually founded by activists socialised into activism by their participation in a wider social movement, often in response to a crisis within that movement (della Porta, 1992b: 12). The Italian Red Brigades, for instance, were in part a response to the (perceived) failure of the student and worker protests of the late 1960s, the gradual co-optation of the Communist Party by the status quo, and the increasingly violent exchanges between police, right-wing organisations, and the Italian Left (della Porta, 1995a). The Provisional IRA was a product of the convergence of a crisis in the Irish nationalist movement, institutionalised discrimination against the wider Catholic community, and increasingly violent encounters between the Catholic civil rights movement which mobilised to end this discrimination, state forces, and Loyalist factions, and the effect these encounters had on nationalist identity (cf. Darby, 1983; Bosi, 2007). Even the disparate, autonomous, amateur 'cells' that carry out operations in the name of al-Qaeda in Europe are part of a wider social movement, however amorphous, transnational and virtual compared to more localised movements, and cannot be fully understood without an analysis of the broader Islamist movement from, and against which, al-Qaeda emerged (cf. Kepel, 2002). Although not unique to SMT – Giles Kepel and John Darby, for instance, are not social movement theorists – an SMT framework provides a strong incentive to explore these links more fully.

Within an SMT framework, violence is studied as one aspect of movement dynamics, and never in isolation. This has a number of consequences. First, violence is conceptualised as one among many possible tactics, enabling the researcher to see violence as part of, and interacting with, a much wider and evolving repertoire of movement actions. This restores fluidity to the concept of violence, both in terms of how it relates to other tactics and in terms of its temporal nature: how it emerges from or morphs into other tactics.

Second, violence is placed within its wider social context, as part of contentions within and around the wider social movement. An SMT framework encourages the researcher to look not just at the tactical or ideological drivers of violence but at the wider social movement, and in particular, at the impact of intra-movement competition, ideological debates in society more broadly, and encounters between the wider movement and the state or counter-movements on the adoption of violent tactics.

Third, such a framework enables the researcher to see the choice to adopt violence as a dynamic process, affected by the experience of activism and the impact of participation in particular organisational structures, rather than simply as a static, individual disposition prior to movement participation, an assumption that underpins the notion of 'profiling' so popular among (some) policymakers and terrorism experts.

The overall result is that terrorist violence is de-exceptionalised, taken out of its sterile box of *sui generis* phenomena, and returned to its living context (see also Alimi, 2006; Toros, 2008b). Within this perspective, using the term 'terrorist organisation' becomes an anomaly, as such terminology exceptionalises terrorist tactics by downplaying the rest of an organisation's action repertoire, its interactions with the wider social movement, and the temporal nature of its recourse to terrorist tactics. While the term 'militant organisation' can similarly be accused of downplaying non-militant behaviour, the dichotomy between militant and non-militant is not usually as rigidly conceived as the terrorist/non-terrorist dichotomy, allowing for more fluidity.

Violence, within such a perspective, is no longer simply an ideological imperative or a tactical choice, but the product of intense debates within the wider movement and of factional power struggles fuelled by differential access to resources and competing interpretations of members' interests and identities. It is shaped in interaction with changing ideological, religious, and cultural attitudes towards violence and other types of protest, and forms part of what Sidney Tarrow (1994) calls 'protest cycles', which are in turn affected by state practices, not just towards the militants, but towards the wider movement and those sections of society with which militants identify.

Hamas militants, for instance, were affected by how the Israeli state or the Palestinian Authority treated not only those loosely affiliated with the Islamic movement but Palestinians more broadly, just as they were influenced by changes in public opinion regarding the utility of suicide bombing and factional competition with other militant groups (Gunning, 2007c: 195–240; Araj, 2008; see also Bloom, 2005: 19–44). Italian Red Brigades members were influenced by debates among the Italian Left about justifications for violence, as well as by the way the Italian police indiscriminately targeted protesters, driving a number of them into the arms of the Red Brigades (della Porta, 1995a). Both organisations turned to more serious violence at the end of a protest cycle, when the mass movements at the centre of these cycles – the Italian student and workers' protests of the 1960s, and the first Palestinian Intifada of the late 1980s – petered out and their leaderships became accommodated by the status quo. Without considering these wider social and political dynamics, the behaviour of militants cannot be adequately explained (for an illustration of the effect of disregarding this wider context, see Kydd and Walter's 2002 analysis of Hamas's suicide bombing campaign; for critiques, see Bloom, 2005: 20–22; Gunning, 2007c: 208–212).

Once chosen, violence usually remains contested, whether in terms of its morality, its utility, or the precise form it should take (e.g. who to target, under what conditions). Furthermore, activists do not remain static. They move across the movement, in and out of militancy, and it is this fluidity that is often obscured by overly focusing on terrorist violence and 'terrorist organisations'. Within both

Hamas and the Italian Red Brigades, violent tactics were contested after they had been adopted, whether by political leaders within, or loosely associated with, the organisation, or by the wider social movement from which they derived. Furthermore, activists moved between different parts of the social movement – some from non-violent activism into militancy (e.g. student activists in both cases), others in the opposite direction (e.g. the *pentiti* in the case of the Red Brigades; former Intifada activists moving into student, professional, or municipal politics in the case of Hamas). Restricting one's canvass to simply the militants or their violence would prevent one from seeing these wider dynamics.

Putting the temporal back into violence

Violence, moreover, does not appear out of nowhere. Usually, there is a long history of contestation, group formation, and increasingly hostile interactions with state or other forces before violence becomes the norm. This history affects the evolution and form of the militant organisation in question and typically concerns the wider community with which militants identify.

The Provisional IRA emerged out of long-drawn-out contestations within the Irish nationalist movement over the future of Irish nationalism, and in response to increasingly violent encounters between the Catholic community in Northern Ireland and local state and Loyalist forces (Darby, 1983; Bosi, 2007). Hamas was a product of long-standing debates within the Palestinian Muslim Brotherhood and (often violent) rivalry with the nationalist movement over the utility of violent resistance, in response to an increasingly desperate economic and security situation in the Palestinian occupied territories (Robinson, 1997: 132–155; Gunning, 2007c: 25–39). The particular form it took was influenced by the institutional evolution of the largely non-violent Brotherhood, as well as by the increasingly violent interactions between Israeli soldiers and nationalist activists, and between the latter and Brotherhood activists. An SMT framework encourages a fuller investigation of these societal and organisational dynamics preceding the establishment of a militant group, or of a particularly violent episode (cf. Theoharis, 2006). While this is not unique to SMT – a number of terrorism scholars have painstakingly grounded their analysis in historical analysis, an excellent example being Martha Crenshaw's *Terrorism in Context* (1995) – an SMT framework offers a particularly dynamic and sophisticated framework for investigating these links.

More broadly, an SMT framework underlines the temporal fluidity of movement tactics. Movements go through phases, during which tactics can evolve rapidly (Tarrow, 1996: 53). Movements at the start of a protest cycle can differ markedly from those emerging later, in terms of tactics, organisational structure, and membership (McAdam, 1996: 31–33). Not to take into account a movement's 'temporal location in the cycle of protest' (Brockett, 1991: 254) when 'comparing even similar movements in different phases of their life cycles can produce a distorted picture' (Tarrow, 1996: 53). An SMT framework pushes researchers to factor this in.

SMT is also ideally suited to analysing why and how organisations move away from violence. Because violence is analysed in the context of changing movement tactics and as part of wider movement dynamics, a ready framework exists to analyse the factors which may lead activists and organisations to reject violence, even if only temporarily. An SMT approach to Hamas's use of violence, for instance, invites the researcher to go beyond suicide bombings and rocket attacks, and investigate the dynamics behind Hamas's non-violent tactics: its ceasefire declarations, its election campaigns, its role in local government, and how these are affected by changes in the prevailing political opportunity structure of Israeli state actions, Palestinian political and economic structures, and changing levels of popular support (cf. Gunning, 2007c).

SMT is obviously not the only possible framework for analysing this. Indeed, terrorism scholars have begun to study pathways out of violence without explicit recourse to SMT (Crenshaw, 1991; Cronin, 2008; Horgan and Bjørgo, 2008). But because SMT encourages researchers to analyse a movement's entire action repertoire, conceptualises movement behaviour as fluid and responsive to contextual changes, and, at least in its synthesised form, advocates an integrated approach combining a focus on structural conditions with an analysis of group dynamics, ideology, and individual motivations, it is particularly well-suited to studying movement transformations. That this is so is underlined by the fact that the two main articles written prior to the 2000s on how terrorism ends were written by a scholar from within the social movement tradition (Gurr in Ross and Gurr, 1989) and by one who had adopted a comparable framework (Crenshaw, 1991).

Finally, seeing violence as part of social movement dynamics enables the researcher to explore how the choice to adopt violence, rather than being simply a prior disposition, is affected by the experience of activism and the particular phase of the 'protest cycle' within which this activism takes place (see also della Porta, 2008). Numerous SMT scholars have shown how the motivations, goals, and perspectives of militants have been forged by movement participation. Donatella della Porta, for example, concluded from her study of Italian militants that 'the experience inside the terrorist organizations was ... what shaped their dispositions.... [T]he real transformation in individual motivations begins within the terrorist organizations' (1992a: 17) – whether through 'political socialization' within the organisation, or the (often violent) interaction between activists and state actors, and the effect this had on the movement's 'protest repertoires' and capacity for militancy (1992a: 7–9, 12–17; see also Braungart and Braungart, 1992: 68–70; Crenshaw, 1992: 31–37; Araj, 2008; and within terrorism studies, Sageman, 2004).

While there are counter-examples of individuals turning to violence without being inside militant organisations, this is a useful corrective to the notion that dispositions are merely individual affairs. For, even those who adopt violence individually are affected by the rhetoric and actions of social movements around them and the state's response to these social movements, while their actual acts of violence are usually enabled, and thus shaped, by a particular social movement organisation and its action repertoire. For instance, those who Jonathan Spyer (2008) categorises as self-radicalised in the context of the Israeli–Palestinian conflict, were still affected by the transnational militant Salafi movement, through both the internet and local preachers, and by the arrests of Hamas leaders, creating a lacuna which these (rival) preachers, and the internet, could fill. An SMT framework encourages researchers to move away from the static notion that socio-economic or psychological characteristics somehow predict militancy, and adopt a dynamic model which sees militancy as the outcome of movement and relational dynamics.

Linking macro, meso and micro explanations

A second key contribution SMT can make is to provide a framework which integrates macro, meso, and micro level explanations, something for which terrorism research has been critiqued for not systematically doing. Della Porta, for instance, critiques orthodox terrorism research for failing to integrate the three levels of explanation and, as a result, failing to adequately explain terrorist violence (1995b: 5–7). Macro functionalist explanations which focus on systemic imbalance have, she notes, 'attributed violence both to too little repression and to too much, to the absence of reform and to abrupt change, to insufficient legitimation and to lack of opposition'. Without additional empirically-grounded analyses of meso and micro factors, it is impossible to explain why repression, reform, or legitimation triggers violence in one case while deterring violence in another. Quintan Wiktorowicz (2004b) mounts a similar critique against research on Islamist movements (both violent and non-violent) – research on which contemporary terrorism studies draws heavily (Jackson, 2007a). This is particularly pertinent to research on militant Islamist organisations.

Micro explanations are often equally disappointing if they assume violence to be either 'caused' by frustration – without adequately explaining why in the majority of cases frustration does not lead to violence – or by psychopathological factors, despite the absence of empirical proof to support such claims (cf. Horgan, 2003; della Porta, 1995b: 6–7). Structural strain explanations do link micro with macro explanations through the notion of individual frustration with structural inequality. But, besides ignoring meso factors, such as the importance of organisational resources, they are typically based on a generalised notion of a hypothetical frustrated individual, rather than an analysis of the actual responses of actual individuals. Here too, more empirically-grounded, ethnographic-type research is needed.

Meso explanations, which focus on the 'ideological characteristics' of militant organisations, are similarly unsatisfactory as they not only fail to explain why a particular ideology is adopted but also too readily assume that 'there is a direct relationship between given aims and chosen means: if the aim is antidemocratic or antisystemic, then the means will be violent' (della Porta, 1995b: 6). Even a cursory review of antisystemic movements shows that this link is not inevitable and thus needs investigation. Gandhi's movement was antisystemic, profoundly radical, but non-violent. Hizb ut-Tahrir shares many of the core values of *jihadi* groups like al-Qaeda, yet has, by and large, refrained from violence (cf. Karagiannis and McCauley, 2006). Meso explanations focusing on organisational characteristics are equally unsatisfactory since, at least within terrorism studies, they usually depict organisational make-up as static and fail to consider the effect of in-movement competition and resource availability on movement structure. Neither ideological nor organisational explanations tend to analyse in detail the role played by state practices, regime type, or socio-economic changes in the evolution of militant movements.

Corroborating these observations, even Lia and Skjølberg's comprehensive overview of the 'causes of terrorism' literature (2004) lists the various levels of explanation separately, without providing a ready way to synthesise them. Within terrorism studies, Crenshaw (1981) has perhaps come closest to advocating an integrated approach by combining a focus on structural conditions with an analysis of group dynamics, ideology, and individual motivations. But even her model lacks the detailed, integrated, multi-level framework offered by a synthesised SMT model.

At its most comprehensive and dynamic – and it must be stressed that much actual SMT-inspired research falls short of this by remaining too wedded to a particular school within SMT, or by privileging structural over agency-based explanations (cf. Goodwin and Jasper, 1999) – SMT provides a framework for not only integrating macro, meso, and micro explanations, but also for analysing the impact the different levels have on each other. Ideological debates, for instance, can be analysed in terms of how they are influenced by changes in the political opportunity structure and in organisational development (cf. Hafez, 2003, 2004). Individual motivations can be studied in the context of group dynamics, state practices towards opposition, and wider socio-economic changes (cf. della Porta, 1992c). The macro findings of econometric studies can be combined with a detailed analysis of organisational and micro-mobilisational dynamics (cf. Opp and Roehl, 1990).

Such a comprehensive framework is also ideally suited for comparative research. Just as SMT scholars have sought to explain the different forms and trajectories the anti-nuclear power movement has taken across different national contexts (Kitschelt, 1986), an SMT framework can help to explain why political violence by Islamist organisations was more widespread in 1990s Algeria than in 1990s Egypt (Hafez, 2003, 2004), or why the militant Italian Left of the 1970s took a different form than their German counter-parts (della Porta, 1995b). Or it can shed light on the way militant *jihadi* and non-violent human rights movements across the Middle East were affected by each other and by differences in regime types and state responses to both (Wiest, 2007).

Linking interests, ideology, and structure

An illustration of the observed lack of multi-level analysis is the tendency of (some) terrorism research to overly focus on either strategic explanations or ideological explanations, and to treat both as relatively autonomous from structural changes. At the extreme end of the first category, militants and militant groups are conceptualised as rational actors maximising their interests, with little reference to ideology, ideas, or identity. At the other extreme, militants are depicted as driven by a static and monolithic ideology, almost regardless of cost-benefit calculations and internal ideological debates. Most research falls in between these two extremes. But too often one explanation drowns out the other, while neither interests nor ideas are linked adequately to structural changes in the external environment.

Both explanations have value. But over-reliance on either obscures not just the multiple other factors at play, but the interplay between ideology and interests. Here again, SMT – at least in its synthesised form[4] – provides a ready framework for integrating both interests and ideology into the analysis, and conceptualising them as fluid and shaped by group dynamics and changing social and political structures.

Illustrating the inadequacy of an interest-based rational choice explanation – and how SMT can help to overcome it – is Carrie Rosefsky Wickham's analysis of Islamist activism in Cairo's suburbs during the 1990s (2004; Wickham does not specifically focus on violent activism). Neither interests nor ideas alone, she argues, can explain Islamist activism, and their relative weight shifts over time (see also Bosi, 2007; Klandermans, 2004). Interests may explain why people joined Islamist networks which were believed to provide a number of 'social, psychological, and emotional benefits' without exposing them to increased risks (Wickham, 2004: 232). They do not, however, explain why people moved from low- to high-risk activities without a clear increase in benefits. To explain this, Wickham turns to the framing processes that took place in the Islamist networks, and in particular to their framing 'activism as a moral "obligation" that demands self-sacrifice and unflinching commitment to the cause of religious transformation' (*ibid.*). It was this framing, drawing on existing ideologies and religious master frames that made high-risk activism seem imperative, whatever the costs.

By drawing on both the rational choice models available from *resource mobilisation* theory, and on the ideational focus of *new social movement* and *framing* theorists, Wickham shows how to move beyond a narrow focus on interests. Note also how, in line with the emphasis within SMT on meso explanations, Wickham's explanation goes beyond the individualistic focus of many rational choice models, embedding individual motivations within group dynamics (see also Crenshaw, 1992; della Porta, 1992a).

Wickham's analysis simultaneously highlights the importance of ideology – a factor which is not always given sufficient attention, within terrorism studies but also SMT circles. One of the critiques *new social movement* theorists hold against other branches of SMT – including *framing* theories – is precisely the perceived lack of importance attributed to ideology (cf. Oliver and Johnston, 2000). Within the literature on violent social movements, Karagiannis and McCauley (2006) similarly argue that SMT models downplay the role of ideology, and in particular of 'religious ideas and interpretations', in shaping political behaviour (see also

Hannigan, 1991). They show that to understand why the transnational Islamist group Hizb ut-Tahrir has so far refrained from adopting violent tactics even though rival groups have done so under similar circumstances, one has to understand its religiously-informed ideological commitments. A mere focus on political opportunity structure, resource mobilisation, and framing, they argue, cannot satisfactorily account for this.

To be fair, a number of SMT-inspired studies of militant organisations have focused on ideology (della Porta, 1995a, 1995b; Hafez, 2003; Robinson, 2004; Gunning, 2007c; Snow and Byrd, 2007; Meijer, forthcoming). However, a focus on ideology by itself is similarly unsatisfactory. Not only does ideology, as we saw above, interact with cost-benefit calculations (which Karagiannis and McCauley largely overlook), but ideology is also in part a product of its environment, as *political process*, *new social movement* and, to a lesser extent, *framing* models, all emphasise. In the example above, Wickham notes that the success of the moral obligation frame was not so much 'a function of the frame's "intrinsic" appeal' as of the way it resonated with 'the life experiences and beliefs' of those targeted, 'the credibility and effectiveness of its agents', and 'its reinforcement through intensive, small-group solidarity at the grassroots level' (2004: 232; see also Snow and Byrd, 2007).

Ideas and ideology cannot be separated from their carriers, the social setting within which they are disseminated and the socio-economic and political context which has shaped those targeted. In the case of the Italian Red Brigades, the development of a more violent, exclusionist ideology was influenced by the increasingly violent state response to the New Left and by the sense of betrayal it felt following the rapprochement between the Communist Party and the Centre Right, developments which facilitated what della Porta (1995a, 1995b) calls 'spirals of encapsulation': militant groups becoming increasingly cut off from their support base, encouraging the development of closed, inward-looking organisational structures and an exclusive, increasingly violent, vanguardist ideology (Hafez observes a similar dynamic in 1990s Algeria; see 2003, 2004). In the case of the EOKA, the militant Cypriot independence organisation, its success in justifying violent tactics cannot be separated from the role played by mainstream authorities such as bishops and political leaders in 'certifying' and 'valorizing' the frames that enabled EOKA to do so (Demetriou, 2007). Hizballah's ideology during the 1980s can similarly not be fully understood without an analysis of the socio-economic changes that underpinned the shift from quietism to activism in the Shia community in Lebanon and the subsequent Israeli invasions (Saad-Ghorayeb, 2003; for structural explanations of Hamas's initial worldview, see Robinson, 1997, 2004; Gunning, 2007c: 25–54).[5]

This is not to deny the causal role played by ideology. Both Hafez and della Porta emphasise that repression alone cannot explain political violence, and that much depends on how repression is interpreted and how the response is framed. The presence of anti-system elements in both 1960s Italian communism and 1980s Algerian Islamism facilitated subsequent developments. But ideology is itself fundamentally shaped by external factors.

Bringing the state into focus

A third contribution SMT can make to the study of terrorism is to bring into sharper focus neglected areas of research. I will focus on two – the impact of state practices on terrorist tactics (see also della Porta, 2008), and the effect of internal dynamics within militant organisations – although there are others to consider, such as the role of the political system more broadly (to be differentiated from the state) or the impact of changing class relations. This is not to say that terrorism studies has ignored these subjects; both state practices and group dynamics have been emphasised as important factors by a number of key scholars (Crenshaw, 1981, 1995; Sageman, 2004; Pape, 2005). But too often, analyses gloss over the exact role of state practices in creating conditions that favour the emergence of anti-system ideologies, exclusivist underground structures, or terrorist tactics, and beyond an acknowledgement that group dynamics are important, too few studies analyse in detail how internal power struggles or organisational culture impact on movement behaviour. An SMT framework both encourages researchers to focus on these aspects, and offers an advanced toolkit for analysing them.

The emphasis on the state stems primarily from the *political process* model. One aspect, which has remained under-studied but is crucial to understanding terrorist violence, is the effect of state practices on the evolution of protest tactics. Bader Araj (2008: 284–288) observes, for instance, that the terrorism literature remains largely silent on the impact of state repression on suicide bombing campaigns, despite (occasional) references to its importance (see, for example, Pape 2005; Bloom 2005). Hafez and Wiktorowicz (2004: 62–65) similarly note that explanations of 'violent episodes of Islamic contention' typically ignore the role of state repression (although there are exceptions, such as Burgat, 2003; Kepel, 2002). Della Porta (1995: 55–56) implies the same in her comparative study of political violence in 1970s Germany and Italy. A rough indication that state repression is indeed under-studied is that out of a total of 1,569 articles in the two main terrorism journals, only seventeen contain the term 'repression' (four of which are reviews, rather than articles).[6] Most, moreover, consider repression quantitatively, as one factor in a multi-factor econometric analysis, rather than qualitatively in a detailed analysis of how repression affects terrorism.

By contrast, the SMT literature contains a number of detailed studies analysing the effects of state repression on protest tactics (cf. Muller, 1985; Gurr and Goldstone, 1986; Lichbach, 1987; White, 1989; Opp and Roehl, 1990; Khawaja, 1993; della Porta, 1995b; Brockett, 1993, 2005; Moore, 1998; Cunningham, 2003; Beitler, 2004; Hafez and Wiktorowicz, 2004; Davenport *et al.*, 2005; Araj, 2008). While conclusions regarding the effect of state repression differ widely, all concur that state practices are an important factor. Because a substantial amount of research has already been carried out, SMT offers a sophisticated conceptual framework for thinking about the impact of state practices.

Hafez and Wiktorowicz (2004: 67–68) note that because different forms of repression produce different outcomes, repression should be categorised in terms of the level of repression used, its timing (pre-emptive or reactive) and its method of targeting (selective or indiscriminate). Other important variables include the institutional context of repression, whether it is perceived as legitimate, how consistently it is applied, and what weight is put on non-coercive, accommodative strategies. Crucially, though, the effect of state practices is mediated through the way oppositional movements interpret them, which in turn is affected by organisational and ideological dynamics (Hafez, 2003, 2004).

Della Porta similarly disaggregates different policing styles, distinguishing between repressive and tolerant, selective and diffuse, preventive and reactive, hard and soft, and 'dirty' and lawful policing (1995b: 57–58). Based on her analysis of the impact of policing in 1970s Italy and Germany, she concludes that:

> a tolerant and soft style of policing favors the diffusion of protest. A repressive and hard protest policing results ... in a shrinking of mass movements and a radicalization of smaller protest groups. Whereas preventive, selective, and legal protest policing isolates the more violent wings of social movements and helps the integration of the more moderate ones, reactive, diffuse, and 'dirty' techniques alienate also the more moderate wings from the state.
>
> (della Porta, 1995b: 82)

However, like Hafez, della Porta underlines that policing practices are 'mediated through organizational processes and individual motivations' and can thus never be studied in isolation. Thus, rather than simply considering – paraphrasing Lichbach – 'does [a particular state practice/regime type] deter or escalate violence', a synthesised SMT analysis would consider 'how does [a particular state practice/regime type] influence the choice of tactics pursued by the insurgents' (Lichbach, 1987: 288–289 quoted in Beitler, 2004: 12–13).

An illustration of how an SMT framework can encourage a focus on the role of the state in helping to create the conditions for violence is my own (preliminary) analysis of how suicide bombing came to be popular among the Palestinian population at particular stages in the Israeli–Palestinian conflict. A widely accepted explanation within the terrorism literature is that the militant organisations employing this tactic succeeded in 'foster[ing] an inverted sense of normality throughout much of Palestinian society', rendering suicide bombing socially acceptable (B. Hoffman and McCormick, 2004; see also B. Hoffman, 2006: 145–165). Hoffman and McCormick concede that other factors, such as intra-Palestinian rivalry and the imbalance between Israeli and Palestinian 'military' capabilities, played a role. But their core claim is that the militants succeeded in inverting normality through social practices, theological justifications, and incessant indoctrination.

Hamas and other groups indeed played a central part in making suicide bombing socially acceptable by bombarding the general population with posters of martyrs, teaching children from kindergarten upwards about the desirability of martyrdom, and according the families of suicide bombers high social status. However, Palestinian militants do not operate in a vacuum. They cannot create the conditions for popular acceptance of extreme methods on their own, but have to do so within particular political opportunity and ideational structures (see also Hafez, 2006). That their message resonated for a specific period with a significant portion of the population was facilitated by, among other things, that population's experiences of Israeli state practices, which encouraged an acute sense of existential threat: border closures, curfews, roadblocks, assassinations, military incursions, state-sanctioned settlement expansions, and the like.

On two occasions, popular support for suicide operations doubled within a very short time frame: once in 1996, following the long-term closure of Palestinian borders by the Israeli state and a series of controversial state-sanctioned incidents, and again in 2000, following the outbreak of the al-Aqsa Intifada (itself a response, in part, to Israeli state actions) and the Israeli state's response to it. In neither case had the militants suddenly become more persuasive or better organised at spreading their ideology (although it was in part in response to their actions that Israel increased its repressive measures). What changed was people's diagnosis of the situation and their prognosis for how to respond as a result of a complex interaction between Israeli state actions and their effect on the economy, Palestinian Authority behaviour, and the activities, including indoctrination, of Palestinian militant groups which tapped into existing cultural, religious and symbolic frames (Gunning, 2007c: 216–220; see also Araj, 2008; Hafez, 2006).[7]

Bringing internal dynamics into focus

An SMT framework similarly enables researchers to open up the 'black box' of the militant organisation and conceptualise the impact of internal dynamics on movement behaviour. Although a focus on organisational form is popular in terrorism studies, the impact of internal power struggles, and how these are influenced by organisational structure, organisational culture, and individual personalities, is far less studied.

SMT has not always lent itself to bringing the internal dynamics within a social movement, let alone a single social movement organisation, into focus (Alimi, 2006: 265–266). Gamson (1990) acknowledges, for instance, that the notion of a social movement organisation had in the past prevented him from 'illuminat[ing] the dynamics among a set of challengers in the same broad movement' because it led him to treat the movement as a monolith (quoted in Alimi, 2006: 266). However, numerous studies use SMT's conceptual tools to illuminate precisely these internal dynamics, both within a social movement organisation and among the different organisations within the wider social movement (cf. Szymanski, 2003; della Porta, 1995b; Wiktorowicz, 2006; Gunning, 2007c).

Analytically, it is crucial to conceptualise the impact of internal dynamics on an organisation's behaviour. Differential access to resources, elites, and bystander publics means that factions are affected by different cost-benefit calculations, identities, and end goal evaluations. Tactical decisions, moreover, are not just about out-foxing the enemy but also about out-manoeuvring rival factions within. Taking the case of Hamas, the political leadership in exile is far removed from the constituencies in the Palestinian occupied territories from which Hamas derives much of its power and legitimacy and, as a consequence, is less influenced by shifts in public opinion than the political leadership inside the territories. The exiled leadership is furthermore geographically closer to the regimes in Syria and Iran, and has close institutional ties with Hamas's paramilitary wing as its primary fundraiser. Without an understanding of these dynamics, Hamas's behaviour makes only partial sense (Gunning, 2007c).

Analytical significance aside, this has important policy implications. If a militant organisation is viewed as a monolith, a typical response is to treat all of its members as equally committed to the most heinous acts perpetrated by members of the organisation (cf. the West's attitude towards Hamas post-2003). However, where there are different factions, a more useful policy would be to engage those willing to contemplate accommodation, while weakening those who remain intransigent by providing visible incentives and addressing, where possible, the main grievances facilitating the justification of violence (cf. the Philippine government's erstwhile policy towards the Moro Islamic Liberation Front; Toros, forthcoming). Failure to do this is likely to drive the accommodationists into the hardline camp (see also Stedman's discussion of total and limited spoilers and his differentiated policy recommendations, 1997).

Deepening terrorism research

'De-orientalise' terrorism research

Employing an SMT framework can serve to de-orientalise the study of non-Western militant organisations. One of the recurring critiques, not just of terrorism studies but of social science research more broadly, is that 'Orientalist' prejudices continue to colour research (Wolff, 1998; Jackson, 2007a: 399–400; see also Riesebrodt, 1998; Hobson, 2007). There has been a marked improvement since Said wrote *Orientalism* (1978). However, one can still find research which too readily assumes that non-Western movements are driven by irrationality, tribal primitivism, ideological fanaticism, or charismatic leaders, and thus lacks either the agency or the structural context that Western movements are assumed to have (cf. Wolff, 1998: 43; for discussion of 'subliminal Eurocentrism' and assumption of non-Western non-agency more generally, see Hobson, 2007: 95–99).

SMT can help to overcome this bias by placing non-Western social movements in the same conceptual universe as Western social movements, subject to the same types of dynamics. It can serve to de-essentialise ideologies and cultures, bring back agency and structure into the equation, and situate non-Western movements not just within their local political and socio-economic context but within the global system and its manifold inequalities.

However, such an approach carries dangers. Because SMT has emerged primarily in a Western academic context to explain Western social movements operating in Western political systems, SMT may encourage researchers to look for structures and dynamics that do not exist in the same form – or, if they do, not necessarily following the same internal dynamics – as they do in (some) Western contexts (see Kurzman, 2004: 297–298). Elections in Lebanon, Pakistan, and the Palestinian territories, for instance, are much more driven by family and clan concerns than is usually the case in the Western democracies most studied. The bulk of the SMT literature assumes the presence of well-established, autonomous civil societies, yet movements in the global South may have to deal with 'weak' or 'deliberately divided civil societies' (Foweraker, 1995: 26–33; Wolff, 1998: 56–57) – although the notion that Western civil societies are inevitably strong and 'non-Western' civil societies inevitably weak is itself in need of problematisation. Movement classifications, such as those found in the *new social movement* literature or in the literature on urban social movements, may furthermore be too particular to be applicable universally (Foweraker, 1995: 25).

There are, nevertheless, three reasons why this problem is not as serious as it appears at first sight. First, political systems and socio-cultural norms differ significantly across 'the West', while there are important similarities between some Western and non-Western contexts and organisations. SMT has successfully managed to accommodate and account for regional and systemic differences between Western national contexts (Kitschelt, 1986; Katzenstein and McClurg Mueller, 1987; Klandermans *et al.*, 1988; Rucht, 1996). It has equally successfully been applied, both comparatively and in single case studies, to non-Western situations (Brockett, 1991; Foweraker, 1995; Kurzman, 1996; Hipsher, 1998; Wiktorowicz, 2004a; Alimi, 2006), and to comparisons between Western and non-Western movements (Pickvance, 1999; Riesebrodt, 1998).

Second, where differences do exist, SMT is particularly capable of accommodating them. SMT provides a thematic framework which focuses and organises what types of questions one should ask. It does not presuppose a particular political or socio-economic system or a particular type of movement organisation, but encourages researchers to analyse their impact on social movement dynamics, regardless of whether the political system is democratic or authoritarian, whether civil society or the middle classes are co-opted, or whether organisations are (in)formal, clan- or class-based.

Third, although an SMT framework is bound to bring in distorting particularist assumptions, the high level of internal critique and self-reflexivity within social movement studies means that the effect of this is lessened. The danger of distortion is obviously there: because of the dominance of certain types of organisational structures in Western studies, an SMT framework may encourage researchers to overlook alternative, more informal networks such as clans (cf. Gunning, 2007c: 149–151). Rational choice proponents within SMT often bring with them assumptions about what it is to be human, derived from a white, male, North American economical perspective (cf. Ferree, 1992). The temptation then is to equate divergent behaviour with irrationality (Wolff, 1998: 56), and to ignore other forms of rationality, for instance, those based on value commitments, group norms, or altruistic considerations (Ferree, 1992: 33, 36–40). *New social movement* theorists similarly smuggle in culturally specific assumptions about what types of protest are considered acceptable, for instance privileging radical non-violent tactics over conventional or violent ones (cf. Johnston *et al.*, 1994: 8).

Similarly, many working within the SMT tradition have until recently worked on the assumption that religious social movements are fundamentally different from non-religious movements, which in turn is derived from culturally specific assumptions about the 'proper' boundaries between the religious and the secular (cf. Hannigan 1991; see also Asad 1993, 2003; Salvatore 1997; Gunning 2007c). Some of these assumptions have their roots in the 'Orientalist' orientations of some of sociology's founders (such as Weber; see Said, 1978: 259–260) which have also inspired assumptions about the presumed propensity of non-Westerners towards violence, irrationality, and fanaticism. More broadly, SMT – and social science more generally – has been unable to conceptualise and study the role of the spiritual in social movement dynamics (Wolff, 1998: 63).

As long as researchers remain aware that what they consider to be universally applicable may in fact be particularist (see also Kurzman, 2004: 297–298), SMT offers a way to study both Western and non-Western social movements. This presupposes a high level of continuous self-reflexivity but also a profound understanding of the specific 'intellectual traditions' and 'types of knowledge' that prevail in the societies from which the militants under investigation hail (Eyerman and Jamison, 1991: 120). Here SMT scholars may have to draw more on ethnographic research methods such as interviews, participant observation, and acquiring a thorough knowledge of the 'deep culture' of a particular situation to better incorporate the voice of the subject and so balance the universalist claims of SMT models with particularist variations.

Increasing self-reflexivity and theoretical rigour

Finally, employing an SMT framework can help to stimulate self-reflexivity and increase terrorism research's theoretical rigour. Lack of self-reflexivity and rigour has long been a critique of terrorism studies (cf. Schmid and Jongman, 1988: 177–179). Graphically, Silke noted that only 1.6 per cent of articles published during the 1990s in the two main terrorism journals dealt with conceptual issues, and then predominantly with the definition of terrorism (Silke, 2004c: 207–209), while Weinberg and Richardson categorised terrorism research as 'largely ... an a-theoretical undertaking' (2004: 138). While the field is gradually becoming more self-reflexive, articles discussing theoretical or methodological issues are still relatively rare.

Engagement with the SMT literature can greatly increase self-reflexivity by providing a wealth of theoretical contention and internal critique. Precisely because SMT consists of competing perspectives which have developed as critiques or elaborations of each other, SMT is theoretically rich and self-reflexive. Much can be learned, for instance, from the critiques levelled by *political process* or *new social movement* theorists against *resource mobilisation* advocates, and vice versa. Ferree's critique (1992) of the rational choice paradigm in *resource mobilisation* is an excellent example, as are the calls by McAdam

(1982) and Tilly (1978) to bring the state back into focus. Another illustration is the exchange between *new social movement* and *framing theory* scholars on the precise relationship between ideology and framing and their respective roles in shaping movement behaviour (Oliver and Johnston, 2000; Snow and Benford, 2000), or Hannigan's plea (1991) to social movement scholars to take religious social movements seriously.

Because SMT is deeply rooted in sociology, it is more explicitly embedded in social and political theory – a key aspect of any critical turn (Toros and Gunning, this volume) – than terrorism studies, with its roots in the more pragmatic traditions of strategic and security studies. It also tends to incorporate more rapidly any theoretical innovations within the wider field of sociology (and the social sciences more generally). Social movement theorists regularly engage in self-reflexive discussions on the state of the theory and its methodological implications, the result of which is a steady stream of publications which combine theoretical reflections with theoretically-informed empirical case studies (see for instance the various volumes of *International Social Movement Research*; Morris and Mueller, 1992; McAdam *et al.*, 1996a). Terrorism research can learn much from this.

Conclusion

In this chapter, I have highlighted a number of areas in which employing an SMT framework can broaden, deepen, and ultimately strengthen terrorism research. The discussion has thrown up a number of key themes.

Engagement with the SMT literature encourages a greater focus on the interplay between militants and the wider social movement of which they form a part, however loosely. What processes encourage activists to move in or out of militancy? How do shifts in popular opinion among the wider constituency, socio-economic changes, and state discrimination against the wider movement or in-movement competition affect militancy? What is the impact of civil society initiatives on militant organisations? Under what conditions are 'spirals of encapsulation' likely to facilitate organisational collapse? Under what conditions are 'spirals of de-encapsulation' likely to emerge, facilitating a move away from violence (research on which is still underdeveloped within the SMT literature; cf. della Porta, 2008)? How do accommodative strategies (state or non-state) towards either militants or the wider social movement influence militancy? What effect do ideological debates in society more broadly have on militant behaviour? What role do 'mainstream' valorisers or detractors have? How does framing affect individual motivations, particularly in the move from low- to high-risk activism?

Employing an SMT framework also encourages researchers to focus more explicitly on movement dynamics, whether organisational or ideational. How is militancy affected by the characteristics of pre-existing networks? What role do organisational structures and changes therein play, such as a shift towards less hierarchical or more transnational structures (research into which is still underdeveloped among SMT scholars; della Porta, 2008)? How do movement narratives affect militancy and how do they develop, for instance from inclusivist, non-violent to exclusivist and violent? What role do collective and individual memories play in this (an area that needs further development within SMT)? More broadly, how are these changes affected by changes in the wider political opportunity structure?

A third focus is on the interaction between militants, state forces and counter-movements, within the context of the prevailing political system, elite alliances, and changing socio-economic conditions. Although the SMT literature provides an impressive database to build on, more research needs to be carried out into the exact impact of repression, both covert (cf. Cunningham, 2003) and overt, and how repressive measures are affected by movement dynamics, such as in-movement competition, organisational characteristics, or the 'temporal location' of both movement and repressive tactics in the cycle of protest. Similarly vital is research into the effect of accommodative strategies and long-term socio-economic programmes on militancy, since research-to-date has focused overly on coercive strategies. In all this, research needs to integrate quantitative studies with in-depth qualitative analyses of particular contexts.

This leads me to a fourth focus: the integration of macro, meso, and micro level explanations. How do political opportunities affect organisational dynamics and individual motivations? How precisely are interests, identities, and structures related? How do structural conditions facilitate the emergence of a particular ideology or organisational structure, and what role do movement entrepreneurs, state practices, and pre-existing social networks play? What function do emotions play in the development of organisational structures, ideas, and behaviour and how are they affected by political opportunity structures? More broadly, and drawing on the burgeoning literature on transnational social movements within SMT, what role do transnational dynamics such as Diaspora communities, transnational economic networks, or transnational counterterrorism alliances play in facilitating or limiting militancy? SMT provides an embryonic framework for integrating these diverse analyses, although putting it into practice remains a challenge for SMT scholars.

A fifth agenda point that suggests itself is a greater focus on comparative research. Of particular importance is research comparing movements across supposedly 'dichotomous divides' – religious v. non-religious, Western v. non-Western, transnational v. national, violent v. non-violent, inclusive v. exclusive systems – in order to challenge prevailing assumptions and gain greater insight into where they overlap, where differ. Here, though SMT offers a ready framework, key themes such as research into religious motivations and structures remain underdeveloped within the SMT community (see also della Porta, 2008), pointing to the need to draw on insights from other disciplines such as religious and ethnographic studies.

Finally, engagement with the SMT literature highlights the importance of making self-reflexivity and theoretical and methodological critique central to research. The very act of drawing on SMT and its myriad debates is likely to make terrorism research more self-reflective, innovative, and theoretically sophisticated. But engagement with SMT should also encourage the field of terrorism studies to become both more self-reflexive within itself, on its own terms, and to contribute more regularly and rigorously to theoretical developments in the social sciences more broadly.

Notes

1 The author would like to thank Donatella della Porta, Carrie Rosefsky Wickham, John Horgan, Magnus Ranstorp, Richard Jackson, and Marie Breen Smyth for their comments on previous drafts.
2 Four of the articles are book reviews. The remaining articles use the terms 'social' or 'movement' without employing an SMT framework, or focus on predominantly non-violent movements. IBSS was accessed on 13 June 2008.
3 This overlaps partially with the shift from grievances to opportunities in civil war studies; however, the model focuses more on organisational dynamics than the unhelpfully labelled 'greed' model developed by Collier and Hoeffler (cf. 2004) and others.
4 Within SMT, a similar division between interests and ideology exists but considerable efforts have been made to synthesise both perspectives (cf. Cohen, 1985; Friedman and McAdam, 1992; Foweraker, 1995: 21–23; Klandermans, 2004).
5 A seminal example of linking ideology to structural changes within the SMT literature is Piven and Cloward's analysis of the American Civil Rights movement (1977: esp. 203–211).
6 That the term 'repression' does not appear more widely does not conclusively prove that the phenomenon is not discussed using different terminology. Search conducted on IBSS on 13 June 2008.
7 More research is needed to establish exactly how people's perceptions changed.

10 The contemporary 'Mahabharata' and the many 'Draupadis'

Bringing gender to critical terrorism studies

Christine Sylvester and Swati Parashar

Introduction

Politically motivated violence aimed at civilians and used by both state and nonstate entities is not new in international relations (IR). The end of the cold war and the 'nervous nineties'[1] facilitated an academic transition within IR from a focus on inter-state wars to intra-state conflicts, particularly those marked by politically motivated violence and terrorism. In some cases, states grappling with diverse ethnic and religious identities confronted powerful internal groups bent on injuring fellow and sister citizens, as in Rwanda, Sudan, and Bosnia. In other cases, unfinished wars left violence simmering and provided the background for people's wars against injustice; the Palestinian Intifada and the Kashmiri insurgency became seemingly permanent 'wars' against state oppression as the international community proved incapable of resolving them. Some wars have been seen as progressive, some are ruthless and regressive: how one categorizes conflicts in Southern Thailand, Mindanao, Aceh, Sri Lanka, Kashmir, North Eastern states in India, Nepal, Chechnya, Palestine and in parts of West Asia and North Africa, depends on the side one supports. There are also state-to-state-to-nonstate actor wars of recent vintage in Afghanistan and Iraq – the terrorism wars.

IR and its cognate field of war studies have been awake to these wars and others of historical importance. Over the years, IR has come to know quite a bit about the weapons and strategies of warfare, world wars and guerrilla wars, imperial wars, independence wars, terrorist, separatist/irredentist wars, and civil wars.[2] IR has long studied the correlates of war, the casualties of wars, the causes of war, the social problems created by wars, and the long-term developmental and environmental consequences of war. What it does not know as well are the ordinary people involved in wars, particularly the women who engage in politically motivated 'terrorist' violence or terrorist acts as gendered 'enactments of masculinity' or as considered acts of agency.[3] That has been left to the feminists to address, and it has been the case until recently that feminism has approached war and terrorism edgily, warily, almost with a sense that women and feminists are outside of war and rarely responsible for it. Feminists and other critical traditions of scholarship and activism regularly speak against war and worry about terrorism, which can leave the field of IR to 'do' those topics.[4]

The events of September 11, 2001 had a significant impact on IR-based studies of terrorism and political violence in general. The state, heretofore threatened with an overwhelming globalization, came into the picture of international relations again. 'Security' was on everyone's lips, along with 'terror', 'terrorism', and 'war on terror'. It seemed that the state was under siege, not by global political economy, but by old-fashioned political opponents bent on taking their grievances and their wars into shadowy netherworlds of state and internations. As a result, sympathy declined for non-state entities that used violence to achieve their goals. Some groups, such as al-Qaeda, were demonized and assigned exaggerated war capabilities. Others, including various Palestinian groups arrayed against heavily armed Israelis, were cut some slack, especially in Europe. In either case, the 'legitimate' power of the state to deal with dissent and political violence was restored. As Gillian Young notes,

> the 2003 Gulf War and its enduring aftermath have emphasized that far from changing the whole character of IR, the era of the war on terror is just as much a story of states and geopolitics, of hegemony, as it has ever been.
> (Young, 2006: 4)

In this ensuing war of states and fugitive non-state 'others' hiding within or behind states, certain individuals have become infamous: the Bin Ladens, Prabhakarans, and Saddam Husseins. Other individuals have been simultaneously marginalized and over-determined by discussions of terrorism. Women are nearly absent from investigations of terrorist participation and wherever visible are marginalized from agency as they have often been in feminist war studies.[5] The chief form of engagement that women have with terrorism is as the pawns of militarized masculinity or victims of the terror moment in international relations.[6] Gender is similarly marginalized and over-determined, such that the ideal-typical terrorist emerges implicitly as a masculine personage, mode, and sphere of conflict, as does 'soldier' in most wars. For the most part, women and femininity are backstage as the necessary homefront dweller in terrorism and war. 'She' is the reason in part why terrorism, counterterrorism, and war are justified: to safeguard the women. We ask: what is wrong with this picture?

The battleground

To answer that knotty question, we can look at the terror moment in international relations through a metaphor from South Asian mythological literature: the battleground 'Kurukshetra', from the great Indian Sanskrit Epic, Mahabharata[7]. The story pits one set of antagonists, the Pandavas, against another called the Kauravas. The Pandavas are descendents of King Bharata of Hastinapur, who have been denied that mythical kingdom by the ruling Kauravas. The two sides eventually fight a fierce battle at Kurukshetra (in Northern India) over territorial claims and other entitlements – ideology, women, throne, and state. One of the central characters of the epic is Draupadi, the wife of the five Pandava brothers.

She is humiliated at the hands of the Kauravas and becomes the immediate cause of a battle that has also been fed by simmering rage and conflict between righteousness or 'dharma', and evil or 'adharma.' In the dominant accounts of the Mahabharata, Draupadi is acted upon and has no voice of her own.[8] She is avenged by the Pandava brothers and returns to a life that is status quo ante, that is, she is now freed from the Kauravas but is still dominated by male rulers and rulings at home.

If we think of today's Mahabharata as the 'war on terror,' which is supposedly being fought between evil and righteousness, we can see a similar line-up of issues. Territorial nation-states fight terrorists and both groups think of themselves as righteous warriors (not as terrorists) full of entitlements – to women, among other 'things.' Terrorists take communitarian exception to the norms of state sovereignty by which international relations has operated for four centuries. The sovereign states are aghast at the audacity and skill of the asymmetrical challenge. Still, nations that do not have states, and identity groups that are bound by non-state or cross-state loyalties, have few legal entitlements in conventional international relations. They are the Pandavas from the epic, brothers who form an identity group or non-state entity to wage war against the conquering and now sovereign Kauravas, masters of Hastinapur. The Pandavas have the support of Krishna, which means that they have righteousness or 'dharma' on their side, while the Kauravas fight with weapons alone.

Modern day Pandavas use violence against states in order to pursue aims they claim are true and just. Not commanding accepted states, they do not/cannot play by state system rules. They are out of bounds, unspeakable, and intolerable for the states or the Kauravas; never mind that Kauravas continuously plot to deny Pandavas their rightful state, doing everything possible to keep them out of political power. War becomes inevitable. The Kauravas mobilize the considerable resources of their kingdom in the firm belief that their authority and power will prevail. The sovereignties and challengers alike insist that they have 'dharma' on their side, symbiotically feeding off one another's insults as well as their own proneness to violence. Each fears defeat against an(other) enemy that is so determined, so certain, and close at hand. Like their mythical counterparts in the Sanskrit epic, today's Draupadis are not heard, even though we often can see them there in the shadows. The story is not about them per se but about how men construct the women as property, cultural capital, and objects of sport. Women's part in the drama is to embody each cause espoused by the men – pure, virginal, subordinated, and ideologically true on one side, and free, autonomous, opinionated, and perhaps subordinated in other ways, on the other.

So far, so familiar. But in the ancient epic of Mahabharata, gender operates in ways that showcase the cruelties of war, terrorism, and men, and that challenge dominant masculinities; even emasculation is common.[9] Draupadi has a central role in exposing the gender set-ups of sovereignties and challengers alike. The Pandavas initially try to wager Draupadi to win back the material possessions they had lost in a game of dice with the Kauravas. The game unfolds and the brothers lose (her). In the wake of their triumph, the Kauravas abuse Draupadi and attempt to disrobe her at the Hastinapur court in the presence of the King and other great warriors, sages, and senior members of the royal family. It is a humiliating scene intended to degrade the Pandava challengers as much as the woman herself. Eventually, though, Krishna rescues Draupadi and that rescue becomes the moral turning point in the story. What had been 'just' a rivalry between the Pandava brothers and the Kauravas turns ferocious over the dishonoring of 'their' woman. The fact that the brothers were willing to put her up as a wager in a game of chance is not seen as problematic: they are just and the Kauravas are decadent. Throughout the ordeals, Draupadi is at the centre of what will be an epochal struggle, and yet she has no script and agency of her own.

How different is Draupadi today in the multifarious realm of terror and the wars on 'it?' Again, the fate of terror women can seem to be in hands other than their own. We know of state veiling and unveilings of women. We hear daily of honor killing of women to preserve the good name of their families. We heard Laura Bush, wife of George W. Bush, speak out early in the post-September 11 lead-up to war about the importance of liberating Afghan women from the Taliban government. Women are taken hostage by insurgent groups in Columbia, the Philippines, Iraq, and elsewhere, and sometimes are rescued by state forces. We have seen women variously disrobed like Draupadi through rapes by UN peacekeepers and ethnic cleansers in the former Yugoslavia (Whitworth, 2004; Hansen, 2001). Today, women can be fought over, humiliated, or protected by states and terrorists alike.

But we also know that women today can take active roles in state wars on terror and in the violent activities of terrorism. British and American women are fighting, being wounded, and some are dying in the wars against 'terror' in Iraq and Afghanistan; some, like Jessica Lynch, are pumped up into overnight celebrities for doing so. Other women join terrorist groups fighting sovereign states and can threaten the lives of school children in Chechnya, wear bombs wired to their clothes in a Moscow theatre, and blow up themselves and others (see Nivat, 2005; Groskop, 2004; West, 2004/5; Skaine, 2006). Women helped to conduct the terror of genocide in Rwanda – indeed, more than 3,000 women are being tried in Rwanda for this. They were pictured gleefully torturing and humiliating prisoners in Abu Ghraib detention center (Sperling, 2006; Drumbl, 2005). Women have been collaborators, informers, human shields, recruiters, sexual baits (in person or over the Internet), and perpetrators of acts of death and destruction (Berko and Erez, 2007). One estimate puts 30 percent of Islamist suicide bombers as women, with their numbers on the increase (Parashar, 2007). In Iraq and Kashmir, where women had appeared to stay away from violence, we now find an unprecedented rise in women's militant activities at different levels. Right wing political and religious movements, and Maoist guerrilla groups in India and Nepal, feature several women cadres (see Sarkar and Butalia, 1996). There are large numbers of women historically involved in radical guerrilla movements in Latin America (see Harris, 1983; Noonan, 1995). Women are everywhere in the terror moment in international relations – in appointed gender roles and in roles that counter social norms. Nevertheless, their voices rarely feature in conventional or critical studies of terrorism.

A dramatic set of readings picturing *World in Collision: Terror and the Future of Global Order*, brought out shortly after 9/11, showcases famous names reciting a 'plurality of viewpoints' needed to think about the odd world we are now experiencing. The index has no entry for 'women' or for 'gender.'[10] This is not unusual: women and femininities are rarely even the understudies for normal international politics, let alone for globally reaching terror, although they might be part of the encircling political economy – as trafficked persons, objects of sex tourism, sex workers around military bases, soldiers in national armies, perhaps aid workers, and so on (see Sylvester, 1998). Most definitely out and about in the world, 'women' of and affected by terrorism are 'burqaed' by scholarly experts, and also by the press and by the power-holders of global governance.

Terrorists themselves can keep women out of the agentic picture. Mohammed Atta's last will and testament, left in a bag that did not get on his self-dooming flight, stipulates that upon the writer's death, 'the person who will wash my body near the genitals must wear gloves on his hands so he won't touch my genitals.' The 'his' is purposive:

> I don't want any women to go to my grave at all during my funeral or any occasion thereafter ... I don't want a pregnant woman or a person who is not clean to come and say good-bye to me because I don't approve of it.

The author of this text did approve though, of serial sexual liaisons in Florida and the Philippines. A chambermaid from the hotel of his choice in Mabalacat, reports that: 'many times I saw him let a girl go at the gate in the morning. ... It was always a different girl' (Kirk, 2001: 1). The obvious point is that the attackers of 9/11 were all men who had visited strip clubs and indulged in lap dancing and drinking hours before they carried out their bloodshed (Brison, 2002).

Perhaps, they were after a 'recovery of manhood from the emasculating politics of globalisation', or they found the West too 'feminised, multicultural, androgynous' (Kimmel, 2002: 22). Perhaps, as Robert McElvaine wrote in the *Washington Post*, it is a matter of being 'terrified of women' (quoted in Brison, 2002). Certainly, the re-masculinization of men and re-feminization of women are simultaneous projects that build on visual gender coding, like beards and short length 'shalwars'[11] for men, and 'niqabs'[12] for women. As for states that seek to defeat the declared terrorist other – and the other's objectionable gender politics – they mobilize their forces without recognizing the gender politics that undergird, inspire, and play out in their own militarized response. IR historically studies the gender politics-avoiding state. Some critical security analyses also sideline gender even as they admirably bring to the fore a range of other neglected issues of security (Sylvester, 2007; see also Roberts, 2008). That some Draupadis of our time do rise and speak out can be subsumed in state, terrorist, and critical security discourses (see Hansen, 2003), rather than given importance of place as operating within, shaping, and being shaped by the gendered politics of contemporary wars. When gender parameters and identities are avoided, critical thinking (some would say emancipated thinking) becomes impossible.[13] There is therefore a pressing need to explore intersections of gender and terrorism in critical terrorism studies, taking into account the multiple and moving frontiers of gendered identities.

Gendered terror

If we were to buy the idea that there is some grand terrorism project in the world today, we might depict it as designed and approved by modern day Pandavas (Osama Bin Laden, Mullah Omar, Abu Musab Zarqawi, Abu Bakar Bashir, Hafiz Saeed, and Vellupillai Prabhakaran), operationalized by manly 'mujahideens' and armed 'tigers' (the Pandava army), whose aim is to purge the world of the evildoers, and countered by heroic males at the helm of state, such as George W. Bush and Tony Blair (the Kauravas),[14] plus countless soldiers (the Kaurava army), who sacrifice their lives to defend their states' sovereignty. When they appear, the Draupadis are hapless victims without any power or agency (see Hunt and Rygiel, 2006: 1), as against the odd warrior woman, whose participation is often explained away by some sort of sadness or perversion. The male suicide bomber is a hero manqué, a rather bold and brave and determined agent of a misguided politics. As Terry Eagleton says of these, 'nothing in their life becomes them like the leaving of it.' (Eagleton, 2005: 98). The woman suicide bomber? Nothing in her life can become her politically, including the leaving of it.

But feminists know that 'for women as much as for men, the experience of violent conflict is not built upon a single discourse' (Moser and Clark, 2001: 5). Terrorists and anti-terrorists hit high profile locations and prosaic places, such as cars, markets, cafes, buses, and trains, where an attack is least expected and the violence is utterly absurd. Markets, in particular, can be places where women and children converge in order to do the family shopping, thereby becoming soft targets relative to targets against 'the' state. Other attacks have occurred on architectures that are exceptionally tall and are identified closely with a powerhouse of business and finance. Survivors of such attacks can be fierce in their retributive convictions, albeit not always violently so: four widows of the 9/11 attack on the twin towers badgered the Bush administration into authorizing a public inquiry into US intelligence failings; RAWA, the 2,000 strong Revolutionary Association of the Women of Afghanistan, documented Taliban atrocities for five years before 9/11 through their own devices and through such dramaturgical mechanisms as the Oprah Winfrey Show (Marsden, 2002: 26). Other survivor women get displaced: the terrorist/terror war refugee is rarely sighted moving away from terror moments in her midst (Caiazza, 2001).

From the point of view of states fighting terrorist or would-be-terrorist states, women are 'collateral damage' in counterterrorist attacks (Rehn and Sirleaf, 2002). Sometimes women do try to prevent that collateral damage from occurring through anti-war activism. Cynthia Cockburn (2007) provides a recent comparative account of women's anti-war mobilizations in countries as different as Sierra Leone, Columbia, India, former Yugoslavia, and Israel. Other anti-war mobilizations range across World Wars I and II, to anti-violence groups that arose in the context of decolonization struggles or in efforts to achieve national independence through liberal methods (Berkin and Lovett, 1980; Tetreault, 1994; Waller and Rycenga, 2000). Most recently, a literature is forming around United Nations Resolution 1325, which calls on member states to bring women into national conflict resolution activities (Naraghi-Anderlini, 2000; Hill et al., 2003). From all these literatures, we can learn about women's militancy and about feminist negotiation styles, forms of mediation, and diplomacy. It is rare, however, to find studies that compare women's anti-terrorist activities with their responses to contemporary wars, such as the Iraq war. One reason is that various forms of conflict merge into one another; for example, we know that terrorist acts can be difficult to differentiate from the background of war in Iraq and around the Gaza Strip. One challenge for critical terrorism studies is to develop a research agenda that foregrounds women joining and refusing to join 'Pandava' v. 'Kaurava' battles, and organizing for and against them today. One suspects that it might be harder than it looks to differentiate the critical position from the uncritical one.

Simona Sharoni (1994) maintains that all women are occupied territories, in the sense that their bodies, minds, emotions, and loyalties can be called upon to play supporting roles in terrorist or anti-terrorist struggles. Some revolutionary movements use 'women' as symbols of liberation and modernization, encouraging them to dress as they wish, to aspire to professional positions, and even to participate in the military. The movement for a separate Tamil homeland in Sri Lanka, for example, officially lists women's emancipation as an aspect of the revolution (Balasingham, 1993).[15] Women there take up arms against those labeled as the oppressors – that is, the Sinhalese people and the Sri Lankan state – with the leadership of the Tamil movement arguing that economic and political freedom can emancipate women from oppressive patriarchal norms through policies that improve their conditions in the private and public spheres. Other ethno-nationalist separatist movements, such as the Basques in Spain and France and the Kurdish Movement in Iraq and Turkey, similarly project women as symbols of contemporaneity and liberation.

Then there are movements in which women become simultaneous symbols of a national culture under threat of destruction or pollution, and a culture of contemporaneity and liberation (Yuval-Davis, 1997). Cases that come to mind include the IRA and Sinn Fein in Northern Ireland where largely male organizations have, over a long conflict, become more attuned to women's issues and to women as comrades and politicians.[16] It also includes the Islamic revolution in Iran where women have political roles that are tightly controlled by the governing forces and that tend to fall into the category of cultural policing. In certain Muslim fundamentalist groups, like al-Qaeda and Hezbollah, men have endeavored to separate themselves from the secular world (computers, planes, and western women excepted), and similarly require or encourage their women to remove their bodies from occasions of insult, impurity, and blasphemy; thus the practice in some communities of forcing women to don the veil and even to remain mostly in the house and quiet

(Mohanty et al., 1991; Messaoudi and Schemla, 1998; Moghadam, 1994). Yet even al-Qaeda has cracked open its patriarchy to recruit women militants, especially in Iraq. The same cannot be said of the Taliban's form of Islamic Sharia rule in Afghanistan which bans women's education, activism, and even physical presence in Afghan society. The religio-political movements in Afghanistan, Iran, Pakistan, Iraq, and India are also known for assigning women the locations and responsibilities of purified 'culture.'[17]

To many in the West, gender-coded rules constitute forms of structural violence against women. Yet women can take up those rules voluntarily to affirm their religious identity, or in the case of clothing, to move about society modestly and with humility. Others refuse to lend their bodies to the practices of sexual objectification that they see rampant in secular societies. And many are hybrids – dressed in plain exteriors that mask western sexy styles and manners; or it can be that they defiantly dress as they please, seeing all of that as irrelevant to their work skills. The question that should be asked is: when are women being forced into confining clothing, locations, or roles in society, and when are women making choices that enable them to control the presentation of their bodies, minds, and religious views rather than conform to prevailing globalized discourse of 'women'? That is another agenda item for critical terrorism studies.

The difficulty comes in figuring out how to penetrate the monolithic images that the Kurukshetra creates of the other in order to see and hear intra-cultural difference. Culture is often talked about as though it were a unified, conformist, and possibly unchanging set of traditions. Whether we are thinking of women's liberation or of women's subservience to men, we can 'reduce women to symbols of either fundamentalist traditions or western hyper modernity' (quoted in Hoogensen and Rottem, 2004: 155). Either tradition can be said to be 'our tradition.' The radical Islamist regime of Ayatollah Khomeini made the re-veiling of women one of its earliest insistences, marking both the end of a different tradition of dress associated with the Shah of Iran and the beginning of the claim that the veil is *the* correct tradition in Iran (Afary and Anderson, 2005). It is also indisputable that Afghanistan has a number of historical traditions with respect to women, including times of cosmopolitan openness before the Taliban imposed the harsh interpretation as the true one. As for Iraq, a recent media discussion of 'Freedom Lost' shows pictures of Iraqi women students at the University of Baghdad in 1976 and women students there in 2006 (Lattimer, 2007). The traditions of dress changed in a span of thirty years, from sweaters, skirts, flowing hair, and unfettered faces to darker clothes and headscarves. Which is the true tradition? Is there such a thing?[18]

To reinforce the sense that there is not such 'a' thing, step back in time to the 1950s. In *Algeria Unveiled*, Frantz Fanon analyzed the symbolism of the veil as it was used during the Algerian anti-colonial war (Duara, 2004). Whereas the veil signifies oppression and 'victimhood' to the West and to modernizers in Muslim countries, as well as to many postcolonial scholars and feminists (see Helie-Lucas, 1990; Mernissi, 1987; el Saadawi, 1982), Fanon saw the veil as a revolutionary instrument – a performance or 'agent' of decolonization. He did so because unveiling had been forced on women during the Algerian war of independence and was resented by many local men and women. Donning a veil could be interpreted as a return to true tradition; or it could be a form of resistance and defiance. We often collapse that nuance today into 'the cult of the veil.' Jeffrey Louis Decker argues that the veil appears and disappears 'as the effect of a dominating power and historical specificity' (Decker, 1990/1: 181). During the Algerian War, it helped to produce the revolutionary subjectivity of women. At other times, it held different or indifferent meanings. Today, it is associated with fundamentalism, resistance to the West, and terrorism as a way of putting that resistance across to the world.

There is a certain irony in critical postcolonial writers bringing women into the framework of revolution or terrorism while feminists can have some difficulty doing likewise. Women as agents of war or terrorism are hard for many feminists to apprehend as healthy and rational people, rather than as distortions of patriarchal power.[19] Their acts can be rationalized. But the agents of those acts can be rejected in a mirror replication of those discourses that equate terror politics with gendered identities. Terrorist violence seems especially horrible to face – to say nothing about being in clear violation of the international laws of war – when it catches up civilians in what can seem to be a nihilist nightmare. When those hit by terrorism are women taking their children to school on the bus, sipping coffee in the cafe, or shopping for the family food at the local market, it can, illogically perhaps, seem beyond the pale of justice of any sort for many feminists. It is also, as Eagleton notes, 'the last word in passive aggression. It is vengeance and humiliation in a single gesture' (Eagleton, 2005: 90). Kill yourself while killing others and, in certain religious readings of the afterlife, patriarchy goes straight to heaven. The vulgar sense has developed in the West that limitless sex with virgins is the ultimate reward motivating the act for men. And for women? What range of heavenly or earth-bound rewards might motivate women suicide bombers? As is often the case, whatever women get out of participation in politics is less publicized. Sex and other rewards need not be a no-go area though, for critical terrorism studies.

Indeed, novelists have fewer qualms. John le Carré describes Bin Laden as a particular kind of man – 'self-adoring,' one who radiates 'narcissism' and 'male vanity.' He predicts that an appetite for 'self-drama and his closet passion for the limelight ... will be his downfall, seducing him into a final dramatic act of self-destruction, produced, directed, scripted and acted to death by [the man] bin Laden himself' (le Carré, 2001: 17, 20). We remember a tape showing him laughing over the unexpected collapse of both World Trade towers and smiling at the knowledge that some of his hijackers were not aware of the nature of the operation until they boarded the planes. Peter Bergen, author of *Holy War, Inc*, a biography of the Bin Laden, reviews the dramaturgy of the tape and points to its grandiose, global ambition to promote resurgent Islam (quoted in Dobbs, 2001: 3). As if any man could do that himself. Do women terrorists have such uber-ambitions? We doubt it, but how can we know without studying the matter seriously?[20]

Women's bodies have long been assigned destructive sex drives, physical weakness, and emotional instability. We remember that Freud thought women were prone to melancholia and hysteria. Feminist analysis has had to work strenuously to correct the impression left even by western philosophers, like Machiavelli and Rousseau, that women are only men's bed and hand-maids – for good (Rousseau) or in ways that cause states to be ruined (Machiavelli). After laboring to establish 'women' as body, mind, and reason, it can be difficult to understand the mind-body relationship of the woman suicide bomber. When women blow their own heads into the ceiling of an Israeli cafe, or march into a theatre in Moscow grasping the cords that will ignite bombs at their waists, where purses often go, the old pathologies of woman repeat. Women are neurotic and irrational. They are pawns in a game they barely understand. Women are the people who excessively grieve dead men and sons.

Little surprise then that many feminists have not wished to issue statements or undertake research on women and terrorism: violent terrorist women can seem to be following old scripts of derangement, rather than resisting them. Acknowledging terrorist women and analyzing their power in a detailed way might be dangerously close to endorsing their methods. There is similar feminist disinclination to tackle the institution of war in the systematic ways applied to trans-historical and trans-cultural institutions of gender, family, and religion. We have studies of militarization, masculinization, women in armed struggles, women serving military men, conflict and development, and gender images in war, among others. There are relatively few feminist IR investigations however, of women who kill in the role of political militant (Tetreault, 1994; Moon, 1997; Nordstrom, 1999). Their motivations therefore, remain sketchy and subject to myth.

Recently, Laura Sjoberg, writing alone (2006) and with Caron Gentry (2007), has been pushing the threshold in feminist writing by taking up the topic of violence and women, and doing so in ways that cannot be construed as disapproving or pandering to patriarchy. Her/their work explores the possibility that violent women are political agents rather than hysterics who succumb to neurosis or demon lovers and other sexualities of terrorism (Morgan, 1989). To have violent women recognized as people who make choices and have influence in their respective spheres of the international is no small matter. As Sjoberg and Gentry put it:

> *women* are not supposed to be violent ... A conservative interpretation of gender sees women as peaceful and apolitical, a liberal view understands women as a pacifying influence on politics, and feminists who study global politics often critique the masculine violence of interstate relations.
> (Sjoberg and Gentry, 2007: 2)

And yet, for all the silencing, subsuming, and assuming around 'women,' women clearly do engage in extraordinary political violence. Feminists are only beginning to enter this area of research, even though there is some recognition of the need to probe linkages between gender and terrorism which have an intimate relationship.[21] Gender may not have a strategy, but the strategy of terror is a 'gendered' one. Women are victims of terror, the bearers of national and cultural identities in terror wars, and, as part of increasing militarization, women participate in 'unfinished wars' and support terrorist activities as patrons, planners, and perpetrators of violence.

Counterterrorist states can also project the sense that they are fighting men and emancipating local women subjected to men's will. The dishonor of women impels war: it is 'dharma' against 'adharma' in Mahabharata.[22] In March 2004, George W. Bush justified continued US presence in Iraq on the grounds that 'the advance of freedom in the Middle East has given new rights and new hopes to women' (Lattimer, 2007: 6). Krista Hunt (2006) warns about 'embedded feminism' in counterterrorist statements and in nationalist and revolutionary movements. At the end of a so-called liberation via foreign intervention, local women can end up worse off; or, if women's liberation was on the agenda of an armed struggle against colonialism, as it was in Zimbabwe, women guerrillas can be marginalized by their societies in the post-conflict period (Sylvester, 2000). Jan Jindy Pettman sees this as the contradictory nature of nationalism: it unsettles older roles and relations by politicizing and radicalizing women, while simultaneously seeking to reinforce women's gendered roles and femininity (Pettman, 1996: 61).

As for terrorist organizations themselves – which, we caution, never call themselves that – there can be military-strategic and not just propaganda reasons for embedding feminist concerns in their strategies. Women are part of revolutionary movements in a number of locations in the Middle East, Latin America, and South Asia, just as they were in the independence or postcolonial struggles of South Africa, Zimbabwe, Mozambique, Angola, Nicaragua, Chiapas, and Chechnya. Women in Kashmir and Pakistan, who have traditionally stayed away from militancy, are now joining up (Ali, 2007; Haq, 2007; Parashar, 2007). Hundreds of women cloaked in the niqaab stormed the Jamia Hafsa seminary in front of the Lal Masjid in Islamabad, Pakistan in 2007, threatening suicide attacks unless their demands were accepted. Farhana Ali contends that militant women pose a potential threat to Pakistan's internal security and also inspire 'other women in patriarchal societies equally disenchanted with their government's alliance with the West and U.S. foreign policies in the Muslim world' (Ali, 2007). Since 9/11, al-Qaeda has 'made the decision to include women, both as support personnel and as jihadic fighters' (Sjoberg and Gentry, 2007: 124), whereas before that time it excluded women from the organization and its activities (Davis, 2003; Bloom, 2005).

Women are killing counterterrorists, themselves, and an indiscriminate range of civilians for their causes. Critical terrorism studies cannot ignore this or give it secondary importance relative to states, individuals, and organizations that have greater visibility and historical centrality in international relations. People embrace cultural assignments and identities while also questioning them in ways that lead to hyphenations like woman-suicide-bomber; understanding that process poses a challenge for critical thinking in terrorist studies, security studies, and feminist and gender studies. In common across all these is the sense that the subject is produced through signifying practices which precede her, while also granting personal and social significance to some of those produced practices (Sylvester, 1994). Critical terrorism studies is well-advised to give plenty of space to what can be termed 'the identities and motivations question in terrorism,' as well as the other issues identified in the final part of this chapter.

Gender and security in critical terrorism studies

Terrorism, gender, and security are intrinsically linked, meaning that gendering the discourse on terrorism implies gendering security debates. Security is one thing that all involved in the terror moment of international relations say they want in some measure or form. The national security state is obviously and intensively security conscious and makes its citizens hyperaware of others around them who could pose threats. New agencies and lingoes define realms of security for us: Homeland Security, National Resilience, Inter/National Security, Aviation Security, Maritime Security, Cyber Security, and trailing somewhat behind, Human Security. Security still comes in the conventional garb of the soldier and the spy, but added to that are various police and private security providers – national police, Interpol police, security guards, and a Special Antiquities Protection Force protecting archaeological sites in Iraq following the 2003 war (Sylvester, 2005). Anything and everything can be securitized on land, air, water, and in cyberspace. Intelligence and surveillance appear on subway platforms, at convenience stores, watching pornographic internet sites, and undercover in public toilets.

September 11, apart from its historical and political impact on international relations, marked the start of what has been called the 'Stockholm Syndrome' in academia (Avishag, 2005). Resources have been flowing to research and teaching about 'new' terrorism and ways to counter it using military, police, intelligence, and surveillance apparatuses. Despite a misinformed claim from critical security specialists in Europe that feminists study war and not security – which shows lack of familiarity with feminist literature (CASE Collective, 2006: 566) – security has engaged feminist IR for thirty years or so, long before the Stockholm Syndrome came to town (see Stiehm, 1984; Cohn, 1987; Tickner, 1992; Hansen, 2006; Sjoberg, 2006). Yet Draupadi Number One remains backstage, her restless mind full of mourning, shame, and humiliation, devotion to Krishna, contempt for the Kauravas, and pride in her five mighty husbands, who she thinks will eventually avenge her honor. She is amidst old props, old actors, old acting methods, old directors, old audiences, and elements of old scripts (Sylvester, 2003). Draupadi Number Two is onstage, active, moving about, securing and insecuring herself and others. With the Mahabharata state elevated above the individual and gendered in the many ways feminists have recorded over the years (Ferguson, 1984; Peterson, 1993; Kaplan, *et al.*, 1999), we cannot see either of these Draupadis, quite. Critical terrorism studies must not only encourage research on the many actors and identities that threaten the national security state, but pay attention to what is found and not assign some of those actors the old back lot position.

Should analysts of gender and terrorism aim for an emancipatory security, as the Welsh School of security studies exhorts? Possibly, but only with caution. Many groups in the world use 'emancipation' as 'the political discourse for inventing humanity' (Booth, 2008: 115) – their own way. Political actors and acts that we associate with terrorism can aim at a kind of cultural emancipation from decadent western trends, identity-submerging globalization, ungodly secular rule, or local injustices. Emancipation can also ring out reasonably among people who have been denied historical recognition by colonial overlords of the past and bloody-minded regimes of the present; or it can be the 'we-know-better' goal of crusaders, colonialists, missionaries, Marxian vanguards, development experts, and those filled with a vague *noblesse oblige*. Some feminist analysts critique the logic linking emancipation and justice to (humanitarian) violence as entirely counter-intuitive (Husanovic and Owens, 2000; Orford, 2003; Butler, 2003; Sylvester, 2005). Yet emancipation has a built-in appeal to those denied opportunities to reach beyond inherited identity into new areas of self-definition, and as a process of removing constraints and conditions associated with counterterrorism operations with names like 'Enduring Freedom' and 'Iraqi Freedom.' The problem is that when a term can be used equally well by people with vastly different and opposed political agendas, it loses rather than gains in power.

Securitization seems to hold down the opposite restrictive pole. It is an omnipresent parental mindset (Burke, 2007b) with practices that can be simultaneously very concrete (such as CCTV cameras), very intrusive (monitoring emails), and also too abstract to turn hyped-up fears into any collective sense of well-being. Surveillance societies put everyone and all politics – emancipatory and otherwise – within a frame labeled 'threat.' Their means are anti-emancipation and all about control. Securitization and emancipation however, are simultaneous tendencies at work today, like pieces of war and pieces of peace existing together on one urban street. Juxtapose those pieces and we form a collage that re-pictures and re-works prior associations. For those interested in Draupadis One and Two, a collage could show the contradictory identities, discourses, and logics that can produce one woman as a silent securitized captive of a larger drama, and another who escapes gender securitization and enters that drama, or goes on the move to circumvent it. The pre-given picture of terrorism or of security is unsettled.

Conclusion: choices and dilemmas

The September 11 attacks and the ongoing war on terror reinforce gender hierarchy and power in international relations. An old habit of rendering women invisible or backstage recurs. We have, as a matter of urgency, thrown more light into the pits to bring out the multiple scenes of gender relations in and around terror, security, wars, and women. Nonetheless, tricks of security and terror are everywhere, even in critical security and critical terrorism studies, where myriad aspects can be seen as more interesting and more germane than gender and women.

We have suggested here several contributions that a gender-attuned approach could make to critical terrorism studies. Among these: it would broaden the personages studied in militant movements; it would render a moving frontier of gendered identities and relations more visible and audible in terrorist thinking and action; it would help clear up confusion over the circumstances in which women choose to become involved in terrorist activities, or to take up fundamentalist social mores, and when women are victims of direct or indirect coercion; it could open up research that compares women organizing against wars of terror and those who enter into them; it could lead terrorism studies to widen its purview, not only with regard to women and gender, but also to include locations that people carve out after terrorist attacks – their places of refuge or displacement, their rewards and their punishments. All these topics have implications both for theory and for empirical research. Finally, and very importantly, critical terrorism studies can learn from a number of 'soft knowledge' fields. It can learn from literary epics of ancient vintage and seemingly tangential content, and from art techniques such as collage, which would have us juxtaposing unexpected or opposing elements (not just emancipation and securitization, but for example, women doctors and women suicide bombers) to see relationships that our discourses and studies might have obscured.

Within that list of contributions and possibilities however, we ourselves find different places of interest. Parashar, who hails from India and studies women militants in Kashmir and Sri Lanka, urges us to problematize what she thinks of as a lingering grand narrative of terrorism, troubling it with multiple narrativizations that reveal how some people grasp meaningful identities and learn to question them too in the challenges of their daily lives. She is interested to know what happens at the fulcrum of accepting and questioning identity interests. Where does that terror-militant woman come from? Which of her many identities are motivating her? Where do we detect her splintered voice in the fragments of violence that she might embrace or reject or conform to? Indeed, can we look at pieces of her wars with forensic eyes or should we turn away from the gore?

Sylvester, immensely tired of the broadsides against the USA that substitute for critical thinking, wants to probe what 'critical' means today. Judith Butler asks a pertinent question in her influential book, *Precarious Life*: 'What has happened to the value of critique as a democratic value? Under what conditions is critique itself censored, as if any reflexive criticism can only and always be construed as weakness and fallibility' (Butler, 2003: 42). She would like to circumvent the stifling climate of exclusion that can surround critical circles and go for more cross-disciplinary democracy. Critical security studies groups in Europe tend to deify their leading thinkers and thereby exclude many others who also think. Conventional terrorism studies reify a state-centric view of the world, unable to think much beyond it. Feminism embraces and avoids: it embraces difficult questions of difference critically, but avoids facing a gun or bomb-toting difference dressed to kill. Sylvester urges democratic criticality within all critical schools of thinking and practice, especially within those that think they already know what it means to be critical. Academic arrogance, correctness, and intellectual listening disorder should not have pride of place in critical terrorism studies.

Parashar and Sylvester agree that new actors and scripts would be enlivening for critical terrorism studies. Mahabharata needs an overhaul so that Draupadis One and Two, who might be the same person with multi-identified senses of shame, humiliation, pride, revenge, diplomacy, and discomfort, can gain places in the larger drama of international relations. That is a large project of simultaneous imagination, juxtaposition, analysis, and interweaving. We place it on the critical terrorism studies agenda and call on philosophers, novelists, painters, playwrights, and flâneurs to join the stolid thinkers of critical theory in pushing into the extraordinary ordinary of wars and terror. People dwell and think in those places and poets and troublemakers wax lyrical there. For us, imagination linked to social sensitivity and international dailiness, rather than narratives of heroics and tragedies, could deliver a more democratic politics of criticality. So democratic, that it can include women.

Notes

1 This term is derived from the game of cricket and denotes the nervousness of the batsmen in their nineties as they get closer towards the century. Tremendous anxiety, nervousness and pressure often results in the batsmen losing their wicket without reaching the century mark. This was also the case in IR in the 1990s when the cold war had ended. The 1990s witnessed a resurgence of intra- state political, ethnic and religious conflicts in large parts of the 'third world.'
2 We concede here the problems in defining terrorism, terrorist and terror. We agree with Anthony Burke (2008: 37), who says it 'seems important to acknowledge the radical instability (and thoroughly politicized nature) of the unifying master-terms of our field: "terror" and "terrorism".' Though there is some consensus on the term as implying a form of political violence, the actors perpetrating this form of violence, and those affected by it, vary according to the nature of the discourse. The suffix 'ism' attached to terror accords it the status of an ideology, although most scholarship and analysis considers it a strategy or even a tactic in the pursuit of political objectives. Burke aptly reminds us that any 'critical' terrorism studies would have to keep the instability and the politicization of the term terrorism at the forefront of any analysis.
3 For masculinity and terrorism see Ferberl and Kimmel (2008). For discussions of violence as more of a choice and act of political agency than the term 'masculinity' implies, see Sjoberg and Gentry (2007).
4 See discussion in Sylvester (2005). IR 'does' war when it is not 'doing' security, a topic area that has expanded so considerably in recent years that it seems to have colonized war studies in IR.
5 Jean Bethke Elshtain is an early exception to that rule. She is entirely interested in women and agency in war in *Women and War* (1987).
6 There are, however, some scholars who have engaged with women's political violence and terrorism, although most of them usually deny any agentive role of the terrorist woman. Notable writers include Bloom (2005), Skaine (2006), Victor (2003), Allison (2004), and Crenshaw (1983). Most writings on women's terrorism are centred around women suicide bombers and women in Latin American guerrilla movements.
7 Mahabharata literally means the Great Tale of the Bharata Dynasty.

Gender & critical terrorism studies 193

8 There are several subaltern/tribal accounts of the Mahabharata that privilege the voice of marginalized characters such as Karna and even Draupadi. See for example, Gayatri Chakravorty Spivak's essay on Draupadi in *In Other Worlds: Essays in Cultural Politics* (1987).
9 One character, Bhishma, is accused of trying to hide his impotency behind his service and devotion to the Hastinapur state. He dies at the hand of a eunuch prince, who had been a princess in her earlier birth, and who wanted to challenge Bhishma's masculinity. Similarly, Pandu, the cursed Kuru King, cannot produce heirs through sexual intercourse and his wife Kunti invokes a 'mantra' granted to her by a sage to beget sons from the gods. The masculinity of the entire Kuru clan is questioned by Draupadi when she expresses her frustration that there is no man in the Hastinapur court who can protect the honor of a woman. And finally, the war itself is a hyper-masculine ambition of the Kuru Prince, Duryodhana.
10 Booth and Dunne (2002: ix). Booth (2007) corrects this oversight in his recent book.
11 Loose pants for Muslim men.
12 The ultra-conservative Muslim women's dress which reveals only a woman's eyes.
13 Swati Parashar thanks Cami Rowe, at Lancaster University, for her insight on this.
14 In the contemporary Mahabharata, we see nonstate collectivities claiming they have resorted to violence as a last resort against injustices of the blind state (Kauravas), which has mobilized military resources against the opponents it has oppressed in the past. The modern day Kauravas' states establish state security and sovereignty as more important than human security and dignity.
15 Balasingham is the wife of late Anton Balasingham, the political speaker of the LTTE. She has supervised the military training of the LTTE women cadres and has spent many years in Jaffna with these women. Extracts of her book are available at www.tamilnation.org/books/Eelam/adeleann.htm#Historical_ Background.
16 We thank one of the reviewers for pointing this out to us.
17 Most of the religio-political movements active in these countries today are Islamist movements with the exception of Sikh separatist movement in India that gained momentum in the early 1980s and which also lost its political base towards the end of the 1980s.
18 Most Islamic societies that are associated with wars against states and forces of globalization, have in recent years imposed dress codes on both men and women. Taliban and al-Qaeda have been at the forefront of imposing the veil on women. Other groups operating in South and South East Asia have also advocated the veil and in some cases forced women to wear them. The Dukhtaran-e-Millat, an all women's radical group in Kashmir, for instance, has been known for throwing acid on women who are not veiled.
19 Cynthia Enloe has long held the latter position. See her *The Morning After: Sexual Politics at the End of the Cold War* (1993).
20 There have been a few studies of women and terrorism, e.g. Neuberger and Valentini (1996), Victor (2003), and Cragin (2009).
21 *Studies in Conflict and Terrorism* brought out a volume on Gender and Terrorism in September 2005 and almost all the articles featured women in combative roles in terrorist and revolutionary guerrilla armies. But its unintended implication was that terrorism can be gendered only by women's direct participation in terrorist activities. It ignored other linkages between gender and terrorism and political violence.
22 'Dharma' or righteousness becomes the rhetorical tool that states use, much as we see in the Mahabharata, the ancient epic. 'Adharma' or evil is what the states claim to be fighting against. But as we have pointed out earlier, the states today are the Kauravas, and in the Mahabharata, the Kauravas were on the side of evil. The Pandavas (the righteous side in the Mahabharata) today are the nonstate actors and terrorist groups, who are referred to as the evil. The discourse of righteousness keeps changing in the contemporary world even as identities are more fixed, with both sides claiming righteousness and 'dharma'.

11 Subjectivities, 'suspect communities', governments, and the ethics of research on 'terrorism'

Marie Breen Smyth

Investigating political violence and terror: ethical and methodological challenges

This chapter examines some of the main ethical and methodological challenges in collecting primary data for the investigation, orthodox or critical, of political violence and terror. These include issues of access, safety, protection of sources and data, risks of seizure or misuse of data collected, and 'contamination' by association with armed (non-state) actors, and conversely the problems of association with governments. The chapter examines the Economic and Social Research Council (ESRC)'s New Security Challenges research funding programme by way of a case study, in order to illustrate some of the issues and elucidate key differences between various disciplines and sectors within the field. The chapter then examines the specific challenges faced by scholars seeking to establish a critical approach within the political atmosphere promulgated by the War on Terror. These include political attack and intimidation, including facing allegations of support for terrorism and the potentially resultant marginalisation, exclusion, and loss of place in scholarly and policy circles, and conversely, the expressions of support, publicity, and camaraderie that can also result. The chapter then draws conclusions on implications for the practice of research and the research agenda for critical scholars of terrorism.

There have been a number of wide-ranging reviews of research on terrorism (see Ranstorp, 2006a; Silke, 2004a; Schmidt and Jongman, 1988; Merkl, 1986; Wilkinson and Stewart, 1989). These reviews have tended to concentrate on research conducted on violent actors, and this provides the main focus for this chapter. For reasons of space, research on victims of violence or the research on the impact of political violence, which raise other sets of complex issues, are not included here, although they are addressed elsewhere (Breen Smyth, 2008a, 2008b), and some of the ethical and methodological issues in victims research are discussed in Breen Smyth (2004). For the same reason, it has been impossible to address the issues of researching the critics or opponents of 'terrorists' which raises substantial methodological issues, since opponents are often part of the status quo and thus more readily accessible to the researcher, and presumed to be closer to the researcher's worldview.

This immediately raises issues regarding the 'objectivity' of research on political violence and terror, and the relationship of the researcher's subjective position, understandings, and insights to the research initiation, process, and outcome. In common with Gunning and Toros (this volume), it is asserted here that research, like theory, is from somewhere and for someone (Cox, 1981: 128), and therefore, that claims to objectivity and value-freedom are highly problematic. Indeed, the very invisibility and irrelevance of the subjective implied in the claim to objectivity obscures a key element in the reader's ability to interpret research, namely, the subjective position of the researcher or author. This element is rarely as crucial as it is in research on political violence and terror. The contemporary researcher operates in a climate where comprehensive processes of 'othering' and demonising the 'terrorist' research subject operate. No researcher can remain immune to contextual influences such as this.

So what are the implications of the ubiquity of this 'othering' and demonisation for the conduct of research on terror? In such circumstances, the claim to objectivity is unsustainable. Indeed, research on violence and harm is invariably conducted within a powerful emotional force-field created and sustained by violence and the reaction to it. The researcher must negotiate this force-field, using their own subjective map of the world, and their subjective understanding of the violence and the actors being studied. The development of empathy with those being studied, an issue that is taken up below, presents particular challenges. Research on political violence and terror (or, following Cox, any research) cannot therefore lay legitimate claim to objectivity in any circumstances.

Surveys of existing research on terrorism throw up a number of perennial criticisms. In 1988, Schmid and Jongman pointed to serious concerns with the methodologies used by researchers to gather data and further concern about the level of analysis that data was subjected to. Silke's (2001) review, which examined research published between 1995 and 2000, found a paucity of primary data, a dearth of fieldwork involving face to face interviews, and that, from a practical perspective, 'terrorist research' had not improved. It was still largely incapable of explaining 'terrorist' events or of predicting the likelihood and impact of such events in the future (see Silke in this volume for an update on this assessment).

After the attacks of 2001 on the World Trade Center, terrorism research proliferated, but, according to Ranstorp (2006b), this increase in quantity did not bring with it a concomitant improvement in quality. Old problems of over-reliance on media, government, and other secondary sources continued. The most enduring of criticisms of the field is the accusation of the dearth of primary research and the resultant derivative nature of many research findings. This lack of, or aversion to, primary research and over-reliance on a limited number of sources has made for a certain narrowing and convergence of views in the field, and the tendency towards over-reliance on state sources has made for a marked degree of state-centricity. Thus, primary research is crucial, since it can expose the gaps in understanding, and the cultural and political biases and misinterpretations in government, intelligence, and media accounts. As Nordstrom (1998) has pointed out, the experiences of those close to political violence 'are frequently worlds apart from the images of political violence (mis)portrayed in public media, formal military texts, the literature, and war museums...', and this discrepancy facilitates the growth of a mythology, which not only mystifies violence, but can disastrously misguide policy and practice. Mahmood (1996: 521) also emphasises how 'face-to-face knowledge can contribute to greater accuracy in judicial and legislative decisions regarding terrorism' in an atmosphere where a fantasy world about the threat of terrorism is manufactured by the media and is extant in public opinion. Primary data is a crucial reality-check therefore, notwithstanding the necessity of corroboration and critical engagement with such data.

The dearth of primary data and obstacles to its collection

The relative scarcity of such primary data is, in a sense, understandable. There can hardly be many more challenging fields in which to conduct primary research. For example, 'finding' and gaining access to one's research subjects when researching armed groups is a task fraught with difficulty, not to mention how to triangulate the data one collects from them. The dangers and difficulties of researching armed non-state actors are perhaps only surpassed by the challenge of researching their state counterparts.[1] Indeed, Sluka points out that both he and Polsky (1967) 'found that most of the risk in his fieldwork came from the authorities rather than from his subjects' (Sluka, 1995: 123).

It has been argued that the very orientation of many scholars in the field of terrorism studies mitigates against the collection of primary data. Brannan *et al.* (2001: 4) point to what they call '*the hermeneutics of crisis management*' within the field of terrorism studies, which they describe as: 'an attitudinal predisposition and framework of analysis – prevalent within the terrorism studies community – that has the researcher approaching her or his research subject antagonistically, as a threat, with a view to facilitate its defeat' (see also, Gunning, 2007b). Brannan *et al.* account for this orientation by referring to terrorism studies' 'communal self-perception of being an adjunct to the various Western counterterrorism agencies, with which terrorism studies enjoys a close working relationship.' Clearly, such attitudes and orientation, (which Brannan *et al.* characterise as a classic exercise in outgroup stereotyping), and any alliance with counterterrorism agencies, comprise serious obstacles to the practice of independent scholarship in general and the collection of primary data in particular. Brannan *et al.*'s account goes some way towards explaining what they term the 'profound reluctance to engage in dialogue with "terrorists"', who are not a research subject, but rather 'research object – an enemy to be engaged in combat rather than a social phenomenon to be understood.'

A further problem is the researcher's anticipation of antagonism on the part of the researched. The RAND working paper, 'Ethical Principles in Social-Behavioral Research on Terrorism' (see RAND, 2007), states in its preface that it is concerned with 'social and behavioral research on terrorism that is frequently carried out in countries or among groups hostile to the United States'. Such anticipated antagonism may prevent researchers, especially those associated with the United States, from attempting to build relationships of sufficient trust with interviewees and may tempt them into some form of deception, which is also discussed in the RAND paper, a practice discussed further below.

Gunning (2007c) has pointed to the dominance of problem-solving and statist attitudes amongst researchers of 'terrorism'. Researchers with strongly antagonistic attitudes are unlikely to wish to embark on an ethnographic or other form of field study of 'terrorist' groups, hence the reluctance noted by Brannan *et al.* Such antagonism also determines the meaning, significance, and value, or lack thereof, of primary data on 'terrorists', since all data will be 'read' through its prism. Researchers are unable to meet the essential criteria of embarking on fieldwork with a relatively open mind, nor can scholars possessing such attitudes make full use of the fieldwork studies of others for similar reasons. Furthermore, a researcher with alliances to the counterterrorism agencies, even if he or she were inclined to do so, would be ill-advised to embark on fieldwork studies of groups regarded as 'terrorist' since such alliances, if discovered by such groups, could mean the end of a researcher's life. Scholars who have formed statist alliances are, in effect, virtually precluded for safety reasons (and by their own disinclinations) from fieldwork, at least with groups that are currently defined as a threat. This state of affairs has resulted in an ever-widening gap in understanding between those whose antagonism to so-called 'terrorist' groups prevents primary research, and those who, because of a desire to understand and in spite of the difficulties, manage to engage in such research.

Within the field of terrorism studies, as it is presently constituted, these two cohorts are not equally well regarded. As Brannan *et al.* (2001: 7) point out:

> The lack of interaction with actual 'terrorists' is evidenced by the literature, and *not* talking to terrorists seems to have become established as a source of scholarly credibility. Based on the notion that the perpetrators of 'terrorist' activities gain legitimacy as well as a propaganda outlet if researchers engage with them in dialogue and allow them to make their own cases, terrorism studies seems to have virtually placed a premium on *avoiding* first-hand contact with the subjects of their research.

Indeed, as Henslin has pointed out, 'people tend to associate the research that a researcher is conducting with the researcher himself' (Henslin, 1972: 55; cited in Sluka, 1995). If you research homosexuality, you are suspected of being homosexual, if you research an armed group, you are suspected of sympathy and support for that group (Sluka, 1995: 289). The researcher risks a kind of 'contamination', 'guilt by association', or a stigma, as a result of undertaking primary research on armed (non-state) actors. Additionally, the security forces become inordinately interested in the research materials, in their contacts, and anything less than a wholesale handing over of research materials, and contacts can be construed as collusion with the armed group.

In spite of these difficulties, some scholars have seen the value of primary research. White (2000), for example, advocates that researchers should seek to *understand* why people engage in small group political violence, by using both qualitative and quantitative methods. He argues that it is crucial, in seeking such understanding, to recognise the activities of all violent actors, including state actors. Some scholars have managed to conduct primary studies of violent non-state groups. Sluka (in this volume) and Avruch (2001) have variously pointed out that anthropology, in particular, has amassed a body of experience of researching violence. Indeed, a body of ethnographic work has been conducted in the context of ongoing violence and terror. However, Avruch identifies the reluctance in past ethnographic research conducted in violent contexts to foreground violence or discuss its impact on the researcher or the study, far less make it the focus of the study. Where violence was mentioned, it tended to be relegated to a foreword on the 'fieldwork setting'. More recent anthropological accounts (C. Taylor, 1999; Simons, 1995a, 1995b; Nordstrom, 2004, 2007) have rectified this to some extent by providing fuller accounts of violence as context.

Perhaps more germane to the concerns of critical terrorism studies, there are also a growing number of studies of armed groups both within and beyond anthropology that utilise a variety of methods, including holistic ethnography, interviews, direct observation, and the like (see, for example, Sluka, 1989/90; Feldman, 1991; della Porta, 1995b; Aretxaga, 1997; Zulaika, 2000; English, 2003; Allison, 2004; Gunning, 2007c). These researchers have taken violent actors as the focus of their fieldwork, and although they do not necessarily foreground the violence itself, they are all concerned with *understanding* and *explaining* those they study within their specific political and historical context.

Furthermore, the existence of many journalistic accounts of armed groups – such as, Moloney's (2007) study of the IRA, Bowyer Bell's (1997) and Taylor's (P. Taylor, 1998) earlier studies of the same organisation, and Trawick's (1997) and Woodworth's (2002) study of ETA, among others – indicates that it is possible to collect primary data on armed groups in a systematic manner and survive not only to tell the tale, but also to produce useful works of scholarship. Researchers (and journalists) who embark on studies of armed groups are often suspected of being adrenalin junkies, or of suffering from Stockholm syndrome (Bejerot, 1974). Researchers who engage in such research have asked themselves if they get 'some kind of thrill' from such research: 'Is there some kind of adrenaline rush to studying violence? Have I become addicted to the excitement of the frontlines? Is there some kind of inescapable perverse fascination in horror?' (Nordstrom, 1997: 19). They also risk being accused by others of 'a personal adventurism rather than a serious academic pursuit' (Bourgois, cited in Mahmood, 1996: 19). In some cases, this might not be without justification, as illustrated by Taussig's admission (cited in Avruch, 2001: 643) that following his study of extreme violence (Taussig, 1987), he was 'a kind of violence junkie'. The individual motivations of researchers engaged in primary research in dangerous fields is beyond the remit of this chapter, save to hazard that those motivations are likely to be diverse, and enthusiasm and fearlessness are unlikely to be ubiquitous. Indeed, fear may be a crucial early warning system for the researcher working in a dangerous field, and its absence can be endangering.

Of course, for some researchers' (Aretxaga, Guelke, Zulaika, and this author, for example), proximity or familiarity with political violence is not a matter of choice, preference, or novelty, since they were born into societies in which political violence was endemic. For others, the risks of violent contexts are less familiar, an occupational hazard rather than a way of life. For the former, whose subjective experience in everyday life has included routine exposure to political violence, the risk of the exoticisation of violence (Breen Smyth, 2008c) is perhaps less than for those with less experience of violent contexts. Indeed, the risk they face may be the reverse, of taking violence for granted. The disposition of researchers in general towards political violence has contributed to a problematic methodological tendency in some of the research to privilege spectacular behaviour over the everyday (see Toros, 2008b; Gunning 2007c), as if the spectacular (violence) can be understood as a free-standing and acontextual phenomenon.

Power and safety

Ranstorp (2006b) recounts an incident in 1990 when the IRA planted two pounds of Semtex explosives under the speaker's podium at a conference on international terrorism in London, in advance of the speech of the British Defence Minister. He cites the incident as an illustration of the dangers of researching terrorism, whereas it better illustrates a point made by Sluka (1995: 280) who notes that there are 'lives [that] are dangerous, and it is dangerous simply being with them.' Being British Defence Minister during an IRA campaign is one such dangerous life, and researchers of terrorism may well find themselves in close proximity to other dangerous lives.

There is a material difference between the kind of safety issues described by Ranstorp and those described by Kovats-Bernat (2002), Sluka (1995), Nordstrom (1997), and others who are operating in dangerous fields, or studying dangerous organisations. Howell's (1990) study of field anthropologists found that: 22 per cent reported 'living through political turmoil' such as revolution, war, or rioting; 15 per cent reported being under 'suspicion of spying'; 42 per cent reported 'criminal interpersonal hazards' such as robbery, assault, rape or murder; and 2 per cent reported 'hostage taking incidents' during their time in the field. Sluka's (1990b) description of the non-fatal shooting, interrogation, and subsequent departure from the field of an anthropologist in Northern Ireland illustrates the risks involved in working in a dangerous field context, and the consequences of a failure to establish trust between the researcher and his or her interlocutors. Similarly, Kovats-Bernat (2002: 216) describes his decision to leave Haiti and abandon his fieldwork after he attracted the close attention and scrutiny of the state's Anti-Gang Unit. The non-fatal shooting by Loyalist paramilitaries in Northern Ireland of Adrian Guelke, an academic and opponent of apartheid in 1991, illustrates the risks that the politically committed scholar can face. In Guelke's case, he believed that the South African security forces acted in collusion with the Loyalist paramilitaries in Northern Ireland in the attack on him (McDonald, 2004).

For those who have grown up with societal violence, whilst other violent contexts can be strangely familiar, one still has to learn how the specific signs of danger are manifest in the particular context. Knowledge of the specific rules places the local interlocutor in a position of power, whilst the lack of such knowledge can render the (outsider) researcher vulnerable. The power relationship usually found between the researcher and the researched is inverted. Kovats-Bernat (2002) points to arrogance in the American Anthropology Association's exhortation in their code of ethics for anthropologists to 'do everything in their power to protect the physical, social and psychological welfare and to honour the dignity and privacy of those studied' (AAA, 2000: 1), and points out that:

> the anthropologist is assumed to be able to control or at least mediate or negotiate danger away from those with whom she or he is working. This is rarely, if ever, the case when working in dangerous fields. More often than not, the circumstances of such fields force a dramatic shift in power – one in which the anthropologist is more likely to rely on local knowledge and the protection extended by interlocutors or other locals in order to safeguard her or his welfare.
>
> (Kovats-Bernat, 2002: 214; see also Toros, 2008b)

The issue of safety, therefore, is not 'merely' a pragmatic set of concerns about the ability of the researcher to negotiate the research field. It also represents a more fundamental set of concerns about who is in charge. On entering the dangerous research field, researchers with any wit will recognise that the hand that holds the gun, or those that command that hand, are those with the rawest and most fundamental form of power. At any stage, working under such conditions may therefore be rendered intolerable for one reason or another.

One common challenge to the researcher is to address the suspicions that they may be a spy. Clearly, members of armed groups and their associates are likely to be hyper-vigilant about the possibilities of infiltration, surveillance, and spying, and their methods of dealing with suspected spies are often interrogation, torture, and execution. Any stranger, researcher, journalist, or mediator entering the field must establish their bona fides before any access will be granted and must ensure that those bona fides are maintained, otherwise there will be real risks to their safety. The significance of sources of funding, affiliations with organisations, and previous track record of research and publication, are all significant, and one must expect these to be questioned or investigated by potential informants. Honesty and transparency are crucial, as is an understanding of the significance of these factors to potential informants. An affiliation that seems perfectly innocent to the researcher may be problematic in the eyes of informants, with resultant consequences for the researchers' work and safety.

Implications for methods and analysis

These configurations of power relationships have implications not only for access to the field and survival within it, but also for the kind of research methods and analysis that is deployed. Kovats-Bernat (2002: 215) describes how 'keeping detailed notes of my interviews could often have jeopardized the lives of myself and my informants'. Sometimes anonymising, coding, encryption, and secreting of data in other locations are not sufficient to protect the identities or shield the data from the eyes of those who would harm those who collect or provide it. Nonetheless, researchers, such as Sluka, Gunning, and this author have used traditional methods such as tape recording when studying Republican and Loyalist paramilitaries in Northern Ireland, or Hamas members in the Palestinian Territories.

Sluka (1995) also advises that certain questions, about planned future operations, the locations of arms dumps, the identity of members of armed groups, and so on, are off limits. The possession of such information places the researcher in an impossible situation, so it is best to avoid knowing these things in the first place.

The conditions under which one works define the parameters of what is possible, what is discoverable, and what must remain undiscovered or unknown. More specifically, informants may impose or negotiate specific conditions that limit or direct the data collection and analysis. Sluka (1989/90) again, describes the 'deal' he made with the Irish People's Liberation Organisation (IPLO) in Belfast after he published his first book about the Irish National Liberation Army (INLA), a splinter group from the Official Irish Republican Army (OIRA), largely engaged in bloody feuding with their own splinter group, the IPLO. In the proposed second piece of research, they agreed that he could interview any member he wished, he could ask questions freely, and he did not have to submit questions in advance, although he admits that he avoided asking questions about weapons, finance, and planned military operations. Two conditions were attached by the IPLO. First, they would review the manuscript of the book before publication. Although they would not have editorial control, Sluka undertook to change anything in the manuscript that compromised the security of any IPLO member or revealed their identity. Second, if there was anything that the IPLO disagreed with in the manuscript, Sluka would give them the right of response within the manuscript.

Sluka saw this as a good deal, where others might worry about the volatility of the organisation that he was dealing with, their internal feuding and frequent changes of leadership, and whether such a deal would 'stick', or whether he too might be drawn into the internecine warfare that characterised that organisation. Furthermore, others might worry about the extent to which the IPLO would tolerate criticism, how this would affect Sluka's ability to be frank and honest in his analysis, and whether the IPLO might not react more robustly than merely exercising the right of reply in the manuscript to criticism that particularly upset them. Was Sluka and his work favoured by a current leader who might be deposed at any time? Any new leader might not like what Sluka was doing, or might not be disposed to honour any deal done with him. These are not only questions about Sluka's work, but about the work of anyone who works closely with an armed organisation. Any such work depends on a degree of trust and mutual confidence. Yet when power lies in the barrel of a gun that could be used at any time, the risks taken by the unarmed researcher can seem enormous. Nonetheless, Sluka is alive to tell the tale, and his is the only published academic work on the INLA,[2] an organisation with a reputation for ruthlessness surpassing that of the IRA.

Received wisdom and training

Kovats-Bernat (2002) points to the inadequacy of the ethical guidance provided to researchers operating in dangerous fields. Similarly, Nordstrom (1997: xvi) bewailed the inadequacy of her training to equip her in a dangerous situation:

> I realised nothing I had read or seen in the literature or media presentations on mobs and political violence resembled what I was observing. I felt momentarily angry that people produced 'truths' about subjects from the safety of their offices, and that I might get into serious trouble because these 'truths' did not match the realities at hand...

Sluka (1990b) highlights the general lack of attention in the literature on research methods and fieldwork to the methodological and ethical issues surrounding the dangers researchers encounter in the field, a situation that, with few exceptions (Peritore, 1990; Lee, 1994) has not much changed in the interim period. Sluka (1995) himself provides advice to the would-be researcher of armed groups, where he summarises the challenges of fieldwork. Following Ellen (1984: 97), he likens researchers working in dangerous environments to professional gamblers who rely on a combination of both skill and luck.

Access

Clearly, identifying and studying those who are fugitives from the law presents many challenges, including establishing access in the first instance. Indeed, the possession of knowledge about non-state actors may in itself be illegal, and certainly will attract the attention of the security forces to the researcher. Indeed, guilt by association is a perennial issue for the researcher. The implications for the collection and protection of data are discussed below, and various researchers have adopted a range of strategies to deal with these difficulties. Access to the armed groups themselves usually depends initially on the establishment of bona fides within their constituent community. Then, Sluka (1995: 288) advises,

> If you want to make direct contact with guerrillas, it is best to make it known that you are interested in this and then wait until they come (or do not come) to you. If you do make contact (which is illegal in most cases), you must be flexible and honest with them.

In my own work, I made it known that I wished to talk to those empowered to speak on behalf of the armed organisation. In this manner, I operated on a 'need to know' basis, and determined that I did not need to know who were members and who were not. Provided they could speak authoritatively on behalf of the organisation, this was knowledge that I judged was too dangerous to possess, and was, in any case, unnecessary for my purposes. Gunning (2000) adopted a similar strategy in his research on Hamas.

Some researchers have not been transparent about their purposes when studying armed groups (see Olawale, 2003), but this course of action is recommended by few if any researchers, although presumably it is a relatively common practice in the security forces, with whom the undercover researcher risks being confused.[3] Overall, the body of experience and practical wisdom accumulated by researchers who have conducted such studies (for example, Allison, 2004; Aretxaga, 1997; Bourgois, 1995; Chaliand, 1969, 1982a, 1982b, 1985, 1988; Chaliand and Pallis, 1984; della Porta, 1995b; English, 2003; Feldman, 1991; Gunning, 2007c; Mahmood, 1996; Nordstrom, 1997; Sluka, 1990a; Taussig, 1987; Zulaika, 2000) is ill-documented.

Protection of sources and data

The researcher studying the armed group risks seizure of data by the security forces, or of it falling into the wrong hands, of which there are many pairs in dangerous fields, and its use for purposes other than those intended by the researcher. In the case of seizure by the state, data could be used, for example, to obtain a prosecution of an informant,[4] a situation that would be difficult and dangerous for all concerned. Both Sluka (1989/90) and Kovats-Bernat (2002) describe the measures they adopted in order to prevent data falling into the wrong hands, such as hiding it in multiple locations, mailing it out of the country at irregular times, and so on. The protection of sources is intimately related to the kind of data collected. As suggested above, the possession of certain information by the researcher will jeopardise both the researcher and informant, so is perhaps best not collected.

Information that is collected may well be compromising and is likely to be of interest to the security forces. The degree of compromise and the extent to which the researcher can honour undertakings of confidentiality – in the face of knowledge about a forthcoming attack, for example – is a substantial ethical and safety dilemma. Whether or not they possess such information, sweeping counterterror laws and robust investigation by the security forces can mean that researchers may find themselves the focus of attention of the security forces or on the wrong side of the law as a result of their research activities. Hence, several researchers report that they experienced the security forces as the greatest threat they faced to their work and themselves. Clearly, the researcher must steer a difficult and fine line between protecting their sources and attempting to avoid prosecution, for example under laws relating to the withholding of information about terrorism.

Academic freedom

Researchers working for government in counterterrorist projects experience the mirror image of these dilemmas. Bhattacharjee (2006) describes a scenario involving scientists working on a risk assessment of the likelihood of a dirty bomb attack on Los Angeles harbour (Rosoff and von Winterfeldt, 2007). The scientists chose to omit some material from their published findings, even though they had used no classified material, in order to comply with the draft guidelines issued by the United States Department of Homeland Security which funds their research centre, and because in their judgement, it was in the interests of national security. As Bhattacharjee (2006) points out, the decision to withhold information has implications, not only for the public's right to have access to the information, but for academic freedom.

In March 2008, Department of Homeland Security (DHS) officials and six university research centres funded by DHS met to consider draft guidelines to control the dissemination of sensitive information generated by their research. The guidelines included recommendations to scrap papers before publication, giving centre directors responsibility for identifying projects likely to produce 'sensitive information', and projects of this nature would attract extra scrutiny. Centre directors, in advance of government regulation, drew up the guidelines as a pre-emptive ploy. The guidelines are likely to have particular implications for the movement and employment of students and researchers who are non-US citizens. Bhattacharjee (2006) has also pointed out that the failure to publish certain studies or certain aspects of a study reduces the chances of another researcher taking the work forward.

In both the example of the scientist assessing the risk of the dirty bomb and the researcher studying the armed group, self-censorship plays a key role in the decision of what to publish. Both are attempting to steer a path around state regulation and practices, and neither is entirely free to 'publish and be damned', out of consideration for the ethics of data collection and source protection on the one hand, and considerations of 'national security' on the other. Furthermore, attaching the labels 'moderate' and 'hardliner' to the researched, can render them targets for assassination, for example. The atmosphere following the declaration of the War on Terror has not eased the burdens or reduced the number of dilemmas faced by researchers of armed groups, or expanded the methods available to them.

Sources of funding

After he returned from his fieldwork studying student politics in Chile, Glazer learned that his funding originated in a United States Army-sponsored research group (Glazer, 1972: 132; cited in Sluka, 1995). For some researchers, this would not present a problem, but for Glazer it did, although Sluka does not explain why Glazer did not know this from the outset or how he responded when he found out. Those studying anti-state politics, particularly as they are manifest in armed groups, must already overcome huge suspicion on the part of those studied as to motivations, affiliations, and trustworthiness. The uncovering by an armed group of a researcher's dependence on military funding, particularly if such funding was not disclosed and agreed at the outset, would be a perilous situation for a researcher to find him or herself in. The chapter now considers a case study of a grant programme launched by the ESRC that illustrates this issue.

Case study: 'combating terrorism by countering radicalisation'

In July 2006, the Economic and Social Research Council (ESRC), together with the Arts and Humanities Research Council (AHRC) and the Foreign and Commonwealth Office (FCO) in the United Kingdom, issued a call for proposals under a joint £1.3m programme entitled, 'Combating Terrorism by Countering Radicalisation'. The programme focused on Europe, Central Asia, South Asia, Southeast Asia, North Africa, and the Gulf, and five specific countries: Turkey, Jordan, Nigeria, Somalia, and Sudan. *The Times Higher Education Supplement* (THES) reported that the programme was 'focused on countries identified by MI5's Joint Terrorism Analysis Centre' or JTAC (Baty, 2006).

JTAC is an intelligence organisation within the United Kingdom's Security Service that provides advice on terrorist threats to the British government and other organisations within the Critical National Infrastructure. JTAC is bound by the provisions of the Intelligence Services Act (1994) and is subject to parliamentary oversight from the Intelligence and Security Committee. The Director of JTAC reports to the Director General of MI5 and heads a staff cohort that includes personnel from MI6, Government Communications Headquarters (GCHQ), Defence Intelligence Staff, the Security Service, and the Metropolitan Police Anti-Terrorist Branch. Six other government departments are also represented by staff seconded to JTAC, who remain under the ultimate authority of their original employing departments.[5]

The ESRC/AHRC/FCO call for proposals identified certain 'key topics', including 'radicalisation drivers and counterstrategies in each of the countries studied' and 'future trends likely to increase/decrease radicalisation.' The programme asked that researchers 'scope the growth in influence and membership of extremist Islamist groups in the past 20 years ... name key figures and key groups ... and understand the use of theological legitimisation for violence' (ESRC/AHRC/FCO, 2006).

The initiative exposed divisions amongst researchers even at the drafting stage. Some accounts say two, while others say four, academics involved in the drafting of the bid resigned from the group charged with advising on the draft. Those who resigned expressed a number of concerns, which were subsequently echoed by others, first, about the safety of researchers working in volatile environments where an association with the British government's counterterrorism operations would jeopardise their safety. Their concerns related not only to those researchers who might obtain research funding through the programme, but also to those who already had funding through the AHRC or the ESRC and who might now fall under suspicion because of this new association between the ESRC, the AHRC, and JTAC, which plays a central role in British government counterterrorism policy. Professor John Sidel of the London School of Economics was quoted as saying:

My concern is the association of researchers with British Counter-terrorism strategy, which is seen in many places as not just controversial but a cause for great anger. It has nothing to do with what one thinks of British counter-terrorism strategy oneself.

(*Times Higher Education*, 2007b).

Second, a number of academics expressed concern that the programme represented an attempt to get researchers to work as spies for the government, handing over names and other information to government, in contravention of basic ethical principles of research. Professor John Gledhill, Chair of the Association of Social Anthropologists, expressed such a view: 'This [research programme] raises fundamental ethical issues. People feel that it smacks of the cold war use of academics in counter-insurgency activities – essentially using academics as spies' (Baty, 2006).

Third, some expressed concern about the influence of government on the design of the programme and the conditionality of government funding, based on the usefulness of the outcomes of the research to government counterterrorist work. An email leaked to the THES revealed that a senior policy manager in the ESRC had confirmed that the FCO had said it would withdraw its share of the funding 'if its interests are not met by the selected projects' (*Times Higher Education*, 2007b).

Fourth, some expressed concern about the independence of any research emanating from the programme. Martha Mundy pointed out that the programme 'started from the premise of a link between Islamism, radicalisation (nowhere defined) and terrorism' (Baty, 2006). Thus, both the selection of projects for funding and the very ideas contained in the project were based on a predetermined interest of the government. The possibility of independent scholarship, she argued, was compromised even before the programme began.

Finally, one researcher alleged that, as a result of the FCO's involvement in the project and their identification of the selected regions, that the programme was: 'designed to meet the needs of its US ally, whose counterterrorism initiatives have been running into an increasing number of difficulties' (*Times Higher Education*, 2007a).

Following these objections and others, the ESRC, AHRC, and the FCO redrafted the bid and reissued it in March 2007. The ESRC website described the new programme as follows:

The aim of the initiative is to produce an informed and critical assessment of the diverse causes of 'radicalisation' and transnational political violence. It will also critically engage with uses of the term 'radicalisation'. Proposals for two kinds of projects are invited. The first will examine social, political and religious dynamics in and across particular countries and regions; the second will concentrate on thematic issues that cut across geographically defined regions and will provide comparisons with different forms of violent and non-violent movements.[6]

Although the second bid appeared to address many of the concerns raised by scholars objecting to the first bid, it remained problematic on a number of grounds. First, it continued to use the problematic term 'radicalisation', implied that radicalisation was a new phenomenon, and placed it within a framework of 'new terrorism', the newness of which is somewhat contested in the field (see for example, Copeland, 2001; Duyvesteyn, 2004). The emphasis in the bid was very heavily on Muslim communities, arguably contributing to a process of demonisation of those communities. The Foreign and Commonwealth Office remained one of the sponsors, contributing 16 per cent of the budget, a further 16 per cent coming from the AHRC, and the remainder from the ESRC. The call explained that the initiative was located inter alia within the FCO's *Prevent* policy, and that through that strategy the FCO seeks to tackle the 'radicalisation of individuals by tackling disadvantage', 'deterring those who facilitate terrorism', and 'engaging in the battle of ideas'. The geographical focus of the bid was on countries outside of the UK, although they listed Europe as one of the target areas. The bid described their 'topics of relevance' as 'the social profile of those who may support or be attracted to violence', 'diverse forms of avowedly Islamist mobilisation, both political and non-political, violent and non-violent', 'the diversity of Islamic schools', and so on. The totality of these factors meant that many scholars remained uncomfortable about the way the call was framed and wary of taking money earmarked for counterterrorism, which the FCO's contribution clearly was. As a result, the idea of submitting a bid to the re-drafted programme seemed to some to be unnecessarily compromising.

On the other side of the argument, from the outset, the Chair of the AHRC, Professor Philip Esler, could see no harm even in the first bid and commented that:

> It is appropriate that the AHRC enables the powerful intellectual resources in the UK to focus on particular public policy issues.
>
> (Baty, 2006)

The ESRC director of research spoke reassuringly of the limited amount of fieldwork involved and the ethical tests that projects in the first bid would be subjected to. The FCO reported that they were working with the research councils to make sure that 'the work was independent, transparent, academically sound and properly peer-reviewed'.

(Baty, 2006)

The ESRC Programme Director responded by email to the author's questions about the first and second bid. When asked about the ethical issues raised by the first bid, he complained that the press coverage in the THES had implied that the programme was aimed at recruiting academics as spies or collecting intelligence, which he believed betrayed a lack of understanding about the way things work. Although such practices were relatively commonplace in the past, he saw this as a ridiculous accusation, because academics were unlikely to possess intelligence not already in the hands of the intelligence services. Rather, he saw the purpose of the programme as academics engaging with government to improve their understanding of particular issues.

In relation to the second bid, the ESRC Programme Director described how some of the objections expressed to him were due to some scholars' ethical aversion to taking government money, or to having any connection with the state whilst other objections were due to some scholars' wish to avoid being associated with UK government operations and policy in Iraq. He found both of these positions unconvincing. He did, however, take on board the issues raised in relation to the safety of researchers, accepting that some researchers might inadvertently attract suspicion whilst conducting fieldwork, and that this could endanger other researchers in the programme. He described how the ESRC ensured that all applicants were briefed about the ethical considerations, and one proposal was rejected on ethical grounds.

When asked about general ethical principles to ensure academic integrity in the context of government funding of research on political violence, he found it strange that some researchers believed that government funding and academic integrity were mutually incompatible. An academic commitment to quality research and the independence of research results resolved the incompatibility, in his view.

Decisions made by researchers – who are not necessarily anti-state – such as when to avail of government funding or accept government commissions and when to forgo such work, are taken, not only in the context of a volatile or dangerous field of research, but also in the context of the source government's domestic and foreign policies at any moment. The current UK government's policies in Iraq and Afghanistan and its involvement on the War on Terror create a situation where acceptance of government sponsorship of research in any of those regions, or on any matter related to Jihadi extremism, may well be taken as support for UK government policies. However, in some contexts, researchers with government funding may be regarded as a useful conduit to government, although if such researchers' findings are not used by government, this may lead to a sense of betrayal and a withdrawal of cooperation. Furthermore, researchers must carefully consider any conditionality attached to the funding, particularly a withdrawal of funding if the results do not suit the government's purpose. Such conditionality could compromise the integrity of the research and hold a metaphorical gun to the head of researchers, who are pressurised to produce the 'right' result. Of course, all grants, whether from government or elsewhere, have conditions attached and researchers exercise judgement when deciding to accept such conditions.

One of the notable features of the ESRC/AHRC case is the division of views it exposed amongst scholars. Some, those who remained involved in drafting and those involved in the ESRC and AHRC, regarded the programme as largely unproblematic, whilst others raised strong objections, resigned from the drafting committee, warned their colleagues of the dangers, and refused to participate in the scheme. In order to explore this division, an audit of all twelve academics who expressed a view, either in favour or in opposition, through the THES was conducted and their disciplinary and regional specialisms noted. These were established by visiting their staff web pages on their employing university's website. An examination of this information reveals that those academics who supported the bid or regarded it as non-problematic tended not to have regional expertise in contemporarily war-torn societies, nor to have an area studies background. Rather they came from strategic or diplomatic studies, or in one case, religious studies. Those academics who opposed the bid had field experience in a developing or war-torn country or a 'suspect community'.

The division of view between the two cohorts almost entirely coincided with their disciplinary bases. Those engaged in primary research in dangerous fields, or with an area studies background, opposed the bids, presumably because they could see potential dangers not only for themselves if they participated in the scheme, but for British academics in general because of the close association of academic research with government counterterrorist initiatives. Even if they did not participate in the scheme, the scheme created the risk that they would be 'tainted' by association with an ESRC or an AHRC, or a British academia in general, which was perceived to be participating in British government counterterrorist operations. Perhaps the most obvious lesson from these events is that field experience or disciplinary base seems to shape the way in which academics perceive ethical and methodological issues, including the recognition and assessment of risk. It raises questions about similar divisions of view between these cohorts in relation to the nature and causes of terrorism itself and in relation to ways to end terrorism.

In summary, the challenge issued by scholars following the first announcement led to recognition being given to their concerns, and the second version was clearly shaped by those concerns. The lesson is clear: it is crucial to involve those with actual field experience when advising on the design and limitations of research programmes aimed at supporting field research. The ESRC/AHRC New Security Challenges experience also raises a number of unresolved issues: why government funding of medical research is relatively unproblematic, whilst government funding for research on political violence raises such sensitivities; and if critical scholars abjure funding from government, does that leave the field wide open for less critical (or less scrupulous) scholars to hold sway unchallenged; and what are the implications for both government policy and academic practice? These are extremely important debates.

Challenges faced by critical scholars

As alluded to earlier, orthodox and critical scholars occupy rather different positions in the world of terrorism studies. Orthodox scholars work in collaborative relationships with government and counterterrorist agencies, they enjoy respectability, and their views are quoted in the popular press and other mainstream outlets. The critical scholar, in comparison, ploughs a rather more difficult and lonely furrow where other difficulties arise. Critical scholars also face the risk of co-option, and studies of armed groups where the researcher is 'embedded', to a greater or lesser extent, present the risk of 'going native' or succumbing to the Stockholm syndrome (Bejerot, 1974), as discussed above.

Researchers studying what Hillyard (1993) refers to as 'suspect communities' run similar risks, but also face a range of ethical dilemmas: overcoming the suspicions of a suspect community and establishing relationships of trust; gaining entry; discharging the ethical responsibility to 'do no harm' given the vulnerability of such communities; creating and maintaining a critical engagement with the community and the various parts or factions of it; and maintaining a balance between participation in order to understand the issues, whilst resisting being drawn into intercommunity conflicts. The researcher must also determine the extent to which it is ethically and professionally appropriate to become an advocate for the community or part thereof. This decision will be influenced to some extent by how the (critical) researcher negotiates the issue of power, how their own power and privilege is understood and owned or disowned, how the position of the researched is perceived, and how the researcher positions him/herself in relation to it. It has been popular amongst critical researchers to aspire to 'speaking truth to power', using their knowledge and position to advocate in the interests of the less powerful. However, a realistic appraisal of the impact of such advocacy has led some to question whether power ever listens to truth and, indeed, whether researchers are capable of entirely defining it (Haas, 2004).

The ESRC/AHRC/FCO programme illustrates some of the difficulties faced by critical scholars in relation to funding. Some sources of funding are off limits to critical scholars, because of the political bias of the sources or the way research is framed, because of the conditions attached, because of the jeopardy for researchers in accepting money from that source, or because of the political predelictions of the funder.

Critical scholars also face political attack and intimidation, which include accusations of 'unpatriotic attitudes', sympathy with terrorists or support for terrorism, or in the case of those who criticise policies of the state of Israel, anti-Semitism. These attacks have been most concerted in the United States where a number of organisations and their associated websites have led an offensive against scholars who express dissident views, particularly about American foreign policy and the War on Terror. Gould-Wartofsky (2008: 1) summarised these developments as follows:

> From Harvard to UCLA, the ivory tower is fast becoming the latest watchtower in Fortress America. The terror warriors, having turned their attention to 'violent radicalization and homegrown terrorism' – as it was recently dubbed in a House of Representatives bill of the same name – have set out to reconquer that traditional hotbed of radicalization, the university.

The task of that 'reconquering' has been assumed by a number of organisations. For example, the American Council of Trustees and Alumni (ACTA) describes itself as 'a nonpartisan, nonprofit, educational organization committed to academic freedom, excellence and accountability at America's colleges and universities.'[7]

ACTA was launched by Lynne V. Cheney, wife of US Vice President Dick Cheney, and Senator Joseph I. Lieberman of Connecticut, amongst others. It claims to work to 'support liberal arts education, uphold high academic standards, safeguard the free exchange of ideas on campus, and ensure that the next generation receives a philosophically-balanced, open-minded, high-quality education at an affordable price' (ACTA, no date). In pursuit of these goals, on 11 November 2001, ACTA issued a report that listed the names of academics along with 117 statements they made, in public forums or in classes, that questioned aspects of the US administration's war on terrorism. On 9 January 2002, Martin Sherwin, the Walter S. Dickson Professor of English and American History at Tufts University in Medford, Massachusetts, placed an advertisement in *The Nation* entitled, 'Tattletales for an Open Society', outing himself as a critical voice and asking for his name to be added to the list (Sherwin, 2002). There followed a stream of scholars offering themselves for inclusion on the ACTA's public list 'of those with the nerve to question aspects of the Bush Administration's war on terrorism' (see Various contributors, 2002).

Daniel Pipes is a neoconservative American historian and political commentator who specialises in the Middle East and Islam. Pipes' think tank, the Middle East Forum, established a website in 2002 called Campus Watch. Through the Campus Watch website, Pipes invited students and academic staff to submit information on 'Middle East-related scholarship, lectures, classes, demonstrations, and other activities relevant to Campus Watch.' Campus Watch was accused of 'McCathyesque intimidation' of professors who criticized Israel when it published 'dossiers' on eight professors it thought 'hostile' to America. The 'Keep Us Informed' section of the Campus Watch website provoked outrage, as it encouraged students to inform on their lecturers, rather than openly engage them in debate and challenge as part of normal academic practice. Those listed on the Campus Watch site attracted death threats and their email was paralysed by a storm of hate mail.

Subsequently, over 100 academics demanded that their names be added to the 'blacklist' (Schevitz, 2002a). In October 2002, Campus Watch removed the dossiers from their website (Schevitz, 2002b) on the grounds that it was distracting people from their main purpose. McNeil (2002) contends that Pipes' purpose is not merely to silence a number of scholars, but to cut off government funding to Middle East area studies programmes in US universities and redirect it to a new Defense Department programme entitled the National Flagship Language Initiative, which establishes courses in Arabic, Farsi, and Turkish, inter alia, and encourages American students willing to make a 'good faith effort' to join the Defense Department, the CIA, or other such US government agencies when they graduate. Continuation of funding was linked to the avoidance of teaching material critical of America (Kramer, 2001).

Whilst the United States has seen the worst of such political witch-hunts, attempts in the same vein have been experienced elsewhere. In 2006, Professor Riaz Hassan of Flinders University received a phone call from the Australian Attorney General warning against interviewing terrorists as part of his research on suicide attacks on the grounds that his original research design contravened Australian anti-terror laws (Shepherd, 2006).

In the UK, THES reported that Police Special Branch were to offer to train academic staff how to monitor students for signs of extremism, on the assumption that Muslim extremists operate on the campuses of UK universities. It was suggested that academic staff have 'a role to play in monitoring and reporting actual and potential extremist activity'. The proposed measures did not meet with universal disapproval from academics. Professor Anthony Glees, Director of the Centre for Intelligence and Security at Brunel University, commented: 'Universities have had to be dragged kicking and screaming, to act on this. There are far too many opportunities for extremists to act on campus' (Sanders, 2006). Glees penned an article for THES in July 2007 in which he variously named Richard Jackson, Bill Durodie, Lord Hoffman, and Sir Ken McDonald, the Director of Public Prosecutions, as some of those who wrongly and dangerously minimize the Muslim terrorist threat. He asserted that: 'the evidence of a link between incitement to extremism of young British Muslims by Islamist preachers and their turning to terrorism is now so convincing that *only academics with a vested interest in denying the facts can dispute it*' (Glees, 2007, emphasis added).

In December 2006, the THES reported (Baty and Shepherd, 2006) that academics with high profile research which challenged UK government policy were 'subjected to concerted campaigns of vilification'. They have had their work publicly rubbished and have been subjected to repeated personal criticisms. The evidence for this emerged shortly after the House of Commons Science and Technology Select Committee voiced 'extreme concerns' that the government had manipulated research findings in order to support its agenda. The House of Commons Committee concluded that the government should desist from making claims that its policies were 'evidence-based'.

Other attacks in the UK have emanated from right-wing journalist, Melanie Phillips, who, as a kind of Daniel Pipes manquée, has published sporadic attacks on her blog at *The Spectator* on all three editors of this book at various times over the past couple of years. Phillips, formerly a leftist, now an ardent Zionist who will brook no criticism of Israel and brands those who criticize Israel as 'Jew-haters', has used uncorroborated, and often false, information passed surreptitiously to her by students to label academics as ultra-leftist, Stalinist, subversive, or accuse them of pedalling hate-filled propaganda against Israel.

Scholars critical of government policy have also been subjected to attacks seemingly aimed at intimidating them, marginalising their work, and ultimately excluding them from academia. Many of these attacks are personal and fail to engage with the substantive issues, such as US or Israeli foreign policy, the advisability of talking to terrorists, and so on. The arguments are not aired, and open debate is not fostered; rather, debate is shut down. Tactics include complaining to the scholar's employing university about a scholar's politics, or the scholars are 'named and shamed' on the Internet to an audience of millions of people, some of whom may be moved to send hate mail, issue death threats or do worse. However, when such attacks occur, almost invariably those attacked have reported that they received substantial numbers of gestures of support and solidarity.

Perhaps it is small wonder, in the light of all this, that a survey reported in *The Times Higher* in October 2006 found that 80 per cent of academics thought that UK scholars could no longer 'speak truth to power'. Yet there are those who persist in doing so, in spite of pressure to desist.

Implications for the practice of research and a critical research agenda

Most reviews of terrorism research have pointed to the second-hand and recycled nature of much of the evidence relied upon by the literature. From this, it is evident that the collection of fresh, first-hand data must be a priority for critical and orthodox scholars alike. Whilst the conduct of primary studies of terror-wielding non-state groups poses many challenges for researchers, these are not insuperable, as several scholars, including Gunning and Sluka in this volume, have illustrated. The knowledge derived from such studies is essential to the task of broadening and deepening scholarship on terrorism, and critical scholars are well placed in terms of their abilities to engage in the field, develop trust, and manage the risks to undertake primary data collection. However, the considerable difficulties posed by the authorities remains a particular difficulty for scholars, in an atmosphere where undertaking research that involves 'talking to terrorists' may attract censure or worse from the authorities, and where certain kinds of results from research are more acceptable than others. The wider political atmosphere of intimidation of scholars expressing certain views is also less than conducive to scholarly enquiry and analysis.

Although critical scholars may wish to distance themselves from certain aspects of government policy, it is crucial that they remain engaged with policymakers, so that policy is informed by a diverse range of views, not merely the orthodoxy. Critical scholars cannot complain about government policy on terrorism if they have not attempted to inform that policy. Even though critical voices may be disregarded or not taken seriously, critical scholars should not let this prevent them from talking to policymakers and government, and speaking 'truth to power', even though 'power' may not listen.

Some worry about accepting government funding, and the case study presented here illustrates how the design of research programmes and the involvement of certain agencies may preclude scholars' participation. However, this does not mean that all government funding is problematic or that it is not possible to accept funding from government and retain one's integrity – and one's safety. Such decisions are made on a case-by-case basis: after all, both governments and research fields change over time.

How do we engage with government and remain critical and independent? The answer is the formation of a community of critical scholars that engages in ongoing debate and consultation with each other about contemporary issues, and seeks second opinions and views from each other. Even though we are at an early stage of the critical turn in terrorism studies, I do not think it is sentimental to say that this community has begun to form. Such a community is important for withstanding the kind of political attack that some critical scholars have been subjected to, and paradoxically and happily, such attacks tend to consolidate such communities, although the concomitant risk is that a ghetto mentality might develop.

The difficulties described above notwithstanding, a renewed support for and involvement in primary research by critical scholars is advocated. Our universities must provide thorough training and preparation for both new and seasoned scholars proposing to work in dangerous fields, through the development of curricula, courses, and bibliographies on the subject, and through exposure to scholars experienced in such fieldwork. Scholars with fieldwork experience must follow Sluka's (1990b) example and draw the lessons from their fieldwork experience and publish them in order to provide advice and stimulation for scholars embarking on fieldwork for the first time. Such literature will also open up and take forward the much-needed debates about ethics and methods in the field.

Finally, it is important to ask who research on terrorism is for. Some critical scholars tend towards a Boothian redefinition of security, focused on the security and well-being of the individual not the security of the state – security as emancipation, with all the difficulties of definition that that raises (see also Toros and Gunning, and McDonald, this volume). Our research ultimately aims at providing a firm knowledge base from which we can understand the political desperation of those who resort to terroristic methods and pre-empt such methods through non-violent, political, and diplomatic means, and through widening and deepening political participation both locally and globally. We must also establish the real effect of contemporary counterterrorist methods, their effects on political attitudes, actual human rights, and the human rights culture, since many suspect they are counterproductive. These are the contributions critical scholars can make to 'solving' terrorism.

Notes

1 See, for example, the difficulties faced by a researcher investigating counterterrorist policing practice in Northern Ireland in Ellison (1997) – subsequently enlarged and published in Smyth and Ellison (1999).
2 There is also one journalistic study of the INLA by Holland and McDonald (1994), and a study of international support (Craig and Geldard, 1988).
3 See the discussion on the practice of deception in research on terrorism in RAND (2007a).
4 Journalist Ed Moloney faced prison in 1999 over a court order to surrender his notes of an interview. The order was taken under the Prevention of Terrorism Act, making the threat of jail more likely than in civil disclosure cases. The notes were of an interview nine years previously with Billy Stobie, a former loyalist paramilitary then charged with the murder in 1989 of human rights solicitor Pat Finucane. Billy Stobie had claimed in the interview that he had told the police that the murder was planned

and they did nothing to stop it. High Court Judge John Foster eventually threw out the order against Moloney, ruling that it was insufficient for police to say that the notes might contain information useful to them; they would have to give stronger reasons for an order. 'I am sure most journalists' notebooks contain material that might be useful to police, especially in Northern Ireland,' the judge said. See www.londonfreelance.org/moloney.html, accessed 12 July 2008.
5 See www.mi5.gov.uk/output/Page65.html, accessed 8 September 2008.
6 See www.esrc.ac.uk/ESRCInfoCentre/opportunities/current_funding_opportunities/New_Security_Challenges.aspx?ComponentId=18575&SourcePageId=5433, accessed 21 July 2007.
7 See https://www.goacta.org/, accessed 13 July 2008.

12 Critical terrorism studies
Framing a new research agenda

Richard Jackson, Marie Breen Smyth and Jeroen Gunning

Introduction

As the chapters in this volume demonstrate, critical terrorism studies (CTS) incorporates and draws inspiration from a rich array of theoretical approaches and research traditions. We would argue that this kind of analytical and disciplinary eclecticism is a real source of strength in terrorism research, because the inclusion of multiple perspectives and diverse voices enlivens and enriches our understanding of the various dimensions of the phenomenon. At the same time, within the different approaches and traditions represented in this book, we believe there is a shared set of concerns and commitments which collectively constitute a discernible and discrete 'critical' approach to the study of political terrorism. More than simply a call for better scholarship, we argue that CTS entails a comprehensive intellectual orientation which speaks to all the important dimensions of research practice: ontology, epistemology, methodology, ethics, and praxis.

The primary aim of this final chapter is to try and summarise the overall argument we have been making for critical terrorism studies and to take stock of what we have achieved thus far and where we aim to be in the future. To this end, the chapter is divided into four main sections. In section one, we summarise what we see to be some of the most serious problems and weaknesses in the orthodox terrorism studies field, drawing largely upon the first four chapters of the volume. The second section outlines and explores what we believe to be the primary intellectual and ethical commitments of a CTS approach. In the third section we attempt to sketch out the outlines of a future CTS research agenda. This is perhaps the most important part of the entire book, as the CTS project will most likely succeed or fail to the extent that it can go beyond critique and deconstruction and generate a clear, achievable, and credible research agenda of its own (in which critique and deconstruction will nevertheless remain a central concern). In the final concluding section, we reflect on some of the potential pitfalls and dangers of the CTS project and make a few suggestions for how they might be avoided.

Problems in terrorism studies

As we argued in the Introduction to this volume, the case for adopting an explicitly critical approach to the study of political terrorism initially rests upon a critique of the existing field. As the first four chapters in this volume, as well as a large number of previous studies, clearly demonstrate (see for example, Stohl, 1979; Herman, 1982; Schmid and Jongman, 1988; Herman and O'Sullivan, 1989; George, 1991a; Reid, 1993; Zulaika and Douglass, 1996; Silke, 2004a; Burnett and Whyte, 2005; Ranstorp, 2006b; Jackson, 2007e; Gunning, 2007a), there are a number of serious problems with the research practices and primary output of the orthodox field of terrorism studies. While some scholars would argue that many of these are neither unexpected nor overly concerning in such a new field (see Horgan and Boyle, 2008; Weinberg and Eubank, 2008), we suggest that many of them are, in fact, deeply problematic on a number of levels and collectively justify the adoption of a different approach. In this section, we briefly summarise a few of the main problems with contemporary terrorism research.

First, it is something of a cliché to note that there is no accepted definition for the field's primary organising concept, 'terrorism', and that there are literally hundreds of different definitions currently in use. We agree that this is not necessarily a serious issue in itself. After all, the sometimes acrimonious definitional debates surrounding a great many key concepts in social science, including 'war', 'violence', 'society', 'culture', 'democracy', 'power', and the like, do not necessarily impede theoretical innovation or empirical analysis (Booth, 2008; Horgan and Boyle, 2008; Weinberg and Eubank, 2008). In fact, it can be argued that there is a general working consensus among the leading terrorism studies scholars about the core defining characteristics of terrorist violence (see Raphael, 2007; Jackson, 2008a). The real problem, as Raphael and others have demonstrated, lies in the way definitions of terrorism are typically applied in a persistently inconsistent manner by scholars in their research, and the subsequent way in which the term is frequently used as a tool of delegitimisation by political actors.

In practice, many terrorism studies scholars tend to identify the groups they want to study first and then apply the definition to them, rather than allow the definition to determine which groups and events to study. What are considered 'terrorist groups' is moreover typically influenced by the (dominant) political climate of the day. This kind of pre-selection has meant that at any given time, the field's overall output tends to be skewed towards examining particular groups (see Raphael, this volume). During the cold war for example, left-wing groups received the most attention, while after 2001 Islamist groups have become the primary focus (see Ranstorp, Silke, this volume). Given that this pre-selection virtually always coincides with the official designation of terrorist groups by leading Western states, this research practice taints the broader field with a certain amount of political bias, associating it with Western counterterrorism policies, and functioning ideologically to legitimise and promote Western state interests and priorities, inadvertently or not (see Raphael, Jackson, this volume).

Related to this, the inconsistent application of the definition and the pre-selection bias has meant that a great many other actions, processes, and actors who fit the definitional criteria have not been systematically studied. In particular, the field has focused almost exclusively on non-state forms of terrorism and has, exceptions notwithstanding, largely failed to examine state terrorism or repression more broadly, including acts of state terrorism carried out by Western states and their allies (Raphael, Jackson, this volume; Blakeley, 2008). In addition, there is an over-emphasis on al-Qaeda, and a noticeable dearth of research in the field on subjects such as: right-wing terrorism; Christian, Jewish, and Sikh terrorism; gender terrorism; and the terrorism experienced in developing regions like Africa, India, the Pacific, and elsewhere (see Silke, this volume). More broadly, the field tends to overly focus on spectacular 'terrorist acts' (by oppositional groups), often paying insufficient attention to the wider conflict and its history, the broader social movement of which militants are typically part and its interactions with the state, the non-violent aspects of both oppositional movements and the state, and other types of violence, such as structural violence (which can be a reason for oppositional violence) or domestic violence (which can be fostered in conditions of political conflict) (Toros and Gunning, Gunning, this volume).

These 'silences' and biases within the broader terrorism studies field function ideologically to construct a particular kind of political 'knowledge' and to promote state and elite hegemonic projects. They serve to downplay state and state-led structural violence on the one hand, and the non-violent and contextual aspects of oppositional groups on the other. They also have serious analytical consequences, in that these gaps and silences limit and distort our understanding of the phenomenon and provide a poor foundation for further research. In particular, as Ranstorp, Silke, and Raphael in this volume imply, the omissions and silences mean that many of the data sets of the field, including the influential RAND database, have dangerous gaps and distortions – most obviously in relation to issues such as state terrorism, terrorism in regions like Africa and the Asia-Pacific, and terrorism by groups allied to Western powers such as the Northern Alliance in Afghanistan. In addition, the political nature of deciding what is and what is not a 'terrorist act', also means that these data sets contain a wide variety of acts that may or may not be comparable under the (falsely) homogenising label of 'terrorism' (Toros and Gunning, this volume). These problems with the data obviously have important follow-on consequences for statistical studies on terrorism (Silke, Toros and Gunning, this volume).

Another crucial weakness with the research practices of many leading scholars in the field is the failure to exercise sufficient critical judgement in regard to official sources of information (see Ranstorp, Raphael, this volume). Rather than recognising the vested interests states have in undermining oppositional groups, and ignoring the numerous documented cases of deliberate misinformation by government officials, many terrorism studies scholars appear to accept official information about terrorist groups with too little questioning. As Ranstorp's cautionary tale about Rohan Gunaratna demonstrates, some scholars unduly privilege unverified secret information originating from the security services over open source information that can be independently verified. This has distorting effects on the field of knowledge, not least in the recycling of false or exaggerated claims, as well as a number of wider ideological effects in society.

Framing a new research agenda 219

Related to the above point, and as Ranstorp, Silke, Toros and Gunning, Sluka, and Breen Smyth note in this volume, there is a more general and widely noted tendency for terrorism studies scholars to over-rely on secondary sources and a simultaneous failure to undertake primary research, particularly in terms of face to face engagement with individuals and groups widely described as 'terrorists'. Primary research which engages directly with the subjectivity of 'terrorists' is still something of a taboo in terrorism studies (Zulaika, 2008) – although there have been some notable exceptions involving face to face interviews in recent years (see, among others, Horgan, 2008, 2005; Stern, 2003; Bloom, 2005) – and a great many terrorism 'experts' have never even met a 'terrorist'. Although not all terrorism-related research topics require primary research of this kind, the notion that there is no need to engage one's research subjects face to face would be unthinkable in cognate disciplines such as anthropology, psychology, and criminology. Clearly, such a situation raises real questions about the veracity and quality of much orthodox terrorism research, and a consequence of these tendencies is that the literature frequently consists of analytically thin, narrative-based, and descriptive accounts of terrorism.

Another concerning issue in terrorism studies can be described as what has in the Critical Security Studies literature been termed the 'fetishization of parts' problem (Wyn Jones, 1999; see Toros and Gunning, this volume). In the context of our field, it concerns the tendency to study terrorism separately from the social movements, state structures, conflicts, history, contexts, and international relations within which it occurs (see Gunning, Toros and Gunning, Dalacoura, this volume). This problem is, in turn, partly a consequence of several other weaknesses, including the broader absence of social theory in terrorism studies, rigid disciplinary boundaries and the lack of theoretical cross-fertilisation, and the tendency to exceptionalise terrorist violence in relation to other forms of violence and political action. A more recent trend is the so-called 'instant expert' problem; that is, the extremely large number of new terrorism scholars following 11 September 2001 who lack adequate grounding in the existing literature, let alone detailed field knowledge, and who can parade as 'experts' in the absence of accepted procedures for 'gate-keeping', particularly if they reinforce the dominant views of orthodox terrorism studies (see Ranstorp, Silke, this volume). The broader de-contextualisation and de-historicisation of terrorism which these tendencies engender, again, has a distorting effect on terrorism 'knowledge' and functions ideologically to reify state hegemony.

As Jackson demonstrates in this volume, one of the consequences of the above problems and weaknesses in terrorism research is the uncritical acceptance and continuous reproduction of a number of 'myths', 'half-truths', and contested knowledge claims about terrorism by a great many scholars. Most notably, the terrorism studies literature demonstrates a persistent tendency to treat the current terrorist threat facing certain Western states as not only objectively 'real', but as unprecedented, highly threatening, and exceptional – notwithstanding some notable voices of dissent about this within the orthodox literature (see Crenshaw, 2003; Tucker, 2001; Mueller, 2006). It also has a tendency, dissenters again notwithstanding, to reproduce a number of dominant myths about, among other things, the role of religion in causing terrorism, the threat of the 'new terrorism' and WMD terrorism, the non-involvement of Western states in the practice of terrorism, and the efficacy of force-based counterterrorism. This widely accepted terrorism 'knowledge' provides a very poor foundation for further research, policymaking, and public debate, and functions ideologically to reify state power and promote particular partisan projects.

In our view, many of the problems described thus far are linked to a general failure by many scholars to adopt a critically reflexive attitude which acknowledges the ontological instability of the terrorism label, remains cognisant of the effects of the cultural context on knowledge production in social science, is sensitive to the politics and consequences of labelling, and recognises the ethical challenges and consequences of conducting research on political violence. Instead, we find that the orthodox terrorism studies literature, particularly its international relations-based sections, tends to treat 'terrorism' as an objective, ontologically stable phenomenon that can be studied in a politically disinterested and unproblematic manner. In part, this particular criticism is rooted in an alternative ontology which recognises the way in which 'terrorism' is constructed as a subject through a series of identifiable discursive practices which also naturalise particular responses to it. But, even if one adopts a positivist ontology, there is nonetheless a frequent failure of many scholars to appreciate and reflect upon the observable 'politics of naming' with regard to 'terrorism', and an insufficient appreciation of the 'real-world' consequences of different modes of representation and definition.

A related weakness in the field is the dominance of what can be called 'problem-solving' approaches to the study of political terror which fail to interrogate the role of the status quo and existing power structures in perpetuating insecurity and violence (Gunning, 2007a). The adoption of a problem-solving approach is in part a consequence of the frequently compromising ethical-political relationships between states and their security agencies, and some scholars and analysts engaged in the study of non-state terrorism (Ranstorp, Raphael, this volume). This is the so-called 'embedded experts' or 'organic intellectuals' problem, whereby the leading scholars constitute an influential epistemic community directly linked to state power (see Burnett and Whyte, 2005; Jackson, 2007f). The dominance of this intellectual network is in part maintained through the operation of closed, static, and self-referential systems of knowledge production which function to exclude scholars with dissenting or counter-hegemonic views (see Reid, 1993). But it is also a function of the dominance of state-centric, realist perspectives among the leading scholars within the field. A particularly deleterious consequence of adopting a problem-solving perspective is the prioritisation of topics tailored to the demands of policymakers for practically useful knowledge in the fight against terrorism, or, the securitisation of research.

Importantly, we detect a failure in the field to adequately reflect upon questions of research ethics, particularly as they relate to the safety of informants and primary researchers, the effects of research on 'suspect communities' and different end-users, and the way terrorism research is frequently called upon by

Framing a new research agenda 221

governments and elites to legitimise certain counterterrorism practices and policies (see Breen Smyth, this volume; Toros, 2008b). There is no getting away from the reality that as with other terms like 'paedophile' or 'rapist', using the 'terrorism' label in relation to other human beings has real consequences on their lives and well-being and that of their families, friends, and wider community. More broadly, and related to the problem of embeddedness and problem-solving in the service of the status quo, we believe insufficient attention is paid to the ethics of advocating, endorsing, or just failing to openly condemn particular counterterrorism policies such as targeted assassination, rendition, torture, internment, shoot-to-kill policies, and harsh prison sentencing. Similarly, there has not been sufficient, rigorous research into the immediate, long-term and wider social effects of these counterterrorism policies, although an increasing number of (non-traditional) scholars have come to question the advisability of such tactics on the basis of empirical research (see Araj, 2008; Hafez, 2003).

Finally, there is the impact of the current war on terrorism, which has had a noticeably chilling and disciplining effect on terrorism research due to the disciplinary nature of the 'you are either for us or against us' rhetoric and the political demands for national unity. This has lead directly to attempts at censorship of certain academics and commentators by some states, other scholars, and media commentators, as well as self-censorship and pressure on academics by state security organisations to inform on their students (see Breen Smyth, this volume). Another effect of the war on terrorism has been the compromising of existing research relationships through the co-option of researchers into government-determined research programmes, and the tainting of researchers with the suspicion that they may be working for the security services. Lastly, the war on terror has created a legal environment in which withholding information about one's informants or possessing certain kinds of widely available materials are now criminal offences.

In short, even this partial and incomplete list suggests that the terrorism studies field has a great many quite serious weaknesses. Far from being trivial or ephemeral, many of these problems are rooted in the ontological, epistemological, methodological, and ethical approaches at the centre of the field's dominant knowledge practices. It is important to note that our critique here is not meant to suggest that the orthodox field has not produced some excellent research in the past few decades, that there has been no real progress on some of the major questions of terrorism (see Ranstorp, Silke, this volume), or that the field as a whole is irredeemable. Nonetheless, the numerous and serious weaknesses that we have highlighted above, we believe, support our argument that terrorism studies is in need of a revitalising and invigorating 'critical turn'.

Some primary commitments for CTS

As we have suggested in some detail elsewhere (Jackson, 2007e; Breen Smyth, 2007; Jackson *et al.*, 2007, forthcoming), we believe that a critical approach to terrorism research can coalesce around a core set of ontological, epistemological, methodological, and ethical-normative commitments. In this section, we briefly summarise some of the most important commitments that we believe make up the CTS approach.

First, at its broadest, CTS can be understood as a critical orientation, a sceptical attitude, and a willingness to challenge received wisdom and knowledge about terrorism. In this sense, we conceive of CTS as a very broad church that allows multiple perspectives, some of which have been considered outside of the mainstream, to be brought into the same forum – with the attendant benefits for intellectual dialogue and debate (in the context of Critical Security Studies, see Krause and Williams, 1997a: x–xi). In other words, CTS is committed to disciplinary and intellectual pluralism and a willingness to engage with a range of perspectives and approaches, including excellent research within the orthodox field which may originate within a problem-solving approach. From this perspective, CTS seeks to practice a 'redemptive hermeneutic' which aims to redeem what is valuable and useful in the views of the 'Other' (Neufeld, 2001), whether this 'Other' is positivist, post-structuralist, 'terrorist', 'counterterrorist', and so on. In short, 'critical' encompasses a diverse set of analytical, ontological, and normative traditions, ranging from positivist or realist perspectives from outside the mainstream, to Frankfurt School Critical Theory, Welsh School Critical Security Studies, Foucauldian discourse analysis, Derridaen deconstruction, and so on. Furthermore, it entails an ongoing process of intellectual engagement (rather than a fixed position or endpoint) with a wide range of perspectives and approaches.

At the same time however, we would argue that CTS research entails a particular ontological position which accepts that 'terrorism' is fundamentally a social fact rather than a brute fact; that its nature is not inherent to the violent act itself, but is dependent upon context, circumstance, intention, and crucially, social, cultural, legal, and political processes of interpretation, categorisation, and labelling (Schmid and Jongman, 1988: 101). Similarly and importantly, the same ontological approach applies to the 'terrorist' label. Such a designation can never be an ontological statement about the nature or status of a particular individual: 'terrorist' is not an identity like 'Amish' or 'Canadian', nor is one 'once a terrorist, always a terrorist' (Schmid, 2004: 205; Toros, 2008b; Toros and Gunning, this volume). We argue that there is little intellectual value to be gained by reducing or essentialising a person or group to what is usually a subset of their overall behaviour, and which, in some cases, does not even accurately describe their behaviour, even by its own definition.[1] For CTS scholars, the acceptance of the ontological insecurity of the 'terrorism' label results in an acute sensitivity to the politics of labelling and extreme care in the actual use of the term during research and teaching, while at the same time rejecting calls to eschew the term altogether.[2] It also leads to the rejection of universalism, essentialism, and exceptionalism in characterising 'terrorism', and instead, prioritises specificity, context, history, and nuance.

This is not to say that, within a CTS framework, there can be no recognition of the actual violence in the 'real world' which is experienced by people as 'terrorism'. Rather, we suggest that there is a discursive, political, and cultural process by which 'real world' experiences of violence are given social meaning through the negotiated application of different kinds of political and intellectual labels. Such labels and meanings are liable to change and contestation; actions and events never just 'speak for themselves'. At the more interpretivist and post-structuralist end of the CTS spectrum, it may be ontologically problematic to talk of 'actual violence'. However, in this volume, Toros and Gunning have put forward the case for adopting a more Frankfurt School-inspired ontology which maintains a 'minimal foundationalism' in which the ontological distinction between subject and object is preserved and discourse and materiality are conceptualised as shaping each other in a dialectical, never-ceasing dynamic (rather than the one being solely constituted by the other). As such, the kind of critical position we are advocating here recognises that there are observable 'regularities' in human activity (what positivists call laws), and that one can distinguish between different acts on the basis of their characteristics, even while recognising that these characteristics, and how we interpret them, are a product of their social context and thus, are not 'objective facts' (in the positivist sense).

The advantage of such an ontology is that it permits both the study of the discourses which produce 'terrorism' as a discursive subject, as well as the material interests which generate and sustain these discourses, and the actual political violence in the 'real' world which has 'terroristic' characteristics. This, and the fact that a Frankfurt School-inspired Critical Theory framework recognises the importance of problem-solving approaches, provides an important bridge to engaging with traditional terrorism studies. At the same time, we are acutely aware that those at the post-structuralist end of the critical spectrum may not be able to find themselves in such an ontology. We return to this problem in the final section.

A third component of the ontology around which CTS appears to coalesce involves a shift from state-centrism and making state security the central concern, to a focus on the security, freedom, and well-being of human individuals (Toros and Gunning, Sluka, this volume). Just as (Welsh School) Critical Security Studies has argued that the primary referent to be secured should be the human individual and not the state – which, after all, is a relatively recent creation and has an ambiguous record of improving the security of human beings – CTS scholars tend to be more concerned with ending the suffering of human beings than with bolstering the state. This does not mean that CTS scholars are necessarily anti-state, or that the state (or other collectivities) should never be the focus of research. What it means is that one of the key yardsticks of legitimacy is whether an act or an organisation (including states and oppositional groups) improves the well-being of human beings.

This leads us to a fourth aspect of what we believe to be a key component of a CTS approach, namely, an explicit commitment to a set of normative values derived from a broadly defined notion of emancipation (Toros and Gunning, McDonald, this volume). Despite post-structuralist objections to the notion of emancipation and its past implication in hegemonic projects, we see an emancipatory commitment to ending avoidable human suffering in most critical research on terrorism. In this, we follow Richard Wyn Jones (2005: 217–220) and Hayward Alker (2005: 192) in positing that all critical research derives from an underlying conception of a different order and thus contains an 'emancipatory' element. Here, we understand emancipation as a process of continuous immanent critique rather than any particular endpoint or universal grand narrative: a process of trying to construct 'concrete utopias' by realising the unfulfilled potential of existing structures, freeing individuals from unnecessary structural constraints, and the democratisation of the public sphere (see McDonald, Toros and Gunning, this volume). Within the context of terrorism studies, we see it as a normative commitment to both ending the use of terrorist tactics (whether by state or non-state actors), and to addressing the conditions that can be seen to impel actors to resort to terrorist tactics.

In addition to a particular ontological position, we argue that critical research on terrorism should also exhibit a deep awareness of key epistemological issues, including the way in which knowledge is produced as a social process, the subjectivity of the researcher, and the link between knowledge and power, and consequently, the ways in which knowledge can be employed as 'a political technology' by elites, institutions, and groups. In other words, a critical approach to terrorism research begins with the fundamental acceptance that wholly objective or neutral knowledge – 'truth' – about terrorism is impossible and there is always an ideological, ethical-political dimension to the research process (Jackson, Toros and Gunning, this volume). This does not mean that all knowledge about the social world is hopelessly insecure, that we reject scholarly standards and procedures in research, or that 'anchorages' – relatively secure knowledge claims – cannot be found and built upon (Booth, 2008; Herring, 2008; Toros and Gunning, this volume). Rather, it suggests that, in addition to a commitment to the highest standards of scholarship, research on terrorism should also be characterised by a continuous and critical reflexivity in regards to its epistemology, ethics, and praxis. Importantly, such reflexivity also opens up new areas of research, starting with the key question: who is terrorism research for and how does terrorism knowledge support particular interests?

The ontological position that terrorism is socially constructed and constituted by its context leads us, epistemologically, to call for a broadening of the focus of terrorism research to include both state and non-state terrorism, counterterrorism, and other forms of violence such as structural or domestic violence, as well as (relevant) non-violent behaviour and social context (see Toros and Gunning, Gunning, this volume). Such a broadening will serve to de-exceptionalise terrorist violence by placing socio-historical context at the heart of the investigation, restoring a past and a future to terrorism, allowing the concept to evolve along with the social world, and seeing (counter)terrorism as part of wider political, societal, and economic dynamics. Engaging social movement theory, specific area studies expertise, and ethnographical methods constitute three practical paths to making context more central to terrorism research (Gunning, Sluka, Dalacoura, Breen Smyth, this volume).

Similarly, a central concern of CTS scholars must be to expand the set of accepted research topics to include those which have been ignored or silenced as a result of dominant ideological commitments. In particular, we would argue that, besides a greater focus on historical context, there is an urgent need to 'bring the state back in to terrorism studies' (Blakeley, 2007a) – to examine the nature and causes of state terrorism, particularly that by Western democratic states. It is also vital to bring gender into terrorism research, as Sylvester and Parashar argue in this volume. In the following section, we outline an expanded research agenda for CTS.

The ontological rejection of traditional theory's 'fetishization of parts' means, among other things, that epistemologically, a critical approach to terrorism should embed the phenomenon in broader social and political theory. Greater inter-disciplinarity – with a view to eventually doing away with disciplinary boundaries altogether – is one way to do this, although we should heed Booth's warning against lowest common denominator inter-disciplinarity (Booth, 2008). The establishment of an explicitly 'critical' field should help to bring in those from cognate disciplines who have so far shunned terrorism studies because of its reputation, earned or not, for political bias and lack of theoretical sophistication (see Gunning, 2007a; Dalacoura, this volume). Another way to embed terrorism research in broader theory is to link terrorism more explicitly to the broader social processes of which it is part, and study it for what it has to say about these broader processes (Gunning, this volume).

One of the consequences of the ontological and epistemological positions we have adopted is a commitment to transparency in regard to the researcher's own values and standpoints, particularly as they relate to the geo-political interests and values of the society in which they live and work. In turn, this implies an abiding commitment to seeking to overcome the Euro/Westo-centric, Orientalist, and masculinised forms of knowledge which currently characterise the terrorism studies and security studies fields and social science more generally (see Toros and Gunning, Gunning, Sylvester and Parashar, this volume). It also implies a commitment to taking subjectivity seriously, in terms of both the researcher and the research subject (see Breen Smyth, this volume). This means being aware of and transparent about the values and impact of the researcher on the process and outcomes of the research, and being willing to seriously engage with the subjectivity of the 'terrorist'. Importantly, this latter point implies an additional commitment to engaging in primary research, as opposed to relying primarily on secondary sources.

In terms of methodological issues, as we have already suggested, CTS is committed to methodological and disciplinary pluralism in terrorism research. In particular, CTS sees value in post-positivist and non-international relations-based methods and approaches, including discourse analysis, post-structuralism, constructivism, Critical Theory, historical materialism, and ethnography. Importantly, CTS refuses to privilege materialist, rationalist, and positivist approaches to social science over interpretive and reflectivist approaches (in the context of critical international relations, see Price and Reus-Smit, 1998: 261), and seeks to avoid an exclusionary commitment to the narrow logic of traditional social scientific explanation based on linear notions of cause and effect. Instead, CTS argues that post-positivist approaches which subscribe to an interpretive 'logic of understanding' can usefully open space for questions and perspectives that are often foreclosed by positivism and rationalism. Furthermore, we would argue that this stance is more than simply methodological; it is also political in the sense that it does not treat one model of social science as if it were the sole bearer of legitimacy (see Smith, 2004: 514).

Another important methodological commitment that flows from our position is a permanent adherence to a set of responsible research ethics which take account of the various end-users of terrorism research, including informants, the 'suspect communities' from which terrorists often emerge, and the populations who bear the brunt of terrorist campaigns and counterterrorism policies – as well as the wider public, other academics, and policymakers. More concretely, this means 'recognising the human behind the [terrorist] label' (Booth, 2008: 73), identifying marginalised and silenced voices, the adoption of a 'do no harm' approach to research, operating transparently as a researcher, recognising the vulnerability of those we research, honouring undertakings of confidentiality and protecting our interviewees, utilising principles of informed consent, and taking responsibility for the anticipated impact of our research and the ways in which it may be utilised. Adopting research paradigms, such as participative action research which aims to establish partnerships with researched populations, particularly when working with 'suspect communities', is a method of attempting to give away or share one's power as a researcher and an academic. As critical researchers, these are all principles, paradigms, and strategies that we ought to explore.

If a critically-informed research praxis is distinguished by its explicit commitment to human emancipation, an important component of CTS research is to try to influence policy. As we have argued both in this volume and elsewhere, not being concerned with policy relevance is not an option for scholars committed to human emancipation (Gunning, 2007b; Toros and Gunning, this volume). However, this does not mean that one should limit oneself to being relevant to state elites. Critical scholars should engage both policymakers and policy-takers, if their primary commitment is to humanity, rather than the state. Engaging policy-takers, furthermore, serves to lessen the risk of co-option by the status quo, particularly if those thus engaged include members of communities labelled 'suspect' by the state, those designated 'terrorists', and so on. However, to be effective, and to work towards realising the potential for immanent change within the status quo, critical scholars must simultaneously strive to engage those who are embedded in the state, members of the 'counterterrorist' forces, the political elite, and so on.

We would argue that a commitment to emancipation in turn implies, among other things: a commitment to praxis as organic intellectuals to help bring about concrete Utopias out of the fissures and contradictions of existing structures (see Herring, 2008; Toros and Gunning, this volume); a continuous process of 'immanent critique' of existing power structures and practices in society; the moral and intellectual questioning of the instrumental rationality paradigm of political violence, whether it be terrorist or counterterrorist violence, state or non-state violence (see Burke, 2008); the prioritising of human security over national security and working towards minimising all forms of physical, structural, and cultural violence (Toros and Gunning, this volume); and the serious scholarly and practical exploration of non-violence, conflict transformation, and reconciliation as practical alternatives to terrorist and counterterrorist violence. From this perspective, we believe that CTS is at heart an anti-hegemonic project, and a kind of 'outsider theorising' which seeks to go 'beyond problem-solving within the status quo and instead ... to help engage through critical theory with the problem of the status quo' (Booth, 2007).

Of course, the adoption of an anti-hegemonic, 'critical' standpoint requires a certain amount of intellectual and moral courage because it invariably engenders vigorous opposition from interests vested in the status quo – as a number of CTS scholars, including ourselves, have experienced (see Breen Smyth, this volume; Herring, 2008). CTS scholars must therefore adopt a prior commitment to refusing to give in to intimidation, abandoning research that is controversial, or to self-censorship. In the current political environment engendered by the war on terrorism, CTS scholars must be prepared to say the unsayable, whether it is to governments, the wider society, particular communities, or terrorists; in a very real sense, we must accept that 'blasphemy is our business' (Booth, 2008: 68).

At one level, CTS can be described simply as a call for much more rigorous and sensitive research. However, we believe that it is more than this. We argue that CTS has a particular approach and orientation that marks it out from much of the orthodox terrorism studies literature in terms of its ontological position, its epistemology, its methodological orientation, its research ethics and praxis, its normative commitment, particularly in regards to emancipation, its reflexivity, and its expanded research foci and priorities. The perspective we have put forward here shares a great deal with and draws heavily upon Frankfurt School Critical Theory and particularly the way the Welsh School of Critical Security Studies has interpreted and applied it (see Toros and Gunning, McDonald, this volume). At the same time, we would argue that it cannot be reduced to a single perspective, and that anything from rigorous positivist critiques to post-structuralist deconstructions has a place. Rather, CTS is an over-arching framework for critiquing existing research on terrorism, embedding terrorism research in broader social and political theory, and generating new kinds of questions and foci for study. As Ken Booth argues regarding Critical Security Studies, we would similarly suggest that CTS is an exciting new approach because it offers an ontology, an epistemology, and an orientation towards praxis (Booth, 2005).

Framing a new research agenda

If CTS is to make a lasting impact on the future development of terrorism studies, its greatest challenge will be to go beyond critique and deconstruction and articulate an alternative, credible research agenda which incorporates both critique of existing research and new empirical research (including deconstructions of dominant political discourses). As we have suggested above, CTS is a call for: (1) *broadening* the study of terrorism to include subjects neglected by the leading scholars of the field and in its main journals, including, among other things, the wider social context of political violence, state violence, non-violent practices, and gender aspects of terrorism; (2) *deepening* terrorism research by uncovering the field's underlying ideological, institutional, and material interests and making the subjectivities and normative commitments of both researchers and researched more explicit; and (3) making a *commitment to emancipatory praxis* central to the research enterprise. More specifically, among an almost infinite field of possibility, we would suggest that an initial CTS research agenda should include some of the following subjects. Many of these suggested topics flow directly from the concerns and issues we raised in previous sections of this chapter, and from the chapters in this volume. We recognise that there is a growing literature on some of these subjects already; however, much of this research occurs largely outside of terrorism studies and does not always engage directly with the issues and concerns of the broader terrorism field. Indeed, one of the tasks of a CTS field is to gather in all these fragmented voices and serve as a tent under whose canvas research from cognate disciplines can coalesce and cross-pollinate (Gunning, 2007a).

First, we would argue that there is a need to examine more thoroughly and systematically the discourses and representational practices of terrorism, and the ontological-discursive foundations – the ideological, conceptual, and institutional underpinnings – which make both terrorism studies, and the practices of terrorism and counterterrorism, possible in the first place. Some important research topics within this broad area include:

- examining the origins and evolution of the terrorism discourse in Western societies, and exposing its ontological and epistemological practices;
- tracing the silences and omissions within the dominant discourses and the ideological consequences they have;
- exploring the ways in which terrorism and counterterrorism, as discursive practices and forms of political violence, co-constitute and reinforce each other;
- uncovering the wider discursive fields and practices upon which terrorism research is predicated, such as the state, sovereignty, just war doctrines, and the like;
- exploring the ways in which different kinds of terrorism discourses and practices – cultural, political, academic, bureaucratic, and legal, among others – reinforce and co-constitute each other;
- looking at the ways in which contemporary terrorism discourses function as a negative ideograph of national identity;
- exploring how terrorism is culturally constructed in the popular imagination, and how it functions in some societies and certain cultural-political

spheres as a social myth (in an anthropological sense) similar to previous social myths such as witchcraft; and
- describing and analysing the micro-physics of the terrorism discourse in different social and bureaucratic settings, including media organisations, security agencies, the police, prisons, and the like.

Second, in addition to exposing and deconstructing the field's 'conditions of possibility', we would suggest that there is also a need to explore in much more detail the political-economic contexts of both the terrorism studies field as a politically-embedded domain of knowledge, and the theory and practice of counterterrorism. In other words, applying historical materialist approaches and taking materiality seriously, there is a need for further exploration of how counterterrorism functions as a form of ideology – how it works to promote certain kinds of material and class interests, maintain political hegemony, and sustain dominant economic relationships. This means rooting critical analyses of the theory and practice of counterterrorism within theories of class, capitalism, hegemony, and imperialism (see Herring, 2008).

Third, as we have already mentioned, there is an urgent need for more systematic research on state terrorism – and state repression more broadly – especially the forms of state terrorism that have remained virtually invisible in terrorism research, such as Western state terrorism (including Israeli state terrorism) and the terrorism practised by Western allies, such as Egypt, Saudi Arabia, Pakistan, Sri Lanka, and Colombia, to name but a few. More specifically, there is a need to build on the pioneering work of Michael Stohl, George Lopez, Alexander George, Noam Chomsky, Frank Gareau, and others, to develop theories, concepts, and typologies about the nature and causes of state terrorism, the social and political dynamics of the use of fear as a form of governance, and the dynamics of violence between state and anti-state militants, particularly the ways in which repressive state actions can produce or quell violent sub-state opposition. There is also an urgent need to construct data sets and publish detailed case studies and comparative studies of state terrorism. In particular, we see great value in a project to build a data set which would systematically document and code instances of state terrorism, in the same way that data sets on non-state terrorism have been constructed. Although it would always be only a partial accounting due to the difficulties of verifying information about events which states do not always want the outside world to know about, it would nonetheless provide a tremendous resource for researchers and over time would contain sufficient data for certain kinds of comparative statistical analyses. Data could be gathered from human rights reports, anthropologists, lawyers, newspapers, and elsewhere. Such a project, if it was done rigorously, consistently, and in a transparent manner, could potentially also have some normative value, as states would be unable to deny their involvement in acts of terrorism and could conceivably be forced to change their behaviour – notwithstanding the depressing track record of most states in this regard.

Fourth, as Toros, Gunning, Sluka, and Breen Smyth argue in this volume, it is imperative to broaden the research agenda to include the wider social context, other forms of violence, and non-violent behaviour in terrorism research. Too little is understood about the interaction between militants and non-militants, and between militant and non-militant action repertoires, within oppositional social movements – or about the role played by bystander publics, political elites, state forces, and wider ideological debates in the evolution of militancy (Gunning, this volume). Similarly, more research is needed into the effect of movement participation on individual motivation and behaviour, or the effect of the internet and transnational (virtual) networks on militancy, the relationship between political and domestic violence, or that between structural and political violence. Here, terrorism research can benefit from cognate disciplines and theories, such as social movement theory, area studies, and anthropology, among many others (Gunning, Dalacoura, Sluka, this volume). Far more detailed and painstaking fieldwork is necessary than has hitherto been carried out, engaging subjects face to face and learning to decipher the 'deep culture' which informs the groups and individuals being studied. Equally important are comparative studies of different contexts, which are rooted in both fieldwork and a robust theoretical framework.

Fifth, as Sylvester and Parashar demonstrate in this volume, we agree that there is a pressing need to take gender much more seriously in terrorism research. A number of topics seem particularly pertinent here: examining the gendered nature of the terrorism studies field itself, the kinds of masculinised forms of knowledge it produces, and the silences it contains about women, gender, and gendered identities; exploring the subjectivities, motivations, ambitions, goals, performativities, and political agency of female participants in terrorism, counterterrorism, and political violence more broadly; applying a gendered gaze to militant groups and movements and exploring how women join, mediate, subvert, and resist such movements; comparative research on women in different societies who join terrorist and counterterrorist groups; and the impact of counterterrorist measures on women and children. In this and other areas, it will be important to open the field up to methodologies and approaches beyond traditional social science – such as art, drama, literature, and so on – so that new perspectives and questions can emerge and old paradigms can be challenged.

Sixth, we argue that there is a real need to expand the study of terrorism to both address the Euro/Westo-centricity prevalent in terrorism research and include the voices and perspectives of those in the global South who have been the most frequent victims of both terrorism and counterterrorism. This is part of a critical scholar's emancipatory mission (see McDonald, Toros and Gunning, this volume). Of particular importance is the need to move beyond culturalist, pathological, or ideological explanations and give non-Western agency and structural explanations an equal place in any research agenda, while at the same time avoiding imposing a universalistic framework which is insensitive to local particularities. Of similar import is the need to deconstruct explanations which focus overly on religion and embed them in broader social and political theory – but, vitally, without overlooking the role of religion and the spiritual (Gunning, this volume). Topics that should be explored in more detail include:

Framing a new research agenda 231

- the Eurocentric and Orientalist underpinnings of the field, and the exclusions and silences of non-Western perspectives it maintains;
- a critical analysis of the different impacts of terrorism and counterterrorism on societies in the South;
- deconstructing local attitudes towards the role of violence in society and identity-construction (including what constitutes legitimate violence and who constitutes a legitimate target) and how these have been influenced by local, state, and international practices;
- exploring the role of Western counterterrorism in the global war on terror as part of broader patterns of dominance and intervention in the South; and
- exploring and listening to the voices of those normally ignored in security analyses.

Finally, we detect a real need to further analyse the ethics, impacts, and efficacy of different approaches to counterterrorism. In addition to finding more transparent and meaningful ways of evaluating the success of counterterrorism measures and interrogating accepted wisdoms (such as 'we do not negotiate with terrorists', or 'decapitation policies are effective'), some of the following subjects urgently need to be explored in greater detail:

- the impact of counterterrorism policies on specific communities, individuals, institutions, the legal order, domestic society, and the international system;
- the effects of counterterrorism policy on human rights, social trust, community cohesion, democratic culture, the academy and academic research;
- the media's role in scrutinising government institutions, and policing culture and practices;
- the role of civil society and socio-economic change in ending campaigns of political violence;
- the efficacy or otherwise of dialogue with those designated 'terrorist';
- the precise role and dynamics of demilitarisation strategies, police reform, truth and reconciliation mechanisms, and the like; and
- the successes and failures of the current war on terror and previous experiences of terrorism.

In particular, the final topic listed here – the impact of the war on terror – is in need of much more systematic research. Given its global reach and size, and the vast areas of social and political life it has thus far impacted upon, there are multitudinous subjects requiring detailed, critical analysis.

In sum, this brief outline demonstrates that CTS is coalescing around a clear, coherent, and systematic research agenda that is informed by its particular ontology, epistemology, and normative position. Furthermore, as scholars begin to explore and engage with the arguments and questions we have posed, and as research gets underway in earnest on some of the topics suggested here, further questions and new research items will arise. It is clear that, more than simply a call for more rigorous research, CTS offers both a way of doing research and a clear research agenda.

Conclusion: dangers, pitfalls and future challenges[3]

There is little doubt that the CTS project is starting to have a discernible impact on the terrorism studies and wider international relations fields. We have noted a growing number of books, peer-reviewed journal articles, conference papers, and doctoral dissertations which cite and engage directly with aspects of the CTS agenda and approach.

Despite the growing level of interest however, we are deeply cognisant that this project may, in the end, fail – and the broader field of terrorism studies will remain largely unaffected by the challenges and provocations offered by the CTS project. After all, as we noted in the Introduction to this volume, calls for more critical approaches to the study of terrorism have been made many times before and thus far they appear to have had little discernible impact on the primary practices and focus of the field. In part, the success of our endeavour will depend upon whether and how we can overcome a number of well-signposted dangers and future challenges. The following list is undoubtedly partial, if only because it is the nature of academic endeavour that as we move forward new problems are revealed and new obstacles arise.

In the first instance, there are perennial thorny issues inherent to the central organising concept of the overall field, 'terrorism'. The employment of such a politically-charged, culturally-laden, and ontologically ambiguous term poses significant challenges for research practice and political praxis, and discourages too many scholars from cognate fields from engaging with the core issues and concerns of the wider terrorism studies field. Scholars who wish to engage in ethnographic studies in communities or groups typically described as 'terrorists' in Western discourse, for example, cannot be associated with the use of the term without risking both their personal safety and the integrity of their research (Breen Smyth, 2004). More fundamentally, acts of 'terrorism' and even the existence of 'terrorist' groups, are typically only one small part of a broader set of contentious political struggles and conflicts. Narrowing the focus of research to a single, sometimes relatively small, aspect of a broader movement or a wider power struggle between state elites and opposition, therefore, risks distortion and misrepresentation while leaving out significant other aspects and their wider social context.

Our response to this conundrum thus far has been to accept that there are genuine reasons for retaining the 'terrorism' label (see endnote 2), whilst arguing that it should always be used and applied with extreme care and sensitivity, with an awareness that its use is a political act which involves a process of demonisation, and therefore that there may be times when it should not be used at all. However, not using it at all is likely to diminish the impact we may have on policymakers and orthodox terrorism studies. Clearly, much more work and intellectual struggle remains to be done regarding this issue, particularly in terms of how the 'terrorism' label impacts upon and structures research, and whether by using it the CTS project becomes simply another, instrumentally-oriented, problem-solving exercise.

Second, we recognise that a large proportion of the current research that is associated with CTS has so far been largely focused on critiquing the orthodox field of terrorism studies and deconstructing its discourses and underlying assumptions. There are some particular dangers that CTS will need to negotiate in this respect. For example, there is the danger that critical scholarship, with its understandable concern for interrogating the discursive foundations upon which the study of terrorism is founded, will become so self-conscious that it becomes simply the study of its own (and other) discourses and progressively disengages from the empirical study of political violence and its foundations in the 'real' world (Weinberg and Eubank, 2008). A related danger is that CTS will come to be viewed as a largely post-structuralist or constructivist project with their associated ontological and epistemological positions, and other approaches – political-economic and historical materialist, (Frankfurt School) critical theory, sociological, psychological, critical realist, and others, for example – will be discouraged from participating in CTS's activities and debates.

At one level, the current shape of the CTS project is simply a reflection of the research interests and focus of the particular group of scholars currently driving it forward through the initiatives we described above. At another level, it must be emphasised that, far from being disengaged from the 'real world' and lost in discursive critiques, the substantial work of many self-identifying CTS scholars involves empirically-grounded 'real world' studies of political violence which adopts historical materialist, ethnographic, and conflict resolution-based approaches, among others (see Gunning, 2007c; Breen Smyth, 2008b, 2008c; Blakeley, 2006, 2007b, forthcoming; Toros, 2008a, 2008b, forthcoming; Stokes and Raphael, forthcoming). We are confident that as more scholars from different disciplines and approaches start to engage with the issues and perspectives articulated by CTS, the field will begin to evidence more diversity and some of the noted gaps in our research focus will start to be filled. Scholars from cognate disciplines who have thus far shunned the world of terrorism studies because of its reputation for being overly state-centric, ideologically biased, and under-theorised, have begun to engage with the field under the more pluralistic umbrella offered by CTS (see, for example, Gunning, 2007c; Booth, 2008; McDonald, 2007, this volume; Dalacoura, this volume; Herring, 2008; Sylvester and Parashar, this volume; Burke, 2008). The challenge remains to increase their number and the methodological and disciplinary diversity of the field.

A third challenge for CTS is to avoid the risk of becoming too eclectic, and breaking down as a result of its internal contradictions and lack of an overarching identity (Gunning, 2007b). This is exacerbated by the fact that CTS, at least in the way we have formulated it, must both be critical in the sense of explicitly challenging the state-centric, problem-solving perspectives that have thus far dominated terrorism research, and be inclusive to enable the convergence of not only explicitly critical perspectives but also the more rigorous traditional, problem-solving perspectives of both traditional terrorism studies and cognate fields. Much of interest has been written by, for instance, traditional conflict resolution scholars who have moved beyond a narrow military understanding of security and placed violence in its wider social context (Toros, forthcoming). Similarly, traditional scholars within terrorism studies have produced significant research that challenges accepted knowledge, findings which we ignore at our peril (Gunning, 2007a).

Conversely, traditional terrorism scholars would benefit greatly from exposure to cognate or critical perspectives. However, further complicating this dynamic is that the term 'critical' – and what it means to be 'critical' in practice – is itself highly contested. In this volume, we have made the case for an inclusive, eclectic approach, inspired by Williams and Krause's take on Critical Security Studies (Williams and Krause, 1997). We accept that our relatively heavy reliance on Frankfurt School Critical Theory, as mediated through Welsh School Critical Security Studies, may put us closer to Booth's more structured, less eclectic, and thus more exclusive, approach to Critical Security Studies (Booth, 2004, 2007), thereby acting as a repellent to those who interpret what it means to be 'critical' differently or who reject the notion of 'emancipation' or the continued use of the 'terrorism' label as hegemonic tools. These issues clearly need much more intellectual struggle and thoughtful dialogue, but we are optimistic that they will not lead to schism or paralysis.

A fourth key challenge for CTS is the risk of bifurcating the broader terrorism studies field into critical and orthodox intellectual ghettos which then refuse to engage with each other's concerns or resort to open intellectual warfare. For CTS, there is the added danger that such an outcome would likely result in a level of intellectual and political irrelevance, since orthodox approaches currently have, for obvious reasons, stronger institutional links to sources of political and cultural power in society. In part, this challenge revolves around the danger that CTS will fail to communicate clearly with orthodox scholars and policymakers about the goals, aims, and approaches of CTS – particularly the willingness of critical scholars to engage in respectful debate about common concerns – or that arguments and counter-arguments will be expressed in polemical, disrespectful terms. We believe that such an outcome can be avoided, and that our willingness thus far to engage in rigorous but respectful debate with scholars who disagree with our approach (see Horgan and Boyle, 2008; Weinberg and Eubank, 2008) sends a powerful signal of our genuine readiness to engage in dialogue. We also strongly believe that critical research has the potential to be the basis for alternative policy recommendations for policymakers and that it can be used to both increase the efficacy of counterterrorism and address (some of) the grievances of those who have resorted to political violence.

At the same time, there is a related danger of dissipating research energy in ongoing debates over what might prove in the end to be irresolvable issues – such as the definitional and ontological status of 'terrorism', the necessity of studying state terrorism, the morality of instrumental violence, or the issue of 'policy relevance' and state-scholar relationships. We view disagreement as healthy and an important way of stimulating new developments and questions. Although there probably will be issues where principled stands will need to be taken, particularly when it comes to key ethical questions, it will be important to try and avoid drawing lines in the sand over conceptual issues of less importance. In this respect, we recognise the danger of drawing too stark a line between critical and orthodox approaches, particularly if this leads to the severing of relations between critically-minded orthodox scholars and self-identified critical scholars. At the same time, we believe in the importance of opening up debate by calling into question accepted practices, frameworks, and taboos. If terrorism scholars on all sides make a commitment to open, respectful, and principled dialogue, we see no reason why disagreements cannot be a source of progress or put to one side when necessary.

Communicating our aims and intentions clearly has one more important dimension, namely, overcoming what might be broadly viewed as an Atlantic divide in terrorism research. It appears that this 'critical' project has so far had far more purchase in Europe and Australasia than it has had in the United States (despite the fact that many of the earliest critical voices within terrorism studies were based in North America), and that the critical-orthodox division largely (but not completely) maps onto the different terrorism studies approaches of US and European scholars. In part, this unfortunate division is sustained through a simple linguistic difference. While the term 'critical' denotes a wide array of approaches to European scholars, there appears to be a perception among many US scholars that it relates specifically to Frankfurt School Critical Theory or some variant of either Marxism or post-structuralism. In this respect, CTS still has some way to go in more clearly articulating what our conception of 'critical' is. We hope that some of the chapters in this volume, particularly the chapters by Gunning and Toros, and McDonald, will go some way towards clarifying our position. Like the critical turn in International Relations Theory, we see the role of CTS as helping 'to re-embed the discipline ... within the broader social sciences' and to increase methodological and perspectival diversity, including in the US (Rengger and Thirkell-White, 2007).

A final set of challenges and dangers lies in the need to continue developing and articulating the CTS normative agenda beyond the initial and necessarily general outline of 'emancipation' given in this volume, and within the confines of the need for both critical distance from the status quo and policy relevance. Such a task is crucial because it has important implications for many of the research practices at the heart of terrorism research, as well as for the relationship between scholars, the state, and security practitioners on the one hand, and research subjects, 'suspect communities', and those designated 'terrorist' on the other. In particular, CTS scholars will need to think through the practicalities, ethics, and modalities of negotiating the delicate balance between normatively-oriented independent scholarship that promotes emancipation and the security of humans in general, and the demands of being 'policy relevant' – and law-abiding in the context of increasingly intrusive anti-terrorism legislation – for the purposes of national security. We believe that it is possible to maintain access to power and critical distance at the same time, but it takes a great deal of care, sensitivity, and intellectual struggle. We agree with Weinberg and Eubank (2008) that government funds may be a legitimate source of funding, just as it has been for research on other pressing social issues, assuming guarantees are in place that the resulting research remains fully independent and that confidentiality clauses are not breached, terrorism laws notwithstanding (see Breen Smyth, this volume). Continuous engagement with policy-takers and 'suspect communities' will similarly help in maintaining a critical distance to power. In addition, we feel that the current political and intellectual climate, in which there is growing disappointment with the effects and outcomes to date of the 'war on terror', and where security practitioners are actively searching for new ideas and approaches to thinking about counterterrorism, provides a ripe moment for critically-oriented scholars to offer their knowledge and expertise.

The CTS project is still in its infancy and there is clearly a great deal of intellectual work left to do at a number of different levels. However, it is our belief that the present interregnum represents a ripe moment for scholars, new and established, to make a genuine contribution to the evolution of this important new field and to the development of new policies and political attitudes. Such a project, moreover, has tremendous intellectual, normative, and practical importance.

Notes

1 Groups specialising in terror and no other forms of political action do sometimes form, but they are extremely rare and typically they remain highly unstable and ephemeral. In reality, most terrorism occurs in the context of wider political struggles in which the use of terror is one strategy among other more routine forms of contentious action (see Tilly, 2004: 6; Jackson, 2007g).
2 Whilst recognising the inherent ontological instability of the term, our contention is that unless we converge under a central concept such as 'terrorism', however problematic it may be in practice, much critical research will remain fragmented, thereby preventing much-needed cross-fertilisation between critical and cognate perspectives. In addition, there are practical reasons for retaining the term, namely, eschewing the 'terrorism' label leaves traditional approaches and policymakers relatively unchallenged, particularly in the race for research funding. In addition, one of the key tasks of CTS is to investigate the political, academic and cultural usage of the term; for this reason alone, it should be retained as a central marker. More pragmatically, the term 'terrorism' is currently so dominant within political structures and the broader culture that CTS cannot afford to abandon it. Academia does not exist outside the power structures and associated dominant discourses of the day. The term 'terrorism', however problematic, dominates public discourse and as such must be engaged with, deconstructed and challenged, rather than abandoned and left to less critical scholars. This explains why we have chosen to employ the term throughout this volume and in the broader CTS project (see also, Jackson et al., 2007).
3 This section draws upon and expands Breen Smyth et al., 2008.

Bibliography

AAA (American Anthropological Association), 2000. Online, available at: www.aaanet.org/committees/ethics/ethcode.htm (accessed 11 July 2008).
ACTA (American Council of Trustees and Alumni), no date. Online, available at: www.goacta.org/about/mission-and-history.cfm.
A Different Future, no date. Online, available at: www.adifferentfuture.org/who01.html.
Ackerman, G., 2005. 'WMD Terrorism Research: Where to from Here?', *International Studies Review*, 7: 140–143.
Afary, J. and K. Anderson, 2005. *Foucault and the Iranian Revolution*, Chicago, IL: University of Chicago Press.
Ahmad, M., 2008. 'Fortress Britain'. Online, available at: www.spinwatch.org/content/view/ 5057/8/ (accessed 23 June 2008).
Alexander, Y., 1989. 'The Terrorist Network', *Defense and Diplomacy*, 7: 36–70.
——, 1986. *State-Sponsored Terrorism: Low Intensity Warfare*, London: Centre for Contemporary Studies.
——, 1985. 'Terrorism and the Soviet Union', in A. Merari, ed., *On Terrorism and Combating Terrorism*, Frederick, MD: University Publications of America.
——, 1980. 'Terrorism and the Media: Some Observations', *Terrorism*, 3(3/4): 179–183.
Ali, F., 2007. 'Dressed in Black: A Look at Pakistan's Radical Women', *Terrorism Monitor*, Jamestown Foundation, 5(8): 9–12.
Alimi, E., 2006. 'Contextualizing Political Terrorism: A Collective Action Perspective for Understanding the Tanzim', *Studies in Conflict and Terrorism*, 29(3): 263–283.
Alker, H., 2005. 'Emancipation in the Critical Security Studies Project', in K. Booth, ed., *Critical Security Studies and World Politics*, Boulder, CO: Lynne Rienner.
Allison, M., 2004. 'Women as Agents of Political Violence: Gendering Security', *Security Dialogue*, 35(4): 447–463.
Amnesty International, 2007. Report 2007, *Iraq*. Online, available at: http://thereport.amnesty.org/page/ 1075/eng/ (accessed 5 December 2007).
——, 2003. *Israel and the Occupied Territories: Israel Must End its Policy of Assassinations,* 4 July 2003. Online, available at: http://web.amnesty.org/library/Index/ENGMDE150562003?open&of=ENG-ISR (accessed 5 December 2007).
——, 2002. *Israel/Occupied Territories: Palestinians Suffer New Collective Punishments*. Online, available at: http://web.amnesty.org/library/Index/ENGMDE151002002?open&of=ENG-398 (accessed 5 December 2007).
——, 1984. *Torture in the Eighties*, London: Amnesty International.

Bibliography

Anselmi, W. and L. Hogan, 2004. 'Scripturing the 21st Century: American Ways to Empire Undone', *College Quarterly*, 7(Fall): 4. Online, available at: www.senecac.on.ca/quarterly/2004-vol.07-num04-fall/anselmi_hogan.html.

Araj, B., 2008. 'Harsh State Repression as a Cause of Suicide Bombing: The Case of the Palestinian–Israeli Conflict', *Studies in Conflict and Terrorism*, 31(4): 284–303.

Aretxaga, B., 1997. *Shattering Silence: Women, Nationalism, and Political Subjectivity in Northern Ireland*, Princeton, NJ: Princeton University Press.

Asad, T., 2003. *Formations of the Secular*, Stanford, CA: Stanford University Press.

——, 1993. 'The Construction of Religion as an Anthropological Category', in T. Asad, ed., *Genealogies of Religion: Discipline and Reasons of Power in Christianity and Islam*, Baltimore MD: Johns Hopkins University Press.

Asprey, R., 1994. *War in the Shadows*, London: Little Brown.

Associated Press, 1982. Interview with Roelef Botha released 30 September 1982. Available online via the subscription services for Nexis UK at www.lexisnexis.co.uk.

Atran, S., 2006. 'The Moral Logic and Growth of Suicide Terrorism', *The Washington Quarterly*, 29(2): 127–147.

Attwood, R., 2007. 'Study of Terrorism Steps Up To New Level', *Times Higher Education*, 22 June 2007.

Aust, S., 1985. *Der Baader Meinhof Complex*, Hamburg: Hoffmann und Campe.

Avishag, G., 2005. 'Terrorism as an Academic Subject after 9/11: Searching the Internet Reveals a Stockholm Syndrome Trend', *Studies in Conflict and Terrorism*, 28(1): 45–59.

Avruch, K., 2001. 'Notes Towards Ethnographies of Conflict and Violence', *Journal of Contemporary Ethnography*, 30(5).

Baaker, E., 2006. 'Jihadi Terrorists in Europe, Their Characteristics and the Circumstances in Which They Joined the Jihad: An Explanatory Study', *Clingendael Security Paper*, Netherlands: The Hague Clingendael Institute.

Baaker, E. and L. Boer, 2007. *The Evolution of al-Qaedaism*, Clingendael: Netherlands Institute of International Relations.

Balasingham, A., 1993. *Women Fighters of Liberation Tigers*, Jaffna, Sri Lanka: Thasan Printers.

Banisadr, M., 2004. *Masoud*, London: Saqi Books.

Barkey, H.J., 2007. 'Turkey and the PKK: A Pyrrhic Victory?', R. Art and L. Richardson, eds, *Democracy and Counterterrorism: Lessons from the Past,* Washington, DC: USIP Press.

Basu, S., 2008. 'Creating SCR 1325: A "War of Position?"', paper presented at the International Studies Association (ISA) Annual Conference, 26–29 March 2008, San Francisco, USA.

Baty, P., 2006. 'Life-risking "Spy" Plan Pulled', *Times Higher Education*, 20 October 2006, 1.

Baty, P. and J. Shepherd, 2006. 'Ministers Vilify Researchers', *Times Higher Education*, 1 December 2006.

BBC, 2005. 'CIA Links Terror Threat to Iraq', 17 February 2005. Online, available at: http://news.bbc.co.uk/1/hi/world/americas/4272287.stm.

——, 1982. 'South African Accounts of Divisions among SWAPO Membership', *Radio Johannesburg*, 28 September 1982, reported by *BBC Summary of World Broadcasts*, 30 September 1982, ME/7144/B/3.

Beitler, R., 2004. *The Path to Mass Rebellion: An Analysis of Two Intifada*s, Lanham, MD: Lexington Books.

Bejerot, N., 1974. 'The Six Day War in Stockholm', *New Scientist*, 61(886): 486–487.
Bellamy, A., 2006. 'No Pain, No Gain? Torture and Ethics in the War on Terror', *International Affairs*, 82(1): 121–148.
Benford, R. and D. Snow, 2000. 'Framing Processes and Social Movements: An Overview and Assessment', *Annual Review of Sociology*, 26: 611–639.
Bergesen, A., D. Snow, S. Byrd, D. Wiest, C. Beck, E. Reid, H. Chen, and J. Goodwin, 2007. 'Researching Terrorism', *Mobilization*, 12(2): 109–203.
Berkin, C. and C. Lovett, 1980. *Women, War, and Revolution*, New York: Holmes and Meier.
Berko, A. and E. Erez, 2007. 'Gender, Palestinian Women, and Terrorism: Women's Liberation or Oppression?', *Studies in Conflict and Terrorism*, 30(6): 493–519.
Berreman, G., 1980. 'Are Human Rights Merely a Politicised Luxury in the World Today?', *Anthropology and Humanism Quarterly*, 5(1), 2–13.
Bhatia, M., 2005. 'Fighting Words: Naming Terrorists, Bandits, Rebels and Other Violent Actors', *Third World Quarterly*, 26(1): 5–22.
Bhattacharjee, Y., 2006. 'Should Academics Self-Censor Their Findings on Terrorism?', *Science*, 19 May 2006, 312(5776): 993–994.
Bilgin, P., 2005. *Regional Security in the Middle East: A Critical Perspective*, London: Routledge.
Bishop, P. and E. Mallie, 1987. *The Provisional IRA*, London: Corgi.
Bjørgo, T., ed., 2005. *Root Causes of Terrorism: Myths, Realities and Ways Forward*, London: Routledge.
Bjørgo, T. and J. Horgan, eds, 2008. *Leaving Terrorism Behind*, London: Routledge.
Black, I., 2008. 'Terror Talks: Would Contacting al-Qaida Be a Step Too Far? Experts Sympathise with Powell's View on Need for Dialogue with the Enemy', *Guardian*, 15 March 2008. Online, available at: www.guardian.co.uk/world/2008/mar/15/alqaida.terrorism.
Blakeley, R., forthcoming. *State Terrorism in the Global South: Foreign Policy, Neoliberalism and Human Rights*, London: Routledge.
——, 2008. 'The Elephant in the Room: A Response to John Horgan and Michael J. Boyle', *Critical Studies on Terrorism*, 1(2): 151–165.
——, 2007a. 'Bringing the State Back into Terrorism Studies', *European Political Science*, 6(3): 228–253.
——, 2007b. 'Why Torture?', *Review of International Studies*, 33(3): 373–394.
——, 2006. 'Still Training to Torture? US training of Military Forces From Latin America', *Third World Quarterly*, 27(8): 1439–1461.
Bloom, M., 2006. 'Dying to Kill: Motivations for Suicide Terror', in A. Pedahzur, ed., *The Root Causes of Suicide Terrorism: The Globalization of Martyrdom*, Oxford: Routledge,
——, 2005. *Dying to Kill: The Allure of Suicide Terror*, New York: Columbia University Press.
Blum, W., 1995. *Killing Hope: US Military and CIA Interventions Since World War II*, Monroe, ME: Common Courage Press.
Bodley, J., 1995. *Anthropology and Contemporary Human Problems*, 3rd edn, Mountain View: Mayfield.
——, 1990. *Victims of Progress*, 3rd edn, Mountain View: Mayfield.
Booth, K., 2008. 'The Human Faces of Terror: Reflections in a Cracked Looking Glass', *Critical Studies on Terrorism*, 1(1): 65–79.
——, 2007. *Theory of World Security*, Cambridge: Cambridge University Press.
——, 2005. *Critical Security Studies and World Politics*, London: Lynne Rienner.

——, ed., 2004. *Critical Security Studies and World Politics*, Boulder, CO: Lynne Rienner.

——, 1999. 'Three Tyrannies', in T. Dunne and N. Wheeler, eds, *Human Rights in Global Politics*, Cambridge: Cambridge University Press.

——, 1997. 'Security and Self: Reflections of a Fallen Realist', in K. Krause and M. Williams, eds, *Critical Security Studies: Concepts and Cases*, London: UCL Press.

——, 1991. 'Security and Emancipation', *Review of International Studies*, 17(4): 313–326.

Booth, K. and T. Dunne, eds, 2002. *Worlds in Collision: Terror and the Future of Global Order*, New York: Palgrave.

Bosi, L., 2007. 'Social Movement Participation and the "Timing" of Involvement: The Case of the Northern Ireland Civil Rights Movement', in P. Coy, ed., *Research in Social Movements, Conflicts and Change*, Amsterdam: Elsevier, 27: 37–61.

Bourcier, N., and C. Lesnes, 2007. 'L'affaire Debat, Un Bluff Américain', *Le Monde*, 22 September 2007.

Bourgois, P., 1995. *In Search of Respect*, New York, Cambridge: Cambridge University Press.

Bowyer Bell, J., 2000. *The IRA 1968–2000*, Ilford: Frank Cass.

——, 1997. *The Secret Army: The IRA*, Edison, NJ: Transaction Publishers.

Boyd, G., 1985. 'Reagan Reports New Latin Threat', *New York Times*, 25 January 1985.

Brannan, D., P. Esler, and N. Strindberg, 2001. 'Talking to "Terrorists": Towards an Independent Analytical Framework for the Study of Violent Substate Activism', *Studies in Conflict and Terrorism*, 24(1): 3–24.

Braungart, R. and M. Braungart, 1992. 'From Protest to Terrorism: The Case of the SDS and the Weathermen', in D. della Porta, ed., *Social Movements and Violence: Participation in Underground Organization*, London: JAI Press, 45–78.

Brecher, R., 2007. *Torture and the Ticking Bomb*, London: Wily-Blackwell.

Breen Smyth, M., 2008a. 'The Other End of the Telescope: Reconsidering the Effects of Political Violence in Context', paper presented at 116th Annual Convention of the American Psychological Association at Boston, Massachusetts, August 2008.

——, 2008b. 'Dealing With the Past: The Politics of Victimhood', in Liam O'Hagan, ed., *Stories in Conflict*, Derry/Londonderry: Yes Publications.

——, 2008c. 'Geographies of Conflict: Meanings and Effects of Political Violence', paper to International Studies Association Annual Convention, San Francisco, March 2008.

——, 2008d. 'Conversations in Critical Studies on Terrorism: Lessons Learned in Counter-Terrorism in Northern Ireland: An Interview with Peter Sheridan', *Critical Studies on Terrorism*, 1(1): pp. 111–124.

——, 2007. 'A Critical Research Agenda for the Study of Political Terror', *European Political Science*, 6(3), 260–267.

——, 2005. 'Insider-outsider Issues In Researching Violent and Divided Societies', in E. Porter, G. Robinson, M. Smyth, A. Schnabel, and E. Osaghe, eds, *Researching Conflict in Africa*, Tokyo: UN University Press.

——, 2004. 'Using Participative Action Research with War Affected Populations: Lessons From Research in Northern Ireland and South Africa', in M. Smyth, and E. Williamson, eds, *Researchers and Their 'Subjects': Ethics, Power Knowledge and Consent*, Bristol: Policy Press, pp. 137–156.

Breen Smyth, M., J. Gunning, R. Jackson, G. Kassimeris, and P. Robinson, 2008. 'Editor's Introduction: Navigating Stormy Waters', *Critical Studies on Terrorism*, 1(2): 145–149.

Bright, M., 2003. 'On the Trail of Osama bin Laden', *Observer*, 11 May 2003.
Brison, S., 2002. 'Gender, Terrorism, and War', *Signs: Journal of Women in Culture and Society*, 28(1): 435–437.
Brockett, C., 2005. *Political Movements and Violence in Central America*, Cambridge: Cambridge University Press.
——, 1991. 'The Structure of Political Opportunities and Peasant Mobilization in Central America', *Comparative Politics*, 23: 253–274.
Brown, C., 1994. '"Turtles All the Way Down": Anti-Foundationalism, Critical Theory and International Relations', *Millennium*, 23(2): 213–236.
B'Tselem, undated. *Population by Year in West Bank Settlements*. Online, available at: www.btselem.org/english/Settlements/Settlement_population.xls.
Burgat, F., 2003. *Face to Face With Political Islam*, London: I.B. Tauris.
Burke, A., 2008. 'The End of Terrorism Studies', *Critical Studies on Terrorism*, 1(1): 37–49.
——, 2007a. 'What Security Makes Possible: Some Thoughts on Critical Security Studies', *Working Paper 2007/1*, Department of International Relations, Australian National University. Online, available at: http://rspas.anu.edu.au/ir/ pubs/work_papers/07–1.pdf.
——, 2007b. *Beyond Security, Ethics and Violence: War Against the Other*, London: Routledge.
Burnett, J. and D. Whyte, 2005. 'Embedded Expertise and the New Terrorism', *Journal for Crime, Conflict and the Media*, 1(4): 1–18.
Butler, J., 2003. *Precarious Life: The Powers of Mourning and Violence*, London: Verso.
——, 1996. 'Universality in Culture', in J. Cohen, ed., *For Love of Country: Debating the Limits of Patriotism – Martha C. Nussbaum With Respondents*, Boston, MA: Beacon Press, 45–52.
Byman, D., 2007. *The Five Front War: The Better Way to Fight Global Jihad*, London: Wiley.
——, 2006. 'Do Targeted Killings Work?', *Foreign Affairs*, 85(2): 95–112.
——, 2003. 'Al-Qaeda as an Adversary: Do We Understand Our Enemy?', *World Politics*, 56(1): 139–163.
Caiazza, A., 2001. *Why Gender Matters in Understanding September 11: Women, Militarism, and Violence*, Briefing Paper, Institute for Women's Policy Research.
Callinicos, A., 2003. *The New Mandarins of American Power*, Cambridge: Polity Press.
Carr, E.H., 1946. *The Twenty Years' Crisis, 1919–1939: An Introduction to the Study of International Relations*, 2nd edn, London and Basingstoke: Macmillan Press and Papermac.
Carr, R., 2003. 'Terror Expert Lists Missed Clues', *Cox News Service*, 10 July 2003.
CASE Collective, 2006. 'Critical Approaches to Security in Europe: A Networked Manifesto', *Security Dialogue*, 37(4): 443–487.
Chaliand, G., ed., 1982a. *Guerrilla Strategies: An Historical Anthology From the Long March to Afghanistan*, Berkeley, CA: University of California Press.
——, 1982b. *The Palestinian Resistance*, Harmondsworth: Penguin Books.
——, 1969a. *The Peasants of North Vietnam*, London: Pelican.
——, 1969b. *Armed Struggle in Africa – With the Guerillas in 'Portuguese' Guinea*, New York, NY: Monthly Review Press.
——, ed. and M. Pallis, trans., 1984. *People Without a Country: Kurds and Kurdistan*, London: Zed Books.
Chalk, P., 2000. *Non-Military Security and Global Order: The Impact of Extremism, Violence and Chaos on National and International Security*, London: Macmillan.

——, 1999. 'The Evolving Dynamic of Terrorism in the 1990s', *Australian Journal of International Affairs*, 53(2): 151–167.
Chandler, J., 2005. 'The Explanatory Value of Social Movement Theory', *Strategic Insights* IV(5). Online, available at: www.ccc.nps.navy.mil/si/2005/May/ chandlerMay05.asp.
Chaze, W., 1981. 'Terrorism: Russia's Secret Weapon?', *US News and World Report*, 4 May 1981.
Chernick, M., 2007. 'FARC-EP: From Liberal Guerrillas to Marxist Rebels to Post-Cold War Insurgents', in M. Heiberg, B. O'Leary, and J. Tirman, eds, *Terror, Insurgency and the State: Ending Protracted Conflicts*, Philadelphia, PA: University of Pennsylvania Press, 51–81.
Chomsky, N., 2006. 'Grievances and Consequences: The Terrorist in the Mirror', *Counterpunch*, 24 January 2006. Online, available at: www.counterpunch.org/chomsky01242006.html.
——, 2001. 'The United States is a Leading Terrorist State', *Monthly Review*, 53 (6): 1019.
——, 1991. 'International Terrorism: Image and Reality', in A. George, ed., *Western State Terrorism*, Cambridge: Polity Press.
——, 1985. *Turning the Tide: US Intervention in Central America and the Struggle for Peace*, London: Pluto Press.
Chomsky, N. and E. Herman, 1979. *The Political Economy of Human Rights, Volume I: The Washington Connection and Third World Fascism*, Nottingham: Spokesman.
Claridge, D., 1999. 'Exploding the Myths of Superterrorism', *Terrorism and Political Violence*, 11(4): 133–148.
Clarke, R. and G. Newman, 2006. *Outsmarting the Terrorists*, London: Praeger Security International.
Cline, R. and Y. Alexander, 1986. *Terrorism as State-Sponsored Covert Warfare: What the Free World must do to Protect Itself*, Fairfax, VA: Hero Books.
——, *Terrorism: The Soviet Connection*, New York: Crane Russak.
CNN, 2002. 'Big Ben "Was September 11 target"'. Online, available at: http://edition.cnn.com/2002/WORLD/europe/06/11/uk.attacks/index.html (accessed 12 June 2002).
Coady, C., 1985. 'The Morality of Terrorism', *Philosophy*, 60(231): 47–69.
Cockburn, C., 2007. *From Where We Stand: War, Women's Activism and Feminist Analysis*, London: Zed Books.
Cohen, J., 1985. 'Strategy or Identity: New Theoretical Paradigms and Contemporary Social Movements', *Social Research*, 52(4): 663–716.
Cohn, C., 1987. 'Sex and Death in the Rational World of Defense Intellectuals', *Signs: Journal of Women in Culture and Society*, 12(4): 687–718.
Cohn, E.G. and D. P. Farrington, 1998. 'Changes in the Most-Cited Scholars in Major International Journals Between 1986–90 and 1991–95.' *British Journal of Criminology*, 38: 156–170.
Cole, D., 2007. *Less Safe, Less Free: Why We Are Losing the War on Terror*, New York and London: The New Press.
——, 2003. *Enemy Aliens: Double Standards and Constitutional Freedoms in the War on Terrorism*, New York and London: The New Press.
Collier, P. and A. Hoeffler, 2004. 'Greed and Grievance in Civil War', *Oxford Economic Papers*, 56: 563–595.
Collins, E., (with M. McGovern) 1997. *Killing Rage*, London: Granta Books.
Coogan, T., 1987. *The IRA*, London: Fontana.

Copeland, T., 2001. 'Is the New Terrorism Really New? An Analysis of the New Paradigm for Terrorism', *Journal of Conflict Studies*, XXI(2): 91–105.

Copson, R. and R. Cronin, 1987. 'The "Reagan Doctrine" and its Prospects', *Survival*, 29(1): 40–55.

Costain, A., 1992. *Inviting Women's Rebellion: A Political Process Interpretation of the Women's Movement*, Baltimore, MD: Johns Hopkins University Press.

Cox, R., 1986. 'Social Forces, States and World Orders: Beyond International Relations Theory', in R. Keohane, ed., *Neorealism and Its Critic*, New York: Columbia University Press.

——, 1981. 'Social Forces, States and World Orders: Beyond International Relations Theory', *Millennium: Journal of International Studies*, 10(2): 126–155.

Crace, J., 2008. 'Just How Expert are the Expert Witnesses?', *Guardian*, 13 May 2008.

Cragin, K., 2009. *Women as Terrorists: Mothers, Recruiters, and Martyrs*, London: Praeger.

Craig, I. and K. Geldard, 1988. *Irish Terrorism: IRA, INLA – Foreign Support and International Connections*, London: Institute for the Study of Terrorism.

Crelinsten, R., 2002. 'Analysing Terrorism and Counter-terrorism: A Communication Model', *Terrorism and Political Violence*, 14(2): 77–122.

——, 1987. 'Terrorism as Political Communication: The Relationship Between the Controller and the Controlled', in P. Wilkinson and A. Stewart, eds, *Contemporary Research on Terrorism*, Aberdeen: Aberdeen University Press, 3–23.

Crenshaw, M., 2007. 'Explaining Suicide Terrorism: A Review Essay', *Security Studies*, 16(1), 133–162.

——, 2003. '"New" Versus "Old" Terrorism', *Palestine–Israel Journal of Politics, Economics and Culture*, 10(1): 48–53.

——, 2000. 'The Psychology of Terrorism: An Agenda for the 21st Century', *Political Psychology*, 21(2), 405.

——, ed., 1995. *Terrorism in Context*, University Park, PA: Pennsylvania State University Press.

——, 1992. 'Decisions to Use Terrorism: Psychological Constraints on Instrumental Reasoning', in D. della Porta, ed., *Social Movements and Violence: Participation in Underground Organizations*, London: JAI Press, 29–42.

——, 1991. 'How Terrorism Declines', *Terrorism and Political Violence*, 3(1): 69–87.

——, 1983. 'Reflections on the Effects of Terrorism', in M. Crenshaw, ed., *Terrorism, Legitimacy, Power – The Consequences of Political Violence*, Middletown, CT: Wesleyan University Press.

——, 1981. 'The Causes of Terrorism', *Comparative Politics*, 13(4), July: 379–399.

Crenshaw, M., [Hutchinson] 1972. 'The Concept of Revolutionary Terrorism', *Journal of Conflict Resolution*, XVI, 3 (Sept., 1972): 383–396.

Critical Studies on Terrorism, 2008. 'Symposium: Critical Terrorism Studies: Foundations, Issues, Challenges', 1(1–2).

Croft, S., 2006. *Culture, Crisis and America's War on Terror*, Cambridge: Cambridge University Press.

Cronau, P., 2003. 'The Legitimizing of Terror Fears: Research or Psy Ops?', *Pacific Journalism Review*, 9.

Cronin, A., 2008. *Ending Terrorism: Lessons for Defeating al-Qaeda* (Adelphi Paper), London: Routledge.

Cunningham, D., 2003. 'State Versus Social Movement: FBI Counterintelligence Against the New Left', in J. Goldstone, ed., *States, Parties, and Social Movements*, Cambridge: Cambridge University Press, 45–77.

Czwarno, M., 2006. 'Misjudging Islamic Terrorism: The Academic Community's Failure to Predict 9/11', *Studies in Conflict and Terrorism*, 29(7): 657–694.

Dalacoura, K., 2003. *Islam, Liberalism and Human Rights: Implications for International Relations*. Revised edition. I. B. Tauris.

Darby, J., 1983. *Northern Ireland: The Background to the Conflict*, Belfast: Appletree Press.

Davenport, C., H. Johnston, and C. Mueller, eds, 2005. *Repression and Mobilization*, Minneapolis, MN: University of Minnesota Press.

Davis, J., 2003. *Martyrs: Innocence, Vengeance, and Despair in the Middle East*, New York: Palgrave Macmillan.

Davis, P. and B. Jenkins, 2002. *Deterrence and Influence in Counterterrorism: A Component in the War on al Qaeda*, Santa Monica, CA: RAND.

Decker, J., 1990/1. 'Terrorism (Un)Veiled: Frantz Fanon and the Women of Algiers', *Cultural Critique*, 17(Winter): 177–195.

Della Porta, D., 2008. 'Research on Social Movements and Political Violence', *Qualitative Sociology*, 31(3): 221–230.

——, 1995a. 'Left-Wing Terrorism in Italy', in Martha Crenshaw, ed., *Terrorism in Context*, University Park, PA: Pennsylvania State University Press, 105–159.

——, 1995b. *Social Movements, Political Violence, and the State: A Comparative Analysis of Italy and Germany*, Cambridge: Cambridge University Press.

——, ed., 1992a. *Social Movements and Violence: Participation in Underground Organizations*, London: JAI Press.

——, 1992b. 'Introduction: On Individual Motivations in Underground Political Organizations', in D. della Porta, ed., *Social Movements and Violence: Participation in Underground Organizations*, London: JAI Press, 3–28.

——, 1992c. 'Political Socialization in Left-Wing Underground Organizations: Biographies of Italian and German Militants', in D. della Porta, ed., *Social Movements and Violence: Participation in Underground Organizations*, London: JAI Press, 259–290.

Della Porta, D. and M. Diani, 1999. *Social Movements: An Introduction*, Oxford: Basil Blackwell.

Della Porta, D. and S. Tarrow, 1986. 'Unwanted Children: Political Violence and the Cycle of Protest in Italy, 1966–1973', *European Journal of Political Research*, 14: 607–632.

Demetriou, C., 2007. 'Political Violence and Legitimation: The Episode of Colonial Cyprus', *Qualitative Sociology*, 30(2): 171–193.

Devetak, R., 2005a. 'Critical Theory', in S. Burchill, A. Linklater, R. Devetak, J. Donnelly, M. Paterson, C. Reus-Smit, and J. True, eds, *Theories of International Relations*, 3rd edn, London: Macmillan.

——, 2005b. 'Postmodernism', in S. Burchill, A. Linklater, R. Devetak, J. Donnelly, M. Paterson, C. Reus-Smit, and J. True, eds, *Theories of International Relations*, 3rd edn, London: Macmillan, 161–187.

——, 1996. 'Critical Theory', in S. Burchill and A. Linklater, eds, with R. Devetak, M. Patterson, and J. True, *Theories of International Relations*, Basingstoke and London: Macmillan Press.

Dobbs, M., 2001. 'Unscripted bin Laden: "Very Dangerous" Man Chuckling at Deaths', *International Herald Tribune*, 15–16 December 2001.

Dodd, V., 2006. 'Police Report: Foreign Policy Helped Make UK a Terrorist Target', *Guardian*, 6 July 2006. Online, available at: www.guardian.co.uk/ attackonlondon/ story/0,,1814756,00.html.

Drumbl, M., 2005. 'Law and Atrocity: Settling Accounts in Rwanda', *Ohio Northern University Law Review*, 31: 41–64.

Duara, P., 2004. *Sovereignty and Authenticity: Manchukuo and the East Asian Modern*, Lanham, MD: Rowman & Littlefield.

Duyvesteyn, I., 2004. 'How New is the New Terrorism?', *Studies in Conflict and Terrorism*, 27(5): 439–454.

Eagleton, T., 2005. *Holy Terror*, Oxford: Oxford University Press.

Egerton, F., forthcoming. *Western Militant Jihadism: Identity and the Imaginary, Movement and Media*, Unpublished Doctoral Thesis, Aberystwyth University.

El Fadl, K., ed., 2002. *Shattered Illusions: Analyzing the War on Terrorism*, Bristol: Amal Press.

El Saadawi, N., 1982. *The Hidden Face of Eve: Women in the Arab World*, translated and edited by S. Hetata, Boston MA: Beacon Press.

Elad, S. and A. Merari, 1984. *The Soviet Bloc and World Terrorism*, Tel Aviv: Jaffee Center for Strategic Studies.

Ellen, R., ed. 1984. *Ethnographic Research: A Guide to General Conduct*, London: Academic Press.

Ellison, J., 1997. *Professionalism in the Royal Ulster Constabulary: An Examination of the Institutional Discourse*, Unpublished Doctoral Thesis, University of Ulster, UK.

Elshtain, J.B., 1987. *Women and War*, New York: Free Press.

Enders, T., 1982. 'Cuban Support for Terrorism and Insurgency in the Western Hemisphere', US Assistant Secretary of State for Western Hemisphere Affairs, *Department of State Bulletin*, August 1982.

English, R., 2003. *Armed Struggle: A History of the IRA*, London: Macmillan.

Enloe, C., 1993. *The Morning After: Sexual Politics at the End of the Cold War*, Berkeley, CA: University of California Press.

Ergil, D., 2007. 'PKK: The Kurdistan Workers Party', in M. Heiberg, B. O'Leary, and J. Tirman, eds, *Terror, Insurgency and the State: Ending Protracted Conflicts*, Philadelphia, PA: University of Pennsylvania Press, 323–357.

Esposito, J., 1999. *The Islamic Threat: Myth or Reality?* New York: Oxford University Press.

ESRC/AHRC/FCO, 2006. *New Security Challenges: Combating Terrorism by Countering Radicalisation*, July 2006.

European Political Science, 2007. 'Symposium: The Case for Critical Terrorism Studies', 6(3), 225–267.

Eyerman, R. and A. Jamison, 1991. *Social Movements: A Cognitive Approach*, Cambridge: Polity Press.

Falah, G., 2004. 'War, Peace and Land Seizure in Palestine's Border Area', *Third World Quarterly*, 25(5): 955–975.

Fanon, F., 1989. *Studies in a Dying Colonialism*, trans. H. Chevalier; with a new introduction by A.M. Babu, London: Earthscan, 1989.

Fay, M., M. Morrissey, and M. Breen Smith, 1999. *Northern Ireland's Troubles: The Human Costs*, London: Pluto.

Feldman, A., 1991. *Formations of Violence: Narratives of the Body and Political Terror in Northern Ireland*, Chicago, IL: University of Chicago Press.

Ferberl, A. and M. Kimmel, 2008. 'The Gendered Face of Terrorism', *Sociology Compass* 2.

Ferguson, K., 1984. *The Feminist Case Against Bureaucracy*, Philadelphia: Temple University Press.

Ferree, M., 1992. 'The Political Context of Rationality: Rational Choice Theory and Resource Mobilization', in A. Morris and C. Mueller, eds, *Frontiers in Social Movement Theory*, New Haven, CT: Yale University Press, 29–52.

Fierke, K., 2007. *Critical Approaches to International Security*, London: Polity.

Fisk, R., 1992. *Pity the Nation: Lebanon at War*, Oxford: Oxford University Press.

Foot, R., 2005. 'Collateral Damage: Human Rights Consequences of Counter-terrorist Action in the Asia-Pacific', *International Affairs*, 81(2): 411–425.

Foweraker, J., 1995. *Theorizing Social Movements*, Boulder, CO: Pluto Press.

Frankfort-Nachmias, C. and D. Nachmias, 1996. *Research Methods in the Social Sciences*, 5th edn, London: Arnold.

Friedman, D., and D. McAdam, 1992. 'Collective Identity and Activism', in A. Morris and C. Mueller, eds, *Frontiers in Social Movement Theory*, New Haven, CT: Yale University Press, 156–173.

Gabelnick, T., W. Hartung, and J. Washburn, 1999. *Arming Repression: US Arms Sales to Turkey During the Clinton Administration*, Joint Report of the World Policy Institute and the Federation of American Scientists, October 1999.

Galtung, J., 1969. 'Violence, Peace and Peace Research', *Journal of Peace Research*, 6(3): 167–191.

Gamson, W., 1992. 'The Social Psychology of Collective Action', in A.D. Morris and C. McClurg Mueller, eds, *Frontiers in Social Movement Theory*, New Haven: Yale University Press, 53–76.

——, 1990. *The Strategy of Social Protest*, 2nd ed., Belmont, CA: Wadsworth.

——, 1975. *The Strategy of Social Protest*, Homewood, IL: Dorsey Press.

Gamson, W. and D. Meyer, 1996. 'Framing Political Opportunity', in D. McAdam, J. McCarthy, and M. Zald, eds, *Comparative Perspectives on Social Movements: Political Opportunities, Mobilizing Structures, and Cultural Framings*, Cambridge: Cambridge University Press, 275–290.

Gareau, F., 2004. *State Terrorism and the United States: From Counterinsurgency to the War on Terrorism*, London: Zed Books.

Garner, R., 1997. 'Fifty Years of Social Movement Theory: An Interpretation', in R. Garner and J. Tenuto, eds, *Social Movement Theory and Research: An Annotated Bibliographical Guide*, Lanham, MD: Scarecrow Press, 1–58.

Garvey, W., N. Lin, and K. Tomita, 1979. 'Research Studies in Patterns of Scientific Communications: III, Information-exchange Processes Associated with the Production of Journal Articles', in W. Garvey, ed., *Communication: The Essence of Science*, Oxford: Pergamon Press.

Gearty, C., 1991. *Terror*, London: Faber and Faber.

George, A., ed., 1991a. *Western State Terrorism*, Cambridge: Polity Press.

——, 1991b. 'The Discipline of Terrorology', in A. George, ed., *Western State Terrorism*, Cambridge: Polity Press, 76–101.

Gerges, F.A., 2005. *The Far Enemy: Why Jihad Went Global*, Cambridge: Cambridge University Press.

——, 1991. 'The Study of Middle East International Relations: A Critique', *British Journal of Middle Eastern Studies*, 18(2).

Girard, R., 1982. *La Violence et le Sacré*, Paris: Grasset.

Glazer, M., 1972. *The Research Adventure: Promise and Problems of Fieldwork*, New York: Random House.

Glees, A., 2007. 'Blind faith', *Times Higher Education*, 20 July 2007.

Gold-Biss, M., 1994. *The Discourse on Terrorism: Political Violence and the Subcommittee on Security and Terrorism 1981–1986*, New York: Peter Lang.

Gold-Wartofsky, M., 2008. 'Repress U: How to Build a Homeland Security Campus in Seven Steps', TomDispatch.com, 10 January 2008. Online, available at: www.truthout.org/docs_2006/0111081.shtml.

Gonzalez, E., B. Jenkins, D. Ronfeld and C. Sereseres, 1984. *US Policy Options for Central America: A Briefing*, Santa Monica, CA: RAND.

Goodwin, J. and J. Jasper, 1999. 'Caught in a Winding, Snarling Vine: The Structural Bias of Political Process Theory', *Sociological Forum*, 14(1): 27–54.

Goodwin, J., J. Jasper and F. Polleta, eds, 2001. *Passionate Politics: Emotions and Social Movements*, Chicago, IL: University of Chicago Press.

——, 2000. 'Return of the Repressed: The Fall and Rise of Emotions in Social Movement Theory', *Mobilization*, 5(1): 65–82.

Gordon, A., 2004. 'Terrorism and Knowledge Growth: A Databases and Internet Analysis', in A. Silke, ed., *Research on Terrorism: Trends, Achievements and Failures*, London: Frank Cass.

——, 2001. 'Terrorism and the Scholarly Communication System', *Terrorism and Political Violence*, 13.

——, 1999. 'Terrorism Dissertations and the Evolution of a Speciality: An Analysis of Meta-Information', *Terrorism and Political Violence*, 11(2): 141–150.

——, 1998. 'The Spread of Terrorism Publications: A Database Analysis', *Terrorism and Political Violence*, 10(4): 190–193.

Gould-Wartofsky, M., 2008. 'Repress U: How to Build a Homeland Security Campus in Seven Steps', *Truthout*, 10 January 2008. Online, available at: www.truthout.org/ article/michael-gould-wartofsky-repress-u-in-seven-steps (accessed 13 July 2008).

Green, L., 1995. 'Living in a State of Fear', in C. Nordstrom and A. Robben, eds, *Fieldwork Under Fire: Contemporary Studies of Violence and Survival*, Berkeley, CA: University of California Press, 105–128.

Grey, S., 2006. *Ghost Plane: The Inside Story of the CIA's Secret Rendition Programme*, London: Hurst/St Martin's Press.

Groskop, V., 2004. 'Chechnya's Deadly "Black Widows"', *New Statesman*, 6 September 2004, 17.

Grosscup, B., 2006. *Strategic Terror: The Politics and Ethics of Aerial Bombardment*, London: Zed Books.

Gunaratna, R., 2003. *Inside Al Qaeda: Global Network of Terror*, 2nd edn, London: Hurst & Co.

——, 2001. 'Blowback', *Jane's Intelligence Review*, 13(8).

Gunning, J., 2008. 'Ignoring Hamas Will Imperil the Peace Process', Interview, *The Hindu*, Chennai, Madras, 4 July 2008. Online, available at: www.hindu.com/nic/hamas.html.

——, 2007a. 'A Case for Critical Terrorism Studies?', *Government and Opposition*, 42(3): 363–393.

——, 2007b. 'Babies and Bathwaters: Reflecting on the Pitfalls of Critical Terrorism Studies', *European Political Science*, 6(3): 236–243.

——, 2007c. *Hamas in Politics: Democracy, Religion, Violence*, London: Hurst.

——, 2004. 'Peace with Hamas? The transforming potential of political participation'. *International Affairs* 80(2): 233–255.

——, 2000. *Re-Thinking Western Constructs of Islamism – Pluralism, Democracy and the Theory and Praxis of the Islamic Movement in the Gaza Strip*, Doctoral Thesis, Centre for Middle Eastern & Islamic Studies, University of Durham, UK.

Gurr, T., 1988. 'Empirical Research on Political Terrorism: The State of the Art and How it Might Be Improved', in R. Slater and M. Stohl, eds, *Current Perspectives on International Terrorism*, New York: St. Martin's Press.

——, 1970. *Why Men Rebel?*, Princeton, NJ: Princeton University Press.

Gurr, T. and J. Goldstone, 1986. 'Persisting Patterns of Repression and Rebellion', in M. Karns, ed., *Persistent Patterns and Emergent Structures in a Waning Century*, New York, NY: Praeger, 324–352.

Haas, P., 2004. 'When Does Power Listen to Truth? A Constructivist Approach to the Policy Process', *Journal of European Public Policy*, 11(4): 569–592.

——, 1992. 'Introduction: Epistemic Communities and International Policy Coordination', *International Organization*, 46(1): 1–35.

Habermas, J., 1984. *The Theory of Communicative Action, Volume 1*, London: Heinemann.

Hafez, M., 2007. *Suicide Bombers in Iraq: The Strategy and Ideology of Martyrdom*, Washington, DC: The United States Institute of Peace.

——, 2006. 'Rationality, Culture, and Structure in the Making of Suicide Bombers', *Studies in Conflict and Terrorism*, 29(2): 165–185.

——, 2004. 'From Marginalization to the Massacres: A Political Process Explanation of GIA Violence in Algeria', in Q. Wiktorowicz, ed., *Islamic Activism: A Social Movement Theory Approach*, Bloomington, IN: Indiana University Press, 37–60.

——, 2003. *Why Muslims Rebel? Repression and Resistance in the Islamic World*, Boulder, CO: Lynne Rienner.

Hafez, M. and Q. Wiktorowicz, 2004. 'Violence as Contention in the Egyptian Islamic Movement', in Q. Wiktorowicz, ed., *Islamic Activism: A Social Movement Theory Approach*, Bloomington, IN: Indiana University Press, 61–88.

Haig, A., 1981. 'Excerpts from Haig's Remarks at First News Conference as Secretary of State', *New York Times*, 29 January 1981.

Haines, H., 1988. *Black Radicals and the Civil Rights Mainstream, 1954–1970*, Knoxville, TN: University of Tennessee Press.

Hannigan, J., 1991. 'Social Movement Theory and the Sociology of Religion: Toward a New Synthesis', *Sociological Analysis*, 52(4): 311–331.

Hansen, L., 2003. 'Domestic Opinion and Identity Politics', *Cooperation and Conflict*, 38(3): 311–317.

——, 2001. 'Gender, Nation, Rape: Bosnia and the Construction of Security', *International Feminist Journal of Politics*, 3(1): 55–75.

——, 2000. 'The Little Mermaid's Silent Security Dilemma and the Absence of Gender in the Copenhagen School', *Millennium: Journal of International Studies*, 29(2): 285–306.

Haq, F., 2007. 'Militarism and Motherhood: Women of the Lashkar-e-Tayyaba', *Signs, Journal of Women in Culture and Society*, 32(4): 1023–1045.

Haqqani, H., 2002. 'Islam's Medieval Outposts', *Foreign Policy*, 133: 58–64.

Harik, J.P., 2004. *Hezbollah: The Changing Face of Terrorism*, London: I. B. Tauris.

Harnden, T., 1999. *Bandit Country: The IRA and South Armagh*, London: Hodder and Stoughton.

Harris, H., 1983. 'Women in Struggle: Nicaragua', *Third World Quarterly*, 5(4): 899–908.

Hayden, N., 2006. 'The Complexity of Terrorism: Social and Behavioural Understanding Trends for the Future', in M. Ranstorp, ed., *Mapping Terrorism Research*, London: Routledge.

Helie-Lucas, M., 1990. 'Women, Nationalism and Religion in the Algerian Liberation Struggle', in M. Badran and M. Cooke, eds, *Opening the Gates: A Century of Arab Feminist Writing*, London: Virago.

Henslin, J.M., 1972. 'Studying Deviance in Four Settings: Research Experiences with Cabbies, Suicide, Drug Users, and Abortionees', in J. Douglas, ed., *Research on Deviance*, New York: Random House.

Herman, E., 1982. *The Real Terror Network: Terrorism in Fact and Propaganda*, Boston: South End Press.

Herman, E. and G. O'Sullivan, 1989. *The 'Terrorism' Industry: The Experts and Institutions that Shape our View of Terror*, New York: Pantheon Books.

Herring, E., 2008. 'Critical Terrorism Studies: An Activist Scholar Perspective', *Critical Studies on Terrorism*, 1(2): 197–211.

Hersh, S., 2006. 'The Next Act', *The New Yorker*, 27 November 2006.

Hill, F., M. Aboitiz, and S. Poehlman-Doumbouya, 2003. 'Nongovernmental Organizations' Role in the Buildup and Implementation of Security Council Resolution 1325', *Signs, Journal of Women in Culture and Society*, 28(4): 1255–1270.

Hillyard, P., 1993. *Suspect Community: People's Experience of the Prevention of Terrorism Acts in Britain*, London: Pluto.

Hipsher, P., 1998. 'Democratic Transitions and Social Movement Outcomes: The Chilean Shantytown Dwellers' Movement in Comparative Perspective', in M. Giugni, D. McAdam, and C. Tilly, eds, *From Contention to Democracy*, Lanham, MD: Rowman & Littlefield, 149–167.

Hiro, D., 2002. *War Without End: The Rise of Islamist Terrorism and Global Response*, London: Routledge.

Hobson, J., 2007. 'Is Critical Theory Always for the White West and for Western Imperialism? Beyond Westphilian Towards a Post-racist Critical IR', in N. Rengger and B. Thirkell-White, eds, *Critical International Relations Theory After 25 Years*, Cambridge: Cambridge University Press.

Hocking, J., 2004. *Terror Laws: ASIO, Counter-Terrorism and the Threat to Democracy*, Sydney: UNSW Press.

Hoffman, B., 2008. 'The Myth of Grass-Roots Terrorism: Why Osama bin Laden Still Matters', *Foreign Affairs*, 87(3): 133–138.

——, 2006. *Inside Terrorism*, 2nd revised edn, New York: Columbia University Press.

——, 1999. 'Terrorism Trends and Prospects', in I.O. Lesser, B. Hoffman, J. Arquilla, D. Ronfeld, and M. Zanini, eds, *Countering the New Terrorism*, Santa Monica, CA: RAND.

——, 1998. *Inside Terrorism*, New York: Columbia University Press.

——, 1992. 'Current Research on Terrorism and Low-intensity Conflict', *Studies in Conflict and Terrorism*, 15(1): 25–37.

——, 1989a. 'The Contrasting Ethical Foundations of Terrorism in the 1980s', *Terrorism and Political Violence*, 1(3): 361–377.

——, 1989b. *US Policy Options to the Hostage Crisis in Lebanon*, Santa Monica, CA: RAND.

Hoffman, B. and G. McCormick, 2004. 'Terrorism, Signaling, and Suicide Attack', *Studies in Conflict and Terrorism*, 27: 243–281.

Hoffman, M., 1991. 'Restructuring, Reconstruction, Reinscription, Rearticulation: Four Voices in Critical International Theory', *Millennium*, 20(2): 169–185.

——, 1987. 'Critical Theory and the Inter-Paradigm Debate', *Millennium*, 16(2):231–249.
Holland, J. and H. McDonald, 1994. *INLA: Deadly Divisions*, Dublin: Poolbeg Press.
Holmes, S., 2005. 'Al Qaeda, September 11, 2001', in D. Gambetta, ed., *Making Sense of Suicide Missions*, Oxford: Oxford University Press.
Honneth, A., 1995. *The Struggle for Recognition: The Moral Grammar of Social Conflicts*, Cambridge: Polity.
Hoogensen, G. and S. Rottem, 2004. 'Gender Identity and the Subject of Security', *Security Dialogue*, 35(2): 155–157.
Horgan, J., 2008. 'Understanding Terrorism: Old Assumptions, New Assertions and Challenges for Research', in J. Victoroff and A. Kruglanski, eds, *Psychology of Terrorism: The Best Writings About the Mind of the Terrorist*, London: Psychology Press.
——, 2005. *The Psychology of Terrorism*, London: Frank Cass.
——, 2003. 'The Search for the Terrorist Personality', in A. Silke, ed., *Terrorists, Victims and Society: Psychological Perspectives on Terrorism and Its Consequences*, Chichester: Wiley.
Horgan, J. and M. Boyle, 2008. 'A Case against "Critical Terrorism Studies"', *Critical Studies on Terrorism*, 1(1): 51–64.
Horkheimer, M., 1992. *Critical Theory: Selected Essays*, New York: Seabury Press.
Howell, N., 1990. *Surviving Fieldwork: A Report of the Advisory Panel on Health and Safety in Fieldwork*, Washington, DC: American Anthropological Association.
Hufford, L., 1985. 'The US in Central America: The Obfuscation of History', *Journal of Peace Research*, 22(2): 93–100.
Hughes, G., 2003. 'Analyse This', *The Age*. Online, available at: www.theage.com.au/articles/2003/07/20/1058545648013.html (accessed 20 July 2003).
Human Rights Watch, 2007a. *Country Summary: Tunisia*, January 2007. Online, available at: http://hrw.org/englishwr2k7/docs/2007/01/11/tunisi14723.htm (accessed 7 December 2007).
——, 2007b. *Israel/Gaza Strip: Rockets and Shelling Violate Laws of War*, 1 July 2007. Online, available at: http://hrw.org/english/docs/2007/07/01/ isrlpa16310.htm.
——, 2006a. *Israel/Lebanon: Israeli Indiscriminate Attacks Killed Most Civilians*, 6 September 2006. Online, available at: http://hrw.org/english/docs/2007/09/06/isrlpa16781.htm.
——, 2006b. Report, *Why They Died: Civilian Casualties in Lebanon During the 2006 War*, September 2006. Online, available at: www.amnesty.org/en/report/info/MDE02/033/2006.
——, 2005. *No Exit: Human Rights Abuses in the Mojahedin Khalq Camps*, May 2005. Online, available at: www.hrw.org/backgrounder/mena/iran0505/index.htm.
——, 2002. *Dangerous Dealings: Changes to US Military Assistance After September 11*, New York: Human Rights Watch.
——, 2001. *The 'Sixth Division': Military–paramilitary Ties and US Policy in Colombia*, New York: Human Rights Watch.
——, 1993. *World Report 1992*, New York: Human Rights Watch.
——, 1990. *World Report 1989*, New York: Human Rights Watch.
Hunt, K., 2006. '"Embedded Feminism" and the War on Terror', in K. Hunt and K. Rygiel, eds, *(En)gendering the War on Terror*, Hampshire: Ashgate.
Hunt, K. and K. Rygiel, eds, 2006. *(En)gendering the War on Terror*, Hampshire: Ashgate.
Husanovic, J. and P. Owens, 2000. 'Emancipation: A "Shrieking in Keeping"? An email conversation on feminism, emancipation and security between Jasmina Husanovic and Patricia Owens', *International Feminist Journal of Politics*, 2(3), 1 October: 424–434.

Hutchings, K., 2001. 'The Nature of Critique in Critical International Relations Theory', in R. Wyn Jones, ed., *Critical Theory and World Politics*, London: Lynne Rienner.

Ilardi, G., 2004. 'Redefining the Issues: The Future of Terrorism Research and the Search for Empathy', in A. Silke, ed., *Research on Terrorism: Trends, Achievements and Failures*, London: Frank Cass.

International Court of Justice, 1986. 'United States' Action Against Nicaragua Contrary to International Obligations', *The Times*, 28 June 1986.

International Crisis Group, 2007. *Pakistan: Karachi's Madrasas and Violent Extremism*. Asia Report No. 130, 29 March 2007.

Jackson, R., forthcoming, 'The Study of Political Terror after September 11, 2001: Problems, Challenges and Future Directions', *Political Studies Review*.

——, 2008a. 'An Argument for Terrorism', *Perspectives on Terrorism*, 2(2): 25–32.

——, 2008b. 'The Ghosts of State Terror: Knowledge, Politics and Terrorism Studies', a paper prepared for the International Studies Association (ISA) Annual Conference, 26–29 March 2008, San Francisco, USA.

——, 2008c. 'Why We Need Critical Terrorism Studies', *e-International Relations*. Online, available at: www.e-ir.info/?p=432.

——, 2007a, 'Constructing Enemies: "Islamic Terrorism" in Political and Academic Discourse', *Government & Opposition*, 42(3): 394–426.

——, 2007b. 'Critical Reflection on Counter-sanctuary Discourse', in Michael Innes, ed., *Denial of Sanctuary: Understanding Terrorist Safe Havens*, Westport, CT: Praeger Security International.

——, 2007c. 'Playing the Politics of Fear: Writing the Terrorist Threat in the War on Terrorism', in G. Kassimeris, ed., *Playing Politics With Terrorism: A User's Guide*, New York: Columbia University Press.

——, 2007d. 'Language, Policy and the Construction of a Torture Culture in the War on Terrorism', *Review of International Studies*, 33: 353–371.

——, 2007e. 'The Core Commitments of Critical Terrorism Studies', *European Political Science*, 6(3): 244–251.

——, 2007f. 'Research for Counterterrorism: Terrorism Studies and the Reproduction of State Hegemony', International Studies Association (ISA) 48th Annual Convention, 28 February – 3 March 2007, Chicago, United States.

——, 2007g. 'Terrorism Studies and the Politics of State Power', International Studies Association (ISA) 48th Annual Convention, 28 February–3 March 2007, Chicago, United States.

——, 2007h. 'Introduction: The Case for Critical Terrorism Studies', *European Political Science*, 6(3): 225–227.

——, 2006. 'Genealogy, Ideology, and Counter-Terrorism: Writing Wars on Terrorism from Ronald Reagan to George W. Bush Jr', *Studies in Language & Capitalism*, 1(1): 163–193.

——, 2005. *Writing the War on Terrorism: Language, Politics and Counterterrorism*, Manchester: Manchester University Press.

Jackson, R., M. Breen Smyth, and J. Gunning, forthcoming. 'Critical Terrorism Studies', in H. Fagan and R. Munck, eds, *Globalization and Human Security: An Encyclopaedia*, Westport, CT: Praeger Security Press.

——, 2007. 'The Case for a Critical Terrorism Studies', American Political Science Association (APSA) Annual Convention, 30 August–2 September 2007, Chicago, USA.

Jasper, J., 1998. 'The Emotions of Protest: Affective and Reactive Emotions In and Around Social Movements', *Sociological Forum*, 13(3): 397–424.

Jehl, D., 1996. 'Iran Tells the Europeans that it Doesn't Back Terrorism', *New York Times*, 8 March 1996.

Jenkins, B., 2003. *Remarks Before the National Commission on Terrorist Attacks Upon the United States*, National Commission on Terrorist Attacks Upon the United States.

——, 2002. '30 Years and Counting'. Online, available at: www.rand.org/publications/randreview/issues/rr.08.02/thirtyyears.html.

——, 2001. 'A Confounding, Complex Tragedy', *San Diego Union-Tribune*, 17 June 2001.

——, 2000/1. 'Colombia: Crossing a Dangerous Threshold', *The National Interest*, 62: 47–55.

——, 1998. 'Will Terrorists go Nuclear? A Reappraisal', in H. Kushner, ed., *The Future of Terrorism: Violence in the New Millennium*, London: Sage.

——, 1985. *International Terrorism: The Other World War*, Santa Monica, CA: RAND.

Jenkins, C., 1983. 'Resource Mobilization Theory and the Study of Social Movements', *Annual Review of Sociology*, 9: 527–553.

Johnston, H., E. Laraña, and J. Gusfield, 1994. 'Identities, Grievances, and New Social Movements', in E. Laraña, H. Johnston, and J.R. Gusfield, eds, *New Social Movements: From Ideology to Identity*, Philadelphia, PA: Temple University Press, 3–35.

Jones, A., 2007. 'Terrorism Studies: Theoretically Under-developed?', *e-IR*. Online, available at: www.e.ir.info/info/?p=151&print=1 (accessed 22 December 2007).

Jones, D., 2006. 'Delusion Reigns in Terrorism Studies', *The Australian*, 15 September 2006.

——, 1999. *Cosmopolitan Mediation? Conflict Resolution and the Oslo Accords*, Manchester: Manchester University Press.

JTAC, 2006. Speech made by the head of JTAC at a conference held at the Swedish National Defence College, October 2006.

Juergensmeyer, M., 2000. *Terror in the Mind of God: The Global Rise of Religious Violence*, University of California Press.

Kaplan, C., N. Alarcon, and M. Moallem, eds, 1999. *Between Woman and Nation: Nationalism, Transnational Feminisms, and the State*, Durham: Duke University Press.

Karagiannis, E. and C. McCauley, 2006. 'Hizb ut-Tahrir al-Islami: Evaluating the Threat Posed by a Radical Islamic Group that Remains Nonviolent.' *Terrorism and Political Violence*, 18: 315–334.

Katzenstein, M. and C. McClurg Mueller, eds, 1987. *The Women's Movements of Western Europe and the United States: Consciousness, Political Opportunity, and Public Policy*, Philadelphia, PA: Temple University Press.

Kegley, Jr., C., ed., 2003. *The New Global Terrorism: Characteristics, Causes, Controls*, New Jersey: Prentice Hall.

Kepel, G., 2002. *Jihad: The Trail of Political Islam*, London: I.B. Tauris.

Khalaf, R. and S. Fidler, 2007. 'From Frontline Attack to Terror by Franchise', *Financial Times*, 4 July 2007. Online, available at: http://news-summary.blogspot.com/2007/07/international-herald-tribune-editorial_05.html.

Khawaja, M., 1993. 'Repression and Popular Collective Action: Evidence From the West Bank', *Sociological Forum*, 8(1): 47–71.

Kimmel, M., 2002. 'Gender, Class, and Terrorism', *The Chronicle of Higher Education*, XLVIII(22).

Kiras, J., 2007. 'Dying to Prove a Point: The Methodology of Dying to Win', *The Journal of Strategic Studies*, 30(2): 227–241.

Kirk, D., 2001. 'Filipinos Recall Hijack Suspects Leading a High Life', *International Herald Tribune*, 5 October 2001: 1.

Kitschelt, H., 1986, 'Political Opportunity Structures and Political Protest: Anti-Nuclear Movements in Four Democracies', *British Journal of Political Science*, 16: 57–85.

Klandermans, B., 2004. 'The Demand and Supply of Participation: Social Psychological Correlates of Participation in a Social Movement', in D. Snow, S. Soule, and H. Kriesi, eds, *Blackwell Companion to Social Movements*, Oxford: Blackwell, 360–379.

Klandermans, B., H. Kriesi and S. Tarrow, eds, 1988. *From Structure to Action: Comparing Social Movement Research Across Cultures*, Greenwich, CT: JAI Press.

Klare, M., 1989. 'Subterranean Alliances: America's Global Proxy Network', *Journal of International Affairs*, 43(1): 97–118.

Klare, M. and P. Kornbluh, 1989. 'The New Interventionism: Low-intensity Warfare in the 1980s and Beyond', in M. Klare and P. Kornbluh, eds, *Low-Intensity Warfare: How the USA Fights Wars Without Declaring Them*, London: Methuen.

Klein, M., 2007. 'Hamas in Power', *Middle East Journal*, 61(3): 442–459.

Kochen, M., R. Crickman, and A. Blaivas, 1982. 'Distribution of Scientific Experts as Recognised by Peer Consensus', *Scientometrics*, 4(1): 45–56.

Kohlmann, E., 2004. *Al-Qaida's Jihad in Europe: The Afghan-Bosnian Network*, Oxford: Berg Publishers.

Kornbluh, P., 2003. *The Pinochet File: A Declassified Dossier on Atrocity and Accountability*, New York: The New Press.

Kovats-Bernat, J.C., 2002. 'Negotiating Dangerous Fields: Pragmatic Strategies for Fieldwork amid Violence and Terror,' *American Anthropologist*, 104(1): 208–222.

Kramer, M., 2001. *Ivory Towers on Sand: The Failure of Middle Eastern Studies in America*, Washington, DC: Brookings Institution.

Kratochwil, F., 2007. 'Looking Back From Somewhere: Reflections on What Remains "Critical" in Critical Theory', in N. Rengger and B. Thirkell-White, eds, *Critical International Relations Theory After 25 Years*, Cambridge: Cambridge University Press.

Krause, K. and M. Williams, 1997a. 'Preface', in K. Krause and M. Williams, eds, *Critical Security Studies: Concepts and Cases*, Minneapolis: University of Minnesota Press.

——, eds, 1997b. 'From Strategy to Security: Foundations of Critical Security', *Critical Security Studies: Concepts and Cases*, Minneapolis: University of Minnesota Press.

Krebs, R. and J. Lobasz, 2007. 'Fixing the Meaning of 9/11: Hegemony, Coercion, and the Road to War in Iraq', *Security Studies*, 16(3): 409–451.

Kriesi, H., 1989. 'The Political Opportunity Structure of the Dutch Peace Movement', *West European Politics*, 12: 295–312.

Kriesi, H., R. Koopmans, J. Duyvendak, and M. Giugni, eds, 1995. *New Social Movements in Western Europe: A Comparative Analysis*, London: University College London Press.

Kupperman, R. and J. Kamen, 1989. 'Bush's Options for Action on Flight 103', *Christian Science Monitor*, 16 May 1989.

Kupperman, R. and W. Taylor, 1985. 'Special Supplement: Low-intensity Conflict, the Strategic Challenge', in G. Hudson and J. Kruzel, eds, *1985–1986 American Defense Annual*, Lexington, MA: D.C. Heath and Company.

Kurzman, C., 2004. 'Social Movement Theory and Islamic Studies', in Q. Wiktorowicz, ed., *Islamic Activism: A Social Movement Theory Approach*, Bloomington, IN: Indiana University Press, 289–303.

——, 1996. 'Structural Opportunity and Perceived Opportunity in Social-Movement-Theory: The Iranian Revolution of 1979', *American Sociological Review*, 61(1): 153–170.

Kydd, A. and B. Walter, 2002. 'Sabotaging the Peace: The Politics of Extremist Violence', *International Organisation*, 56(2), Spring 2002: 263–296.

Laffey, M., and J. Weldes, 1997. 'Beyond Belief: Ideas and Symbolic Technologies in the Study of International Relations', *European Journal of International Relations*, 3(2): 193–237.

Laqueur, W., 2003. *No End to War: Terrorism in the Twenty-First Century*, New York: Continuum.

——, 1999. *The New Terrorism: Fanaticism and the Arms of Mass Destruction*, New York: Oxford University Press.

——, 1977. *Terrorism*, London: Weidenfeld and Nicolson.

Laraña, E., H. Johnston, and J. Gusfield, eds, 1994. *New Social Movements: From Ideology to Identity*, Philadelphia, PA: Temple University Press.

Lattimer, M., 2007. 'Freedom Lost', *Guardian G2*, 13 December 2007: 6–11.

Leach, E., 1977. *Custom, Law, and Terrorist Violence*, Edinburgh: Edinburgh University Press.

Le Carré, J., 2001. 'The War that Came in From the Cold', *The Australian*, 17–20.

Lee, R., 1994. *Dangerous Fieldwork*, Thousand Oaks, CA: Qualitative Research Methods Series, Sage Publications.

Lee Koo, K., 2007. 'Security as Enslavement, Security as Emancipation: Gendered Legacies and Feminist Futures in the Asia-Pacific', in A. Burke and M. McDonald, eds, *Critical Security in the Asia-Pacific*, Manchester: Manchester University Press.

Leheny, D., 2002. 'Symbols, Strategies, and Choices for International Relations Scholarship After September 11', *International Organisation*, 57–70.

Leiken, R., 1982. *Soviet Strategy in Latin America*, Washington Papers 93, New York: Praeger.

Leitenberg, M., 1999. 'Aum Shinrikyo's Efforts to Produce Biological Weapons: A Case Study in the Serial Propagation of Misinformation', *Terrorism and Political Violence*, 11(4): 149–158.

Lentini, P., 2008. 'Review Essay – Understanding and Combatting Terrorism: Definitions, Origins and Strategies', *Australian Journal of Political Science*, 43(1): 133.

LeoGrande, W., 1984. 'Through the Looking Glass: The Kissinger Report on Central America', *World Policy Journal*, 1(2): 251–284.

——, 1981. 'A Splendid Little War: Drawing the Line in El Salvador', *International Security*, 6(1): 27–52.

Lia, B., 2007. *Architect of Global Jihad: The Life of Al-Qaeda Strategist Abu Mus'ab al-Suri*, London: Hurst.

——, 2005. *Globalisation and the Future of Terrorism: Patterns and Predictions*, London: Routledge.

Lia, B. and K. Skølberg, 2004. 'Causes of Terrorism: An Expanded and Updated Review of the Literature', FFI-report 2004/04307.

——, 2000. 'Why Terrorism Occurs – A Survey of Theories and Hypothesis on the Causes of Terrorism', FFI-report 2000/02769.

Lichbach, M., 1987. 'Deterrence or Escalation? The Puzzle of Aggregate Studies of Repression and Dissent', *Journal of Conflict Resolution*, 31(2): 266–297.

Linklater, A., 2007. 'Towards a Sociology of Global Morals with an Emancipatory Intent', *Review of International Studies*, 21(1): 135–150.

——, 2005a. 'Discourse Ethics and the Civilizing Process', *Review of International Studies*, 31(1): 145–154.
——, 2005b. 'Political Community and Human Security', in K. Booth, ed., *Critical Security Studies and World Politics*, Boulder, CO: Lynne Rienner.
——, 2001. 'The Changing Contours of Critical International Relations Theory', in R. Wyn Jones, ed., *Critical Theory and World Politics*, Boulder, CO: Lynne Rienner.
——, 1998. *The Transformation of Political Community*, Columbia: USC Press.
——, 1996. 'The Achievements of Critical Theory', in S. Smith, K. Booth and M. Zalewski, eds, *International Theory: Positivism and Beyond*, Cambridge: Cambridge University Press.
Livingstone, N., 1984. 'Fighting Terrorism and "Dirty Little Wars"', *Air University Review*, XXXV(3): 4–16. Online, available at: www.airpower.maxwell.af.mil/airchronicles/aureview/1984/mar-apr/livingstone.html.
——, 1983a. 'Terrorism: A National Issues Seminar', *World Affairs*, 146(1): 92–98.
——, 1983b. 'The Wolves Among Us: Reflections on the Past Eighteen Months and Thoughts on the Future', *World Affairs*, 146(3): 7–22.
——, 1980. 'Terrorism: The International Connection', *Army*: 14–21.
Livingstone, N. and T. Arnold, 1986. 'The Rise of State-Sponsored Terrorism', in N. Livingstone and T. Arnold, eds, *Fighting Back: Winning the War Against Terrorism*, Toronto: Lexington Books.
Lum, C., L. Kennedy, and A. Sherley, 2006. 'The Effectiveness of Counter-Terrorism Strategies: A Campbell Systematic Review'. Online, available at: www.campbellcollaboration.org/doc-pdf/Lum_Terrorism_Review.pdf (accessed January 2006).
Lustick, I., 2006. *Trapped in the War on Terror*, Philadelphia, PA: University of Pennsylvania Press.
McAdam, D., 1996. 'Conceptual Origins, Current Problems, Future Directions', in D. McAdam, J.D. McCarthy, and M. Zald, eds, *Comparative Perspectives on Social Movements: Political Opportunities, Mobilizing Structures, and Cultural Framings*. Cambridge: Cambridge University Press, pp. 23–40.
——, 1982. *Political Process and the Development of Black Insurgency, 1930–1970*, Chicago, IL: University of Chicago Press.
McAdam, D., J. McCarthy, and M. Zald, eds, 1996a. *Comparative Perspectives on Social Movements: Political Opportunities, Mobilizing Structures, and Cultural Framings*, Cambridge: Cambridge University Press.
——, 1996b. 'Introduction: Opportunities, Mobilizing Structures, and Framing Processes – Toward A Synthetic, Comparative Perspective on Social Movements', in D. McAdam, J. McCarthy, and M. Zald, eds, *Comparative Perspectives on Social Movements: Political Opportunities, Mobilizing Structures, and Cultural Framings*, Cambridge: Cambridge University Press, 7–20.
McCarthy, J. and M. Zald, 1977. 'Resource Mobilization and Social Movements: A Partial Theory', *American Journal of Sociology*, 82(6): 1212–1241.
McDonald, H., 2004. 'The Underbelly of a City of Assassins', *Observer*, 3 October 2004. Online, available at: www.guardian.co.uk/uk/2004/oct/03/ northernireland.northernireland1.
McDonald, M., 2007. 'Emancipation and Critical Terrorism Studies', *European Political Science*, 6(3): 252–259.
——, 2005. 'Constructing Insecurity: Australian Security Discourse and Policy Post-2001', *International Relations*, 19(3): 297–320.

McNeil, K., 2002. 'The War on Academic Freedom', *The Nation*, 11 November 2002. Online, available at: www.thenation.com/doc/20021125/mcneil (accessed 13 July 2008).

MacPherson, M., 1986. 'The Mystique of Terror: Neil Livingstone, Wheeling and Dealing in the Security Game', *Washington Post*, 20 August 1986.

McSherry, J., 2002. Tracking the Origins of a State Terror Network: Operation Condor, *Latin American Perspectives*, 29(1), 38–60.

McWilliams, M. and J. McKiernan, 1993. *Bringing it Out in the Open: Domestic Violence in Northern Ireland*, Belfast: HMSO.

Mahajan, R., 2003. *Full Spectrum Dominance: U.S. Power in Iraq and Beyond*, New York: Seven Stories Press.

——, 2002. *The New Crusade: America's War on Terrorism*, New York: Monthly Review Press.

Mahmood, C., 1996. *Fighting for Faith and Nation: Dialogues with Sikh Militants*, Philadephia, PA: University of Pennsylvania Press.

Mallie, E. and D. McKittrick, 2001. *Endgame in Ireland*, London: Hodder and Stoughton.

Maoz, I., 2004. 'Peacebuilding Activities in Violent Conflict: Israeli–Palestinian Post-Oslo People-to-People Activities', *International Journal of Politics, Culture and Society*, 17(3): 563–574.

Marcus, B., ed., 1982. *Sandinistas Speak: Speeches, Writings and Interviews with Leaders of Nicaragua's Revolution*, New York: Pathfinder Press.

Marsden, P., 2002. *The Taliban: War and Religion in Afghanistan*, London: Zed Books.

Martin, G., 2003. *Understanding Terrorism: Challenges, Perspectives, and Issues*, Thousand Oaks: Sage.

Martin J. and A. Neal, 2002. 'Defending Civilization: How our Universities are Failing America and What can be Done About it', American Council of Trustees and Alumni Report. Online, available at: www.goacta.org/publications/Reports/ defciv.pdf.

Maskliunaite, A., 2004. 'Theories of Terrorism and Their Position in Social Sciences', *Lithuanian Political Science Yearbook 2004*, (1).

Mayer, J., 2008. *The Dark Side: The Inside Story of How the War on Terror Turned Into a War on American Ideals*, New York: Doubleday.

Meijer, R., forthcoming. 'Commanding Good and Forbidding Evil as a Principle of Social Action: The Case of the Jama'at al-Islamiyya', in R. Meijer, ed., *Global Salafism: Islam's New Religious Movement*, London: Hurst.

Melucci, A., 1985. 'The Symbolic Challenge of Contemporary Movements', *Social Research*, 52(4): 789–816.

Merari, A., 2000. 'Terrorism and Threats to US Interests in the Middle East', Testimony before the Special Oversight Panel on Terrorism of the House of Representatives Committee on Armed Services, 13 July 2000.

——, 1991. 'Academic Research and Government Policy on Terrorism', *Terrorism and Political Violence*, 3(1): 88–102.

Merkl, P., ed., 1986. *Political Violence and Terror: Motifs and Motivations*, Berkeley, CA: University of California Press.

Mernissi, F., 1987. *Beyond the Veil: Male–Female Dynamics in a Modern Muslim Society*, Bloomington, IN: Indiana University Press.

Messaoudi, K. and E. Schemla, 1998. *Unbowed: An Algerian Woman Confronts Islamic Fundamentalism*, trans., Anne C. Vila, Philadelphia, PA: University of Pennsylvania Press.

Miall, H., O. Ramsbotham, and T. Woodhouse, 1999. *Contemporary Conflict Resolution: the Prevention, Management and Transformation of Deadly Conflicts*, Cambridge: Polity Press.

Middle East Report, 1998. 'Under Western Eyes: Violence and the Struggle for Political Accountability in Algeria: An Interview with Hugh Roberts', 206 (Spring): 39–42.

Milliken, J., 1999. 'The Study of Discourse in International Relations: A Critique of Research and Methods', *European Journal of International Relations*, 5(2): 225–54.

Mills, T., 2008. 'Evan Kohlmann; "The Doogie Howser of Terrorism?"'. Online, available at: www.spinwatch.org/content/view/4850/8/ (accessed 29 April 2008).

Minter, W., 1994. *Apartheid's Contras: An Inquiry into the Roots of War in Angola and Mozambique*, Johannesburg: Witwatersrand University Press.

Mishal, S. and M. Rosenthal, 2005. 'Al Qaeda as a Dune Organization: Towards a Typology of Islamic Terrorist Organizations', *Studies in Conflict and Terrorism*, 28(4): 275–293.

Moghadam, A., 2006. 'Suicide Terrorism, Occupation and the Globalization of Martyrdom: A Critique of Dying to Win', *Studies in Conflict and Terrorism*, 29(8), 707–729.

Moghadam, V., 1994. *Gender and National Identity: Women and Politics in Muslim Societies*, London: Oxford University Press.

Mohanty, C., A. Russo, and L. Torres, 1991. *Third World and the Politics of Feminism*, Bloomington, IN: Indiana University Press.

Moloney, E., 2007. *A Secret History of the IRA*, Harmondsworth: Penguin.

Montagu, A., 1997. *Man's Most Dangerous Myth: The Fallacy of Race*, 6th edn, New York: Oxford University Press.

Moon, K., 1997. *Sex Among Allies: Military Prostitution in US–Korea Relations*, New York: Columbia University Press.

Moore, W., 1998. 'Repression and Dissent: Substitution, Context, and Timing', *American Journal of Political Science*, 42(3): 851–873.

Morgan, R., 1989. *The Demon Lover: On the Sexuality of Terrorism*, London: Methuen Press.

Morris, A., 1984. *The Origins of the Civil Rights Movement: Black Communities Organizing for Change*, New Jersey, New York: Prentice Hall.

——, 1981. 'Black Southern Sit-Ins: On Analysis of Internal Organization', *American Sociological Review*, 45: 744–767.

Morris, A. and C. Mueller, eds, 1992. *Frontiers in Social Movement Theory*, New Haven, CT: Yale University Press.

Morris, B., 1999. *Righteous Victims: A History of the Zionist–Arab Conflict, 1881–1999*, London: John Murray.

Moser, C. and F. Clark, 2001. *Victims, Perpetrators or Actors: Gender, Armed Conflict, and Political Violence*, London: Zed Books.

Mueller, J., 2006. *Overblown: How Politicians and the Terrorism Industry Inflate National Security Threats and Why We Believe Them*, New York: The Free Press.

Muhammed Ally, S., 2008. 'When Did the Conflict With al Qaeda Start? Two Visions at Guantanamo', Human Rights First. Online, available at: www.humanrightsfirst.org/blog/gitmo/2008/07/when-did-conflict-with-al-qaeda-start.html (accessed 30 July 2008).

Muller, E., 1985. 'Income Inequality, Regime Repressiveness, and Political Violence', *American Sociological Review*, 50(1): 47–61.

Murphy, C., 2007. 'The Promise of Critical IR, Partially Kept', in N. Rengger and B. Thirkell-White, eds, *Critical International Relations Theory After 25 Years*, Cambridge: Cambridge University Press.

——, 2005. 'A Scholarly Look at Terror Sees Bootprints In the Sand', *Washington Post*, 10 July 2005: D01.
Nagangast, C., 1994. 'Violence, Terror, and the Crisis of the State', *Annual Review of Anthropology*, 23: 109–136.
Naraghi-Anderlini, S., 2000. *Women at the Peace Table Making a Difference*, New York: UNDP.
National Bipartisan Commission on Central America, 1984. *Report of the National Bipartisan Commission on Central America*, Washington, DC, 10 January 1984.
Neuberger, L. and T. Valentini, 1996. *Women and Terrorism*, London: Palgrave Macmillan.
Neufeld, M., 2004. 'Pitfalls of Emancipation and Discourses of Security', *International Relations*, 18(1): 109–123.
——, 2001. 'What's Critical About Critical International Relations Theory?', in R. Wyn Jones, ed., *Critical Theory and World Politics*, London: Lynne Rienner.
Newman, E., 2006. 'Explaining the Root Causes of Terrorism', *Studies in Conflict and Terrorism*, 29(8): 749–772.
Nietschmann, B., 1987. 'The Third World War', *Cultural Survival Quarterly*, 11(3): 1–16.
Nivat, A., 2005. 'The Black Widows: Chechen Women Join the Fight for Independence – and Allah', *Studies in Conflict and Terrorism*, 28(5): 413–419.
Noonan, R., 1995. 'Women Against the State: Political Opportunities and Collective Action Frames in Chile's Transition to Democracy', *Sociological Forum*, 10(1): 81–111.
Nordstrom, C., 2007. *Global Outlaws: Crime, Money, and Power in the Contemporary World*, Berkeley, CA: University of California Press.
——, 2004. *Shadows of War: Violence, Power, and International Profiteering in the Twenty-First Century*, Berkeley, CA: University of California Press.
——, 1999. 'Wars and Invisible Girls, Shadow Industries and the Politics of Not-Knowing', *International Feminist Journal of Politics*, 1(1).
——, 1998. 'Deadly Myths of Aggression', *Aggressive Behaviour*, 24: 147–159.
——, 1997. *A Different Kind of War Story*, Philadelphia, PA: University of Pennsylvania Press.
Nordstrom, C. and J. Martin, eds, 1992. *The Paths to Domination, Resistance, and Terror*, Berkeley, CA: University of California Press.
Norris, P., M. Kern, and M. Just, 2003. 'Framing Terrorism', in P. Norris, M. Kern, and M. Just, eds, *Framing Terrorism: The News Media, The Government, and The Public*, London: Routledge.
Northern District of New York, 2006. USA v. Aref and Hossain. Online, available at: www.websupp.org/data/NDNY/1:04-cr-00402-282-NDNY.pdf.
Norton, A.F., 2007. *Hezbollah*, Princeton, NJ: Princeton University Press.
O'Brien, B., 1993. *The Long War: The IRA and Sinn Fein*, Dublin: O'Brien Press.
O'Brien, K., 2001. 'The Use of Assassination as a Tool of State Policy: South Africa's Counter-revolutionary Strategy 1979–92 (part II)', *Terrorism and Political Violence*, 13(2): 107–142.
O'Doherty, M., 1998. *The Trouble with Guns: Republican Strategy and the Provisional IRA*, Belfast: The Blackstaff Press.
O'Hagan, J., 2004. 'The Power and the Passion: Civilizational Identity and Alterity in the Wake of September 11', in P. Goff and K. Dunn, eds, *Identity and Global Politics*, London: Palgrave.

Olawale, I., 2003. 'Community Conflicts in Nigeria', in M. Smyth and G. Robinson, eds, *Researching Violently Divided Societies: Ethical and Methodological Issues*, Tokyo: UNU Press.

Oliver, P., and H. Johnston, 2000. 'What a Good Idea: Frames and Ideologies in Social Movements Research', *Mobilization: An International Journal*, 5: 37–54.

Oliverio, A., 1997. 'The State of Injustice: The Politics of Terrorism and the Production of Order', *International Journal of Comparative Sociology*, 38(1–2): 48–63.

Omang, J., 1984. 'Soviets Using Terrorism, Shultz Asserts', *Washington Post*, 25 June 1984.

Opp, K. and W. Roehl, 1990. 'Repression, Micromobilization, and Political Protest', *Social Forces*, 69(2): 521–547.

Orford, A., 2003. *Reading Humanitarian Intervention: Human Rights and the Use of Force in International Law*, Cambridge: Cambridge University Press.

O'Sullivan, N., 1986. 'Terrorism, Ideology and Democracy', in N. O'Sullivan, ed., *Terrorism, Ideology And Revolution*, Brighton: Wheatsheaf.

Pape, R., 2005. *Dying to Win: The Strategic Logic of Suicide Terrorism*, New York, NY: Random House.

Parashar, S., 2007. 'Gender, Jihad and Jingoism: Women as Perpetrators, Planners and Patrons of Militancy in Kashmir', paper presented at a conference entitled, 'Women and Al Qaeda', 10 April 2007, Jebsen Center for Counter Terrorism Studies, Tufts University, USA.

Parker, T., 2007. 'Fighting an Antaean Enemy: How Democratic States Unintentionally Sustain the Terrorist Movements They Oppose', *Terrorism and Political Violence*, 19(2): 155–179.

Paz, R., 1998. 'Is There an "Islamic Terrorism?"', International Policy Institute for Counter-Terrorism (ICT) Publication, Herzilya, Israel, 7 September 1998. Online, available at: www.ict.org.il/articles/articledet.cfm?articleed=46 (accessed 12 October 2001).

Pearce, J., 1982. *Under the Eagle: US Intervention in Central America and the Caribbean*, London: Latin American Bureau.

Pentagon and State Department, 1983. *Grenada: A Preliminary Report*, Washington, DC, 16 December 1983.

Peritore, N., 1990. 'Reflections on Dangerous Fieldwork', *The American Sociologist*, 21(4): 359–372.

Pessin, A., 2005. 'Congress Maintains Restrictions on US–Indonesian Military Relations', Voice of America News, 17 November 2005. Online, available at: www.voanews.com/english/archive/2005-11/2005-11-17-voa83.cfm?CFID= 186768642 &CFTOKEN=27358202.

Peterson, V., ed., 1993. *Gendered States: Feminist (Re)Visions of International Relations Theory*, Boulder, CO: Lynne Rienner.

Petras, J., 1981. 'White Paper on the White Paper', *The Nation*, 28 March 1981.

Pettman, J.J., 1996. *Worlding Women: A Feminist International Politics*, London: Routledge.

Piazza, J., 2008. 'A Supply-Side View of Terrorism: A Cross-National Study', *The Journal of Politics*, 70(1): 28–39.

Pickvance, C., 1999. 'Democratisation and the Decline of Social Movements: The Effects of Regime Change on Collective Action in Eastern Europe, Southern Europe and Latin America', *Sociology*, 33(2): 353–372.

Pierre, A. and W. Quandt, 1995. 'Algeria's War on Itself', *Foreign Policy*, 99 (Summer): 131–148.

Piven, F. and R. Cloward, 1977. *Poor People's Movements: Why They Succeed, How They Fail*, New York, NY: Pantheon.

Polsky, N., 1967. *Hustlers, Beats and Others*, Harmondsworth: Penguin.

Powell, J., 2008. *Great Hatred, Little Room – Making Peace in Northern Ireland*, London: The Bodley Head.

Price, R. and C. Reus-Smit, 1998. 'Dangerous Liaisons? Critical International Theory and Constructivism', European Journal of International Relations, 4(3): 259–294.

Purvis, T. and A. Hunt, 1993. 'Discourse, Ideology, Discourse, Ideology, Discourse, Ideology…', *British Journal of Sociology*, 44(3): 473–499.

Rabasa, A. and P. Chalk, 2001. *Colombian Labyrinth: The Synergy of Drugs and Insurgency and its Implications for Regional Stability*, Santa Monica, CA: RAND.

RAND, 2007. Proceedings Editors, T. Bikson, R. Bluthenthal, R. Eden, and P. Gunn, 'Ethical Principles in Social-Behavioral Research on Terrorism: Probing the Parameters'. Document Number: WR-490-4-NSF/DOJ. Online, available at: www.rand.org/pubs/working_papers/WR490-4/.

——, 2006. 'RAND-MIP Terrorism Incident Database Project'. Online, available at: www.rand.org/ise/projects/terrorismdatabase/index.html (accessed 16 March 2008).

——, 2004. *A Bibliography of Selected RAND Publications: Terrorism, 1980–2004*, Santa Monica, CA: RAND.

Ranstorp, M., 2007. *Mapping Terrorist Research: State of the Art, Gaps and Future Direction*, Abingdon: Routledge.

——, ed., 2006a. *Mapping Terrorism Research: State of the Art, Gaps and Future Direction*, London: Routledge.

——, 2006b. 'Mapping Terrorism Research: Challenges and Priorities' in M. Ranstorp, ed., *Mapping Terrorism Research: State of the Art, Gaps and Future Direction*, London: Routledge, 2–24.

——, 1998. 'Interpreting the Broader Context and Meaning of Bin-Laden's *Fatwa*', Studies in Conflict and Terrorism, 21(4): 321–330.

Raphael, S., forthcoming. *Legitimating US Coercive Interventions in the Global South: The Ideological Function of Terrorism Studies*, Unpublished Doctoral Thesis, University of London.

——, 2008. 'Who are the Key Figures in Terrorism Studies?', in H. Chen, E. Reid, J. Sinai, A. Silke, and B. Ganor, eds, *Terrorism Informatics: Knowledge Management and Data Mining for Homeland Security*, New York: Springer-Verlag.

——, 'Putting the State Back in: The Orthodox Definition of Terrorism and the Critical Need to Address State Terrorism', British International Studies Association (BISA) Annual Conference, 17–19 December 2007, University of Cambridge, UK. Online, available at: www.bisa.ac.uk/2007/tuesday.htm.

Rapoport, D., 1984. 'Fear and Trembling: Terrorism in Three Religious Traditions', *American Political Science Review*, 78(3): 658–677.

——, 1971. *Assassination and Terrorism*, Toronto: CBC Merchandising.

Reagan, R., 1985. 'Excerpts from the President's Address Accusing Nations of "Acts of War"', *New York Times*, 9 July 1985.

Rehn, E. and E. J. Sirleaf, 2002. 'Women, War and Peace: The Independent Experts' Assessment on the Impact of Armed Conflict on Women and Women's Role in Peace-Building, United Nations Development Fund for Women (UNIFEM)'. Online, available at: www.unifem.org/resources/item_detail.php?ProductID=17.

Reid, E., 1997. 'Evolution of a Body of Knowledge: An Analysis of Terrorism Research', *Information Processing and Management*, 33(1): 91–106.

——, 1993. 'Terrorism Research and the Diffusion of Ideas', *Knowledge and Policy*, 6(1): 17–37.
——, 1983. *An Analysis of Terrorism Literature: A Bibliometric and Content Analysis Study*, PhD dissertation, University of Southern California, Los Angeles.
Reid, E. and H. Chen, 2007. 'Mapping the Contemporary Terrorism Research Domain', *International Journal of Human-Computer Studies*, 65: 42–56.
Rengger, N., 2001. 'Negative Dialectic? The Two Modes of Critical Theory in World Politics', in R. Wyn Jones, ed., *Critical Theory and World Politics*, Boulder, CO: Lynne Rienner.
Rengger, N. and B. Thirkell-White, 2007. 'Still Critical After All These Years? The Past, Present and Future of Critical Theory in International Relations', *Review of International Studies*, 33(Special Issue): 3–24.
Reuters, 2004. 'War on Terror Threatens Aid Priorities', 10 May 2004. Online, available at: www.alertnet.org/thefacts/reliefresources/108418153847.htm.
Riesebrodt, M., 1998. *Pious Passion: The Emergence of Modern Fundamentalism in the United States and Iran*, Berkeley, CA: University of California Press.
Ripley, A., 2008. 'Future Revolutions – 4. Reverse Radicalism', *TIME Magazine*, 13 March 2008.
Robben, A.C.G.M., 2005. *Political Violence and Trauma in Argentina*, Philadelphia, PA: University of Pennsylvania Press.
Roberts, A., 2005. 'The "War on Terror" in Historical Perspective', *Survival*, 47(2): 101–130.
Roberts, D., 2008. *Human Insecurity: Global Structures of Violence*, London: Zed.
Robinson, G., 2004. 'Hamas as Social Movement', in Q. Wiktorowicz, ed., *Islamic Activism: A Social Movement Theory Approach*, Bloomington, IN: Indiana University Press, 112–142.
——, 1997. *Building a Palestinian State: The Incomplete Revolution*, Bloomington, IN: Indiana University Press.
Rogers, P., 2007. *Why We're Losing the War on Terror*, Cambridge: Polity.
Rose, G., D. Byman, and K. Pollack, 2001. 'Beef Up the Taliban's Enemy', *Los Angeles Times*, 20 September 2001.
Ross, B., 2007. 'Clinton, Pelosi, Greenspan, Powell, Bloomberg, Gates, Annan Also Say Interviews "Fakes"', *ABC News*, 13 September 2007.
Ross, J., 2004. 'Taking Stock of Research Methods and Analysis on Oppositional Political Terrorism', *The American Sociologist*, 35(2): 26–37.
Ross, J. and T. Gurr, 1989. 'Why Terrorism Subsides', *Comparative Politics*, 21(4): 405–426.
Rosoff H., D. von Winterfeldt, 2007. 'A Risk and Economic Analysis of Dirty Bomb Attacks on the Ports of Los Angeles and Long Beach', *Risk Annal*, 27(3): 533–546.
Roy, S., 2007. *Failing Peace: Gaza and the Palestinian–Israeli Conflict*, London: Pluto Press.
——, 2006. 'Humanism, Scholarship and Politics: Writing on the Palestinian-Israeli Conflict', in S. Roy, ed., *Failing Peace: Gaza and the Palestinian-Israeli Conflict*, London: Pluto Press.
——, 2003. 'Hamas and the Transformation(s) of Political Islam in Palestine', *Current History*, 102(660): 13–20.
Ruane, J. and J. Todd, 2005. 'Communal Conflict and Emancipation: The Case of Northern Ireland' in K. Booth, ed., *Critical Security Studies and World Politics*, Boulder, CO: Lynne Rienner.

Bibliography

Rucht, D., 1996. 'The Impact of National Contexts on Social Movement Structures', in D. McAdam, J. McCarthy, and M. Zald, eds, *Comparative Perspectives on Social Movements: Political Opportunities, Mobilizing Structures, and Cultural Framings*, Cambridge: Cambridge University Press, 185–204.

Saad-Ghorayeb, A., 2003. 'Factors Conducive to the Politicization of the Lebanese Shi'a and the Emergence of Hizbu'llah', *Journal of Islamic Studies*, 14(3): 273–307.

——, 2002. *Hizbu'llah: Politics and Religion*, London: Pluto Press.

Sageman, M., 2008. *Leaderless Jihad: Terror Networks in the Twenty-First Century*, Philadelphia, PA: University of Pennsylvania Press.

——, 2004. *Understanding Terror Networks*, Philadelphia, PA: University of Pennsylvania Press.

Sageman, M. and B. Hoffman, 2008. 'Does Osama Still Call the Shots?: Debating the Containment of al Qaeda's Leadership', *Foreign Affairs*, July/August 2008.

Said E., 2000. *The End of the Peace Process: Oslo and After*, New York: Pantheon Books.

——, 1988a. 'Identity, Negation and Violence', *New Left Review*, 171: 46–60.

——, 1988b. 'The Essential Terrorist', in E. Said and C. Hitchens, eds, *Blaming the Victims: Spurious Scholarship and the Palestinian Question*, London: Verso, 149–159.

——, 1978. *Orientalism*, London: Penguin.

Salvatore, A., 1997. *Islam and the Political Discourse of Modernity*, Reading: Ithaca.

Sanders, C., 2006. 'Staff Must Identify Extremism', *Times Higher Education*, 20 July 2007.

Sarkar, T. and U. Butalia, eds, 1996. *Women and Right Wing Movements: Indian Experiences*, London: Zed Books.

Saxton, J., 2000. 'Terrorism and Threats to US Interests in the Middle East', Opening Statement before the Special Oversight Panel on Terrorism of the House of Representatives Committee on Armed Services, 13 July 2000.

Scarry, E., 2004. 'Five Errors in the Reasoning of Alan Dershowitz', in S. Levinson, ed., *Torture: A Collection*, Oxford: Oxford University Press.

Schevitz, T., 2002a. 'Professors Want Own Names Put on Mideast Blacklist – They Hope to Make it Powerless', *San Francisco Chronicle*, 28 September 2002. Online, available at: www.sfgate.com/cgi-bin/article.cgi?file=/chronicle/archive/ 2002/09/28/ MN227890.DTL (accessed 13 July 2008).

——, 2002b. '"Dossiers" Dropped from Web Blacklist', *San Francisco Chronicle*. Online, available at: www.campus-watch.org/article/id/209 (accessed 13 July 2008).

Schmid, A., 2007. 'Farewell Words for Prof. Paul Wilkinson', speech given on the occasion of the retirement of Professor Paul Wilkinson at the University of St Andrews. Online, available at: www.st-andrews.ac.uk/~wwwir/research/cstpv/ about/staffprofiles/ pwretiral101007.pdf.

——, 2004. 'Frameworks for Conceptualising Terrorism', *Terrorism and Political Violence*, 16(2): 197–221.

Schmid, A. and A. Jongman, 1988. *Political Terrorism: A New Guide to Actors, Authors, Concepts, Databases, Theories and Literature*, Amsterdam: North Holland Publishing Company.

Schueller, M. and A. Dawson, 2007. Introduction, *Social Text 90*, Special Issue on the Perils of Academic Freedom, 25(1): 1–15.

Sciolino, E. and E. Schmitt, 2008. 'A Not Very Private Feud Over Terrorism', *New York Times*, 8 June 2008.

Scraton, P., ed., 2002. *Beyond September 11: An Anthology of Dissent*, London: Pluto.

Shafritz, J.M., E.F. Gibbons, Jr., and G.E.J. Scott, 1991. *Almanac of Modern Terrorism*. Oxford: Facts on File.

Shapcott, R., 2001. *Justice, Community, and Dialogue in International Relations*, Cambridge: Cambridge University Press.

Sharoni, S., 1994. 'Homefront as Battlefield: Gender, Military Occupation and Violence Against Women', in T. Mayer, ed., *Women and the Israeli Occupation: The Politics of Change*, London: Routledge.

Shepherd, J., 2007. 'The Rise and Rise of Terrorism Studies', *Education Guardian*, 3 July 2007.

——, 2006. 'Just Who is Listening In?', *Times Higher Education*, 2 November 2006.

Sherwin, M., 2002. 'Tattletales for an Open Society'. Open letter to Dr. Lynn Cheney and Senator Joseph Lieberman, published as a back cover advertisement in *The Nation*, 21 January 2002.

Shultz, R. and A. Vogt, 2003. 'It's War! Fighting Post-11 September Global Terrorism through a Doctrine of Preemption', *Terrorism and Political Violence*, 15(1): 1–30.

Sick, G., 1998. 'Rethinking Dual Containment', *Survival*, 40 (1): 5–32.

Silke, A., forthcoming. *Suicide Terrorism: Understanding, Controlling, Preventing*, Chichester: Wiley.

——, 2006. 'The Impact of 9/11 on Research on Terrorism', in M. Ranstorp, ed., *Mapping Terrorism Research: State of the Art, Gaps and Future Direction*, London: Routledge, 175–193.

——, ed., 2004a. *Research on Terrorism: Trends, Achievements and Failures*, London: Frank Cass.

——, 2004b: 'An Introduction to Terrorism Research', in A. Silke, ed., *Research on Terrorism: Trends, Achievements and Failures*, London: Frank Cass, 1–29.

——, 2004c. 'The Road Less Travelled', in A. Silke, ed., *Research on Terrorism: Trends, Achievements and Failures*, London: Frank Cass, 186–213.

——, 2004d. 'The Devil You Know: Continuing Problems with Research on Terrorism', in A. Silke, ed., *Research on Terrorism: Trends, Achievements and Failures*, London: Frank Cass, 57–71.

——, ed., 2003. *The Road Less Travelled: Recent Trends in Terrorism Research*, London: Routledge.

——, 2001. 'The Devil You Know: Continuing Problems with Research on Terrorism', *Terrorism and Political Violence*, 13(4): 1–14.

——, 1998. 'Cheshire-cat Logic: The Recurring Theme of Terrorist Abnormality in Psychological Research', *Psychology, Crime and Law*, 4: 51–69.

Simons, A., 1995a. *Networks of Dissolution: Somalia Undone*, Boulder, CO: Westview.

——, 1995b. 'The Beginning of the End', in C. Nordstrom and A. Robben, eds, *Fieldwork Under Fire*, Berkeley, CA: University of California Press.

Sjoberg, L., 2006. *Gender, Justice, and the Wars in Iraq: A Feminist Reformulation of Just War Theory*, New York: Lexington.

Sjoberg, L. and C. Gentry, 2007. *Mothers, Monsters, Whores: Women's Violence in Global Politics*, London: Zed.

Skaine, R., 2006. *Female Suicide Bombers*, Jefferson, NC: McFarland & Company.

Sloan, S., 2006. *Terrorism: The Present Threat in Context*, Oxford: Berg.

Sluka, J.A., 2008. 'Terrorism and Taboo: An Anthropological Perspective on Political Violence Against Civilians', *Critical Studies on Terrorism*, 1(2): 1–17.

——, ed., 2000a. *Death Squad: The Anthropology of State Terror*, Philadelphia: University of Pennsylvania Press.

——, 2000b. '"For God and Ulster": The Culture of Terror and Loyalist Death Squads in Northern Ireland', in J. Sluka, ed., *Death Squad: The Anthropology of State Terror*, Philadelphia: University of Pennsylvania Press, 127–157.

——, 1995. 'Reflections on Managing Danger in Fieldwork: Dangerous Anthropology in Belfast,' in C. Nordstrom and A. Robben, eds, *Fieldwork Under Fire: Contemporary Studies of Violence and Survival*, Berkeley, CA: University of California Press.

——, 1992. 'The Anthropology of Conflict', in C. Nordstrom and J. Martin, eds, *The Paths to Domination, Resistance and Terror*, Berkeley: University of California Press, 18–36.

——, 1990b. 'Participant Observation in Violent Social Contexts', *Human Organization*, 49(2): 114–126.

——, 1989/1990. *Hearts and Minds, Water and Fish: Support for the IRA and INLA in a Northern Irish Ghetto*, London: JAI Press.

Smith, S., 2004. 'Singing Our World into Existence: International Relations Theory and September 11', *International Studies Quarterly*, 48(3): 499–515.

——, 1996. 'Positivism and Beyond', in S. Smith, K. Booth, and M. Zalewski, eds, *International Theory: Positivism and Beyond*, Cambridge: Cambridge University Press.

Smyth, J., and G. Ellison, 1999. *The Crowned Harp: Policing Northern Ireland*, London: Pluto Press.

Snow, D., and R. Benford, 2000. 'Clarifying the Relationship Between Framing and Ideology in the Study of Social Movements: A Comment on Oliver and Johnston', *Mobilization: An International Journal*, 5: 55–60.

Snow, D. and S. Byrd, 2007. 'Ideology, Framing Processes, and Islamic Terrorist Movements', *Mobilization*, 12(1): 119–136.

Snow, D., S. Rochford and R. Benford, 1986. 'Frame Alignment Process, Micromobilization, and Movement Participation', *American Sociological Review*, 51: 464–481.

Souaïdia, H., 2001. *La Salle Guerre*, Paris: La Découverte.

Spence, A., 2006. 'The Problems of Evaluating Counter-terrorism', *UNISCI Discussion Papers*, 12(October): 181. Online, available at: http://redalyc.uaemex.mx/redalyc/pdf/767/76701212.pdf.

Sperling, C., 2006. 'Mother of all Atrocities: Pauline Nyiramusuhuko's Role in the Rwandan Genocide', *Fordham Urban Law Journal*, 33(2): 637–664.

Spivak, G., 1987. *In Other Worlds: Essays in Cultural Politics*, London: Routledge.

Spyer, J., 2008. 'Self-radicalization', *Jerusalem Post*, 30 July 2008.

Stampnitzky, L., 2007a. 'Disciplining an Unruly Field: Terrorism Experts and Theories of Scientific/Intellectual Production', Unpublished manuscript.

——, 2007b. 'The Rise of the Terrorism Expert: Discourse and Expertise from Munich to the "War on Terror"', Unpublished manuscript.

State Department, 2000. *1999 Country Reports on Human Rights Practices*, February 2000. Online, available at: www.state.gov/g/drl/rls/hrrpt/1999/.

——, 2000. *Patterns of Global Terrorism 1996*, April 2000. Online, available at: www.state.gov/www/global/terrorism/1996Report/1996index.html.

——, 1985. *'Revolution Beyond Our Borders': Sandinista Intervention in Central America*, Special Report No. 132, September 1985.

——, 1983. *Informal Briefing*, 25 May 1983.

——, 1981. *Communist Interference in El Salvador: Documents Demonstrating Communist Support of the Salvadoran Insurgency*, 23 February 1981.

Stedman, S., 1997. 'Spoiler Problems in Peace Processes', *International Security* 22(2): 7–16.

Sterling, C., 1981. *The Terror Network: The Secret War of International Terrorism*, Holt, Ronehart, and Winston.

Stern, J., 2003. *Terror in the Name of God: Why Religious Militants Kill*, New York, NY: HarperCollins.

Stiehm, J., 1984. *Women's and Men's Wars*, Oxford: Pergamon Press.

Stohl, M., 2008. 'Old Myths, New Fantasies and the Enduring Realities of Terrorism', *Critical Studies on Terrorism*, 1(1): 5–16.

——, 2006. 'The State as Terrorist: Insights and Implications', *Democracy and Security*, 2(1): 1–25.

——, 2005. 'Knowledge Claims and the Study of Terrorism', in J. Victoroff, ed., *Tangled Roots: Social and Psychological Factors in the Genesis of Terrorism*, Proceedings of the NATO Advanced Research Workshop on Psychology and Terrorism, Castelvecchio Pascoli, Italy, 14–17 September 2005.

——, 1988. *The Politics of Terrorism*, New York, NY: Marcel Dekker.

——, 1979. 'Myths and Realities of Political Terrorism', in M. Stohl, ed., *The Politics of Terrorism*, New York: Marcel Dekker, 1–19.

Stokes, D., 2006. '"Iron Fists in Iron Gloves": The Political Economy of US Terrorocracy Promotion in Colombia', *The British Journal of Politics & International Relations*, 8(3): 368–387.

——, 2005. *America's Other War: Terrorising Colombia*, London: Zed Books.

——, 2003. 'Countering the Soviet Threat? An Analysis of the Justification for US Military Assistance to El Salvador, 1979–92', *Cold War History*, 3(3): 79–102.

Stokes, D. and S. Raphael, forthcoming. *Transnational Empire, Oil and Human Rights: Understanding US Intervention in the Age of Terror*, Baltimore, MD: The Johns Hopkins University Press.

Stone, D., 1996. *Capturing the Political Imagination: Think Tanks and the Policy Process*, London: Frank Cass.

Suarez-Orozco, M., 1992. 'A Grammar of Terror: Psychocultural Responses to State Terrorism in the Dirty War and Post-dirty War Argentina', in C. Nordstrom and J. Martin, eds, *The Paths to Domination, Resistance, and Terror*, Berkeley: University of California Press, 219–259.

——, 1990. 'Speaking the Unspeakable: Towards a Psychosocial Understanding of Responses to Terror', *Ethos*, 18(3): 353–383.

——, 1987. 'The Treatment of Children in the "Dirty War": Ideology, State Terrorism, and the Abuse of Children in Argentina', in N. Scheper-Hughes, ed., *Child Survival: Anthropological Perspectives on the Treatment and Maltreatment of Children*, The Netherlands: Reidel, 219–259.

Sylvester, C., 2007. 'Anatomy of a Footnote', *Security Dialogue*, 38(4): 547–558.

——. 'The Art of War/The War Question in (Feminist) IR', *Millennium: Journal of International Studies*, 33(3): 855–878.

——, 2003. 'Global "Development" Dramaturgies/Gender Stagings', *Borderlands e-journal*, 2(2).

——, 2000. *Feminist International Relations: An Unfinished Journey*, Cambridge: Cambridge University Press.

——, 1998. 'Homeless in International Relations? "Women's" Place in Canonical Texts and in Feminist Reimaginings', in A. Phillips, ed., *Feminism and Politics*, Oxford: Oxford University Press.

——, 1994. *Feminist Theory and International Relations in a Postmodern Era*, Cambridge: Cambridge University Press.

Szymanski, A., 2003. *Pathways to Prohibition: Radicals, Moderates, and Social Movement Outcomes*, Durham, NC: Duke University Press.

Tamimi, A., 2007. *Hamas: Unwritten Chapters*, London: Hurst and Co.

Tarrow, S., 1996. 'States and Opportunities: The Political Structuring of Social Movements', in D. McAdam, J. McCarthy, and M. Zald, eds, *Comparative Perspectives on Social Movements: Political Opportunities, Mobilizing Structures, and Cultural Framings*, Cambridge: Cambridge University Press, 41–61.

——, 1994. *Power in Movement: Social Movements and Contentious Politics*, Cambridge: Cambridge University Press.

Taubman, P., 1983. 'US Officials say CIA Helped Nicaraguan Rebels Plan Attacks', *New York Times*, 16 October 1983.

Taussig, M., 1992. 'Terror as Usual: Walter Benjamin's Theory of History as a State of Siege', in M. Taussig, *The Nervous System*, London: Routledge, 11–36.

——, 1987. *Colonialism, Shamanism, and the Wild Man: A Study of Terror and Healing*, Chicago, IL: University of Chicago Press.

——, 1984. 'Culture of Terror – Space of Death: Roger Casement's Putumayo Report and the Explanation of Torture', *Comparative Studies in Society and History*, 26: 467–497.

Taylor, C., 1999. *Sacrifice as Terror: The Rwandan Genocide of 1994*, Oxford: Berg.

Taylor, P., 1998. *The Provos: The IRA and Sinn Fein*, London: Bloomsbury.

Teti, A., 2007. 'Bridging the Gap: IR, Middle East Studies and the Disciplinary Politics of the Area Studies Controversy', *European Journal of International Relations*, 13(1): 117–145.

Tetreault, M., 1994. *Women and Revolution in Africa, Asia, and the New World*, Columbia: University of South Carolina Press.

Theoharis, J., 2006. '"Alabama on Avalon": Rethinking the Watts Uprising and the Character of Black Protest in Los Angeles', in P. Joseph, ed., *The Black Power Movement: Rethinking the Civil Rights–Black Power Era*, London: Routledge, 27–53.

Tickner, A., 1992. *Gender in International Relations: Feminist Perspectives on Achieving Global Security*, New York: Columbia University Press.

Tilly, C., 2004. 'Terror, Terrorism, Terrorists', *Sociological Theory*, 22(1): 5–13.

——, 1984. 'Social Movements and National Politics', in C. Bright and S. Harding, eds, *Statemaking and Social Movements: Essays in History and Theory*, Ann Arbor, MI: University of Michigan Press, 297–317.

——, 1979. 'Collective Violence in European Perspective', in H. Granham and T. Gurr, eds, *Violence in America: Historical and Comparative Perspectives*, New York: Praeger, 4–45.

——, 1978. *From Mobilization to Revolution*, Reading, MA: Addison Wesley.

Times Higher Education, 2007a. 'On Her Majesty's Secret Disservice', 9 February 2007.

——, 2007b. 'ESRC "Ignores" Danger Fears', 20 July 2007.

Toolis, K., 1995. *Rebel Hearts: Journeys Within the IRA's Soul*, London: Picador.

Toros, H., forthcoming. *Talking to 'Terrorists:' Conflict Transformation in Northern Ireland and Mindanao*, Unpublished Doctoral Thesis, Aberystwyth University, UK.

——, 2008a. '"We Don't Negotiate With Terrorists!": Legitimacy and Complexity in Terrorist Conflicts', *Security Dialogue*, 39(4): 407–426.

——, 2008b. 'Terrorists, Scholars and Ordinary People: Confronting Terrorism Studies with Field Experiences', *Critical Studies on Terrorism*, 1(2): 279–292.

Trawick, M., 'Reasons for Violence: A Preliminary Ethnographic Account of the LTTE', *Journal of South Asian Studies*, 20(1): 153–180.

Tucker, D., 2001. 'What is New About the New Terrorism and How Dangerous is It?', *Terrorism and Political Violence*, 13(3): 1–14.
US Department of State, 2007. Country Reports on Terrorism, 30 April 2007. Online, available at: www.state.gov/s/ct/rls/crt/2006/82736.htm (accessed 6 December 2007).
Usher, G., 2005. 'The New Hamas: Between Resistance and Participation', *Middle East Report Online*, 21 August 2005, p.3 of printout. Online, available at: www.merip.org/ mero/ mero082105.html (accessed 19 September 2005).
USA v. *Adham Amin Hassoun, Kifah Wael Jayyousi, Jose Padilla*, 2007a. The United District Court, Southern District of Florida, Miami Division, Case 04–60001-CR-COOKE, *USA* v. *Adham Amin Hassoun, Kifah Wael Jayyousi, Jose Padilla*, Miami, Florida, 29 June 2007. Transcript of Jury Trial Proceedings before The Honorable Marcia G. Cooke, United States District Judge, Day 35.
——, 2007b. The United District Court, Southern District of Florida, Miami Division, Case 04–60001-CR-COOKE, *USA* v. *Adham Amin Hassoun, Kifah Wael Jayyousi, Jose Padilla*, Miami, Florida, 10 July 2007. Transcript of Jury Trial Proceedings before The Honorable Marcia G. Cooke, United States District Judge, Day 39.
Vallis, R., Y. Yang, and H. Abbass, 2007. 'Disciplinary Approaches to Terrorism: A Survey', Defence and Security Applications Research Centre (DSA), Australian Defence Force Academy, Canberra: Unpublished manuscript.
Van Bruinessen, M., 1996. 'Turkey's Death Squads', *Middle East Report*, 26(2): 20–23.
Various contributors, 2002. 'Tattletales For an Open Society', *The Nation*, 10 January 2002.
Victor, B., 2003. *Army of Roses: Inside the World of Palestinian Women Suicide Bombers*, New York: Rodale.
Waller, M. and J. Rycenga, eds, 2000. *Frontline Feminisms: Women, War and Resistance*, New York: Garland Publishing.
Walter, E.V., 1969. *Terror and Resistance: A Study of Political Violence with Case Studies of Some Primitive African Communities*, New York: Oxford University Press.
Weinberg, L., 2008. 'Two Neglected Areas of Terrorism Research: Careers After Terrorism and How Terrorists Innovate', *Perspectives on Terrorism – Under-investigated Topics in Terrorism Research*, Special Issue – June. Online, available at: www.terrorismanalysts.com/pt/index.php?option=com_rokzine&view=issue &id= 15&Itemid=54.
Weinberg, L. and W. Eubank, 2008. 'Problems with the Critical Studies Approach to the Study of Terrorism', *Critical Studies on Terrorism*, 1(2): 185–195.
Weinberg, L. and L. Richardson, 2004. 'Conflict Theory and the Trajectory of Terrorist Campaigns in Western Europe', in A. Silke, ed., *Research on Terrorism*, 138–160.
Weitzer, R., 1990. *Transforming Settler States: Conflict and Internal Security in Northern Ireland and Zimbabwe*, Berkeley: University of California Press.
West, J., 2004/5. 'Feminist IR and the Case of the "Black Widows": Reproducing Gendered Divisions', *Innovations: A Journal of Politics*, 5.
Whitbeck, J., 2001. '"Terrorism": The Word Itself is Dangerous', *Daily Star* (Lebanon), 7 December 2001. Online, available at: www.pugwash.org/ september11/ whitbeck.htm.
White, R., 2000. 'Issues in the Study of Political Violence: Understanding the Motives of Participants in Small Group Political Violence', *Terrorism and Political Violence*, 12(1): 95–108.
——, 1989. 'From Peaceful Protest to Guerrilla War: Micromobilization of the Provisional Irish Republican Army', *American Journal of Sociology*, 94(6): 1277–1302.
Whitworth, S., 2004. *Men, Militarism & UN Peacekeeping*, Boulder, CO: Lynne Rienner.

——, 2001. 'The Practice, and Praxis, of Feminist Research in International Relations', in R. Wyn Jones, ed., *Critical Theory and World Politics*, London: Lynne Rienner, 149–160.

Wickham, C., 2004. 'Interests, Ideas, and Islamist Outreach in Egypt', in Q. Wiktorowicz, ed., *Islamic Activism: A Social Movement Theory Approach*, Bloomington, IN: Indiana University Press, 231–249.

Wiest, D., 2007. 'A Story of Two Transnationalisms: Global Salafi Jihad and Transnational Human Rights Mobilization in the Middle East and North Africa', *Mobilization* 12(2): 137–160.

Wiktorowicz, Q., 2006. 'Anatomy of the Salafi Movement', *Studies in Conflict and Terrorism*, 29(3): 207–239.

——, 2005. *Radical Islam Rising: Muslim Extremism in the West*, London: Rowman & Littlefield.

——, ed., 2004a. *Islamic Activism: A Social Movement Theory Approach*, Bloomington, IN: Indiana University Press.

——, 2004b. 'Islamic Activism and Social Movement Theory', in Q. Wiktorowicz, ed., *Islamic Activism: A Social Movement Theory Approach*, Bloomington, IN: Indiana University Press, 1–33.

Wilkinson, P., 2003. 'Rising in the East', *Sunday Herald*, 12 January 2003.

——, 2002. *Terrorism Versus Democracy: The Liberal State Response*, London: Frank Cass.

——, 1985. 'The Real-world Problems of the Terrorist Organisation and the Problem of Propaganda', in A. Merari, ed., *On Terrorism and Combating Terrorism*, Frederick, MD: University Publications of America.

——, 1984. 'State-sponsored International Terrorism: The Problems of Response', *The World Today*, 40(7): 292–298.

——, 1981. 'Proposals for Government and International Responses to Terrorism', in P. Wilkinson, ed., *British Perspectives on Terrorism*, London: Allen & Unwin, 161–193.

——, 1977. *Terrorism and the Liberal State*, NY: Wiley

——, 1974. *Political Terrorism*, Hampshire: Macmillan.

Wilkinson, P. and A. Stewart, eds, 1989. *Contemporary Research on Terrorism*, Aberdeen, Scotland: University of Aberdeen Press.

Williams, M. and K. Krause, eds, 1997. *Critical Security Studies*, Minneapolis: University of Minnesota Press.

Wolff, K., 1998. 'New Orientalism: Political Islam and Social Movement Theory', in A. Moussalli, ed., *Islamic Fundamentalism: Myths & Realities*, Reading: Ithaca, 41–73.

Woodworth, P., 2002. *Dirty War, Clean Hands: ETA, The GAL and Spanish Democracy*, New Haven, CT: Yale University Press.

Wyn Jones, R., 2005. 'On Emancipation: Necessity, Capacity, and Concrete Utopias', in K. Booth, ed., *Critical Security Studies and World Politics*, Boulder, CO: Lynne Rienner.

——, 1999. *Security, Strategy and Critical Theory*, Boulder, CO: Lynne Rienner.

Yee, A., 1996. 'The Causal Effects of Ideas on Politics', *International Organization*, 50(1): 69–108.

Young, G., 2006. 'Feminist International Relations in the Age of the War on Terror: Ideologies, Religions and Conflict,' *International Feminist Journal of Politics*, 8(1): 3–18.

Yuval-Davis, N., 1997. *Gender and Nation*, London: Sage Publications.
Zald, M. and R. Ash, 1966. 'Social Movement Organizations: Growth, Decay, and Change', *Social Forces*, 44: 327–340.
Zayyat, M., 2005. *The Road to Al-Qaeda: The Story of Bin Laden's Right-Hand Man*, London: Pluto Press.
Zinn, H., 2002. *Terrorism and War*, New York: Seven Stories Press.
Zulaika, J., 2008. 'The Terrorist Subject: Terrorism Studies and the Absent Subjectivity', *Critical Studies on Terrorism*, 1(1): 27–36.
——, 2000. *Basque Violence: Metaphor and Sacrament*, Reno, NV: University of Nevada Press.
——, 1995. 'The Anthropologist as Terrorist', in C. Nordstrom and A. Robben, eds, *Fieldwork Under Fire: Contemporary Studies of Violence and Survival*, Berkeley: University of California Press, 206–223.
——, 1988. *Basque Violence: Metaphor and Sacrament*, Reno: University of Nevada Press.
Zulaika, J. and W. Douglass, 1996. *Terror and Taboo: The Follies, Fables, and Faces of Terrorism*, New York and London: Routledge.
Zunes, S., 2005. 'Hurricane Katrina and the War in Iraq', *Foreign Policy in Focus*, 2 September 2005. Online, available at: www.fpif.org/fpiftxt/491.

Index

9/11 25, 31, 45–6, 47–8, 78, 116, 179, 189; Commission Hearing 30

Abbass, H. 24, 32
academic freedom 152, 203–4
academic influence, US policy 39–51
academic networks 2–3, 49–51, 81
Afghanistan 60, 121–2, 183, 185
African National Congress (ANC) 115
al-Qaeda 22–3, 27–30, 31–2, 41–3, 45, 71, 72, 73, 134–5, 161, 184–5, 188, 218
Alexander, Yonah 19, 52, 53–8, 63
Algeria 126–7, 131, 185–6
American Anthropology Association 200
American Council of Trustees and Alumni (ACTA) 116, 152, 210–11
Americas Watch 60
Amnesty International 58
analysis: implications of power relationships 200–2; trends in 38–43
Angola 60
antagonism, researchers/informants 196–7
anthropology 138–55, 198; and critical terrorism studies 140–2
anti-terrorism rhetoric 144–6
anti-war activism 183–4
area studies, Middle East 124–36
Arts and Humanities Research Council (AHRC) 205–9, 210
asylum seekers 119
Atta, Mohammed 182
Aust, Stefan 20
authoritarian regimes, cooperation with 117–18

Bergen, Peter 186
Bhattacharjee, Y. 203–4
bin Laden, Osama 23, 186
book: aims 3–4; overview 4–8
Booth, Ken 15, 89, 90, 98, 99, 101, 103, 105, 111–14, 121–2
Borge, Tomas 55, 56
Brannan, D. 196, 197
Breen Smyth, Marie 1–8, 141–2, 194–214, 216–36

British International Studies Association (BISA) 2–3

Cabinet Committee to Combat Terrorism, US 20–1
Campus Watch website 211
Central America, US intervention 49–64
Centre for the Study of Radicalisation and Contemporary Political Violence (CSRV) 3, 18
Chalk, Peter 52, 53–8, 61–2, 63
Chemical, Biological, Radiological, and Nuclear weapons (CBRN) 44–5, 71, 76
CIA 21, 29–30
Cline, Ray 52, 53–8, 63
Coady, C. 125–6
Cold War 53–8, 60, 62, 72
collaborative research, lack of 39
Colombia 57, 59, 60, 63
Combating Terrorism Center, US 17
Combating Terrorism by Countering Radicalisation programme 205–9
conceptual issues 45–6
conferences 2, 3, 21
Contras 56, 60, 63
counter-hegemony 131–3
counterterrorism 95–6; methods 73–4: as moral duty 144–6; UK 142–3; US 49–64, 142–4
Cox, Robert 77, 87–8, 89, 92, 103, 132, 157
Crace, J. 27
Crenshaw, Martha 14, 18, 19, 163, 164, 166
critical analysis 74–81
critical cultural deconstruction 146–8
critical perspectives as support for terrorism 150–2
critical scholars, challenges faced by 209–13
critical security studies 111–14
Critical Studies on Terrorism Working Group (CSTWG) 2–3
critical terrorism studies 111–14; and anthropology 140–2; case for 1–8; future challenges 232–6; new research agenda 227–32; primary commitments 221–7
critiques, absence of 14–15

Cronau, Peter 29
Cuba 54–8

Dalacoura, Katerina 7, 124–36
data gathering: obstacles to 196–9; trends in 38–43
data: dearth of 196–9; protection of 203
Debat, Alexis 26–7
debates 14, 15–19
dehumanisation 144–6
della Porta, D. 164, 165, 168, 169, 170
descriptive statistics 40–1
detention facilities, interviews conducted in 29–30
detention practices 117
Different Future (ADF) 120
discourse analysis 67–9, 74–81
discourse and state hegemony 129–31
Douglass, William 80, 145–8, 150–1

Economic and Social Research Council (ESRC) 2, 194, 205–9, 210
Egypt 127, 133–4
El Salvador 55–6, 58, 62, 63
ELN 57
emancipation 111–14, 141–2, 190; commitment to 226–7; dangers and possibilities 121–2; definition of 112–13; framework 99–104
emancipatory critical terrorism studies, key questions 114–21
embedded academics 25, 30, 81, 197, 209–10
EOKA 168
epistemological issues 224–5
Esler, P. 196, 197
ETA 56, 151
ethics 226; academic freedom 203–4; access to terrorists 202–3; challenges 194–6, 209–13; funding sources 204–9; power and safety 199–202; primary data/data collection 196–9; protection of sources and data 203; received wisdom and training 202
ETIM 115
Eurocentrism 103–4
evidence, art of masquerading 25–31
expert witnesses 27–30
experts: embedded 25, 30, 81, 197, 209–10; identification of 51–3; legitimisation role 62–4; reliance on 53–8; silencing of 58–62

Fanon, Frantz 185–6
FARC 57, 94
femininity 182
feminism 186, 187–8, 190
fieldwork 105–6; power relationships/safety issues 199–200; researchers' motivation for 198–9
first order critique 68, 74–7, 91–2, 100, 113–14, 116–18
FMLN 55–6
force-based terrorism responses 74, 76–7, 94, 95–6, 117

Foreign and Commonwealth Office (FCO) 205–9, 210
foreign dissidents, state assassinations of 58–9
framing theory 159, 167–8
Frankfurt School 87, 88, 98–100, 104, 110
freedom fighters, terrorists as 142–4, 148–50
funding: lack of 39–40; sources of 204–9

Gearty, C. 36
gender: battleground 179–83; choices and dilemmas 190–2; and security 189–90
gendered terror 183–9
Gentry, C. 187
'going native' 105, 210
Gould-Wartofsky, M. 210
government sponsorship of research 204–9; sponsorship of terrorism 58–62
grassroots terrorism 16
grounded theory approach 68
Guatemala 55
Guelke, Adrian 199
Guevara, Che 148–9
Gunaratna, Rohan 25, 28–30, 73, 218
Gunning, Jeroen 1–8, 17, 24, 77, 87–107, 156–77, 197, 216–36
Gurr, Ted 19, 20, 158, 164

Hafez, M. 168, 169–70
Hamas 61, 72, 101, 128–9, 130, 160, 162–3, 164, 165, 170, 171–2
hegemony 79–81; of counter-hegemony 131–3; and discourse 80–1, 129–31
Hero (Historical Evaluation and Research Organization) 21
Hezbollah/Hizballah 57, 62, 63, 128, 129, 130, 132–3, 168, 184–5
historical context 23–4, 45–6, 96–8
Hizb ut-Tahrir 168
Hoffman, Bruce 16–17, 22, 25–6, 31, 52, 53–8, 59, 61, 63, 70, 128, 170
Honduras 55–6
Horkheimer, M. 88, 89, 92–3, 98–100, 103
human diversity 102–3
Human Rights Watch 56, 59, 60, 131
human security 93–5
humanisation 148–9
Hurricane Katrina 119

ideological characteristics 165–8
ideological functions 51, 52–8, 62–4, 77–9
immanent critique *see* first order critique
inferential statistics 40–1
Institute for Scientific Information (ISI) 20
intelligence studies 32
interdisciplinarity 98–9
internal dynamics, social movements 169–72
International Bibliography of the Social Sciences (IBSS) 35, 157
International Court of Justice 56
international relations theory (IR) 23–4, 178–9

272 Index

International Studies Association (ISA) 2
Iran 57, 59, 130, 132, 133, 184, 185
Iraq 59, 61, 121–2, 126, 185, 188, 189
Irish National Liberation Army (INLA) 142–3, 201–2
Irish People's Liberation Organisation (IPLO) 201–2
Irish Republican Army (IRA) 35–6, 47, 96–7, 101–2, 118–19, 142–3, 160, 161, 163, 184, 199
Islam 76, 90–1, 128–9
Islamic Salvation Front (FIS) 127, 131
Islamist terrorism 22–3, 43, 73, 132–3, 167–8
Israel 59, 61–2, 63, 90, 91, 126, 128–9, 132–3, 142, 145, 162, 171
Italian Red Brigades 96, 160, 161, 162–3, 164, 168

Jackson, Richard 1–8, 17, 66–82, 140–1, 216–36
Jamaat-e-Islami 27
Jenkins, Brian 14, 19, 52, 53–8, 59, 60–1, 63
Joint Terrorism Analysis Centre, MI5 205
Jongman, Berto 13, 14, 30, 36–7, 52, 195
journalism and academic expertise 26
journals 3, 15, 24, 34–48
Juergensmeyer, Mark 72

Kamen, J. 62
Kashmir 188
Kauravas 179–83
knowledge 69–74
Kornbluh, P. 59
Kovats-Bernat, J.C. 199–201, 202, 203
Kupperman, Robert 52, 53–8, 62
Kurdistan Workers' Party (PKK) 94, 96, 118–19, 134

Laqueur, Walter 19, 52, 53–8, 59, 61, 62, 70, 73
Leach, Edmund 138, 144–6
Lebanon 59, 61, 62, 129, 130, 132–3, 173
liberal democracy, promotion of 117–18
Libya 54–8, 59, 130
Linklater, A. 88, 100, 102, 103, 110, 113
literature: proliferation of 17–18; review of 34–48
Livingstone, Neil 52, 53–8, 62–3

McDonald, Matt 6–7, 109–22
macro explanations 165–6
Mahabharata 179–83
Mahmood, Cynthia 148–9, 151, 196
masculinity 182
Merari, Ariel 52, 53–8
meso explanations 165–6
methodological challenges, political violence/terror 194–6
methodological issues 225–6
methodology 51–3; implications of power relationships 200–2

micro explanations 165–6
Middle East: non-state actors and hegemony of counter-hegemony 131–3; problem-solving 133–5; religion and terrorism 128–9; research 22–3; state hegemony 129–31; states and the 'terrorist' label 125–7
Mills, T. 27
minimal foundationalism 92–3
Mojahedin-e Khalq (MKO) 133
Moro Islamic Liberation Front (MLF) 97, 172
Muhammad Ally, S. 27–8
multidisciplinary research, need for 24–5, 32
multiple identities 96–7

narrative 69–74
National Consortium for the Study of Terrorism and Responses to Terror (START) 18
national culture, women as symbols of 184–5
national security 93–5, 189–90; strengthening institutions of 79
Network of Activist Scholars of Politics and International Relations (NASPIR) 3
new research agenda 227–32
New Right 142, 145–6
new social movement theory 159, 160–1, 166–7, 173–5
'new terrorism' thesis 71–2, 76, 97
Nicaragua 54–8, 60
non-combatants: targeting 93, 143; treatment of 126–7
non-state actors, and counter-hegemony 131–3
non-violent protest 103, 160
non-violent responses 73–4
non-Western social movements 172–4
normative agenda 99–104, 223–4
Norwegian Defence Research Establishment (FFI) 17

Office of Military Commission (OMC), US 27–8
ontological approach 222–3
Operation Condor 59
Orientalist prejudices 172–4
orthodox studies, problems with 216–21
Oslo process 61–2

Pakistan 173, 188
Palestine 61–2, 91, 119, 126, 128–9, 132–3, 142, 162, 163, 170–1, 172, 173
Palestine Liberation Organisation (PLO) 55–6
Palestinian Muslim Brotherhood 163
Pandavas 179–83
Pape, Robert 15–16, 76
Parashar, Swati 7–8, 178–92
peer assessment 51–3
peer-review 15
policing styles 170
policy: academic influence on 49–51; legitimisation of 51, 52–8, 62–4, 77–9
policy-makers, engaging 104–6
policy relevant research 77–8

political attacks on researchers 210–13
political dissidents 119
political process model 159–60, 168, 169, 174–5
political systems 173
political violence/terror, challenges to 194–6
post-9/11 terrorism studies 22–5
power relationships 199–200; implications for methods and analysis 200–2
praxis 104–6, 226–7
primary data 17, 195–6, 219; dearth of 196–9; *see also* fieldwork
problem-solving theory 77–8, 91, 92
protest cycles 162, 163, 164
psychological abnormality 72, 76

radicalisation 72, 76, 205–9
RAND 19, 20–1, 59, 71, 81, 196–7, 218
Ranstorp, Magnus 5, 13–33, 195, 199
Raphael, Sam 5–6, 49–64
rational choice 166–8, 173
realism 89, 91, 103
reconstruction 99–106
refugees 119
relative deprivation model 158
relativity 149–50
religion 73, 76, 128–9
religious social movements 174
religious terrorism 90–1; *see also* Islamist terrorism
research: art of masquerading evidence 25–31; barriers to entry 15; broadening 95–9, 161–72; 'de-orientalising' 172–4; deepening 89–95, 172–4; emergence and legacy of 19–22; framing new agenda 227–32; future challenges 232–6; future directions 31–3; narrative and knowledge in 69–74; post-9/11, 22–5; problem-solving in 133–5; problems in 216–21; quality of 36–7; relevance of SMT 160–1; time to publication 37; violation of standards 25–31
research inventories 13–14
researchers: numbers of 37, 38–9, 40; one-time 21–2
resource mobilisation theory 158–9, 167, 174–5
Revolutionary Association of the Women of Afghanistan 183
Roosevelt, Franklin D. 154–5
rumor intelligence (RUMINT) 26
Russia 53–9, 73

sacralisation 144–6
safety issues, fieldwork 199–200
Sageman, Marc 16–17, 22, 71, 73, 128
Said, Edward 87, 89, 147, 152
St Andrews Centre for Studies in Terrorism and Political Violence 81
Sandanistas 54–6, 60, 63
Schmid, Alex 13, 14, 19, 30, 36–7, 52, 195

second order critique 68–9, 77–80
secondary sources 17, 219
secular goals 16
security and gender 189–90
security sector 79
security studies 111–14
self-censorship 204
self-reflexivity 174–5
sensitive information 203–4
Sikh militants 148–9, 151
silencing, problem of 58–62
Silke, Andrew 5, 17, 18, 34–48, 77, 78, 174, 195
Sinn Fein 184
Sjoberg, Laura 187
Sluka, Jeffrey A. 7, 138–55, 196, 197–8, 199, 201–2, 203, 214
social context 96–8, 102, 161–3
social movement theory: overview of 158–60; relevance to terrorism studies 160–1
social scientific methodologies 70–1
socio-cultural norms 173
sources, protection of 203
sourcing, problem of 53–8
South Africa 57, 115
Sri Lanka 76, 184
Stamnitzky, Lisa 14–15, 20–1
state-centrism 93–5
state hegemony 129–31
state practices, impact of 169–71
state terrorism 70, 75, 78–9
state violence 95–6
states: impact on terrorist tactics 169–71; and terrorist label 125–7
statistical analysis 40–1
status quo 91
Sterling, Claire 20, 73
Stern, Jessica 71–2, 128
Stockholm Syndrome 189–90, 198, 210
Stohl, Michael 14, 74
strategic goals 16, 166–8
structural changes 166–8
studies *see* research
Studies in Conflict and Terrorism (journal) 22–3, 37–8, 51–3, 81, 156–7
subjectivity 149–50
Sudan 130
suicide terrorism 23, 43–4, 76, 170–1, 181
suspect communities 104–6, 119, 210
Sylvester, Christine 7–8, 178–92
Syria 57, 58–9, 130

Taliban 185
Tamil Tigers 76, 184
Taussig, Michael 144–5, 198
teaching 2, 18
temporal aspect of violence 163–5
terrorism: critical perspectives as support for 150–2; de-exceptionalising 96; defining responses to 116–17; definitions of 36, 58, 70,

terrorism *continued*
  114–15, 125–6, 217–18; myth of 146–8; nature and study of 70–1; origins and causes of 72–3; responding to 73–4
Terrorism and Political Violence (journal) 22–3, 37–8, 51–3, 81, 156–7
Terrorism Research Initiative (TRI) 3
terrorist label 125–7
terrorist tactics: impact of state 169–71; research on 43–5; temporal fluidity of 163
terrorists: access to 202–3; as freedom fighters 142–4; humanising 148–9
'terrorologists' 30–1
theoretical commitments 67–8
theoretical rigour 174–5
theories, challenging orthodoxy of 15–19
threat narrative 71–2, 76
Times Higher Education Supplement (*THES*) 205–6, 207–9, 212, 213
Toros, Harmonie 6, 87–107
transformation, locating possibilities for 104–6; potential for 99–106
Tunisia 131
Turkey 59, 60, 118–19, 120, 134

UK 142–4, 205–9, 212
United Nations (UN), Resolution 1325 184
University of Goteborg Resistance Studies Network 3
University of Michigan ITERATE project 21
US: challenges faced by researchers 210–12; in global South 49–64; interventions 142–4; in Middle East 130–1

US State Department 57, 70, 130
USA v. *Aref and Hossain* 27
USA v. *Hassoun, Jayyousi and Padilla* 28, 29, 30

Vallis, R. 24, 32
veiling, women 185–6
violence: de-exceptionalising 162; forms of 95–6; retaining category of 92–3; temporal aspect of 163–5
vulnerability 118–19

'war on terror' 74, 114–21, 130, 135–6, 152, 180, 181
weapons of mass destruction (WMD) *see* chemical, biological, radiological, and nuclear weapons (CBRN)
Welsh School 88–9, 91–2, 93–4, 95, 96, 99–104, 111–14, 118, 119–20, 122, 157–8, 190
Western exceptionalism 78–9
Western social movements 172–4
Whitbeck, J. 150, 152–3
Wickham, Carrie R. 167
Wiktorowicz, Q. 165, 169–70
Wilkinson, Paul 19, 52, 53–8, 73, 151–2
Wyn Jones, Richard 95, 98, 99, 101, 104, 111, 113, 114, 120, 121, 157–8

Zulaika, Joseba 80, 145–8, 150–1

Lightning Source UK Ltd.
Milton Keynes UK
UKOW07f0246270115

245180UK00006B/152/P